PELICAN B

W. B. Y

Joseph Hone, the author and critic, was born in
Ireland in 1882. He was educated at Wellington
College and Jesus College, Cambridge. In 1943,
four years after the poet's death, he published
Yeats, which is now recognized as the standard
biography. His other books include *Bishop Berkeley*, *The Life of George Moore*, *The Moores of
Moore Hall*, *Henry Tonks* and an edition of the
letters of John B. Yeats. He lived in Dublin and
was elected President of the Irish Academy of
Letters in 1957. He died in 1959.

JOSEPH HONE

W. B. Yeats

1865-1939

PENGUIN BOOKS

Penguin Books Ltd, Harmondsworth, Middlesex, England
Penguin Books Australia Ltd, Ringwood, Victoria, Australia
—
First published by Macmillan & Co. Ltd., 1943
Published in Pelican Books 1971
Copyright © Mrs. W. B. Yeats, 1962
—
Made and printed in Great Britain
by Hazell Watson & Viney Ltd
Aylesbury, Bucks
Set in Linotype Georgian

Contents

Prefatory Note to the First Edition

In the first place I am deeply indebted to Mrs W. B. Yeats, with whose sanction the biography has been written. She has placed her recollections at my disposal as well as the relevant records, manuscripts and letters in her possession. Next I must acknowledge similar kindnesses on the part of W. B. Yeats's sisters, Lily Yeats and Elizabeth Yeats, and on that of his brother, Jack B. Yeats.

My grateful thanks are due to Mr Jack Grene for helping me to revise the manuscript and for various suggestions, and to Mr Cecil Salkeld, to Mr Oliver Edwards and Mr Monk Gibbon for their advice and assistance in regard to certain chapters; and among Yeats's friends who have talked and/or corresponded with me on the subject of his life and work, I should mention especially Madame Gonne MacBride (Maud Gonne) and, after her, the late F. R. Higgins, T. Sturge Moore, Dr F. P. Sturm, Captain Dermot MacManus, Miss Edith Shackleton, Miss Norah Heald, Sir William Rothenstein, Dr M. Rossi, Miss Edith Sitwell, Mrs Stuart (Iseult Gonne), General Sir Ian Hamilton, Miss Ethel Mannin, Mrs Llewelyn Davies and Richard Best.

I am under great obligation to the following: Dr Thomas Bodkin, Mr G. R. Barnes, Mr L. A. G. Strong, Dame Edith Lyttelton (the Hon. Mrs Alfred Lyttelton); to Dr Bodkin for accounts of Yeats's work as a Senator; to Mr Barnes for a description of Yeats's broadcasting; to Mr L. A. G. Strong for his picture of Yeats's life at Oxford; and to Dame Edith Lyttelton for a passage on Yeats and Psychical Research.

Letters written by the late Robert Bridges are quoted by permission of his executors; letters written by the late George Moore, with acknowledgements to Mr C. D. Medley; letters by John Butler Yeats, with acknowledgements to Jack B.

Yeats and Miss Lily Yeats. In the case of Yeats's own letters the permission has been given by Mrs Yeats. In reproducing these I have frequently corrected the spelling. There were certain quite common words which up to the end of his life he always spelt wrong.

Various other obligations are acknowledged in the Bibliography to be found at the close of the book.

J. H.

Blackrath, Kilkenny
May 1942

Publisher's Note to the Second Edition

JOSEPH HONE'S *W. B. Yeats* was first published on February 12th, 1943, four years after the poet's death. The restrictions on book production in war-time meant that only a limited number of copies could be produced, and this admirable biography went out of print within five months of first publication.

No subsequent accounts of Yeats's life has replaced it. In the twenty-three years since his death there have been a number of critical works of a very high order, but no one since Hone has had such free access to the papers dealing with Yeats's personal life, and the assistance which only Mrs Yeats could offer.

Unhappily the author did not live to prepare the present edition himself, as he died on March 26th, 1959, at the age of seventy-seven.

In 1943 Yeats's body still lay at Roquebrune. A short epilogue to this edition therefore describes his subsequent interment at Drumcliff. Some corrections and other changes of less importance have also been made to the text.

MACMILLAN & CO. LTD

February 1962

[1]

Family and early associations

Yeats family in Dublin and Sligo – J. B. Yeats; Sandy-
mount Castle and the Corbets – Birth of the poet (1865) –
J. B. Yeats in London as art student – The Pollexfens
– W. B. and his grandparents – The Middletons

━━

> *He that in Sligo at Drumcliff*
> *Set up the old stone Cross,*
> *That red-headed rector in County Down,*
> *A good man on a horse,*
> *Sandymount Corbets, that notable man*
> *Old William Pollexfen,*
> *The smuggler Middleton, Butlers far back,*
> *Half legendary men.*

¶

MUCH information concerning William Butler Yeats's
family and early life can be agreeably acquired from his own
telling and from that of his father. He descended on his
father's side from a certain Jervis Yeats – the old merchant
'free of the ten and four' of his poem on ancestors* – who
towards the close of the seventeenth century was established
in the wholesale linen business in Dublin, and enjoyed the
privilege of being exempt from certain duties by the Irish
Parliament. The name Yeats was then common in Yorkshire
and it has been presumed that Jervis Yeats was a settler from
that county. He died in 1712, and was succeeded by his son
Benjamin, a member of the mercantile community which
accepted Dean Swift as its leader and struck the first note of
Irish Protestant Nationalism. The family business appears
to have flourished; for, in Grattan's Dublin, at the close of

* In the volume *Responsibilities* (1914).

the eighteenth century, a second Benjamin Yeats, the grandson of Jervis, lived in William Street, at that time a street of handsome houses, the abodes of rich men of business. This Benjamin Yeats married Mary Butler, daughter of John Butler of the War Office in Dublin, and, all her brothers dying unmarried, Mary Butler inherited and brought into the family the lands of Thomastown in Co. Kildare, a small property, which remained in its possession up to the poet's time, together with a beautiful silver cup with the Ormonde crest upon it, already old at the date 1534, when the initials of some bride and bridegroom were engraved on the lip. The poet looked back with pride to Butlers, Butlers (Earls of Ormonde) being next to Fitzgeralds the most illustrious of the Anglo-Irish medieval families. For a time he supposed that some of them fought on the Irish side at the Boyne:

> . . . You that did not weigh the cost,
> Old Butlers when you took to horse and stood
> Beside the brackish waters of the Boyne,
> Till your bad master blenched and all was lost . . .*

Through the Butlers the Yeats family was attached to the older Ireland, and also – like many Irish Protestant families of distinction – to Huguenot immigrants. Mary Butler's great-grandmother was a Voisin, and tradition says that, when dying, she requested to be buried at Donnybrook near the famous Archbishop King, the friend of Swift.

With the second Benjamin Yeats the commercial history of the family ended. In his will, dated 1795, Benjamin wishes 'to dispose of the small remains of his property that may be saved from the wreck of disappointments and the unforeseen misfortunes of this world'. His widow, however, was by no means badly off, for she had a pension of £900 from the War Office, as well as the income from Kildare lands. Her son John Yeats, born in 1774, was sent to the Dublin University, where, after winning Bishop Berkeley's gold medal for Greek, and generally distinguishing himself, he took orders in the

* See note on p. 486.

Church of Ireland. In 1803 he married Jane Taylor, the daughter of a Dublin Castle official, and two years later was appointed to the living of Drumcliff, in Co. Sligo, where he remained until his death in 1846. It was in this way that the long association of the poet's family with Sligo began.

Drumcliff, a place of high antiquity, is a large parish in the barony of Carbury, lying between mountains and a bay of the Atlantic. The church, at the fourth milestone on the road leading from Sligo to Ballyshannon, is built on the site of a monastery, either founded by St Columba, or dedicated to him after his death. The yard contains a sculptured Celtic cross, and, near by on the road to the Rectory, are the remains of the only Round Tower in Sligo and of a ruined castle of the O'Connors.

John Yeats's Rectory survives to this day, set on a field rising from the river; a three-storied narrow house. Flat-topped Ben Bulben, that strange and beautiful mountain, famous in Irish legend for the encounter of Diarmuid with the enchanted boar, 'sets the scene' and other hills run in an easterly direction from this range into the lovely valley of Glencar:

> Where the wandering water gushes . . .
> In pools among the rushes
> That scarce could bathe a star.

In John Yeats's day, and for long afterwards, Sligo was in the firm possession of a small number of great landlords, all Protestant and mostly dating from Cromwellian and later invasions: Ormsbys, Gore-Booths, Parkes, Wynns, Coopers. This was not the Connaught where numbers of the older Roman Catholic and Anglo-Irish gentry survived and lived in the irresponsible extravagant manner that is depicted in the novels of Lever and Maria Edgeworth. The distinguishing features of the county are well indicated by Lennox Robinson in his biography of Major Bryan Cooper, the friend and political colleague of the poet in post-Treaty Ireland (1922–30).

. . . The English soldiers who settled in it were gradually to make it unique, were to make it something curiously contradictory even in this country of sharp contrasts. They were destined to become a kind of island, bounded on the south by the banished Irish, on the north by Ulster and on the east by the Irish of Roscommon. On the west was the wild Atlantic, and what could the little colony do save dig itself in, intermarry and consolidate its position? It was its fate to impinge, little perhaps as it knew it at first, on a country very rich in Gaelic folk-lore and history and tradition. There seems to be hardly a barony in County Sligo that is not linked with fairy legend or religion or ancient battle . . .

Sligo extorted the admiration of even so prejudiced a visitor as Carlyle, who, on his Irish tour of 1849, saw nothing in other parts of Connaught but beggary and stone walls. When Carlyle first comes in view of the environs of Sligo, at Dromore, on the road from Ballina, a change comes over him and he writes in his diary: 'Country suddenly alters here . . . beautiful view of the sea, of Sligo bay, with notable mountains beyond . . . decidedly a pleasant region, with marks of cultivation everywhere.' And on the high ground over the town with the full panorama expanding before him – the mountains of Ben Bulben, Cashengal and Knocknarea, the undulating pasture lands and tillage fields of Magherow, diversified with woods – he is moved to add 'Sligo at last . . . *beautiful town and region altogether*'.

'Parson Yeats' of Drumcliff, a fine scholar, loved outdoor life and the entertainment of friends. He fished; kept two racehorses in his stable because he liked the look of them; and when he died left a wine bill of £400 for his heirs to pay. In religion he was scriptural, but with the quiet good sense and breadth of sympathies that Froude found in an Irish evangelical household; he did not think of himself as a Saint of God. He mixed on genial terms with the Roman Catholics; and on one occasion, having come back from a protracted sojourn in Dublin, bonfires blazed all over the countryside, lit by order of the French-educated priest, a reader perhaps of Gibbon and of Voltaire. 'This parson's name is still popular as that of a straightforward, high-principled man', says the Roman Catholic author of the history of Sligo, the Rev. T. O'Rorke.

It is told of him that when he with Sir Robert Gore-Booth's agent . . . and a bailiff . . . went among Sir Robert's tenants, asking them to send their children to the Protestant school, and was told by a man named James O'Hara, that a child of his would never darken the door of that school house, Mr Yeats commended him for his spirit and observed that he was the honestest man they had come across that day.

The parson reared a long family, several members of which remained in Sligo after his death. His eldest son, William Butler, the poet's grandfather, was educated at Trinity College (B.A. 1831), where he earned distinction as a racket-player, and was co-editor, with Isaac Butt, of the famous *Dublin University Magazine* in which Carleton, Carlyle's 'genuine bit of old Ireland', published his *Traits and Stories of the Irish Peasantry*. Another son, Thomas, a first-class mathematician, never beaten in the Honours Examination, having taken his degree, sought the canal boat to Mullingar, and from Mullingar drove over the Curlew Mountains into Sligo, which he never left again, devoting himself entirely to the support of near relatives. 'Tom Yeats buried in Sligo, fancy that', Sir William Wilde, Oscar Wilde's father, used to say. 'The Yeatses were the cleverest and most spirited people I ever met.'

On leaving college William Butler became Curate in the parish of Moira, Co. Down. In 1836, while still a curate, he married Jane Corbet of Sandymount, Co. Dublin, sister of the Governor of Penang, and soon after his marriage was appointed rector of the large parish of Tullylish, near Portadown. He was very tall, red-headed and the most eloquent of preachers; like his father before him, an Irish gentleman of the old school, and a sociable scholar. When Macaulay's *History* came out he bought it, threw the parish to his curate and went to bed until he had read all the volumes. At the

time of the great famine he went with another Irish clergyman to collect relief in England; but he disliked Presbyter-
ians, his son tells us, and could never come to an understanding with the aggressive North, because his Evangelicalism
belonged to the cultivated classes, and instead of being a
hatred of human nature was 'an intense pity mixed with an
affectionate and human delight'.

2

That remarkable man, John Butler Yeats, artist, author and
philosopher, was born at Tullylish in 1839, the eldest of a
large family, all of them high-spirited, handsome, full of
health. At twelve years of age he went to school at the Atholl
Academy in the Isle of Man, kept by a Scotchman; it was
here that he made a dear friend in the son of a shipowner
and miller from the town of Sligo, George Pollexfen, whose
sister he afterwards married. He was attracted, he has told
us in *Some Chapters of Autobiography*, by the boy's melancholy:

> George Pollexfen was melancholy as a boy and as a man. I
> think it was his melancholy that attracted me, who am a cheerful
> and perennially hopeful man. It always mortifies me to think
> how cheerful I am, for I am convinced it is a gift I share with all
> the villains; it is their unmistakable buoyancy that enables these
> unfortunates to go on from disaster to disaster and remain
> impenitent.

It had been intended that J. B. Yeats should become a
clergyman, but it was not long before he discovered himself
to be without religious beliefs: at Dublin University Butler's
Analogy, the classic of Anglican apologetics, had been put
into his hands; he found the premises sound, but drew from
them conclusions precisely opposite to those of the Bishop;
the Bar was then spoken of. Someone once described J. B.
Yeats as 'singularly incurious about God and immortality';
and certainly he neither sought a substitute for Christianity

nor felt any hostility to religion. In one of his letters to his son he says: 'The mission of the Church is not to teach truth but to impose on such as wish to be imposed on, as we all do while listening to ghost stories.'

He read classics, and in his last year at college metaphysics and logic; after taking his degree he won a prize in political economy. He resisted the prevalent worship of Carlyle, but J. S. Mill's gentle and liberal spirit captivated him, and reminded him of the quality which he found in his own father, the Rector of Tullylish, of whom he has left this description:

My father was sweet-tempered, and affectionate, also he constantly read Shelley, and, no less, Shelley's antidote, Charles Lamb. To be with him was to be caught up into a web of delicious visionary hopefulness. Every night, when the whole house was quiet, and the servants gone to bed, he would sit for a while beside the kitchen fire and I would be with him. He never smoked during the day, and not for worlds would he have smoked in any part of the house except the kitchen; and yet he considered himself a great smoker. He used a new clay pipe, and as he waved aside the smoke with his hand, he would talk of the men he had known – his fellow students – of Archer Butler the Platonist, and of a man called Gray, who was, I think, an astronomer, and of his friend Isaac Butt. . . . And he would talk of his youth and boyhood in the West of Ireland where he had fished and shot and hunted, and had not a care . . .

While J. B. Yeats was at the University, his father retired from his Co. Down parish and came to live at Sandymount, the 'great pasture by the Sea' of Dublin's medieval chroniclers, then becoming a modernized and terraced suburb, which was to be the poet's birthplace. The attraction at Sandymount for the retired Rector was his brother-in-law, a charming and hospitable man, Robert Corbet, owner of Sandymount Castle, one of the several country houses, secluded in their gardens, which had grouped themselves round the old village in the eighteenth and early nineteenth centuries.

Sandymount Castle was J. B. Yeats's Capua during his

college days. It was an eighteenth-century house, but already altered beyond recognition by Gothic additions: battlements, clock tower and a cloister. Corbet employed four or five men on the extensive grounds to grow wonderful fruit and flowers and himself spent much time in cutting trees to make 'vistas' of Dublin Bay and of the mountains. There was a sheet of water called the pond with duck and swans and an island to which two eagles were chained; deer ran about the park. When he became a bankrupt and was obliged to leave the Castle, gardens, vistas and even the lake soon vanished, and the house was adapted to the uses of a boys' school. The Castle still exists, a long low building facing the whole length of one side of Sandymount Green, the fields much built over and a nursery garden at the back.

The prize in political economy, valued at £10, was J. B. Y.'s first earnings; with the money in his pocket and his heart full of his father's memories he visited Sligo and stayed with his school friend, George Pollexfen. His father had often talked to him of Sligo with great affection, and of how he would like to go there and visit all the places he had known, and then go away before his sister Mary or his brothers Tom and Matthew were awake; only thus could he visit a place where he had been so happy and young. Long afterwards he recalled the evening of his arrival:

Five miles from the town, at the mouth of the river, is a village called Rosses Point, and the Pollexfens were staying there for the summer. George and I walked on the sand-hills which were high above the sea. The sign of happiness in the Pollexfens has always been a great talkativeness, – I suppose birds sing and children chatter for a similar reason. George talked endlessly – what about I forget, excepting that he several times sang one of Moore's melodies, which he had lately heard at a concert. Indeed, I think the talk was mostly about that concert. The place was strange to me and very beautiful in the deepening twilight. A little way from us, and far down from where we talked, the Atlantic kept up its ceaseless tumult, foaming around the rocks called Dead Man's Point. Dublin and my uneasy life there, and Trinity College, though but a short day's journey, were obliterated, and I was again with my school friend, the man self-centred and tranquil and on that evening so companionable.

The Rev. W. B. Yeats died in 1862. He had been taking lunch at Corbet's Castle in Sandymount and was thought to have gone to some meeting of clergy in Dublin, but the butler came in and found him dead in his chair. His friends cherished the memory of a man of 'great personal charm, an accomplished mind, and courtly manners'; it was Rose Butt, Isaac Butt's daughter, who so described him to his grandchildren. As eldest son J. B. Y. inherited the settled estate in Kildare, which consisted of 626 acres with a valuation of £464 (de Burgh's *Landowners of Ireland*, 1878). This was enough on which to marry; George Pollexfen's prettiest sister, Susan, had other suitors; so it seemed better not to delay. ('Your mother married me', J. B. Y. once explained to his son, 'because I was always there and the family helped.') The wedding took place at St John's Church, Sligo, on 10 September 1863, and was posted at some length in the local newspaper. The six bridesmaids who attended the 'eldest and accomplished daughter of William Pollexfen of the firm of Middleton & Pollexfen' included two sisters of the bridegroom, one sister of the bride, and a cousin, Elizabeth Dawson, who was the first woman to enter the medical profession in England.

3

The young married pair settled in a recently-built, six-roomed, semi-detached house at the head of Sandymount Avenue, about half a mile from the castle of uncle Robert Corbet. 'Georgeville' was the most genteel house in the avenue, with stone steps up to the hall door and plate-glass windows; but Corbet with his grand ideas looked on the address with scorn and used to send his letters to 'The Quarry Hole', because he remembered the quarry hole upon which the house was built. At Georgeville, late at night on 13 June 1865, the poet was born. The child's fine 'os frontis' was remarked upon by the doctor. He was given the name of William Butler and baptized a month later at Donnybrook Church. His first outings in the perambulator were in the grounds of Sandymount Castle; his nurse reported that he was much frightened by the deer.

The Yeatses remained at Sandymount for about a year and a half, during which time J. B. Y. completed his terms. He was considered by his friends to be a young man of uncommon ability, but flighty in his ideas – very flighty. His distinguished friends included Edward Dowden, the young professor of English literature at T.C.D., George Fitzgerald, the scientist (a predecessor of Einstein), and Isaac Butt, former Tory leader, now the magnanimous defender of the Fenian prisoners, and later the founder of the 'Home Rule' movement. One day the great advocate was at Sandymount Castle, and the butler Michael, while serving him with wine at luncheon, said: 'Now, sir, Mr Johnnie is a barrister and you ought to do something for him,' and Butt answered, 'Michael, I will.' It was too late, as J. B. Y.'s repugnance to the 'malodorous law courts on the Liffey' had already become insurmountable. His description of Butt, written years later to his son, is worth quoting for the light which it throws on his own philosophy of life:

It used to be a curious experience to listen to Isaac Butt when speaking at the Four Courts on some case which had appealed to him – at times he would stand perfectly still and begin to *chant* his sentences and it would be quite evident to everyone present that he had forgot all about the Jury and the judge and the opposing counsel, or that he was in a court of justice at all ... the black eyes luminous with kindness which nothing could tire – nothing could tire, because with a profound conviction went in his case a profound hopefulness – and a belief that all men were good men – the belief itself a vision – he certainly was of the race of poets – like the true poet he sought obscurity – his visions haunted him, and my father told me it was always impossible to draw Butt into an argument, always he had other things to think about. But alas for his amazing career in T.C.D. and his amazing success at the Bar, a leading Q.C. before he was thirty, his early brilliancy in Politics, when Disraeli would walk with him in the lobby of the House with his arm through his, promising to make him a cabinet minister, finally the vision of a regenerated Ireland. All these drew him away – and the poor Muse could only visit him in strange places – in brothels and gaming houses she would meet her son, herself an exile; in those days banished by the respectable poets and Bishops and all the old mumbling bigotries of religious and social hatred. Butt, who loved humanity too much to hate any man, and knew too much of history to hate any opinion – besides how can a self-centred man, with visions to follow, hate? The career of Butt and its disasters is enough to prove the necessity of the Irish poetical movement.

Since he had been a small child J. B. Y. had sketched, with a growing delight in his gift, and there exists a sensitive drawing, done in the early years of their married life, of his wife in Victorian cloak and bonnet, which already shows a certain accomplishment. Dublin possessed an Academy of Painting (the Royal Hibernian Academy), but no society of artists to speak of; and after making his resolve to abandon the law for art it seemed best to remove to London. Besides J. B. Y. did not care to remain in Dublin after the collapse of Robert Corbet and the sale of Sandymount Castle, with all that glory spent. He spoke constantly of the Corbets, of turreted house, gardens and ponds to his children, and one day he read Morris's 'Golden Wings' to Willie and said it made him think of that old house where he had been very happy. The verses ran in the child's head for years, and became for him the best description of happiness in the world.

> Midways of a walled garden
> In the happy poplar land
> Did an ancient castle stand,
> With an old knight for a warden.
>
> Many scarlet bricks there were
> In its walls, and old grey stone;
> Over which red apples shone
> At the right time of the year.

In 1900 the poet made a pilgrimage to Sandymount, his sister having shown him old photographs from Corbet's time, with top-hatted young gentlemen and crinolined beauties in a rural scene. 'One can recognise in the remnant of the garden – now the school playing grounds – an old avenue of trees', he wrote to her after the visit. 'The house is manifestly a really old house, very quaint and twisted within. The young man who brought us there on the way out showed me a house where he said the neighbours said I had been born . . .'

1868 saw the Yeatses established at 23 Fitzroy Road, Regent's Park, which was their London home for seven years and the birthplace of the poet's two brothers, Robert and John Butler ('Jack'), and of the younger sister, Elizabeth ('Lolly'). The elder sister, Susan Mary ('Lily'), was born at Enniscrone, near Sligo, while Mrs Yeats was on a visit to her parents. 'My first memories', writes the poet in *Reveries over Childhood and Youth,*

are fragmentary and isolated and contemporaneous, as though one remembered some first moments of the Seven Days. . . . I remember sitting upon somebody's knee, looking out of an Irish window at a wall covered with cracked and falling plaster, but what wall I do not remember, and being told that some relation lived there. I am looking out of a window in London. It is at Fitzroy Road. Some boys are playing in the road and among them a boy in uniform, a telegraph boy perhaps. When I ask who the boy is, a servant tells me that he is going to blow the town up, and I go to sleep in terror.

At this time J. B. Y. was working at Heatherley's Art School, Newman Street. Here he made the acquaintance of Samuel Butler. Though not politically-minded, he was very conscious of national differences, and Butler excited his curiosity as a man of some social standing and at the same time of emancipated intellect. He had not met an Englishman of that kind before. The other students called each other briefly by surnames without prefix of the Mr – Butler was always Mr Butler.

From Heatherley's J. B. Y. went on to the Academy
School, where he studied under Poynter. He was a diligent
pupil, working from morning to night; but he was slow to
make a start as a professional painter, and when time passed
and he failed to show a 'picture of the year' at the Royal
Academy Exhibition, or any picture at all, his relatives-in-
law became critical. Expenditure at 23 Fitzroy Road soon
outran income, J. B. Y. being without money sense and excessively generous to friends. In the society in which he had
been brought up, the master spirit (he has told us) was for
enjoyment, meaning by that the gratification of the affections and of the sympathies, and of the spirit of hopefulness.
With the Pollexfens, on the other hand, rule and strictest
order was the ideal, especially in money matters.

4

The Pollexfens, though it was not their custom to endow
their daughters on marriage, were hospitable people, and the
Yeatses frequently stayed with them for long periods. Sligo,
indeed, not London, was looked upon by the children as
their home, and the human being who first loomed large in
the poet's life was not father or mother, but grandfather
William Pollexfen, 'the silent and fierce old man' of another
poem on ancestors: 'In Memory of Alfred Pollexfen' (1916).
The Pollexfens had an interesting family history. Though
the name was known in seventeenth-century Galway, William was born at Brixham in Devonshire; he was the son
of Antony Pollexfen, a barrack-master of probable Cornish
extraction, and of an Irishwoman from Co. Wexford. He
took to sea as a boy; prospered, and became the owner of
many sailing ships. In 1833 he sailed into Sligo on *The
Dasher* in order to offer his services to a cousin, Mrs Middleton, the widow of a certain William Middleton of Dromahair, Co. Leitrim, whose daughter Elizabeth he subsequently
married. The Middletons were millers and shipowners and
William acquired a partnership in the firm which still bears

the Pollexfen name.* When his first grandson, the poet, was born he sent a notice of the event to a Devonshire newspaper; but he was never known to visit his English relatives, or to speak of them, and only crossed to England to take the waters at Bath now and again. Yet he mixed little with Sligo neighbours; his only friends appeared to be two correspondents, Campbell of Ismay, who had befriended him and his crew after shipwreck, and Captain Webb of Channel swimming fame, who had been a mate in his employ.

The Middletons had also been seafarers; there is a tradition that they were once engaged in the trade between Galway and Spain. The first of them of whom anything definite can be ascertained is William Pollexfen's father-in-law from Dromahair, who, it is said, spoke Irish. This William Middleton, who was born in 1770, lived an early life of risk and hazard as shipowner, trader and smuggler between London, the Channel Islands and South America, where once he was placed under arrest and escaped with difficulty. In 1810, putting in at Jersey on a Sunday morning, he attended the Reverend Charles Pollexfen's church, where his eye fell upon the clergyman's daughter,† whom he carried off to Sligo forthwith, a girl-bride of fifteen. This bold-spirited man, the poet's great-grandfather, inspired the timid with his example of charity during the cholera epidemic which decimated the town in 1832; his death (which, as has been said, brought William Pollexfen to Sligo) was due to his having contracted the disease from a dying pauper whom he picked up in the street and brought to his own house. He was succeeded by a son, another William Middleton, Pollexfen's brother-in-law and partner in the firm, and by a brother named Walter, who welcomed the first steamship that arrived at Sligo in verses beginning 'Hail, majestic Monster'.

The Middleton and Pollexfen enterprises prospered and contributed towards making Sligo the busy little town which

* W. and G. T. Pollexfen, Ballisodare.

† Antony Pollexfen, the barrack-master, and the Reverend Charles are thought to have been brothers, but this is not certain.

it became in the latter part of the nineteenth century. When the poet first stayed with his grandparents, old William Pollexfen was a rich man and lived in a large house, 'Merville' (now the Nazareth convent), a little beyond the town, on the south side of the river, with Knocknarea rising behind it, and a view across the estuary to Ben Bulben. The country people say that Knocknarea is a haunted mountain and that Maeve, Queen of the western Sidhe, who led the hosting of Connaught into Ulster, lies buried under the cairn of stones on the smooth summit.

> Caoilte, and Conan, and Finn . . .
> Came to the cairn-heaped grassy hill
> Where passionate Maeve is stony-still . . .*

There were sixty acres of land round Merville; the house contained fourteen bedrooms, a stone kitchen, offices, a glorious laundry redolent of soap, and a storeroom like a village shop, with windows and fireplaces, shelves and drawers and a strong smell of ground coffee.

The earliest recollections of J. B. Y.'s children may be said to have consisted of a multitude of Sligo relatives: Pollexfens, Yeatses (children and grandchildren of Parson Yeats of Drumcliff) and Middletons. It was a little patriarchal society. 'I think,' writes the poet in *Reveries over Childhood and Youth*, 'I confused my grandfather with God.... Even today when I read *King Lear* his image is always before me, and I often wonder if the delight in passionate men in my plays and in my poetry is more than his memory.' The old man, fresh-complexioned and bearded, broad-built but not stout, with very blue eyes, was kind, but inspired fear and admiration rather than love. He kept a hatchet at his bedside for burglars; and Willie once saw him hunt a party of malefactors with a horsewhip. He never went to a shop for any of his clothes, and his shoes were made to a pattern of his own, without laces or buttons; it thrilled the children to watch him, as he stood firm and square on a sheet of paper,

The Wanderings of Oisin.

while Andy the shoemaker with trembling hand ran round his foot with a pencil.

William Pollexfen's wife was a kind, gentle and patient woman who read the Bible regularly, but kept a warning mark against the 109th Psalm. She was ambitious for her large family of sons and daughters, and for her grandchildren, and suffered much when one of her sons, a clever man who had designed the Sligo quays, had to be placed in an asylum. The poet could recall this uncle as the owner of a model turret ship in a glass case kept in a bedroom at the end of a long stone passage. When Mrs Pollexfen got a letter from the asylum her husband always went out of the room that she might read it alone. Husband and wife were devoted; when she sat near him he was at peace.

Other uncles and aunts came and went. The youngest uncle had a tongue of leather over the keyhole of his door at Merville to keep the draught out; and there was an artistic aunt who went to London and might have married Oliver Madox Brown, if that wonderful boy had not died. The especial friend of J. B. Y., George Pollexfen, was seldom seen at Merville, as he worked at Ballina for the firm, but he would put in an appearance for a race meeting, and once he excited his nephew by arriving in Sligo accompanied by two postillions dressed in green. He was a fine amateur rider and raced under the name of Paul Hamilton. 'George on a race-course,' his brother-in-law records, 'above all if mounted on a wild and splendid horse, was a transformed being. The Puritanism of the family was shattered ... then he loved all men, he loved humanity, he loved even himself. ... I never saw any man on horseback to compare with him, horse and man made a unity of grace and strength. ...'

Always J. B. Y. loved to meditate on the Pollexfens; of all the people he ever knew he seems to have considered his brothers-in-law and his sisters-in-law as most worthy of the attention of a philosopher. The references to them in his letters are endless. 'Talking to any of them, even to that mental simpleton Alfred, I feel he has something greater than either of us ... and George in one swing will say more luminous things than all these nervous energy people will say in a dozen weeks. He crawls; but is all the time a sort of glowworm.' And again (of George): 'Had the destinies permitted he might have become a great student and a recluse and buried himself in a university. His expression was strangely wistful, his eyes seemed to peep at you like stars in the early twilight.' To a sister-in-law, Agnes, is ascribed that 'mysterious energy which is the pulse of immortal life'. Once J. B. Y. defined W. B.'s lyrical gift ('The lyrical gift gives personal sensations detached from nature') as Yeats, but his poetical heredity as Pollexfen. The Yeatses have 'knowledge of the art of life and enjoyment', but the Pollexfens are 'full of the materials of poetic thought and feeling'. 'By marriage with the Pollexfens I have given a tongue to the sea cliffs.' Yeats has written that this last sentence was the only compliment that ever turned his head.

5

The following is the earliest of the letters now extant in which the poet is mentioned. It was written by J. B. Y. to his wife while she was in Sligo with her children during the winter of 1872–3. He had remained in London, sharing the house in Fitzroy Road with George Wilson, the water-colour artist.

Nov. 1st, 1872. 23 Fitzroy Rd. ... I am very anxious about Willy, he is never out of my thoughts. I believe him to be intensely affectionate, but from shyness, sensitiveness and nervousness, difficult to win and yet he is worth winning. I should of course like to see him do what is right but he will only develop by kindness and affection and gentleness ...

Bobby is robust and hardy and does not mind rebuffs – but Willy is sensitive, intellectual and emotional, very easily rebuffed and continually afraid of being rebuffed so that with him one has to use sensitiveness which is so rare at Merville. ... I wish greatly Willy could be made more robust by riding or other means – *not by going to school.* I was very sorry he could not have the pony more – but perhaps he might ride that donkey about which he used to tell me. Above all keep him from that termagant [Aunt] Agnes who is by no means as indulgent to other people's whims and foibles as she is to her own. . . . Willy is only made timid and unhappy and he would in time lose frankness . . .

I am getting on at Poynter's well – Wilson is here and will remain I fancy as long as I like. . . . I am very worried about some matters and so must write again tomorrow or next day. Tell Willy not to forget me.

Some of Willie's unhappiness was due to fear of old William Pollexfen, some of it to loneliness and a curious sense of the ignominy of childhood. Once he suffered a night of misery when, having prayed for several days that he might die, he began to be afraid that he was dying and prayed that he might live. 'I remember little of childhood but its pain', he was to write when he was fifty; '. . . I have grown happier with every year of life as though gradually conquering something in myself.'

The little boy did not lack a courage of his own; for he was only seven or eight when, roused out of sleep by one of his uncles, he consented to get his pony and carry a message to a cousin, who lived six miles away. The uncle wanted to borrow a railway pass; William Pollexfen had one, but would have thought it dishonest to let another use it; the cousin was not so conscientious. Willie was let out through a gate that opened on a little lane out of earshot of the house, and rode through the moonlight, and awoke his cousin by tapping on the window with his whip. He was not home until the small hours, when he found the coachman waiting for him in the lane.

His education commenced under his aunts, who found it difficult to teach him to read, and supposed that his intelligence was defective; whereas really he was unable to attend to anything less interesting than his own thoughts. He was then sent to a dame-school in the town, but did not there receive the benefit that was expected. The next attempt to teach him was made by his father, when J. B. Y. made a long stay at Merville in the spring of 1873, and startled his children by not attending church; of which his son says:

That gave me courage to refuse to set out one Sunday morning. I was often devout, my eyes filling with tears at the thought of God and of my own sins, but I hated church. . . . My father said if I would not go to church he would teach me to read. I think now that he wanted me to go for my grandmother's sake and could think of no other way. He was an angry and impatient teacher and flung the reading-book at my head, and next Sunday I decided to go to church. My father had, however, got interested in teaching me, and only shifted the lesson to a week-day till he had conquered my wandering mind.*

There was a room, called library, at Merville which contained a few novels and an encyclopedia, bought in London by great-grandfather Middleton on his wedding trip in 1817. The first reading that Willie undertook on his own account was in this encyclopedia, and he picked up from it an interest in natural history and in geology, which gradually made him understand his father's agnosticism. His father introduced him to imaginative literature by reading aloud to him out of Scott and Macaulay; *The Lay of the Last Minstrel* gave him his first wish to be a magician.

Early in 1873 his brother Robert died at Merville. It had been said of Robert by his father that he would 'love ideas and have enthusiasms and ardours and go through more experiences in a month than another in ten years.' The ships in the harbour had their flags at half-mast; presently Willie was sitting with his sister at the table drawing ships with their flags half-mast high. The next day at breakfast he heard people telling how a servant had heard the banshee crying the night before Robert died.

Later that year there was a wedding of a Pollexfen aunt, at which Willie appeared as a page, dressed in a vivid blue sailor suit and carrying roses.

* Reveries over Childhood and Youth.

6

In his autobiography the poet groups passages about his ancestors round great-aunt Micky (Mary) Yeats, a daughter of the Drumcliff parson and a great authority on the history of the family. She lived on the top of a hill in a little cottage called 'Seaview' on the Ben Bulben side of the Channel – the tidal river between the town of Sligo and Rosses – and owned the silver cup with the Ormonde crest. The widow and children of John Yeats, County Surveyor, Kildare, had a home near Aunt Micky's; and some miles away, in a house by a ruined mill, with a stream flowing in front of it, lived another of Parson Yeats's sons, Matthew, a land agent, father of several boys and girls all 'very well-bred and very religious'. From time to time his grandmother used to take Willie to pay duty calls upon these relatives, although there was little love lost between them and Pollexfens, for the Yeatses, having come a little down in the world, were all the more inclined to belittle people enriched by trade.

Middletons figured more prominently than Yeatses in the poet's memories of childhood. William Middleton, son of the smuggler, 'a cleverer man than my grandfather', frequently came to Merville for dinner, which was at the hour of four, walking back with Pollexfen from the office in town. He would sit at one side of the lady of the house, Pollexfen at the other. There would be no talk as the Yeats family understood talk, only statements about ships and cargoes; but once William Middleton said, 'We should not make light of the troubles of children', and Willie resolved that when grown up he would never talk of the happiness of childhood. He was a wealthy man, who had purchased for £17,000 all the land at Rosses Point lying between the Sligo and Drumcliff estuaries. He built lodges and 'developed' this beautiful site which is now the chief watering-place in Sligo and widely known for its golf links. He owned two houses, 'Elsinore' at Rosses, reputed to be haunted by smugglers, and 'Avena' at Ballisodare, near the family flour mills, where there is a river breaking over the rocks in a most romantic manner in many pretty falls. His family was a large one, his youngest son Henry being only a little older than Willie, who was delighted when invited to join his cousins at Rosses and at Ballisodare. At Rosses there was the river-mouth, in which to row or to be taken sailing in a heavy schooner yacht; and at Ballisodare there was a cleft among the rocks to be passed with terror because inhabited by a murderous monster that made a buzzing sound like a bee.

The Middletons lived close to the soil and pretended to nothing that they did not feel. They took the nearest for friends, and were always in and out of the cottages of pilots and tenants. The poet's mother resembled them in her tastes; and Yeats says that it was from the Middletons 'perhaps' that he got his interest in country stories; certainly the first fairy stories that he heard were in the cottages about Rosses and at Ballisodare. They were 'psychic', and at Elsinore they used to listen for the smuggler's three raps upon the drawing-room window, which set all the dogs of the neighbourhood barking. Willie heard the raps once, and later, when he was in his teens, and at Ballisodare, he shared with them the experience, related in *Reveries* – mysterious sounds and lights following one another, all in one day – which started him off on an inquiry into raths and fairy hills and the primitive beliefs of the countryside.

George Moore has told how a French count once discovered in Yeats a Finnish sorcerer – a throw-back to some non-Aryan ancestor a thousand years ago. If there was indeed in certain movements of the poet's mind, in the form taken by his mysticism, in his nose so broad between the eyes, in his swarthy complexion and deep-set slanting eyes, something out of character with the accepted features of the Aryan strains which have gone to make up the peoples of these islands, it is likely that these attributes were inherited from the seafaring Middletons and Pollexfens rather than from the home-loving Yeatses.

Yeatses, Pollexfens and Middletons, numerous as they

once were, are now all gone from Sligo. One of the last of these names to be found in the county was that of Henry Middleton, Willie's playfellow and the original of John Sherman in the novel of that name. Henry was very good-looking, as dark as Willie, but with very blue eyes, and he had the poet's taste for a little colour in dress. He became a noted eccentric, and when Yeats visited Sligo with his young wife in 1919, was living entirely alone at Elsinore behind a locked gate:

> My name is Henry Middleton,
> I have a small demesne,
> A small forgotten house that's set
> On a storm-bitten green.
> I scrub its floors and make my bed,
> I cook and change my plate,
> The post and garden-boy alone
> Have keys to my old gate . . .

Yeats climbed the wall and walked into the sitting-room, littered with cheap novels, with a butter-churn in the middle. His cousin was there, beautifully dressed in a summer suit of white. 'You see,' he said, after they had exchanged a few words, 'that I am too busy to see anyone.'

Schooldays

———

What matter if I live it all once more?
Endure that toil of growing up;
The ignominy of boyhood; the distress
Of boyhood changing into man;
The unfinished man and his pain
Brought face to face with his own clumsiness.

When I think of all the books I have read, and of the
wise words I have heard spoken, and of the anxiety I
have given to parents and grandparents, and of the
hopes that I have had, all life weighed in the scales of
my own life seems to me a preparation for something that
never happens.

I

WHEN Willie was nine his father and mother moved from
Fitzroy Road to a house in West Kensington, 14 Edith Villas,
near Burne-Jones at North End. Fetched from Sligo, Willie
was brought, not to Edith Villas, but to Burnham Beeches,
where his father had gone to paint in company with some
friends – one of them Farrar, the American landscape artist.
The men were out all day, but Willie found delightful adventures alone, wandering about the country after moths
and butterflies, or dawdling round ponds where he could
imagine ships going in and out and think of Sligo and of
the fine ship he would launch when he grew up. Sometimes
he would forget to return to the lodging for the midday

meal, and often, with so much to entrance, fail to fix his mind on the lesson which his father set him before going out and heard in the evenings.

J. B. Y. was painting a large picture of a pond. He began it in the spring and painted it all through the year; the picture altered with the seasons, and was given up unfinished when the snow appeared upon the heath-covered banks. On Willie's leaving Sligo an aunt had said to him, 'In England you will be nobody at all', conveying a reproach to his father for not having yet made a success. Under fire of the Pollexfen criticism for his want of common-sense, J. B. Y. used to quote Poynter, who had said, 'He is right to work so long at the school and at studying instead of painting pictures – he works like a nigger.' Unfortunately J. B. Y. would never be satisfied, would never make himself say that a picture was finished. Also, he missed opportunities. 'A gentleman,' he would say, 'is such simply because he has not the doctrine of *getting* on and the habit of it. The contest is not against material things, but between those who want and those who don't want to get on, having other important things to attend to.' By preference he consorted with charming persons who were bound to miss the mark. Rossetti admired one of his works at the Dudley, and despatched three messengers inviting him to his house. J. B. Y. never went to Rossetti; whom he admired nevertheless. When Browning, who was pleased with a design that he had made for *Pippa Passes*, called on him, he was out. A friend wanted to take him to George Meredith, but this chance he also threw away. But his portfolios were already full of interesting, imaginative designs, and he had had a few commissions for portraits, one from the Herberts of Muckross, where he had been painting a young bride at the time that he was called to Sligo by the death of his son Robert. As the girl ran away from her husband immediately afterwards, the portrait was not wanted by the family, and J. B. Y. had not the heart to ask for payment. It was bought by Dowden, and is now in the possession of Mrs W. B. Yeats.

'I have no worries', J. B. Y. wrote to his wife during one of her absences in Sligo, 'except the abiding ones about my work and want of money, and absence from a quiet home of peace and happiness.' The rents from the Butler property in Kildare were no longer paid with regularity. Everything was talked over in the presence of the children, and the girls had a rag doll that they called Mrs Finnerty, after a Kildare tenant, and whipped when they heard their father complain of the recalcitrant rent-payer. The painter could protect himself against worries by his work; with his wife it was very different – she had no defence, not even an instinct of self-interest. 'Self-interest and self-preservation', J. B. Yeats once wrote to his son, 'are the death of poetry, and your mother had less of these things than anyone I ever met.' As a girl in Sligo Mrs Yeats had known no cares, and now she was unable to face the task of housekeeping for a poor man. At no time did she pretend to take any interest in painting; she never entered a studio, never visited an exhibition. Though physically strong she was never well, and soon after marriage she developed a cataract in one eye. When Sir William Wilde was consulted all he said to her was, 'You are married, leave it alone; but don't forget to ask your husband when his uncle Thomas is going to send me those fishing-rods.' In his autobiography the poet tells us that his mother left little impression upon his first childhood. When in good spirits (a rare fit for her) she could show a rich capacity for joy, and her letters to her husband would overflow with pleasure in her children and in scenery, especially in the movements of the waves and the clouds. Of these she would write at length.

The father took command of the household, terrifying Willie by descriptions of his moral degradation, putting him to tests of physical endurance far beyond his strength, shouting at him during lesson-time. He would suddenly say, 'You need more oxygen', and order the boy and his sister Lily to walk to the National Gallery and back, giving each of them a penny. At the Gallery Willie always went straight

to Frith's 'Derby Day', although he had heard at home of
better things. Exhausted and hungry, the children would
stop in the Park on the way forth or back to eat their penny
rolls and rest. Yet J. B. Y. could not bear that other children
should have the cry over his own. Willie had brought from
Sligo a model boat, 'The Rose', which he used to sail in the
Round Pond, Kensington Gardens. One's friends were made
according to the size of one's boat, and when J. B. Y. noticed
that 'The Rose' was treated with contempt and lowered his
son's social status among the other boys, he at once ordered
an expensive model of the famous yacht, 'Sunbeam', from
a shop in Holland Park Walk. Willie spent days in the little
courtyard watching the progress of the work; he was very
observant when interested, and once he came home with
an account of how he had seen 'Miss Knowles', the proprietor's daughter, aged four, toasting bread on the point
of her fingers. With this yacht, the name of which he
changed to 'Moonbeam',* he became Commodore of the
Model Yacht Club in the gardens, and his father's ambition
for him was for the time satisfied.

In 1876, after two years at Edith Villas, the family moved
to one of the new houses in Bedford Park. Bedford Park,
Norman Shaw's 'village', originated in the aestheticism of
William Morris; J. B. Y. had described it in glowing terms
to his family as a little city protected by walls against newspapers and the infections of commercial progress. There
were winding streets, big trees, and only the better houses
had then been built. The Yeatses' house, 8 Woodstock Road,
had a bathroom, Morris paper on the walls, and a garden
with apple trees, and all were thrilled. 'We could imagine',
the poet has said in *Reveries*,

people living happy lives as we thought people did long ago,
when the poor were picturesque and the master of a house would
tell of strange adventures over the sea. We went to live in a
house like those we had seen in pictures, and even met people

* It is interesting to notice that he preferred moon to sun when he
became astrologer. 'Banished heroic mother moon and vanished.'

dressed like people in the story-books. The newness of everything, the empty houses where we played at Hide-and-seek, and
the strangeness of it all, made us feel that we were living among
toys.

The boy had begun to take notice of his father's friends.
Most of them were artists who had been influenced by the
pre-Raphaelite movement, but had lost their confidence.
Wilson, Page, J. T. Nettleship, Potter, the painter of 'The
Dormouse', were constantly in and out of the house. Farrar
came in one day to describe the funeral of Potter, who died
from semi-starvation. The model, Nelly Whelan, half Irish,
half Italian, had tried to help Potter by finding a position
for herself in a board school, and Willie had seen her sitting
in the North End studio, a book in her hand, learning a
Latin lesson from J. B. Yeats. He preserved a memory of
her pre-Raphaelite beauty; and she remembered him and
sent him a telegram of congratulation on his seventieth
birthday.

2

Willie was now attending a day school, the Godolphin,
Hammersmith. This was a school for the sons of struggling
professional men, and it is characterized in the autobiography as 'rough' and 'cheap'. An inquiry made some
time ago elicited the information that 'the last headmaster
having died, no one knows where the school records are'.
Yeats wrote in 1911 that 'without being sure of exact dates',
he was at the Godolphin 'from about 1875 to 1880'. He kept
among his papers four of his reports from the Godolphin,
also a timetable of the lessons, drawn up by himself. The
last date on a report is Christmas Term 1878, when he was
in Form IIA. Here his 'general work' is described as 'very
good'; he was eighth in a class of thirty-one for Latin, his
best subject. The reports for Lent 1878 and Michaelmas
1877 refer to frequent absences which have interfered with
his progress. A fourth report is headed Summer Term; no

year is given; he is in Form II, as in the Michaelmas Term of 1877. 'A very good boy', writes his form master. 'Tries to do as well as he can. He does best in Latin and History, with perseverance he will do better. Conduct very good.' His mathematics are 'very poor', and in French he is *'faible, sans énergie'*. On the timetable of lessons, which is undated, and probably early, his subjects are described as 'Scripter', 'Riting', 'Reading', 'Inglish', 'Gramar', 'Arithmithick'. Spelling always bothered him; he gradually improved, but there were many common words he never got right (*e.g.* he wrote to the end 'exausted' for 'exhausted').

He was a gentle boy, and the masters had never the heart to be harsh with him. But there was some bullying out of school, and his physical strength was inadequate to make his resistance a success. 'I had a harassed life,' he says in *Reveries*, 'and got many a black eye and had many outbursts of grief and rage.... I was ashamed of my lack of courage, for I wanted to be like my grandfather, who thought so little of danger that he jumped overboard in the Bay of Biscay after an old hat.' But he was less unhappy than might have been expected, and he had the advantage of enjoying the protection of one of the finest athletes in the school, Cyril Vesey, who shared his passion for moths and butterflies. Vesey used to go home for the midday meal, often followed in dog-like devotion by Willie, who would sit in Mrs Vesey's garden and miss his own dinner (paid for as an extra by his parent) at the Godolphin. Should there be an extra pudding at the Veseys', Cyril would say to his mother, 'Can Yeats have some?' and Willie would come through the window. In his last term Willie won a race for a silver cup. Vesey started from scratch, and Willie kept looking round to see where his friend was. A mother was heard to say, 'Look at that boy. I wish I had the feeding of him.'

Visits to Sligo were now limited to a yearly holiday of a few weeks. The family – all but the father – detested London, and the poet has told in *Reveries* how once at the drinking-fountain near Holland Park, Lily and he came close to tears. 'I remember with wonder, for I had never known anyone that cared for such mementoes, that I longed for a sod of earth from some field I knew, something of Sligo to hold in my hand.' His mother would have thought such displays of emotion vulgar and English. Had she not mocked at tourists seen kissing at Irish railway stations, and taught her son to feel disgust at such lack of reserve? But it was she who kept alive the feeling for Sligo by telling stories told to her in her girlhood by the fishermen and pilots at Rosses Point.

There was romance in feeling oneself a foreigner from a disturbed country, and this sentiment helped Willie to preserve his self-respect at school. He was ignorant of the Irish national argument; his father, although a Liberal, and, in devotion to Isaac Butt, a Home Ruler, did not encourage an interest in politics, which he regarded as an inferior form of human activity. But when J. B. Y. spoke of English people, it was always detachedly, with a touch of disdain, unless they were artists. The Pollexfens were loyal Protestants and active Freemasons,* who suspected, and looked down upon, Roman Catholics and Nationalists; yet they too seemed to have an anti-English prejudice, as if they were an elect breed. The attitude was common enough among the Protestant and Unionist minority in the nineteenth century, and rather illogical when accompanied, as it usually was in the upper class, by a fervent British patriotism and a readiness to provide the Empire with its soldiers, sailors and administrators. The Yeatses (except distantly through the Corbets) were without military tradition and sentiments; J. B. Y. scoffed at the English fetish of 'character', telling his son that the fights among the boys at the school were another instance of English absurdity; and when Willie read of some English victory in class, he did not believe that he read of his own people. 'They thought of Cressy and Agincourt and the Union Jack and were all very patriotic, and I,

* Members of 'Light of the West' Lodge.

without those memories of Limerick and the Yellow Ford that would have strengthened an Irish Catholic, thought of mountain and lake, of my grandfather and of ships.'

When he arrived at the Clarence Basin, Liverpool, on his way to Sligo for the holidays, he felt he was among his own people. The sailors on the ship knew him, for as a little boy he had often gone down to Sligo quay to sail his boat; and the ss. *Sligo* and the ss. *Liverpool* belonged to the company of which his grandfather and William Middleton were directors. The voyage between Sligo and Liverpool took thirty hours and was often very uncomfortable, as the ships were small. But in fair weather there were lovely moments; the cliffs of Donegal seen at dawn, Tory Island, and the run-up past Rosses through Sligo Bay to the quays of the little town. However early the young people arrived, and whatever the time of year, a servant from Merville always awaited them at the pier, and Miss Lily Yeats retains a memory of a wintry morning when Ellie Connolly's cry 'The Lord love you, Master Willie', rang out through the darkness as the ship berthed. Mrs Pollexfen kept a large staff, and when one of the young maids, as often happened, emigrated to America, the children were awakened at four in the morning to be kissed and cried over. Willie was a particular pet, especially with Ellie Connolly, who forgave all his absences of mind, and was never angry when he upset the water-jug or let the fire out.

The poet's later childhood in Sligo has been thus depicted by his own hand:

I no longer cared for little shut-in places, for a coppice against the stable-yard at Merville where my grandfather lived or against the gable at Seaview where Aunt Micky lived, and I began to climb the mountains, sometimes with the stable-boy for companion, and to look up their stories in the county history . . .

One night just as the equinoctial gales were coming, when I was sailing home in the coastguard's boat, a boy told me a beetle of solid gold, strayed maybe from Poe's 'Gold Bug', had been seen by somebody in Scotland, and I do not think that either of us doubted his news. Indeed, so many stories did I hear from sailors along the wharf, or round the fo'castle fire of the little steamer that ran between Sligo and Rosses, or from boys out fishing that the world seemed full of monsters and marvels. The foreign sailors wearing earrings did not tell me stories, but like the fishing boys, I gazed at them in wonder and admiration. . . .

I had still my red pony, and once my father came with me riding too, and was very exacting. He was indignant and threatening because he did not think I rode well. . . . He himself, some Pollexfen told me, though he rode very badly, would go hunting upon anything and take any ditch. . . . Left to myself, I rode without ambition, though getting many falls, and more often to Rathbroughan where my great-uncle Mat lived, than to any place else. His children and I used to sail our toy-boats in the river before his house, arming them with toy cannon, touchpaper at all the touch-holes, always hoping but always in vain that they would not twist about in the eddies but fire their cannon at one another. I must have gone to Sligo sometimes in the Christmas holidays, for I can remember riding my red pony to a hunt. He baulked at the first jump, to my relief, and when a crowd of boys began to beat him, I would not allow it. . . . I fished for pike at Castle Dargan and shot at birds with a muzzle-loading pistol until somebody shot a rabbit and I heard it squeal. From that on I would kill nothing but the dumb fish.

3

The Yeatses returned to Ireland in 1880, partly for financial reasons. The Land War had caused a complete stoppage of rents from the Kildare farms. They settled in Howth, the all-but-island promontory which runs out into the Irish Sea, and serves to form the bay of Dublin on the north-east. Here for one winter J. B. Y. had the loan of a thatched cottage on the cliffs, called Balscadden. It was intended for summer use, and in the winter the sea sprayed the windows and sometimes soaked the beds. But it was convenient to the city, where J. B. Y. had taken a studio at 7 Stephen's Green. At the beginning of 1881 Willie was placed in the High School, Harcourt Street, and every morning father and son set out together for Dublin, eight miles distant by train. They breakfasted together at the studio and Willie returned to his father for a midday meal of bread and butter. At the High School, a foundation of Erasmus Smith, the Puritan philanthropist of the seventeenth century, most of the boys worked hard. No one asked, as they had done at the Godolphin, 'Who's your father?' for no one cared. The principal members of the staff were two brothers, William and George Wilkins, able men, with scornful tongues. William, the head master, had won honours at Trinity in literature as well as in mathematics; he wrote competent verse in his spare time. George, who resembled Henry VIII in appearance and was something of a sybarite, became a Fellow of Trinity later on, and caused surprise by taking orders.

The brothers were kind enough at first to the tall gaunt-looking lad with dark locks, who either would prepare his lessons and forget his note-books, or bring his note-books with nothing in them. He showed more interest in mathematics than in other subjects, but as a task-learner he was a failure, especially in Greek and Latin. Some of his deficiencies were attributed to his father, who made himself a great nuisance to Wilkins. J. B. Y. tried to browbeat the master into accepting his peculiar views on education. 'Don't you know', he would say, 'that geography and history are no training for the mind, and that all needed of them can be picked up in general reading?' After one of these interviews the head master turned on Willie: 'I am going to give you an imposition because unfortunately I can't give one to your father'. Yeats was worst of all in literature. He had the impression that Shakespeare was being read for the grammar only. If he had an ambition it was to excel as an entomologist. He would arrive at school his pockets stuffed with little cardboard pill-boxes, filled with his victims. Once while in class a beetle escaped and crossed the floor; with a bound Willie was after it and sprawling on the ground. The interruption of the lesson caused great commotion, and Yeats was made to report to Wilkins, who severely admonished him, and set him a task which occupied him for several hours after school time.*

After one winter at Balscadden Cottage J. B. Y. moved with his family to a small house called Island View above the old harbour of Howth, where at night the fishermen's smacks could be seen passing in and out under their coloured lights. The children still frequented Sligo with their mother. Lough Gill was frozen over in the winter of 1881–2, and all learned to skate. In summer Willie went boating at Rosses with the Middleton cousins, and once walked the five miles to Merville to carry into the drawing-room a conger-eel, its tail trailing along the carpet. Howth was a paradise for the entomologist, and when there he kept late hours chasing moths (once he caught a Death's Head, a thrilling experience) over the hill. He caused a sensation among a little group of intellectual boys at his school by announcing that he was a follower of Darwin and Wallace, Huxley and Haeckel, and shocked Cyril Vesey, who spent a holiday with him at Island View, by his arguments in refutation of Adam and Noah and the Seven Days. Vesey was a mere hobbyist and collector of facts; Yeats wanted to generalize, and there was no arguing with the athlete 'who still collected his butterflies for the adventure's sake, and with no curiosity but for their names'. Vesey fell further in Yeats's estimation by refusing to sail to Lambay Island and go without his dinner; so the friendship cooled. Yet when, many years later, Vesey came home from India on leave, his first thought was to seek out the poet. Both looked forward to the meeting with some excitement. But they had pitiably little to say to each other when they met in the hall of a London club.

The first book that Yeats planned was 'about the changes through a twelve-month among the creatures of some hole in the rock'. He had planned a hypothesis, which afterwards he could not recall, as to the colour of sea-anemones. There was general agreement in the family that he would become

* This story is taken from an anonymous article by a former schoolfellow which appeared in *T. P.'s Weekly* (June 1912).

a writer though perhaps not a poet. But when at seventeen he first began to write verses, his father remembered how, as a little boy, 'knowing no Latin and no Greek either', he had loved to repeat the phrase, *Magna est veritas et prævalebit*, and how on a Devonshire holiday in the summer of 1879 he had murmured for days the phrase of a village boy, 'I saw thee and the little brother and the maids at church'. His father talked nothing but literature to him now, beginning at breakfast before Willie made his way to school, when he read out passages from the poets, 'and always from the play or poem at its most passionate moment'. J. B. Y. would rail against Tennyson and Wordsworth, but probably these two poets received more of W. B.'s youthful admiration than he would have admitted at the time to his father's face. Fifty years afterwards he was asked, 'Whom did you venerate as a young man, Mr Yeats?' His answer came without hesitation, 'Tennyson'. On the question being repeated by the inquirer, who had not expected this answer, the reply was the same with the addition of 'Wordsworth'.

J. B. Y. had fixed ideas upon art in relation to humanity. He once wrote:

I don't think we have had in England a great poet since Shakespeare and Milton; and this because there has not been a great man. By a great man I do not mean a man great in virtue – the definition of virtue varies in every age – but somebody great in *humanity*, what I think might be better named character, energy. In this sense we use the word 'great' when we apply it to God, and think of his infinite love, infinite pity, infinite justice – even when we speak of his infinite power. Shakespeare was great because of his vast humanity. . . . Wordsworth, notwithstanding his genius, is to my mind a dull dog and his intensities and enthusiasms have something forced and factitious in them. . . . Shelley again has always seemed a little crazy, a little of a fanatic. . . . Byron, – talent rather than genius. . . . Browning was the non-conformist conscience trying to make itself vocal and musical – all *his* humanity gone away into some such channels; he thought poorly of human nature. . . . The stripling Keats, had he not died of consumption, would have died spiritually in the intellectual penury of the time; and as to Tennyson and his musical inanities – whom do they grip?

I do not of course expect you to answer all these statements which will probably appear to you too wild and paradoxical – but I write them because I want to say that I believe poets will ultimately find their salvation in writing plays for the public theatre. In this medium the greatest poets have worked. Homer did not write plays, but he wrote that his verses might be recited for heroes and warriors to listen to them . . . simple men with big imaginations.

Apparently Willie was not wholly influenced by his father's criticism, but it is interesting to find the father of the founder of the Abbey Theatre writing – 'Poets will ultimately find their salvation in writing plays for the public theatre'.

For a while longer Willie roamed about the hill of Howth, his green net slung across his shoulder. His pleasure in insects and in flowers on the hill did not fade, but his thought was now founded on literature, not on science. It was possible to spend a whole day in fairy glades, or upon the hill paths, and not see the face of one's kind. Sometimes he would trespass in the dark hours, exploring the grounds of Howth Castle, while his sisters sat up to greet him with a cup of cocoa on his return. The shores of the hill are rocky and precipitous and abound in gloomy caverns, and one of these he discovered and named MacCrom's Cave after an evicted tenant who had lived there for many years. On one warm night he slept in the cave; and when he found lovers there on a bank holiday he was disconsolate until he heard that the ghost of MacCrom had been seen a little before dawn, stooping over the fire in the cave mouth.

He began to act the sage and the magician. Sometimes he was Hamlet, 'an image of heroic self-possession'; at other times, as he climbed along a narrow ledge, Manfred on his glacier. Or he thought of Prince Athanase and his solitary lamp, or of Alastor whose melancholy he must share, disappearing at last from everybody's sight, as he disappeared drifting in a boat. ... His notion of women was founded on his favourite poets. They were victims of brief tragedy and loved in wild passion. Irish mythology was still a closed book to its future poet. His father knew nothing of the patriotic work in Celtic scholarship accomplished in modern times by O'Donovan and Curry and by countless obscure Irish linguists. Yet there was a mass of ancient tradition and folklore to be gathered by the wanderer on Howth. It had been a great resort of the Druids, and on the highest point of the hill is a cairn which marks the grave of Crimthann, a king of Ireland. Ireland's Eye, off Baily lighthouse, is the island of the sons of Nessan, called Innisfallen by Ossian. A cromlech in the demesne of Howth Castle is reputed to have been the first resting-place of Diarmuid and Grania, whose flight from Finn ended at Ben Bulben in Sligo.

Of Yeats's early writings, or at least of such of them as he printed, only 'The Ballad of Moll Magee' and the sketch 'Village Ghosts' in *The Celtic Twilight* are associated with the years at Howth. He told Agnes Tobin that he was seventeen when he wrote the ballad, but no doubt it was often rewritten before it appeared in *The Wanderings of Oisin, and Other Poems* five years later. It was suggested by a sermon heard in the Roman Catholic Church, and there is internal evidence that it came early, as it is his only poem in which are found 'vulgar' Anglo-Irish expressions, such as 'say' for sea, 'childer' for children. An unpublished poem of 1882 in broken metres had for subject a thicket between three roads, some distance from any of them, where he used to spend a great deal of his time. This thicket, he wrote long afterwards, gave him his first thought of what a long poem should be, 'a region into which one might wander from the cares of life', with characters 'no more real than the shadows that people the thicket'. He got the story 'Village Ghosts' from the servant at Island View, a fisherman's wife, with whom his mother used to talk over a cup of tea in the kitchen. His mother loved the activities of the fishing village; indeed the fishing people of Howth, and the pilots and

fishing people of Rosses Point, were the themes outside the
family that seemed of interest to her. J. B. Y., a sociable
man, brought his son to call on well-known Dublin people
who had villas on the western slopes of the hill. Willie went
unwillingly and felt shy and awkward. He would rather have
stayed at home, listening to his mother and the servant ex-
changing 'stories that Homer might have told'.

4

Holidays in the West were the happiest events in his life;
but now he no longer stayed with his grandparents, but with
his uncle George Pollexfen, who had come from Ballina to
fill the place of his grandfather, who had retired from business. Old William Pollexfen was not as rich as he had been
and had moved to a smaller house called Rathedmond,
which overlooked the port of Sligo. He occupied himself
with ordering his tomb at St John's Churchyard, where he
walked almost daily to superintend the work. Jack lived
with the grandparents and had replaced Willie in their
grandmother's affections. Jack had known how to come to an
understanding with 'the silent and fierce old man', and seated
happily together the pair would sometimes be seen driving
in a trap through Sligo, Jack holding a dinner-bell with
which to clear the traffic. He had begun to draw pilots and
tandems and donkey-races, but was always at the bottom
of the class at school, his grandmother said, 'because he is
too nice to compete'.*

George Pollexfen, a confirmed bachelor, rented an ugly
house, 'Thornhill', which might have grown in a terrace,
two miles outside the town – an old three-storied house with
a small garden in front and a yard and a field at the back.
In J. B. Y.'s portrait, painted at this time, his brother-in-law
has a long skull, small very blue eyes, and looks the sports-
man. George Pollexfen was still a member of the racing

* York Powell, the famous historian, said of Jack Yeats, 'He is the
best educated man I have ever met.'

confraternity and kept horses in his field, but he had almost ceased to ride, having become a hypochondriac. He lived in great discomfort at Thornhill in winter, and spent the summer in a draughty house at Rosses, near the little pier, with a view across 'Memory Harbour' to Knocknarea.*

In spite of the low spirits which he cultivated, George Pollexfen could be excellent company. He had a wonderful faculty for keeping one absolutely entranced by the skill with which he could describe an incident in itself trifling. He was also an excellent listener and a man of sensitive and artistic tastes; he read poetry: Tennyson's *Idylls of the King* gave him particular pleasure. When first he visited London at the age of forty-five it was to see the exhibition at the Royal Academy. His only other journeys were to races; he never missed the Grand National at Liverpool. Yeats soon held his uncle in great affection, confiding to him dreams and ambitions undisclosed to his more argumentative and impatient father.

It was during one of his early visits to Thornhill that Yeats planned the night walk of thirty miles round Lough Gill, which is thus described in *Reveries*:

My father had read me some passage out of *Walden*, and I planned to live some day in a cottage on a little island called Innisfree, and Innisfree was opposite Slish Wood where I meant to sleep. I thought that having conquered bodily desire and the inclination of my mind towards women and love, I should live, as Thoreau lived, seeking wisdom. . . . I set out from Sligo about six in the evening, walking slowly, for it was an evening of great beauty; but though I was well into Slish Wood by bedtime, I could not sleep, not for the discomfort of the dry rock I had chosen for my bed, but from my fear of the wood-ranger.

He returned exhausted next day with an account of his experience, and for months afterwards his uncle's general

* 'Memory Harbour', the title of an early picture by Jack B. Yeats, showing houses and anchored ship, the Metal Man (pointing where the water is deep enough for ships) and the bearded pilot. The picture was used as the frontispiece to *Reveries*.

servant brought blushes to his cheeks by bursting into laughter whenever the walk was alluded to. She could not be convinced that he had not been out with a girl.

In Tadhg Kilgannon's *Guide to Sligo* there is a photograph marked, *Innisfree, Yeats' bed in the foreground*. In a letter dated Savile Club, 30 November 1922, replying to the girls of the present Northgate School, Ipswich, who had asked 'Is Innisfree a real Island?', Yeats wrote:

Dear Ladies,

Yes, there is an island called Innisfree, and it is in Lough Gill, Co. Sligo. I lived in Sligo when I was young, and longed, while I was still as young as you, to build myself a cottage on this island and live there always. Later on I lived in London and felt very homesick and made the poem, 'The Lake Isle of Innisfree'.

Another time, when Yeats was with his uncle at Rosses Point, he woke his cousin, Henry Middleton, at midnight and asked him to get his yacht out. He wanted, having already imagined his poem, *The Shadowy Waters*, to find what sea-birds began to stir before dawn. He was then eighteen, and it was in the same year, at Ballisodare, while staying with the Middletons, that he had the ghostly experience already recorded, when his mind took the ply which it ever afterwards retained. Now, instead of arguing against 'Adam and Noah and the Seven Days', he asked himself whether one should not believe in all that had ever been believed, or at least put the onus of disproof on the disbeliever; and when one night, near Rosses, a fire blazed on a green bank on his right side, and another fire answered from Knocknarea, he did not doubt that he saw again the mysterious lights that he had previously seen by the river at Ballisodare. Except perhaps for Drumcliff, Ballisodare was reputed to be the most 'gentle' (that is, the most haunted) spot in Sligo, and henceforth, whenever he went with his cousins to the cottages, he was on the lookout for stories of the supernatural. The conversation of his uncle's housekeeper, Mary Battle, who had second sight and a speculative mind (she had a theory of the nearness together of heaven, hell and purgatory), assembled further 'phantoms of the human mind' for his delectation. He has acknowledged the debt of his *Celtic Twilight* to her humour and rich turn of speech. Gradually he acquired a considerable knowledge of country beliefs and of prehistoric traditions in Sligo; but some time passed before he thought of making verses and stories out of the knowledge or formed the modest ambition of doing for Sligo what William Allingham had done for Ballyshannon.

5

At the Dublin High School he now stood ostentatiously aloof from the generality of the boys. He wrapped himself up in a dream of superiority, as an artist and the son of an artist, and made no attempt to conquer prejudice. A class-mate, who characterized himself as one of the 'vulgar herd', wrote of him when he became famous* that 'there was something quietly repellent in his manner at school which affected even his relations with the masters'; a sentence which drew from J. B. Y. the comment, 'The creature found your manners repellent: I should rather hope it – *with him*; who is he at all?' It became known that W. B. wrote verse, and the classical master, probably aware that his own metrical productions were slighted by this pupil, sneered, and made ambiguous jokes about the 'nights out' on Howth, of which exaggerated accounts had reached Harcourt Street. But 'Willie Yeats', as he was called, found a few admirers among those whom John Eglinton, who was at the school with him, has called 'unlikely boys', mostly younger than himself. To these he was gracious. His essays began to excite the attention of his more bookish fellows. 'They used to impress me', Canon Jourdan writes, 'as full of imagery and fancy, such as I now know forecast the poet's powers of imagination and creative thought.' John Eglinton remem-

*T. P.'s Weekly, June 1912.

bers that he held his manuscript thrust out in front of him and declaimed his sentences just as he did those of Demosthenes, and that, curiously enough, no one laughed. He never got a prize because the essays were judged by the handwriting and spelling alone. Among those who perceived and acknowledged his superiority were Charlie Johnston, a handsome youth and brilliant classical scholar, and a boy from Sligo named Fred Saunders, who recalls that 'in those days' he did not walk with his eyes on the ground but gazed upwards. 'In the exercise yard the boys would play hurley, the forerunner of hockey, and the masters used to parade up and down to keep themselves warm – gowns flapping in the wind.' Mr Saunders adds, 'I don't think W. B. ever bent down to pick up a ball! I don't remember ever having seen him run!'

6

Eighteen-eighty-three was Yeats's last year at the school, and during it his attendances were intermittent. He came to regret that his father had not taken him away earlier and taught him only Greek and Latin, the subjects in which he was weakest, so that he would not have had to look at the classics through the poor mechanism of translations, nor face authority 'with the timidity born of excuse and evasion'.

Some friends of the family thought that Willie should complete his education at the University. But there was a doubt whether he could pass the entrance examination, and the fees at Trinity being another consideration, he was put to attend classes at the Metropolitan School of Art in Kildare Street. It was J. B. Y.'s opinion that every boy, whatever he might intend to do in after life, should have a training in art. A rich Dublin woman, who was an artist, reproached J. B. Yeats for not preparing his son for a profession. 'You can make the boy a doctor for fifteen shillings a week', she said. 'Listen to this', he replied, and read out some of Willie's verses. She had to admit they were good and said no more.

At the art school the boy showed some promise, but met

with little encouragement from his teachers. 'I do not believe that I worked well', he says in his autobiography.

. . . The work I was set to bored me. When alone and uninfluenced, I longed for pattern, for pre-Raphaelitism, for an art allied to poetry, and returned again and again to our National Gallery to gaze at Turner's 'Golden Bough'. Yet I was too timid, had I known how, to break away from my father's style and the style of those about me. I was always hoping that my father would return to the style of his youth, and make pictures out of certain designs now lost, that one could still find in his portfolios.

The warmest influence upon him at the school was that of George Russell (AE), the poet and mystic, a tall slip of a lad from the north who sketched his religious visions instead of drawing from the model. A mad and pious student came in with a daisy-chain hung round his neck, and to him Russell lent a little theosophical work, *Light on the Path*. The student stayed away for some days and then returned looking very troubled. He gave the book back saying, 'You will drift into a penumbra'. In the modelling class, to which Yeats presently went, were two serious workers, John Hughes and Oliver Sheppard, afterwards distinguished sculptors. Sheppard had been in Paris, and wore a loose tie, like a French artist. Yeats took him aside and inquired with great earnestness where such ties could be bought in Dublin; both he and Russell wanted one, he said. Yeats's tie, when he found it, was scarlet, and it lit up his sallow face effectively. In other details of his dress he was negligent. His clothes bore the marks of the studio; once he was seen scrubbing at a paint stain with olive oil, which he took to be turpentine. As he modelled he would sway backwards and forwards, reciting his verses; and Oliver Sheppard remembers that once while so engaged he stepped back into the modelling clay with disastrous results to his very short trousers, which were said at the school to have been his grandfather's.

Though he proposed to earn a living by art, Yeats continued to write poetry, mostly plays on romantic far-away things in the manner of Shelley and Edmund Spenser. These

works were passed from hand to hand, and a good many
people were interested, one of the first to feel sure of his
talent being T. W. Lyster, the Dublin librarian, who afterwards showed him how to correct proofs. From the first he
composed aloud; there is a reference to this habit, never lost,
in a letter written by his father to Edward Dowden:

> Jan. 7th, 1884
>
> Could you send me Willie's MS. – his railway ticket is up so
> that he is a prisoner at Howth and cannot go for it – if you rolled
> it up and put a stamp on it would it not come safely – he wants it
> for a rehearsal which is to come off immediately.
>
> Of course I never dreamed of publishing the effort of a youth
> of eighteen – The only passage in it which seems to me finally to
> decide the question as to his poetic faculty is the dialogue be-
> tween Time and the Queen – There was evidence in it of some
> power (however rudimentary) of thinking – as if some day he
> might have something to tell.
>
> I tell him prose and verse are alike in one thing – the best is
> that to which went the hardest thoughts. This also is the secret
> of originality, also the secret of sincerity – so far I have his con-
> fidence – That he is a poet I have long believed – where he may
> rank is another matter.
>
> That the doubt may have a chance of resolving itself I favour
> his wish to be an artist – his bad metres arise very much from his
> composing in a loud voice, manipulating of course the quantities
> to his taste.

Yeats and Russell wrote in rivalry; for one play they took
for subject a magician who sets up his throne in Asia, and
expresses himself with Queen Mab-like heresy. 'His great
drama, *The Equator of Olives*, is finished', Russell wrote to a
friend at about this time. 'The episode of the Sculptor's
Garden is in it. You should get practice by writing continuously. ... Yeats does so, and so do some other literary
acquaintances of mine, they do not mind tearing up.' Russell,
whose memory for words was extraordinary, had every page
written by heart.

Towards the end of 1884 a high-class literary and political
periodical, the *Dublin University Review*, was established in

Dublin, and in it Yeats made his first appearance before the
public (in March 1885) with two lyrics, the one beginning

> A man has a hope of heaven
> But soulless a fairy dies

being probably inspired by the eschatology of Paddy Flynn,
a figure in *The Celtic Twilight* who was the great teller of
tales in the Middleton village of Ballisodare, and knew 'how
to empty heaven, hell and purgatory, fairy-land and earth,
to people his stories'. 'Voices', the second of the lyrics, a
precious example of the poet's early work, has, with some
changes ('make' for 'weave' in the first line, and 'I make the
cloak of Sorrow' for 'The cloak I weave of Sorrow'), happily
been preserved in collected editions under the title 'The
Cloak, the Boat, and the Shoes'.

> 'What do you make so fair and bright?'
> 'I make the cloak of Sorrow:
> O lovely to see in all men's sight
> Shall be the cloak of Sorrow,
> In all men's sight.'

> 'What do you build with sails for flight?'
> 'I build a boat for Sorrow:
> O swift on the seas all day and night
> Saileth the rover Sorrow,
> All day and night.'

> 'What do you weave with wool so white?'
> 'I weave the shoes of Sorrow:
> Soundless shall be the footfall light
> In all men's ears of Sorrow,
> Sudden and light.'

Both lyrics were taken from an arcadian play, *The Island
of Statues*, which was subsequently published in the *Dublin
University Review*. Shelley and (to a lesser extent) Spenser
were still the poet's exemplars, and after being reprinted in
The Wanderings of Oisin, and Other Poems (1889) the play

was cast away as a work too much influenced by the romantic vocabulary of *Prometheus* and as weak in the handling of the longer metres. He read books on prosody, but could never remember what was in them. 'You will notice', he wrote in old age to a friend, Edith Shackleton, sending her a poem, 'how bothered I am when I get to prosody, because it is the most certain of my instincts, [but] the subject of which I am most ignorant. I do not even know if I shall write the mode of accent or stress thus ' or thus.'

The family was now at 10 Ashfield Terrace, Harold's Cross, variously described in the autobiography as 'the Terenure house', 'the Harold's Cross house' and 'the Rathgar house', Terenure, Harold's Cross and Rathgar being adjoining suburbs. By living near Dublin J. B. Y. could meet and dine with leaders of the Bar and College celebrities, who might give him commissions for portraits. He was always hoping to 'get a judge', and never failed to put in an appearance at the dinners in King's Inn, for which he kept his old barrister's gown. He had many friends, of whom the most important from his son's point of view was Edward Dowden, an obliging neighbour with a comfortable house in Rathgar lined with books. Dowden frequently asked J. B. Y. and Willie to breakfast and paid friendly attention to the verses which Willie read out to him after the meal. The dark good looks of the professor, his self-possession and rich store of knowledge, employed at this time on his Life of Shelley, made due impression on the young poet. A little later J. B. Y. brought his son to the Contemporary Club, of which the founder was Hubert Oldham, editor of the *Dublin University Review*, a political economist and leader of a small group of intellectual Protestant Home Rulers in Trinity College. It was in Oldham's College rooms that Yeats read 'The Island of Statues' to a large audience which included young Professor Bury (afterwards Acton's successor in the chair of History at Cambridge), who gave his vote in favour of publication. Both Unionists and Nationalists used the club, and though one was there supposed to be out of hearing of party

yells of hatred, the debates were often harsh and violent,
even when non-political questions were being discussed.
Yeats presently began to intervene in the debates. He says
that he spoke easily when not interrupted, but when someone was rude he would fall into silence or talk wildly. Then
he would spend hours in going over his words and putting
the wrong ones right. It was his secret ambition to 'be able
to play with hostile minds as Hamlet played, to look in the
lion's face, as it were, with unquivering eyelash'. He met at
the club, and also at Dowden's house, where argument was
always conducted with sobriety and taste, other young
writers, notably Douglas Hyde, Stephen Gwynn, T. W.
Rolleston and W. F. Stockley, most of them a little older
than himself. 'Some of us', says Stephen Gwynn, 'were recognized as counting for something and likely to count for
more. But every one of us was convinced that Yeats was
going to be a better poet than we had yet seen in Ireland;
and the significant fact is that this was not out of personal
liking.'

7

George Russell was never seen at Dowden's, nor at the Contemporary Club, but he would often spend an evening at
Ashfield Terrace with the Yeats household. When all the
rest of the family had retired to bed, Willie and he would
sit in the kitchen, cook a meal, and then chant their verses
to each other. It was supposed upstairs that they were trying
to disincarnate themselves. The elder Yeats was a little
critical of this friendship, for he detected in Russell, already
spoken of as the religious leader of the future, the ethical
complacency of the Ulster Protestant. 'A saint but raised in
Portadown', he would say, or 'He has no love, no admiration
for the individual man. He is too religious to care for really
mortal things, or rather, for he does care, to admire and love
them.' J. B. Y. would tell Willie that in him there was no
trace of religion: 'You can only pretend it – your interest is

in mundane things, and Heaven to you is this world made better, whether beyond the stars or not.'

Ernest Boyd tells in *Ireland's Literary Renaissance* how the Theosophic Movement in Dublin originated one afternoon at Dowden's house, when, Yeats being present, somebody spoke of a strange book which had just appeared – A. P. Sinnett's *Esoteric Buddhism*. Yeats procured a copy of the book and recommended it to Charlie Johnston, the brilliant High School boy, who at the time wanted to be a Christian missionary. Johnston read the book and it converted him to Esoteric Buddhism, after which he and a few others joined with Yeats, who had a love for closed circles, for everything that is secret and intimate (inherited no doubt from the Freemason Pollexfens), in taking a room at the top of a dilapidated house in York Street, to 'outwatch the Bear, with thrice-great Hermes'. 'A Society', wrote the *Dublin University Review*, 'has been started in Dublin to promote oriental religions and theosophy generally. It has been called the Hermetic Society. The name is a peculiar one. But as its business will be with a philosophy which, until latterly, has been entirely secret, or only revealed in symbolism, it may be considered appropriate.'

In the next year, 1886, Johnston crossed to London to interview Madame Blavatsky, and returned to form the famous Dublin Lodge, which for many years had rooms in Ely Place. Yeats was never a member of the Lodge, though he was in and out of the rooms a great deal, chiefly to see George Russell, who quickly assumed leadership of the little community. At the first meeting of the Hermetic Society Yeats had proposed that whatever the great poets had affirmed in their finest moments was the nearest one could get to an authoritative religion, and this one unshakable conviction he found no one to share. The Orient, however, laid a strong hold upon his imagination, and he was fascinated by a Bengali Brahmin, Babu Mohini Chatterji, who visited Dublin at the time that the Theosophical Lodge was being founded. The Brahmin had been one of the earliest members of the Theosophical Society in India,* and possessed a wide knowledge of the different schools of Indian philosophy, as well as of Western philosophy and religion. He taught that everything we perceive, including so-called illusions, exists in the external world; that this is a stream which flows on, out of human control; that we are nothing but a mirror and that deliverance consists in turning the mirror away so that it reflects nothing. This philosophy satisfied Yeats until William Blake drove it out of his head; he made the verses, not reprinted:

> Long thou for nothing, neither sad nor gay.
> Long thou for nothing, neither night nor day,
> Not even, 'I long to see thy longing over,'
> To the ever longing and mournful spirit say.

Somebody asked Mohini Chatterji if one should pray, and he answered, 'No, one should say before sleeping: "I have lived many lives, I have been a slave and a prince. Many a beloved has sat upon my knees and I have sat upon the knees of many a beloved. Everything that has been shall be again"': words which forty years later Yeats turned into verses, which the Brahmin, then an old man and blind in London, had his daughter read to him.

> I asked if I should pray,
> But the Brahmin said,
> 'Pray for nothing, say
> Every night in bed,

* He is mentioned in a passage of *The Personal Memoirs of H. P. Blavatsky*. H. P. B. wrote to Mr Sinnett late in 1883 that 'Olcott will probably sail for India on various business and Mahatma K. H. sends his chila, under the guise of Mohini Mohun Chatterji, to explain to the London Theosophists of the Secret Section every or nearly every *mooted* point. . . . Do not make the mistake of taking the *Mohini you knew* for the Mohini who will come. There is more than one *Maya* in this world of which neither you nor your friends are cognisant. The ambassador will be invested with an *inner* as well as with an *outer* clothing. *Dixit*.'

"I have been a king,
I have been a slave,
Nor is there anything,
Fool, rascal, knave,
That I have not been,
And yet upon my breast
A myriad heads have lain".'

A story told by Yeats in his autobiography shows that he was accounted a guiding spirit in this movement towards the East. He chanced upon his former High School master in the street, and the latter begged him to desist from spoiling the career of his prize pupil, Charlie Johnston, who had been expected to make a brilliant entry into the Indian Civil Service. Yeats was in great alarm, but managed to stammer out a text from the Bible about the children of light, and Wilkins went off with an angry sneer. Johnston, however, passed his examinations successfully, after which he went to Russia to marry Madame Blavatsky's niece. Only one member of the Lodge, a lady, approved. She said, 'Oh, that beautiful young man. How wicked of Theosophists to try and prevent people from falling in love.'

'The Indian upon God', 'The Indian to his Love', 'The Sad Shepherd' and the quatrain quoted above, were spontaneous expressions of Yeats's new philosophic convictions. With a few other short poems, not reprinted, an article on Sir Samuel Ferguson and the dramatic poem, *Mosada*, they appeared in the *Dublin University Review* during the course of 1886. *Mosada*, a Moorish story with an Inquisitor as the principal character, was regarded as Yeats's most important production to date, and J. B. Y., assisted by Dowden, collected a few subscribers, so that it might be brought out as a pamphlet in stiff covers by a firm of Dublin printers. The young English priest, Gerard Manley Hopkins, then a lecturer at the Catholic University College, writing to Coventry Patmore about the 'odds and ends' of poets and poetesses he had been meeting in Dublin, added to his list a 'young Mr Yeats who has written in a Trinity College publication some

striking verses'. . . . 'I called', Hopkins went on, 'on his, young
Yeats' father, by invitation, and with some emphasis he
presented me with *Mosada, A Dramatic Poem*, by W. B.
Yeats, the young man having finely-cut features, and his
father being a fine draughtsman. For a young man's pamphlet this was something too much; but you will understand
a father's feeling.' Fortunately Hopkins was not required to
praise what presumably he had not then read. But he had
read a poem ('The Two Titans') about a young man and a
sphinx on a rock in the sea, and could say (although the
allegory seemed to him 'strange and unworkable') that he
liked this.*

Thirty years were to pass before much of Hopkins's own
work was published. When 'sprung verse' became the fashion
and his influence replaced that of Bridges and of Hardy,
Yeats recalled in his Oxford *Modern Verse* 'a sensitive and
querulous scholar', met on several occasions in his father's
studio, and (in conversation) 'a religious Englishman, which
is in itself an absurdity'. The principal subscriber to *Mosada*
was Edward Dowden's brother, the Bishop of Edinburgh,
who, on hearing some years later of Yeats's rising fame and
of the rarity of this early work, jingled his episcopal keys
and sent his daughter up to the Palace library to search for
his twelve copies. Not one could be found.

8

Yeats's article on Samuel Ferguson was a eulogy of a poet
lately dead, whose work had been the largest effort yet made
to interpret through the medium of English the history and
the spirit of Celtic Ireland. In reading Ferguson, Yeats is
reminded of 'some aged king, sitting among the inland
wheat and poppies – with the savour of the sea about him

---

* *Further Letters from Gerard Manley Hopkins*, edited by Charles
Collier Abbott. 'The Two Titans' was omitted from Yeats's later
collections.

and its strength'. Here is 'an author who brings a clear glass once more as when the world was young', whose 'nature descriptions are not a mask behind which go the sad soliloquies of the nineteenth century.' Ferguson is the greatest modern poet Ireland has produced, because 'the most central and the most Celtic'; and the race, 'now so widely spread and so conscious of its unity', will find its morning in this writer of 'antique quality, breadth and sincerity'.

Ireland owed to Ferguson an example of solid, slow-wrought, well-founded workmanship, drawing its inspiration from a real study of the Irish mythology, legend and history. He had been neglected during his lifetime and now after his death was being over-praised by the patriotic school. Hopkins, who had been set to read him by his colleagues at the University, observed that, like the rest of the Irish poetical fellowship originating in the Young Ireland movement of 1848, he lacked 'species', individual beauty and style. Yeats's article was rhetorical, and he did not stand by it at a later date. Its interest resided in its character of a manifesto, in which a young man of Protestant and 'Anglo-Irish' upbringing, whose first work had appeared in a Trinity College publication, came out definitely on the side of an entity known as 'Celtic Ireland', avowed his faith in a distinctive national literature, written in English but deriving from native sources, and attacked the culture of Trinity College and of the educated classes as academic and servile to English notions.

It was at the Contemporary Club that Yeats met John O'Leary, who became a chief stimulating impact upon his life and awakened in him the desire of intellectual leadership in Ireland. This lean and bearded man, with pathetic eyes and grave and noble head, was still under sixty, but seemed venerable to Yeats, and the more so when he heard his story. O'Leary was the son of a small property-owner in Tipperary, and while a medical student at Trinity College, had come across the poems and essays of Thomas Davis of the *Nation*, and these had altered the world for him, making him feel that for better or worse his fate was linked with that of his country. He joined Young Ireland clubs, and afterwards became one of the Triumvirate with Stephens and Luby in the Fenian conspiracy which succeeded Young Ireland as the non-transacting force in Irish politics. He served a sentence of five years' penal servitude, of which he would never speak ('I was in the hands of my enemies, why should I complain?'), and was an exile in Paris for fifteen years; when he came back to Dublin he won the respect of all, perhaps particularly of the Protestants and Unionists. Once when Yeats was defending a certain Irishman who was making a great outcry about his prison treatment, by showing that it was done for propaganda, he said, 'There are things a man must not do to save a nation'. He condemned the Irish-American dynamite party and disliked the gainful Nationalism of the Land League. 'Your average bourgeois', he would say, 'may make a good sort of agitator ... a rebel, however, you can never make him, for here the risk is immediate and certain, and the material advantage distant.' He never underrated English character and intelligence, and would maintain that there was never a cause so bad that it was not defended by good men and for worthy motives. 'He admitted no ground for reform outside the moral life', says Yeats.

He had no philosophy, but things distressed his palate, and two of those things were International propaganda and the Organised State, and Socialism aimed at both, nor could he speak such words as 'philanthropy', 'humanitarianism', without showing by his tone of voice that they offended him. The Church pleased him little better ...

His sister, who wrote poetry, kept house for him in Leinster Road, and the first time Yeats called several middle-aged women were playing cards. They suggested his taking a hand and gave him a glass of sherry; the sherry went to his head and he was impoverished by the loss of sixpence. Ellen O'Leary described her brother's life, the Fenian movement and the arrests and sentences, without rancour. Yeats was moved, and when O'Leary lent him the poems of Davis and of other patriots, of whom he knew nothing, he read them eagerly. He knew that the most of their work was poor poetry, yet it brought to light a congenital sentiment, and he who had never wanted to see the houses where Keats and Shelley had lived would ask everybody what sort of place Inchedony was, because Callanan had named after it a bad poem. O'Leary, a genuine bookman with a sense of the religion of letters, recognized that much of what passed for national literature among patriotic Irishmen was third-rate stuff. He despised what he called the spurious Irishry of Thomas Moore's songs and knew that the interest of Thomas Davis in poetry had not been equal to his patriotic inspiration. On the other hand, as a disciple of Montaigne and a man whose literary taste was founded on eighteenth-century criticism, he could share but few of the enthusiasms of his young political disciple. O'Leary frowned upon Yeats's interest in the preternatural, and Yeats used often to ask himself how he could have won this friendship and why O'Leary, who probably cared for no English poet since Pope, should have believed in his talent. No doubt it was Yeats's integrity that attracted O'Leary, and they were moreover both agreed in wishing that Irish Nationalism should not be strengthened by second-rate literature or second-rate morality.

O'Leary had two other disciples, T. W. Rolleston and J. F. Taylor; the one an accomplished scholar from Trinity and the other, J. F. Taylor, an unsuccessful barrister of ungainly appearance and disagreeable manners but a notable orator, who became when he spoke like a great actor in a poor play. Rolleston, who wrote one lovely poem, was ready to work with Yeats, but he was constantly disappointing, as if he had no desires but measured everything by some foot-rule made in University or Department. Taylor, the opposite of all this, was invariably rude to Yeats, mistaking, from his habit of religious and political apologetics, the search for style and wisdom for effeminacy or affectation. Yet Yeats remembered with pride that Taylor once stopped him in the street to say, 'If you and Rolleston were born in a small Italian principality in the Middle Ages, he would have friends at Court and you would be in exile with a price on your head.'

9

In Sligo, as a boy, Yeats had enjoyed no social acquaintance with Nationalists and Catholics; now he went to their houses in Dublin where he was perhaps happier than in the company of his father's friends, legal and academic luminaries, who were apt to be critical of his absences of mind, his untidiness and lack of worldly sense. He became definitely a Nationalist, and henceforward never thought of the English – even if there were times when he preferred to live among them – as anything but foreigners. A patriotic society met in the lecture hall of a workmen's club with O'Leary for president, and there four or five Catholic students and himself and, occasionally, Taylor spoke on Irish history and on Irish literature.

I began to plot and scheme how one might seal with the right image the soft wax before it began to harden. I had noticed that Irish Catholics among whom had been born so many political martyrs had not the good taste, the household courtesy and decency of the Protestant Ireland I had known, yet Protestant Ireland seemed to think of nothing but getting on in the world. I thought we might bring the halves together if we had a national literature that made Ireland beautiful in the memory, and yet had been freed from provincialism by an exacting criticism, an European prose.*

He was now publishing work in the *Irish Monthly* and the *Irish Fireside*, two periodicals which chiefly circulated in Roman Catholic households. Here he published 'The Meditation of the Old Fisherman', 'The Fairy Doctor', 'The Fairy

* *Reveries over Childhood and Youth.*

Pedant', and his first Sligo poem, 'The Stolen Child'; he would write no more about Spanish Inquisitors and Greek islands. In spite of his Quietist philosophy learned from the Indian, he wanted to make ballads for his country, caring less who made the laws. Hugo still ruled the spheres, and for a time Yeats believed that, while refraining from putting political opinion in their verse, Irish poets should write out of 'a gusty energy that would put all straight if it came out of the right heart'.* His love of literature and his belief in nationality came together easily enough. He had more difficulty in finding a relation between them and his particular form of thought.

Father Matthew Russell, the editor of the *Irish Monthly*, had praised *Mosada* as 'the voice of a new singer of Erin, who will take a high place among the world's future singers'. Father Russell was a kindly, courteous man who was not afraid to publish poems about fairies by a Protestant. He had gathered a bevy of poets around him, among them the talented Katharine Tynan, a girl with red-gold hair, religious and of eager admiring disposition, daughter of a fine old-fashioned type of Irish farmer, prominent in Parnellite politics. Yeats had been taken to see her by Hubert Oldham in the summer of 1885, and after that they met at John O'Leary's house, as she shared his admiration for the old Fenian. They became friends, and read books together; she introduced him to her own little literary circle, where he was tireless in his talk of poetry, as interested in others' work as in his own. He was made welcome at 'Whitehall', her father's hospitable house under the Dublin hills, and he would tramp the five miles to it in all weathers, once arriving like a snowman, unconscious of his plight, to be warmed and dried and fed. He was much more quickly at ease in the society of women than in that of men, and in Katharine Tynan's various books of memories he is portrayed as the gentlest of creatures, the most sympathetic and helpful of critics. 'How little you care for your own fair youth', she

* *Vide* 'What is "Popular Poetry"?' in *Ideas of Good and Evil.*

wrote when they were both middle-aged, and he had become a many-sided Goethean personality, a realistic politician, and rather formidable to her and to others of his early friends.

$$\lceil 3 \rceil$$

London (1887-91)

Early commissions – *The Wanderings of Oisin* – William
Morris – Meeting with Maud Gonne – Madame
Blavatsky; Magic – Writing for the theatre and on Blake
– 'Innisfree'; The Rhymers' Club

———

Who will go drive with Fergus now,
And pierce the deep wood's woven shade,
And dance upon the level shore?
Young man, lift up your russet brow,
And lift your tender eyelids, maid,
And brood on hopes and fear no more.

I

DURING the six years at Howth and in Rathgar, J. B. Y. had
painted several fine portraits and made many good friends.
Yet in 1887 he decided to pack up once more and see what
luck held for him and his children (now all grown up except
Jack) in London. With their faithful servant Rose and a
black cat named Daniel O'Connell, the family sweltered
during the torrid June of Jubilee at 58 Eardley Crescent,
Earl's Court. Little Jack alone was happy, for he possessed a
free ticket for the American Exhibition near by,* which he
visited every day and all day. J. B. Y. sought to get black-
and-white work taken by the magazines while Willie en-
deavoured to make acquaintance with editors and publishers. Nothing prospered, and towards the end of the
summer Mrs Yeats suffered the paralytic stroke which affected her mind. Her elder daughter, Miss Lily Yeats, brought

* The promoters provided residents of the Crescent situated within
hearing of the Exhibition with free tickets as a compensation for the
pandemonium.

her for the winter to a Pollexfen aunt, wife of a vicar in a remote Yorkshire parish, where they were snowed up for several weeks. She seemed to get better, but after their return to London had a second stroke and fell downstairs. Soon she was living entirely in one room, forgetful at last of money troubles, occasionally able to read a little, never allowing it to be said that she was an invalid, and finding happiness in feeding the birds at her window.

A note in Katharine Tynan's diary shows W. B. in Dublin again: 'December 1887, W. B. brought a boy, George Russell, with him. Fond of mysticism and extraordinarily interesting. Another William Blake.' W. B. wore a feather in his cap: his poem 'King Goll' had been printed in *The Leisure Hour*, the first English magazine to publish him. The poem was illustrated; a drawing of himself (he wore a beard) by his father depicted him as the King driven mad and made a wanderer by mysterious presences in the winds and waters. He tears the strings out of a harp, his eyes are dreamy and he has a great mass of black hair; but there is no record of any young girl having fallen in love with him.

> I wander on, and wave my hands,
> And sing, and shake my heavy locks.
> The grey wolf knows me; by one ear
> I lead along the woodland deer;
> The hares run by me growing bold.
> They will not hush, the leaves a-flutter round me, the
> beech leaves old.

After a stay in Sligo Yeats returned to London where he found the family once more established at Bedford Park. John Todhunter, poet and doctor, best known as the author of a school Algebra, helped J. B. Y. to find the house, 3 Blenheim Road, and saw that it had a good boiler, the Yeats family being greatly addicted to hot baths. 'The house', W. B. wrote to Katharine Tynan, 'is fine and roomy ... everything is a little idyllic.' He was still 'in all things pre-Raphaelite', but the charm had gone that he had felt when as a schoolboy he played among the unfinished houses and passed the co-operative stores, with their little seventeenth-century panes. At the back of the house was his study which opened on a little balcony, and the ceiling of the room was presently covered with a map of Sligo painted by himself and his brother, with a ship at each corner.

A Dublin publisher commissioned him to make a selection from the work of contemporary Irish poets, and brought out the collection, *Poems and Ballads of Young Ireland*. He included from his own work 'The Madness of King Goll', 'The Old Fisherman', 'The Stolen Child', and a love song from the Gaelic; and T. W. Rolleston contributed the dedication to John O'Leary and the beautiful 'Dead at Clonmacnoise'. The fee from the Dublin publisher did little more than cover the price of a return ticket to Sligo, where still he most wanted to be. In all adversity J. B. Y. felt himself born to easy spending and the home was frequently in the throes of a financial crisis: the last of the Butler farms had been sold. There was no income to be made out of poetry and Willie felt that he might help his family best by completing his study of art in London. The memory of the Dublin art school caused him to put off the evil day and O'Leary wrote him innumerable postcards urging him to give all his time to literature. Professor Oliver Elton, one of several good neighbours in Bedford Park, offered to recommend him for a sub-editorship of a provincial newspaper; while he was considering what he should reply he saw his father sitting in great gloom. It meant an immediate income; but the paper's politics were Unionist. At last he told his father that he could not accept, and J. B. Y. replied, 'You have taken a great weight off my mind'. He had almost finished his *Wanderings of Oisin* but the chances of finding a publisher for this long poem appeared to be slight. Presently J. B. Y. suggested that he should write a story, partly of London, partly of Sligo, and he began *Dhoya*. His father said, 'I meant a story about real people', and he began *John Sherman*, into which he put his cousin Henry Middleton and his own longing for

Sligo. Then came some commissions from London publishers; he edited for a popular series a volume of Carleton and a book of Irish fairy stories, and was paid seven guineas for the Carleton and twelve for the fairy stories. The work took him to the British Museum and he would often walk the whole way from Bedford Park so as to save his pennies for a cup of coffee in the afternoon. He did not mind the rents in his boots as he had formed an ascetic ideal, but he had to struggle with his senses, and this made him shy on the subject of sex. The romantic poets had given him a vision of perfect love. Perhaps he would never marry in church, but would love one woman all his life. He wrote many letters to Katharine Tynan and one day he overheard somebody say that she was the sort of woman who might make herself very unhappy about a man, and he began to wonder if it was his duty to propose to her. Yet she never gave him reason to believe that she thought of him otherwise than as a friend.

His face being not so much dreamy as haunting – 'if one were to meet him on an Irish mountain side', wrote an acquaintance of these days, 'one would hasten away to the nearest fireside with a ghost story' – London was ready to accept him as an authority on fairy lore. George Russell helped by copying for him in the Dublin Library. The contents of *Fairy and Folk Tales of the Irish Peasantry* were not all dug out of old books, as he published in it examples of his own fairyland verse and certain translations made by Douglas Hyde from modern Gaelic country stories. In his notes on the various kinds of folk-faith he refused to rationalize a single fairy or ghost. 'The various collectors of Irish folk-lore have', he wrote in a charming introduction, 'one great merit. ... They have made their work literature rather than science, and told us of the Irish peasantry rather than of the primitive religion of mankind, or whatever else the folk-lorists are on the gad after. ... They have caught the very voice of the people, each giving what was most noticed in his day.'

A curious piece of work which came his way in 1888 was

the transcription of a rare (Caxton) volume of Aesop which Alfred Nutt wished to reprint. He went to Oxford, as it was supposed that the only existing copy of the book was to be found in the Bodleian. 'There is a most beautiful country about here', he wrote to Katharine Tynan.

I walked about sixteen miles on Sunday, going to the places in Matthew Arnold's poems – the ford in the *Scholar Gipsy* being the most interesting. How very unlike Ireland the whole place is – like a foreign land (as it is). One understands – (a long *s*, I notice, has been got out of the book I am copying) – English poetry more from seeing a place like this.

His host at Oxford was York Powell, the Regius Professor of History, who had a house in Bedford Park where he spent weekends. York Powell looked more like a retired mariner than a man of vast erudition, and the Yeatses, particularly the father and Jack, were devoted to him. Indeed, J. B. Y. gave Powell place in his admirations beside Isaac Butt, as a man of magnanimous mind and imagination, all of whose vast learning and industry was for the benefit of his friends.

Another employment found for Yeats by O'Leary was correspondence, chiefly on Irish matters, for two Irish-American papers, the *Providence Journal* and the *Boston Pilot*. The first of his prose contributions to these papers was an article on William Allingham's poetry, written in September 1888, and the last was a letter on the foundation of the Irish National Literary Society in 1892. The poems that he contributed to these journals have not been reprinted in his collected works; one, 'The Legend of the Phantom Ship', was greatly admired by his father. In 1933 he gave Horace Reynolds permission to bring out the prose contributions (not the poems) in a little volume called *Letters to the New Island*. This book does not testify to early powers of critical expression, but is interesting because it shows him at work on those ideas about Ireland, poetry and philosophy which were to possess his later life.

2

He was in Sligo late in the summer of 1888, staying with his grandparents, when he finished *The Wanderings of Oisin* and broke down after reading it to his uncle George. The poem, which was intended to be but a beginning of a whole 'Légende des Siècles', is based on translations of an eighteenth-century Irish work and of some poems in Middle-Irish reporting the dialogue between St Patrick and the Pagan (Macpherson's Ossian) who has come back, bent, blind, but unregenerate, to Christian Ireland after three hundred years in wonderland with his fairy bride.

The completion of the poem, which is in rhymed verse of different lengths (irregular iambics in the first part, heroic couplets in the second, and anapaests in the third, with lyrical passages and dramatic dialogue interspersed), was a great relief. Never, Yeats told Katharine Tynan, had any poem given him so much trouble, and he added that the last part was, of the three sections, the most artistic but the least inspired, and that something of its spirit could be traced to his nearness to 'old and reticent people'. The work was to be judged in contrast to 'The Island of Statues', as poetry of 'insight and knowledge'. 'Under disguise of symbolism I have said several things to which alone I have the key. The romance is for my readers. They must not know that there is a symbol anywhere.'

The Wanderings of Oisin, and Other Poems was published by private effort, chiefly John O'Leary's. O'Leary scraped together most of the subscriptions which induced Kegan Paul to launch a new poet. The shorter pieces in the volume, especially those in which a love and knowledge of the more minute kind of natural beauty were conspicuous, pleased everybody. Letters of warm congratulation reached Bedford Park from Edward Dowden and Father Matthew Russell, and there were good reviews in the English press. *The Guardian* placed Yeats above all other writers on Irish myth, except Tennyson in 'The Voyage of Maeldune'. Professor

Elton was very encouraging, and William Morris, meeting Yeats in the Strand, said, 'You write my kind of poetry', and would have said more had he not suddenly caught sight of a building that he disliked. On the other hand, T. W. Rolleston wrote a severe criticism of *Oisin*, which he found weak in the handling of the longer metres and defective in expression in many passages. The poem was vastly improved in later revision to which many of its greatest delights are due. Even then some felt that their pleasure in the colour and imaginative energy of the narrative was interrupted by the theosophical hints and suggestions, and asked whether it was in this manner that Irish saga, objective as the Greek, endowed things with dream shape and magical significance. One critic saw in the poem the English romantic movement in process of decomposition, and certainly the influence of Coleridge, Keats and Shelley is apparent in some of the loveliest lines:

> . . . found on the dove-grey edge of the sea
> A pearl-pale, high-born lady who rode
> On a horse with bridle of findrinny;
> And like a sunset were her lips,
> A stormy sunset on doomed ships.
>
> In a sad revelry he sang and swung
> Bacchant and mournful, passing to and fro
> His hand along the runnel's side, as though
> The flowers still grew there.
>
> Where many a trumpet-twisted shell
> That in immortal silence sleeps
> Dreaming of her own melting hues,
> Her gold, her ambers and her blues,
> Pierced with soft light the shallowing deeps.*

It is strange that Yeats in his critical writings and letters scarcely mentions Coleridge, a poet to whom the early Yeats has often been compared. In one of his later note-books he asks, 'Why does Coleridge interest me more as man than

* The quotations are from the revised work.

poet?' and answers that it is because from 1807 onwards
Coleridge seems to have had some kind of illumination
which was only in part communicable.

Henley also conveyed his encouragement to the young
poet. After *Oisin* Henley liked best 'King Goll', 'Song of
the Last Arcadian', 'The Old Fisherman' and 'The Island
of Statues'. The redoubtable editor of the *Scots Observer*,
afterwards the *National Observer*, lived about a quarter of
an hour's walk from Bedford Park; Yeats, after a few calls
on Sunday evenings, began to contribute to the *Scots
Observer*, where appeared what he afterwards called 'my
first good lyrics' – 'A Cradle Song', 'The Lake Isle of Innisfree' and 'The Man who dreamed of Faeryland', also a
number of the *Celtic Twilight* stories which were to enchant
that part of the British public not captured by Rudyard
Kipling, another of Henley's young men. Yeats's poems
were sometimes revised by Henley, who was much quicker
to see the bad things than the good ones. He would cross out
a stanza or a line now and again and put in one of his own
as happened (perhaps) in the case of 'A Cradle Song', where

> The angels are sending
> A smile to your bed,
> They weary of tending
> The souls of the dead.

became

> The angels are bending
> Above your white bed,
> They weary of tending
> The souls of the dead.*

Charles Whibley, Kenneth Grahame, Barry Pain, R. A. M.
Stevenson, George Wyndham, were members of the little
group which gathered round Henley. 'He got the best out
of us all', Yeats wrote of him,

* 19 April 1890. The first version is given in a letter to K. Tynan,
13 January 1889. Yeats wrote a third and final version of the stanza
for his *Poems*, 1901 (Fisher Unwin).

because he had made us accept him as our judge and we knew that his judgment could neither sleep, nor be softened, nor changed, nor turned aside. When I think of him, the antithesis that is the foundation of human nature being ever in my sight, I see his crippled legs as though he were some Vulcan perpetually forging swords for other men to use.

Yeats met Oscar Wilde at Henley's, and although he went with his father and sisters to Lady Wilde's extraordinary parties, Wilde affected to believe that he was a lonely young man without family and once invited him to a Christmas dinner at his Chelsea house. Wilde made him tell long Irish stories and compared his art to that of Homer.

3

In his teens W. B. Yeats had set his father above all men. From him he learned to put certain passages in Shakespeare above all else in literature, and to admire Balzac; Scott and Balzac were the novelists upon whom J. B. Y. brought up his children, telling them long stories out of both when he brought them out for walks in Sligo. The poet had first broken away from his father by taking up occult science, and now their conflicts of opinion were frequent. One night at Bedford Park W. B. expressed an appreciation of Ruskin's *Unto This Last*. He was put out of the room so violently that he broke the glass of a picture with the back of his head. Another night when they had been in some similar argument, J. B. Y. squared up and wanted to box, and, when Willie said that he could not fight his own father, replied, 'I don't see why you should not'. For a while everything became a form of ethics with the young poet, and as he walked the streets, he used to believe that he could define exactly the bad passions or moral vacuity that had created, after centuries, every detail of architectural ugliness. He had met William Morris when Morris had been in Dublin on some Socialist errand; and now he began to go to the Socialist lectures for working men at Kelmscott House and soon he was one of the visitors who used to be invited to remain for supper. In this way he met Bernard Shaw, Sidney Cockerell, Walter Crane and Prince Kropotkin, the anarchist. He quarrelled with the young working men because they preferred Michael Davitt to Parnell, but was pleased when Kropotkin, on the one occasion when they talked together, explained how the French Revolution, by sweeping away old communal customs and institutions in the name of equal rights and duties, had left the French peasant at the mercy of the capitalist. There was a project among Morris's young Socialists of a mission of some sort to Paris, and a French class was started, really because Morris wanted to find employment for a needy old Frenchwoman. Yeats was the teacher's favourite pupil; he studied hard and made progress until, on his father's insistence, his sister Lily joined the class. Then he had no longer the exciting novelty of strange faces and soon became idle and careless.

From the start Morris, with some trick of manner that reminded him of his grandfather, was a wonder and a delight. But on finding that the Socialists made no effort to understand his thought, he ceased after a while to attend the debates and lectures and seldom saw Morris, who, however, remained an enduring literary influence and was perhaps the only nineteenth-century poet to whose mood he could always adapt himself. He once described the prose romances *The Sundering Flood* and *News from Nowhere* as 'the only books I ever read slowly so that I might not come quickly to the end'. An author whose work never touches philosophy, Morris, as George Russell once suggested, may have become a sort of resting-place for Yeats's imagination, insecure in the mid-world which he really loved, because he saw things both higher and lower than Morris ever saw.

Miss Lily Yeats became an embroideress under May Morris, and then her assistant. Elizabeth became a student mistress at Chiswick High School and worked as a student at Froebel College. Jack Yeats prospered; a batch of his drawings was accepted by a paper called *The Vegetarian*, and a little later he invented for a Harmsworth publication a wonderful horse, Signor MacCoy, which was more widely known then than any of his brother's productions. This animal, always depicted with a daisy hanging from its mouth, became so famous that a horse at Olympia was called after it. A thought of his life as a householder in Bedford Park may have been with J. B. Y. when, many years later, he wrote this passage in an article entitled 'Back to the Home':

The typical Irish family is poor, ambitious and intellectual, and all have the national habit, once indigenous to 'Merrie England', of much conversation. . . . A bright boy . . . becomes the family confidant, learning all about the family necessities; with so much frank conversation it cannot be otherwise. . . . His intellect is in constant exercise. He is full of intellectual curiosity, so much conversation keeping it alive. . . . He is at once sceptical and credulous but, provided his opinions are expressed gaily and frankly, no one minds. With us intellect takes the place which in the English home is occupied by the business faculty.

4

There was a herald of spring in the air on a day soon after the publication of *The Wanderings of Oisin*, when a hansom drew up at the door of 3 Blenheim Road, and a lady of great height, as radiant as Flora herself, alighted to present an introduction from John O'Leary, and to say that she had cried over passages of the poem. In that period, memorable for lack of taste in ornament and building, homage was paid to the women of classic beauty; and Maud Gonne, who was the visitor, had had her fill of admiration since, as a motherless girl of sixteen travelling with a French governess, an Italian proposed to her and she accepted because it was moonlight in the Coliseum. Maud Gonne was the daughter of an English Colonel, who had died in a Dublin barracks of the cholera, leaving independent incomes to her and to a sister almost as lovely. Recalled from the Continent after the affair in the Coliseum, she figured for a time in Castle society in Dublin, but soon wearied of being told at the dinner-tables of judges and of doctors that she was a 'daughter of the gods, divinely tall and most divinely fair', and escaped from the guardianship of a dry and unimaginative uncle to join a troupe of actors as leading lady. Then, at the time that the agitation against the coercive régime of Mr Balfour was at its height, she decided to dedicate her life to the last breath to Irish political and social revolution.

The whole family was present when she called at the house in Blenheim Road. To the ladies, much impressed by her beautiful French clothes, she addressed gracious looks, but conversed almost entirely with J. B. Y. and Willie. She praised war; which vexed J. B. Y., disciple of Mill. But Willie agreed with her that there was something a little grey in the prospect of a perpetual Victorian peace. How could a young man do otherwise than support so beautiful a woman? But what he was best to remember of this first meeting was her figure as she stood by the window playing with a spray of flowers, the light on her golden-brown hair and delicate face. Twelve years afterwards he put the impression into verse:

> I thought of your beauty, and this arrow,
> Made out of a wild thought, is in my marrow.
> There's no man may look upon her, no man,
> As when newly grown to be a woman,
> Tall and noble but with face and bosom
> Delicate in colour as apple blossom.
> This beauty's kinder, yet for a reason
> I could weep that the old is out of season.

Yeats was now twenty-three and the trouble of his life had begun. The young woman asked him to dine with her that evening in her rooms in Ebury Street and he dined with her frequently during her short stay in London. There was such excitement in her ways that it seemed natural she should give her hours in one flowery abundance. She was surrounded with cages of singing birds, with which she always travelled, taking them even upon short journeys. She was now about to visit Paris on some political expedition.

She spoke of her wish for a play that she could act in

Dublin. Somebody had suggested Todhunter's *Helen of Troy* but he had refused. Yeats told her of a story he had found when compiling his *Fairy and Folk Tales* and offered to write for her the play called *The Countess Cathleen*. He told her he wished to become an Irish Victor Hugo, and he was not wholly sincere – for had he not begun to simplify himself with great toil? – but he had seen upon her table *Tristan de Lionnesse* and *Les Contemplations* and it was tempting to commend himself by claiming a very public and declamatory talent, for her beauty as he saw it in those days seemed incompatible with private intimate life. She, like himself, had received the political tradition of Davis, with an added touch of hardness and heroism from the hand of O'Leary; when she spoke of William O'Brien in jail making a prolonged struggle against putting on prison clothes, she said, 'There was a time when men sacrificed their lives for their country but now they sacrifice their dignity'. But mixed with the feeling for what is permanent in human life there was something rhetorical about her mind. She confessed her desire for power and when she talked of politics, dwelt on the effectiveness of the winning of this or that election. Her five-and-twenty years had taken some colour, it seemed, from Boulangist adventurers and journalists, *arrivistes*, whose acquaintance she had made in France. Yeats was full of the thought of the 'Animula Vagula' chapter in *Marius*, and from the young Brahmin who had come to Dublin he had learned that 'only the means can justify the end'. She meant her ends to be unselfish but she thought almost any means justified in their service. The poet and she were seeking different things; she, some memorable action for final consecration of her youth, and he, after all, but to discover and communicate a state of being. Perhaps even in politics it would in the end be enough to have lived and thought passionately and have, like O'Leary, a head worthy of a Roman coin. How important it all seemed to him then! What would he not have given that she might think exactly right on these questions!

He perceived that she possessed great generosity and courage but felt sure that her mind had no peace. When she and all her singing birds had gone, his melancholy was not the mere melancholy of love. He had what he thought was a clairvoyant perception, but it was, he knew later, but an obvious deduction of awaiting disaster. He was compiling at this time a selection from some Irish novelists for an American publisher; the deliberation of their humour but reminded him of the dread. They too, according to a fashion of the early Victorians, had been so often thrown without father or mother or guardian into a world of deception. They too were incurably romantic. Yeats was in love; but he had not spoken of love and never meant to speak. The months passed and he grew master of himself again. What wife would she make, he thought – what share could she have in the life of a poor student?

5

Very soon after arriving in London Yeats, with introduction from Charlie Johnston, had sought the acquaintance of the London theosophists. These, like Morris's young workers, thought little of those that did not share their belief, and talked a great deal of the improvement of mankind. Yeats would say that so much in life had no aim but itself, and there would be an evening of argument. From Madame Blavatsky herself came no argument, only statements. When he took off his beard she promised him a bad illness within six months through the loss of the mesmeric forces that collect in the beard. For a period he called on her every six weeks, and felt for her the same kind of admiration which he gave to William Morris. Unlike those about her, he had read the Psychical Research Society's charges of fraudulent miracle-working, and yet she seemed to him to surpass all others in honesty, as she sat there talking, vast and shapeless of body, perpetually rolling cigarettes, inconsequent and incomprehensible. 'All her life is but sitting in a great chair with a pen in her hand', Yeats wrote to O'Leary. 'For years she has written twelve hours a day. I have no theories about her, she is simply a note of interrogation. "Olcott is much honester than I am", she said to me one day. "He explains things. I am an old Russian peasant." That is the deepest I ever got into her riddle.'

In the society he soon reached the esoteric section, or inner ring of devout students who met to study tables of oriental symbolism. There he learned that every organ of the body has its correspondence in the heavens, and that the seven principles, which compose the human soul and body, corres-pond to the seven colours of the planets and the notes of the musical scale. He was always longing for evidence; having induced the other members of the section to attempt an experiment, he was called before an official and told with great politeness to resign. He said, 'By teaching an abstract system without experiment you are making your pupils dogmatic, and taking them out of life'. The official was a clever man and he admitted what Yeats said but added that Madame Blavatsky had told them that 'no more super-natural help would come to the movement after 1897', when some cycle or other ended.

Maud Gonne was predisposed to a belief in the doctrine of rebirth and on a later appearance in London she accom-panied Yeats readily to his London Lodge. She was pleased when Madame Blavatsky told her that the Dublin theo-sophists were talking nonsense when they said that political activities, such as cattle-driving, need not exclude one from the ranks of theosophists. John O'Leary thought it all very silly and said that Maud Gonne and Yeats were behaving like a pair of children. He sent postcards to both. Yeats excused himself on the ground that he was getting a great deal of entertainment out of the politics of the Lodge. 'Madame Blavatsky', he wrote to O'Leary on 7 May 1889,

has expelled Mrs Cook . . . and expelled also the president of the lodge for flirtation; and expelled an American lady for gossip about them. Madame Blavatsky is in great spirits, she is purring

and hiding her claws as though she never clawed anybody. . . .
You need not be afraid of my going in for mesmerism. It interests
me but slightly. Madame Blavatsky is very much against them,
and hates spiritualism violently.

From the Theosophists Yeats passed into the circle of
MacGregor Mathers where he hoped to get proof that 'the
sage Ahasuerus dwells in a sea cavern 'mid the Demonesi',
and to learn more of those Masters whose representative
Madame Blavatsky claimed to be; and by Mathers he was
initiated into a society called the Golden Dawn,* an order of
Christian Cabalists. Liddell was Mathers's first name but he
soon became under the touch of Celticism, MacGregor
Mathers, and then plain MacGregor. He was a well-made
man, lean of visage, who talked in a deep voice and pretended to know much more than he did. As a reader in the
British Museum, where he was copying the *Mysterium Mag-
num* of Boehme, and as author of *The Kabbalah Unveiled*,
he had excited Yeats's curiosity some time before a friend
introduced them. He was ten years older than the poet; very
little is known of his early life, but his name is found on the
books of Bedford School, where he reached the Upper Fifth
Form and achieved fame as a runner. Like Madame Blavatsky, he could throw himself with great dramatic power into
a part, and he managed to invest the origins of his Order
with a mystery which was afterwards found not to be there.
Soon after his first meeting with Yeats he became curator of
a private museum at Forest Hill and married the very attractive sister of Henri Bergson, then an obscure professor.

MacGregor Mathers attributed the rituals and teachings
of the Order to secret sources and to his own clairvoyance.
To Yeats the rituals seemed full of the symbolism of the
Middle Ages and the Renaissance. A fellow-student showed
Yeats how to allow his reveries to drift, following the sugges-
tion of the symbol, and he was soon able to summon images

---

* Yeats gives the date of his initiation as May or June 1887, but it
must surely have been a year or two later. For a note on the Order
and the source of its teachings, see p. 486.

from, as he thought, a deeper source than conscious or unconscious memory. He found that these images began to
affect his writing, making it more sensuous and vivid; and
he believed that with the images would come more profound
states of the soul, and lived in vain hope. In MacGregor
Mathers's conversation there was no exhortation to alarm
one's dignity and no abstraction to deaden the soul. 'We
only give you symbols', Mathers said to him, 'because we
respect your liberty', and now Yeats made a curious discovery. After he was moved by ritual he formed plans for
deeds of all kinds, and wished to find public work in Ireland, whereas when he had returned from the theosophist
meetings he had no desire but for more thought, more
discussion.

By joining the Order of the Golden Dawn Yeats braved
the reproaches of George Russell and the Dublin visionaries
as well as of O'Leary. Russell believed that by the practice of
austerities and concentration he could develop faculties of
power over himself and a superior insight into Nature, but
thought the attempt to compel men or non-human spirits to
do one's will wrong and irreligious. This is, indeed, the rough
distinction between mysticism and magic, for in magic,
though it is the oldest form of religion, there is, as Hegel
observes, no question of worship or of reverence for a
spiritual being, for what has an absolute objective existence
of its own. The process is rather the exercise of lordship over
Nature – the sway of the magician over those who do not
know: * in short, all magic is black magic. Whether Russell
had a greater facility for seeing visions than Yeats, who shall
say, but it is certain that Yeats had a stronger feeling for the
rights of individuality, for distinctions, for the antinomies,
than is proper to mysticism where dreams lose their dramatic
evidence and absolute worth. Perhaps it was the instinctive
repugnance of an artist to the featureless unity that sent him
to the shabby temples of the magicians, then to the spirit-
ists, and lastly to Kant, Hegel and the great European

* *Philosophy of Religion*, Part II, Div. 1, chap. i.

philosophers, 'to the kind of exact analysis that drives me
back to poetry with my vigour renewed', as he wrote once to
Dr Rossi, an Italian friend.

6

A neighbour of some literary consideration in Bedford Park
was John Todhunter, the well-to-do doctor turned poet, who
had bought J. B. Y.'s pictures when the latter was still a pre-
Raphaelite. He was a Dublin man and a protestant Home
Ruler and he became, with W. B., a member of the patriotic
Southwark Irish Society. W. B. would cross miles of streets
with the doctor, a young harper of old days side by side with
a middle-aged Brehon, to address the clerks, shop-boys and
shop-girls who chiefly composed the Society. 'Gradually he
became one of ourselves', says a pamphlet on the history of
the Club.

. . . Some of us thought that we had a tolerable acquaintance
with the ways and doings of the Irish fairies, but Yeats's first
lecture (of course it was on the good people) was something of a
revelation to us – in fact he spoke as one who took his information
first-hand. His only error was to speak unduly of the *soulths* and
sheogues of his own country, but the south had a sturdy cham-
pion in John Augustus O'Shea who gave it as his experience
that there were more fairies in a square foot of Tipperary than
in all the County Sligo.

Everybody in the Society had said all he had to say many
times over, and when, on another occasion, Yeats attacked
the Renaissance for making the human mind inorganic, and
pleaded that Ireland should lead a counter-movement, his
lecture was much applauded.

Todhunter shared Yeats's interest in projects for the
reform of the modern theatre. Shelley's *Cenci* had just been
played for the first time and Yeats used to argue with Todhunter that *The Cenci*, and Tennyson in *Becket*, were deliberately oratorical; where they should have created drama in
the mood of the *Lotos-Eaters* and the *Epipsychidion* they

tried to escape their characteristics, that is, thought of the theatre as outside the general movement of literature. In his new play, *The Countess Cathleen*, for which he made in the first instance two complete versions in prose, he was endeavouring to avoid every oratorical phrase and cadence. The work is mentioned in a letter to Katharine Tynan of April 1889:

I have been doing rather well lately. I told you about the man who came and asked me to do literary notes for the *Manchester Courier*.* They give me very little trouble and are fairly profitable. I got £7 for an article in *Leisure Hour* and have two in *Scots Observer*. . . . These matters have made 'The Countess' fare badly. Fortunately my constitutional indolence brings my thoughts perpetually swinging back to it by their own weight. I am not half industrious enough to drive my thoughts. They go their own road; and that is to imaginative work.

In June 1890 Todhunter's *Sicilian Idyll* was performed on the little stage of the Bedford Park clubhouse. This was an event of note in Yeats's life, as it was then that he first saw Florence Farr (Mrs Emery) act, and was enchanted by her subtle gestures and fine delivery of the verse. Florence Farr was the sister-in-law of another Bedford Park neighbour, the black-and-white artist Henry Paget, and lived in lodgings at Brook Green some twenty minutes' walk from the Yeats's house. She had made an unhappy marriage and was separated from her husband. Yeats knew her already, and, until he met Maud Gonne, had been accounted in love with her by his sisters. After the performance in *A Sicilian Idyll* he thought of her as a collaborator in the theatre, essential, by reason of her unfashionable art, to the plays that he would one day write. They formed an enduring friendship in which were at times tender passages, and always on his side some exasperation because she seemed to set a higher value on her wit and intellectuality than on her incomparable sense of rhythm and her musical voice.

* He abandoned this work when Oscar Wilde said that writing literary gossip was not a fit occupation for a gentleman.

Yeats had been encouraged by his father in an enthusiasm for William Blake, and about the time that he commenced *The Countess Cathleen* he engaged upon the study of the Prophetic Books with a view to producing a comprehensive edition of Blake's mystical writings, with all the original illustrations to the Books and an elaborate commentary. Quaritch offered by way of payment thirteen large-paper copies to each editor – the other editor was Edwin J. Ellis, poet and painter and friend of his father's, who had been under Rossetti's influence when Gilchrist published Blake's *Life*. Though not a very good poet or a very good painter, Ellis was often a profound critic; and, indeed, in some private notes for an autobiography dated 1922, Yeats goes so far as to say that he may have owed his mastery of verse to the instruction of Edwin Ellis. The conversation, witty and extravagant, of this student of Blake, Boehme and Swedenborg, had but two themes, religion and sex. Ellis had a curious psychic sensitiveness, and early in their collaboration Yeats, finding in his studio on a sheet of paper a series of Blake's attributions of the different districts of London to the human faculties, recognized certain attributions of the cardinal points which he heard of among the Cabalists. Ellis's wife was a little moody, and would sometimes drive Yeats out of her house, saying that he was casting a spell on her husband; then he would be forgiven and fed with very rich cakes which neither pleased his palate nor suited his digestion, and once she sent him a small sum of money anonymously. Visits to the Linnells, three old men and a sister, descendants of Blake's patron, were more agreeable. The Linnells lived at Redhill in Surrey, and their house, full of Blake relics, was a most hospitable place. The sister thought Yeats looked delicate, and gave him good meals and port to sip while he copied. It was a great joy to the collaborators when they discovered in the Linnells' house 'Vala', a manuscript of two thousand lines which had been barely mentioned by Rossetti.

The toil was hard and long, but Yeats did not begrudge it,

being convinced that, as a student of the magical tradition, he was at an advantage over earlier interpreters of Blake's visionary and paradoxical philosophy. The text was ready in 1891, but some change of plan occurred which delayed publication for two years. Eventually there were three sumptuous volumes, *The Works of Blake, Poetic, Symbolic and Critical*, of which Mr Godfrey Keynes gives the following description in his definitive Blake bibliography:

The chief value of these volumes lies in the interpretation of the symbolism, the paraphrased commentaries and the lithographic reproductions which they contain. The memoir introduces a new theory of Blake's ancestry, according to which he is supposed to be of Irish origin. The value of the printed texts is reduced by the large number of inaccuracies which occur in them; some of these are intentional alteration, but the majority are mistakes made in copying. This appears in particular in the poems from the Rossetti MS.

The mistakes made in copying may have been due in part to Yeats's defective eyesight. His was the responsibility for turning Blake into an Irishman, but not for the passage in the commentary which animadverted upon Swinburne's failure to grasp the doctrine of the four Zoas. Swinburne, however, when he reprinted his own book on Blake thirteen years afterwards, seized an opportunity to insult Yeats and the Irish movement by remarking that the alleged strain of Irish blood in Blake would account for the parts of the Prophetic Books, such as those containing the doctrine of the Zoas, where 'fever and fancy take the place of reason and imagination'. Whereupon J. B. Y. denounced Swinburne as 'that turgid and monotonous poet, with his intellectual underbreeding and inferior kind of pride, that aristocratic cad. . . . That man without sweetheart, wife or mistress.'

7

To the period of Yeats's collaboration with Ellis belong two of the most charming of the early poems, 'The Lake Isle of

Innisfree' and 'The Man who dreamed of Faeryland'. Both were published in Henley's *National Observer*, the one in December 1890, and the other in the February following. 'See', said Henley when the fairyland poem appeared, 'what a fine thing has been written by one of my lads.' 'The Lake Isle' was not only generally popular but it set the professors agog by the arrangement of the vowel sounds ('I scarcely knew', said Yeats, 'what a vowel was'):

> And I shall have some peace there, for peace comes
>   dropping slow,
> Dropping from the veils of the morning to where the
>   cricket sings;
> There midnight's all a glimmer, and noon a purple glow,
> And evening full of the linnet's wings.

A letter came from R. L. Stevenson in far-off Samoa. Stevenson said that he had been three times laid under a spell; first by the early Swinburne, then by a stanza in 'Love in a Valley', and then by 'Innisfree'. 'It is so quaint and airy, simple artful, and eloquent to the heart.'*

In the novelette *John Sherman*, which was published a few months after 'Innisfree', there is this passage:

Delayed by a crush in the Strand, he heard a faint trickling of water near by; it came from a shopwindow where a little water-jet balanced a wooden ball upon its point. The sound suggested a cataract with a long Gaelic name, that leaped crying into the Gate of the Winds at Ballah. Wandering among these memories a footstep went to and fro continually, and the figure of Mary Carton moved among them like a phantom. He was set dreaming a whole day by walking down one Sunday morning to the border of the Thames – a few hundred yards from his house – and looking at the osier-covered Chiswick eyot. It made him remember an old day-dream of his. The source of the river that passed his garden at home was a certain wood-bordered and islanded lake, whither in childhood he had often gone blackberry-gather-

---

*Yeats would never allow his publishers to quote the letter. It appeared, however, in Stevenson's *Letters*.

ing. At the further end was a little islet called Innisfree. Its rocky centre, covered with many bushes, rose some forty feet above the lake. Often when life and its difficulties had seemed to him like the lessons of some elder boy given to a younger by mistake, it had seemed good to dream of going away to that islet and building a wooden hut there and burning a few years out, rowing to and fro, fishing, or lying on the island slopes by day, and listening at night to the ripple of the water and the quivering of the bushes – full always of unknown creatures – and going out at morning to see the island's edge marked by the feet of birds.

Fisher Unwin placed *John Sherman* in his Pseudonym Series, between the same covers as *Dhoya*, a wonder story, also of Sligo, and the little book earned £40 for the author. 'It is West rather than National', Yeats wrote to Katharine Tynan. 'Sherman belongs, like Allingham, to the small gentry, who in the West at any rate, love their native place without perhaps loving Ireland.' *John Sherman* is a homely story in which Yeats succeeded in keeping the characters from turning into eastern symbolic monsters (he told O'Leary that this had been the temptation), which would have been 'a curious thing to happen to a curate and a young man from the country'.

He still cherished his boyish ambition to live like Thoreau, but with the foundation in 1891 of the Rhymers' Club, life in London became more tolerable. The Club met in an upper room of the 'Cheshire Cheese', and with several of the members he was already acquainted. Ernest Rhys, a Welshman, had set him to compile tales of Irish fairies, and it was perhaps on Rhys's suggestion that he called on Lionel Johnson one afternoon, at an old house in Charlotte Street. Herbert Horne, afterwards the great authority on Botticelli, Selwyn Image, and an architect, MacMurdo, shared the house and a manservant with Johnson. Rhys, T. W. Rolleston and Yeats played the chief part in founding the Club, and when Johnson joined he brought Ernest Dowson, Horne and Selwyn Image with him. John Davidson, Le Gallienne, Edwin Ellis and Todhunter came constantly for a time, Arthur Symons less constantly, while William Watson joined but never came, and Francis Thompson came once but never joined. They were 'The Tragic Generation'. From the first Yeats devoted himself to Johnson, attracted by a certain stateliness of mind that seemed to be the counterpart of a little and beautifully formed body, of a distinction, as of a Greek carving, in his regular features. He was a disciple of Walter Pater, and he had taken from Pater certain famous phrases which came to mean much to Yeats, such as 'hieratic', 'marmorean', 'life should be a ritual'. These phrases led Yeats to form a new ideal picture of a poet, a more artificial composition than that suggested by Shelley, Hugo or Walt Whitman, and may have encouraged him to cultivate that air of authority and dignity to which he attained in middle-age. An intimate friend of his later life, Edmund Dulac, has written of 'the world of aristocratic beings, cultured, refined, linked by a certain elegance of expression, a certain ritualism of dress and behaviour, that he had once realised about him, and always thought he might find again round the corner.' 'I have need of ten years in the wilderness,' Johnson would say to him; 'you need ten years in a library.' Johnson was not yet a Catholic, but he scoffed at Yeats's magical practices and unorthodox speculations – Yeats thought because he half believed in them – yet they had a bond in that the Winchester and Oxford man, on some ground of ancestry, counted himself an Irishman and sang of Irish martyrs. There were about a dozen regular members of the Club, and these read their verses aloud – Dowson's moved Yeats most – and criticized one another's work; the talk owed its chief distinction to Arthur Symons, who knew Paris and its excellent talkers. Yeats led the attack on Victorianism, by which was meant (he has said) 'irrelevant description of nature, the scientific and moral discursiveness of *In Memoriam*', and when other Irish members were present, there was lively and animated debate during which Johnson would sit in gloomy disapproval of this overflow of reasons. On such occasions Yeats was made to feel that he was an incurable provincial – that he 'was one of those doomed to imperfect achievement, and under a curse, as it were, like some race of birds compelled to spend the time, needed for the making of the nest, in argument as to the convenience of moss and twig and lichen.'

Death of Parnell and after

Maud Gonne in London and Dublin – Parnell's funeral –
Publication of *Countess Cathleen* – Books for Young
Ireland – The Gaelic League

═══

> *The Bishops and the Party*
> *That tragic story made,*
> *A husband that had sold his wife*
> *And after that betrayed;*
> *But stories that live longest*
> *Are sung above the glass,*
> *And Parnell loved his country,*
> *And Parnell loved his lass.*

I

IN a book of selections from Irish novelists, Maria Edgeworth, Lover, Lever, Gerald Griffin and others, published in
1890 in London and in New York, Yeats closed his introduction with the prophecy of an intellectual movement in Ireland at the first lull in politics. Though Captain O'Shea had
already filed the petition for divorce which named the Irish
leader as co-respondent, Parnell was still at the height of his
power; no one yet imagined that the affair would cause the
split in the Irish parliamentary party which eventually
turned the better part of Ireland from politics – at least of
the material and party kind – and so contributed to a rebirth of more spiritual conceptions of nationality, going
back, on the one hand, to Gaelic tradition, and, on the other,
to the modern nation of Swift and Wolfe Tone and Grattan.

Irish literature had fallen into disrepute in Land League
times; rarely did an educated man buy an Irish book; and
the ironic Dowden used to say that one could be known by

the smell of its rotten glue. No Irish writer of the patriotic
sort had ever shown ardour in seeking out and rendering the
expression of his own feelings, the passion of the artist for
the one word. Yet Young Ireland poetry had done more than
answer the traditional slanders and start an apologetic habit.
It had created sensible images for the affections, vivid
enough to follow men to the scaffold. Yeats began by trying
to do the same thing but in a more profound and enduring
way. His mind was hospitable to chimeras, and he dreamed
that it might be possible to create an heroic and passionate
conception of life, worthy of the study of men elsewhere and
at other times, and to make that conception the special
dream of the Irish people.

In his contributions to the *Pilot* he continually set
nationalism against internationalism. He drew attention to
Douglas Hyde's Gaelic translations and the romances of
Standish O'Grady. He wrote of now forgotten poetesses,
Ellen O'Leary and Rose Kavanagh. 'There is no fine literature without nationality', he reiterated. He believed that a
writer needs 'subject matter', and in this he was upheld by
his friends of the Rhymers' Club, where one was a scholar
in music-halls, another a Grecian or an authority on the age
of Chaucer. The Rhymers in their search for new subject
matter, new emotions, marked the reaction from that search
for merely new forms, which had distinguished the close of
the Tennysonian epoch. 'Sonnets are played out and ballads
and rondeaus are no longer novel', he declared in one of his
letters, 'and nobody has invented a new form. All, despairing, cry of the departing age, but the world still goes on, and
the soul of man is ever young, and its song shall never come
to an end ...'

His influence in Ireland was not wholly confined to the
patriotic group. A North of Ireland girl, who had been at the
Dublin art school, sent him her verses. Some of the views
that he expressed in his careful and courteous reply gave
place to others later on. One remembers his judgement in
favour of occasional *dull* words :

30.1.89 *To Miss Elizabeth White*

I have in the first place to apologize for slight damage to your MS. My study window was open and the wind blew your MS. into the fender where a red-hot coal somewhat charred one corner.

The poems seems to me musical and pleasant – There are some really poetic phrases such as 'breathing light' in the blank verse lines and what the 'Marrow' says about 'The landfields, dark and still' and that other line about the sea lying dim ('dim' and 'hill' by the way are too nearly rhymes without being so, to come so close together as they do in this verse –) I very much like the verse on the trees that saw naught beyond autumn 'and breathed half timidly soft love songs through their crimson-stained leaves'. It is the most poetic of your details perhaps, but I like the 'Marrow's Lament' best as a whole – Blank verse is the most difficult of all measures to write well. A blank verse should always end with a slight pause in the sound.

You should send these poems to the *Irish Monthly*, the editor is the Rev. Matthew Russell . . .

You will find it a good thing to make verses on Irish legends and places and so forth. It helps originality – and makes one's verses sincere, and gives one less numerous competitors – Besides one should love best what is nearest and most interwoven with one's life.*

When he found Maud Gonne in Dublin, she and he would take long walks together in the mountains, and he would seek to assure her of his patriotism by discoursing in mystical strain of his hopes of a great Irish literature. Might he not, with health and good-luck to aid him, create some new *Prometheus Unbound*: Patrick or Columcille, Oisin or Fionn, in Prometheus' stead, and in place of Caucasus, Croagh Patrick or Ben Bulben? Had not all races their first unity from the polytheism that marries them to rock and hill? In Ireland there were imaginative stories, known and even sung by the uneducated classes, and might not these stories be made current among the educated Nationalists, and, at last, so deepen the political passion of the nation,

* The letter written to his sister has been preserved by Professor Oliver White of Trinity College. 'My earliest recollection', he says, 'is of my sister putting me to sleep with *King Goll*.'

that all, artists and poets, craftsman and day labourer, would accept a common design? Might not these images, once created and associated with river and mountain, move themselves, and with some powerful, even turbulent life?

In London what a curious sight they must have presented to the Cockneys – the young poet and the European beauty: the poet, with pale face and long hair and rich melancholy eyes, held her cloak and superintended the transport of the bird-cages beneath the high sooty arch of Victoria Station; beside him Maud Gonne, as tall as he, eyes fiery from her Parisian politics, her clothes swirling with her long strides and wide gestures. Either alone would have arrested attention: together with cloaks and bird-cages, amid the fuss and paraphernalia of a railway station, they set the platform astare. Once he had to carry a full-grown Donegal hawk to her compartment. She still retained some ties with the Army society in which she had been brought up; and it was said in a German paper that Kitchener himself had proposed to her and had been accepted on condition that he took off the Queen's coat. He could not go so far as that (the paper continued), but he always carried the image of the beautiful Maud Gonne in his heart. Evidently, one could not expect so fine a lady to travel in trams; consequently, John O'Leary used to send Yeats fatherly warnings against extravagance. 'I hope', he wrote on one postcard, 'that you are not paying for the hansoms.' Yeats replied that his friend always insisted on paying her share.

Yeats was now in a position of importance in Mathers's Order of the Golden Dawn, and Maud Gonne had passed four initiations and learned several Hebrew words. Yeats spoke to her of the magician Nicolas Flamel and his wife Pernella, and when she told him of an apparition, a woman in grey, remembered from her infancy, he was persuaded that he must make this woman visible, for he believed that it was an evil spirit troubling his friend's life, weakening affections and creating a desire for power and excitement. If it were made visible, it would put the temptation into words

and could be faced. Mrs MacGregor Mathers therefore
made a symbol for him according to the rules of the Order,
considering it as an inhabitant of the fifth element, with
another element subordinate, and almost at once it became
visible. It was a 'sport' personality now seeking for reunion.
Miss Gonne had been a priestess in Tyre, and under the influence of a certain priest had given false oracle, and because
of this the personality of that life had split off from the soul,
and remained a half-living shadow. The vision, corroborated
by a dream constantly recurring with her, showed Miss
Gonne going off into the desert to die alone, and also connected her with someone who lived in the desert and bore a
curious resemblance to Yeats himself, just as a rather similar
vision of George Russell's had done. Yeats would have interpreted all this as symbolic event, expressing a psychological
state, or spirit – Rahib in William Blake is an 'eternal state'
– but for a coincidence: when he had been in the esoteric
section of the London theosophists he was taught as one of
the secrets of the initiation that such a separated half-living
body might have no soul in its new life, and must seek a reunion that would always be refused.

There were some interesting people in the Order besides
Mathers and his wife: Wynn Westcott, the London coroner,
Florence Farr, Algernon Blackwood, Brodie, the Astronomer Royal of Scotland, and an old clergyman who had made
what he believed to be the elixir of life thirty years before. A
travelling French mystic had held the bottle containing the
elixir up to the light, and had said it was properly made, but
the clergyman had been afraid to drink it, and now it had
all evaporated. Most of the members, however, surprised
Maud Gonne by their air of British commonplace, and she
quickly grew restless. 'Aren't they an awful set?' she said to
Mathers and to Yeats, and Mathers replied that no doubt
the same complaint had been made about the early Christians. When Mathers spoke of the great changes to come,
streets running with blood, for no great spiritual change
comes without political change, she was excited, but she

began to suspect that the ritual was tainted with Free-masonry, and that anything of significance in the Order had been transmitted from that source. Yeats denied it vigorously. He spoke of not-to-be-revealed sources in Aus-trian and German Rosicrucianism, but without effect, and she resigned from the Order on the ground that Free-masonry is one of the mainstays of the British Empire.

In spite of this discouragement Yeats persisted in the study which he had determined to make, next to his poetry, the most important pursuit of his life. 'It is merely absurd to hold me "weak",' he wrote to John O'Leary ...

Whether it be, or be not, bad for my health can only be decided by one who knows what magic is and not at all by any amateur. ... If I had not made magic my constant study I could not have written a single word of my Blake books, nor would The Coun-tess Cathleen have ever come to exist. The mystical life is the centre of all that I do and all that I think and all that I write. It holds to my work the same relation that the philosophy of Godwin holds to the work of Shelley ... the revolt of the soul against the intellect.

2

On a visit to Ireland in the summer of 1891, Yeats, hearing that Maud Gonne was in Dublin, called upon her at the hotel in Nassau Street, where she always stayed. At first sight of her, when she entered the room, he was overwhelmed with an emotion which was like an intoxication of pity. Their talk became intimate, and her hints of some personal unhappi-ness or disillusionment made him think more than ever of her need for protection and peace. Later on, he learned that some of his Nationalist friends and acquaintances in Dublin, who had been at first flattered by a high-bred lady's descent among them, were beginning to gossip about her, gracious though she was to all, to women as well as to men. She was proud. One of her admirers ventured to report some slander and to advise her against defying conventions. 'People may say what they choose about me but not to me', was her answer. Even John O'Leary was critical but on different grounds. William O'Brien and John Dillon had lately persuaded the townsmen of Tipperary, who were fighting their landlord, to build a new town on a neighbouring plot of land, and it was discovered that the old landlord, by some grip in a forgotten lease, could turn them out of the new town also. O'Leary not only owned property in the old town, but he disliked those two politicians above all others. 'They want', he said, 'to influence English opinion at the moment, so that a Home Rule Bill will come before they are found out.' Miss Gonne had been to the formal opening of the new town. 'She is no disciple of mine,' O'Leary said; 'she went there to show off her new bonnet.' When Yeats reached Sligo he was amongst Unionists, and some young landlord told him how he was peeping through a hotel window at a public meeting which had been called to support his tenants against him. Somebody shouted 'Shoot him!' and a beautiful girl near the platform, whom he believed to be Maud Gonne, had clapped her hands. George Pollexfen said, 'It's wonderful what some people will do for notoriety'.

In July Yeats spent a week at Ballykilbeg, the Co. Down home of Charlie Johnston's father, a well-known Orange M.P. He appears to have recovered his spirits, for he was able to find amusement in making fire-balloons of Charlie's examination papers and chasing them over the countryside, the chase becoming longer as his and Charlie's skill in the manufacture of the balloons improved. A letter from Maud Gonne drew him back to Dublin, and it was then that he made his first proposal of marriage. No, she said, she could not marry; there were reasons, but in words that had no conventional ring she begged him for his friendship. They went out to Howth together, spent a day walking over the well-remembered cliff paths, and dined at a little cottage, where her old nurse lived. He overheard the nurse asking her whether she was engaged. He read her his unpublished *Countess Cathleen*, and told her that he had come to interpret the life of a woman who sells her soul as a symbol of all

souls that lose their peace, their fineness, in politics, serving
but change. The expedition cost him ten shillings, and it
was a great sum for him, but the day was never forgotten.*

She was at this moment without political work, and she
had plenty of time to give to the poet. Then suddenly she
told him in confidence that she must go to France on the
orders of some revolutionary group to which she belonged.
She had come to look upon the members of the group as self-
seekers, but could not disobey the first summons that had
come from it. Yeats stayed on in Dublin, drifting between
the Theosophical house in Ely Place, O'Leary's lodgings and
the Tynan farm at Clondalkin. At Clondalkin he discovered
a cobbler who read Carlyle when he was 'wild with the neighbours' and, better still, an old woman who had seen a vision
of St Joseph with 'a lovely shiny hat upon him and a shirt
buzzom that was never starched in this world'. In Dublin,
with some sense of superiority to the virtuous inmates of the
Theosophical house, he penetrated into a society of black
magicians, which surprisingly existed in a respectable street
of the city. 'A whole colony of them,' he wrote cheerfully
enough to Lionel Johnson,

of the most iniquitous kind. They are great mesmerists and
thorough blackguards, but picturesque in their hideous costumes
of black cloth which covers all but their eyes. They have the
inverted pentagram upon their foreheads and are followers of
the goddess Isis. Certain good Theosophists aver to seeing them
in visions of the night and do in truth shake in their shoes at the
mention of their name. . . . The black magicians have invited me
to drop in an incantation now and again as a compliment to my
knowledge of the black art. They have not got enough in the
way of souls left to cover an old sixpence but that does not matter
much for the present.

Under the thatched roof the Tynan farmhouse literature
had given way before politics. It was a fateful hour for Ireland; the proud inscrutable Parnell, battling for his life

Last Poems: '. . . Maud Gonne at Howth station waiting a train,
Pallas Athene in that straight back and arrogant head.'

against English nonconformists and Irish bishops, with the
Fenians at his side, was the overmastering topic. O'Leary
had disapproved of many things in Parnell's policy. Now he
said, 'You cannot depose a man for gallantry', and the Ty-
nans and their Dublin friends, devout Roman Catholics all,
made the same choice without hesitation. '... We spoke of
Parnell', Yeats says in his autobiography.

We told each other that he had admitted no man to his
counsel; that when some member of his party found himself in
the same hotel by chance, that member would think to stay
there a presumption, and move to some other lodging; and,
above all, we spoke of his pride, that made him hide all emotion
while before his enemy.

Miss Tynan has left us in her memoirs a most graphic and
moving account of the loyalty of an impassioned few to a
doomed leader.

In October, when the news of Parnell's death flashed from
Brighton, Yeats was with O'Leary in the latter's lodgings in
Temple Street. On the 11th, a morning melancholy with
clouds and mist, he went to Kingstown pier to meet the mail
boat that arrived at six. He was expecting Maud Gonne,
and he met as well the body of Parnell. He did not go to the
funeral, as he shrank from the vast crowd, but she went. She
told him on her return of the star that fell in broad daylight
as Parnell's body was lowered into the grave. Years after
Standish O'Grady was to write:

I state a fact – it was witnessed by thousands. While his
followers were committing Charles Parnell's remains to the
earth, the sky was bright with strange lights and flames. Only a
coincidence possibly, and yet persons not superstitious have
maintained that there is some mysterious sympathy between the
human soul and the elements, and that storm, and other elemental disturbances, have too often succeeded or accompanied
great battles to be regarded as fortuitous. ... Those flames recall
to my memory what is told of similar phenomena, said to have
been witnessed when tidings of the death of St Columba overran
the north-west of Europe.

Yeats had already composed a poem for the occasion, 'Mourn – and then Onward', and he enclosed a copy of it in a letter which he wrote that evening from the Theosophical house to his sister Lily:

The Funeral is just over. The people are breathing fire and slaughter. The wreaths have such inscriptions as 'murdered by the Priests' and a number of Wexford men were heard by [a] man I know promising to remove a Bishop and seven priests before next Sunday. Tomorrow will bring them cooler heads I doubt not. Meanwhile Healy is in Paris and the people hunt for his gore in vain. Dillon and he are at feud and the feud is being fought out by the *Freeman* and *National Press* in diverse indirect fashion. Tell Jack I have no more fairy articles at present but will get some done soon. I have finished 'Countess Cathleen' and am doing stray lyrics and things . . .

He printed 'Mourn – and then Onward' in *United Ireland*, a Dublin weekly journal, which Parnell some months before his death had taken by force out of the hands of his enemies. From devotion, for the work was unpaid, W. B. had already become a contributor to this paper, writing articles on controversial questions of Irish literary interest; here a little later appeared the narrative poem 'The Death of Cuchulain', outstanding in his early work, also a eulogy of Maud Gonne's oratory, 'The New Speranza'. His lines on Parnell had little merit, and many years passed before he again attempted 'occasional' political verse. Lionel Johnson's and Katharine Tynan's were much better, and so were those of Edmund Leamy, the editor, a pleasant and indolent man, author of a book of fairy stories. In the office of *United Ireland* was John MacGrath, who wrote a famous article accusing the anti-Parnellites of having literally murdered Parnell. The young man was friendly to Yeats's thought and used to help him to promote literary discussions among the Parnellites. The Ireland of Thomas Davis and John Mitchel, MacGrath told his readers, had been reborn of the tragedy.

In the months following Parnell's death Yeats passed the greater part of his time in Ireland, where he was engaged in laying the foundation of the National Literary Society and in affiliating thereto various clubs throughout the country, wherever the Young Ireland tradition survived. The members of the Society included several of his father's old Nationalist acquaintances in the Contemporary Club, such as John O'Leary, J. F. Taylor, Hubert Oldham, formerly of the *Dublin University Review*, who kept many photographs of Maud Gonne upon his mantelpiece, Dr Sigerson, a provincial bard with some Irish scholarship, and Richard Ashe King, Irish correspondent of *Truth*, a gentle and devoted friend. Younger men and women, some of whom afterwards became local celebrities, joined in. The patriotism of the group was extreme, but by it many of the members were undone, being driven to form opinions on matters beyond their experience. A poet in such company was bound to encounter formidable opposition because his truths could be outfaced by deductions from premises which nearly all accepted. How, for instance, could one prove to a man like J. F. Taylor that certain wavering rhythms were nearer to the soul than the resolute rhythms of political oratory? Yeats's nationalism was mixed up inextricably with his desire of art, and was based upon the belief that art if it were to flourish must be upheld by an authoritative ideal of life. Lionel Johnson came once or twice to Dublin, and as a learned convert to Catholicism, Yeats designated him critic, or theologian of the movement, hoping that parish priests would not dare to question his orthodoxy. Yeats wished to avoid a quarrel with the Church, which already showed some signs of suspicion of his work; a Tipperary priest accused him of attributing degraded beliefs to the peasantry in his Introduction to the book of fairy and folk tales. But his chief trouble was with Nationalists, who supposed that if one questioned the merits of Thomas Davis's poetry one was defending the Danes or Oliver Cromwell.

The indispensable figure in the Society was John O'Leary, its first president, and Yeats was sure of his support. O'Leary's long imprisonment, his association with famous figures of the past, his lofty character and perhaps his distinguished head had given him great authority. But he was not an easy ally, and Yeats might not have had him for an ally had they not lodged together in the same old eighteenth-century house. It often took a whole day to convince O'Leary of the propriety of some resolution. Taylor, his disciple, was perpetually occupied with impassioned argument, to which he brought great historic erudition. He saw the world, as it were, in mathematical forms, and being impatient of compromise, he hated, and would always hate, what existed. He was enraged; he seemed at times to live in rage; it was useless for Yeats to quote from Blake, 'Those who cannot defend the truth shall defend an error that enthusiasm and life may not cease'. The most important man for the future was certainly Dr Douglas Hyde, whose lecture to the Society at the end of the first year had led to the foundation of the Gaelic League. Dr Hyde's faculty was by nature narrative and lyrical, and at the committees, especially if Taylor or O'Leary were speaking, he gave an impression of muddle or confusion. His perpetual association with peasants, whose songs and stories he had taken down from early childhood when he learned Irish, had given him the habit of diplomacy, and he evaded as far as he could prominent positions and the familiarity of his fellows that he might escape jealousy and detraction. He once told Yeats, who was on a brief visit to him in Roscommon, that he was the only man from Dublin who had ever stayed in his house. 'They would draw me into their quarrels,' he said.

In the effort to organize an Irish literary life Yeats had definite plans for himself and for his own work; having finished *The Countess Cathleen*, he wanted to create an Irish Theatre, and thought of a travelling company to visit the country branches of the Dublin National Literary Society. But the 'popular imaginative literature' was to come first; and when Fisher Unwin printed the first meagre version of the play in the summer of 1892, along with *Various Legends and Lyrics*, there was little hope of its possible early production on the stage. The reviews were coming in while Yeats was in Sligo with his uncle; a good one from Lionel Johnson, a bad from John Davidson, with whom Yeats had been at quarrel. A letter from J. B. Y. on the reception of the book has survived.

Last night I sent you the *D. Chronicle* and the *Star,* the poison and the antidote. Who could have written the *D. Chronicle* criticism? Was it Davidson as a *tit* for your *tat*? The tats were provoking and rather unnecessary, and since probably totally unexpected therefore the more bewildering and enraging to the fiery Scot. I would like to write and ask him if he wrote it and also whether he *really* thought so badly of the poems. Apart that is from the tits for tats business – the criticism was a very effective piece of coarse journalism but by its nature only appealed to the merest vulgar and not likely to do you or anybody any harm – I send you today's *Chronicle* and have marked a passage which will show that the good *Daily Chronicle* has returned to its sober senses. I laughed very much and without bitterness over the offending criticism and assuming Davidson to be the author liked him all the better – It is a good sign when a man does not know how to wound. I showed it today to York Powell who of course entirely disagreed with it – he said beauty of diction and lyrical quality are exactly what distinguish 'The Countess Kathleen'. When I showed York Powell your book he said he hated plays and would not read it – but he was into it at once as silent and busy as a bee buried in a flower – merely calling out from time to time – 'This is very good', 'This is a great improvement' and several times over – 'There are some fine lines here'. He never stopped till he had finished the whole book – he said then by the way of general conclusion that you had learned to compress – and again that the whole book was full of fine lines.

In the greater number of the lyrics in the volume Yeats was still a poet of fairyland and the successor of Allingham. But included in the volume was the group of poems, afterwards called 'The Rose', work more original than Yeats had yet accomplished, both in form and content. The rhythms still echo Morris, but the Platonism of Shelley and Spenser is no longer literally accepted. As Yeats himself noted when making a comment on the group in his autobiography, the quality symbolized in such poems as 'The Rose of the World', 'The Rose of Peace' differs from the intellectual beauty of Shelley and of Spenser in that it is imagined as suffering with man and not as something pursued from afar. The sufferings and aspirations of Ireland,

> That country where a man can be so crossed,
> Can he so battered, badgered and destroyed,

(the lines are from the later version of the originally somewhat sentimental 'Dedication to a Book of Stories selected from the Irish Novelists') are interpreted in the light of this philosophy.

> Come near, I would before my time to go
> Sing of old Eire and the ancient ways:
> Red Rose, proud Rose, sad Rose of all my days.

'I am delighted to hear you were pleased with my review,' Lionel Johnson wrote to him, 'though those abominable misprints still grieve me. The Rhymers have been meeting, with some good results in the way of rhyme: but do come back, and put some new life into us. Sligo must have inspired you sufficiently by this time.'

During the autumn of 1892 occurred the deaths of both the Pollexfen grandparents. Old Mrs Pollexfen had asked to see Yeats, but by some mistake he was not sent for in time. She had heard that he was much about with a beautiful admired woman and feared that he did not speak of marriage because he was poor; she wanted to say to him, 'women care nothing about money'. He went to Sligo for the funeral, and stayed at his uncle's for the few weeks during which William Pollexfen was dying. Before the old man gave way he believed that his wife had been brought to his bedside. The incident is mentioned in *Reveries over Childhood and Youth*, and also in a letter written to Miss Lily Yeats:

... I am afraid that grandpapa's death will make mamma worse. Please let me know how she is now and then. Grandpapa died quite painlessly. He said, 'George, fetch your mother' (thinking that Uncle George was there), and then after a pause held out his hands saying, 'Ah, there she is', and with that he died.

3

The Countess Cathleen is a drama of old days when a terrible famine laid waste Ireland. Two demons tempt the peasants to sell their souls for food. The Countess Cathleen sacrifices all her goods that her poor tenants may not make so dreadful a contract; and at the last, pity-crazed by the decay of character around her, disposes of her own soul at a great price in order that the people may not be forced by starvation to sell theirs. The old angels at the end of the play were imitated from a drawing by some French artist of an angel standing against the sky. The angels were old and wingless and armed like a knight. Yeats's father thought nothing of the drawing because it was out of proportion, and generally a judgement from his father would put him off anything, but this time the image remained.

Stories of how Maud Gonne had appeared as a sort of miracle-worker among the poor in Donegal associated themselves in the poet's thought with the legend, and made the play a symbolical song of his pity. Maud Gonne had given of her substance to the evicted tenants: exhausted by the effort, she had been told by her French doctor that she was threatened with serious illness, and must spend a winter among the pine trees at St Raphael. Here one day, upon opening her post, she found a letter from Yeats enclosing a poem recently printed by Henley. It bore the discouraging title, 'An Epitaph', and began:

> I dreamed that one had died in a strange place
> Near no accustomed hand;
> And they had nailed the boards above her face,
> The peasants of that land . . .

Maud Gonne made a good recovery, and returned to Paris where she took a little flat in the Avenue de la Grande Armée and occupied herself with plans which boded ill for the British Empire. She founded a French society called the

Friends of Irish Freedom, comprised of descendants of those who had accompanied Hoche's expedition to Ireland in 1796. She extended her acquaintance among French Nationalist politicians and members of the military party, who regarded England rather than Germany as the hereditary enemy, and who thought it desirable to encourage Germany's colonial and maritime ambitions as a bargain for the return of Alsace and Lorraine. But she still frequently came to Ireland, and Yeats had many opportunities of seeing her in London and in Dublin. She had not lost sight of the cause of the evicted tenants, forgotten by most in the dispute between Parnellites and anti-Parnellites, and the cause of the dynamite prisoners in the English jails was also near her heart. This work kept her continually on the move. Yeats and she went together to gatherings presided over by John O'Leary, who criticized the oratory, particularly hers and W. B.'s. In O'Leary's lodgings, where books were piled on the chairs and about the floor, Yeats would say that there must be more books – new books for the new generation – and the thought would intrude on her mind, 'Who had ever read these dusty volumes? What we need is surely action, not literature.' O'Leary saw but a beautiful woman seeking excitement, and the artist Miss Sarah Purser, painting her in that character, said to Yeats, 'Maud Gonne talks politics in Paris, and literature to you, and at the Horse Show she would talk of a clinking brood mare'. Though full of disquiet Yeats never failed to defend her; he would say, 'None of you understands her force of mind'. Miss Gonne lived, as ever, surrounded by dogs and birds, and he was aware of many charities – old men and old women past work were always seeking her out – and of a pattern beyond his reach in her handling of birds and of hearts.

4

In London Yeats prepared a scheme for the publication of a series of books on the lines of the old National Library of Thomas Davis. He engaged Fisher Unwin's interest, and

then found that Sir Charles Gavan Duffy, a survivor of
Young Ireland, who had come home after a successful political career in Australia, had suggested a like scheme to one
of the young Southwark Irishmen. The sales were to be
organized through the London Irish Literary Society, which
T. W. Rolleston, with some assistance from Yeats, had lately
founded. Unlike Yeats's Dublin organization, the Irish
Literary Society included Unionists and anti-Parnellites
among its members, and presently Rolleston intervened and
collected a group of learned men, many of them Yeats's
political opponents, who decided that the one really necessary thing was to raise money for the publication of books
of Irish scholarship. Not having set his thoughts on books
for scholars but on popular imaginative literature, Yeats
crossed to Ireland in a passion. The first man he sought out
in Dublin was a butter merchant, whose name had been
given to him by a Southwark friend. The butter merchant
agreed with his views, and Yeats went off to lecture in a provincial town, where a workman's wife, who wrote patriotic
stories in a weekly newspaper, invited him to her house. She
made a little speech in which she said that what she wrote
had no merit, but that it paid for her children's schooling;
and she finished her speech by telling her children never to
forget that they had seen him. He was compared in another
house to Thomas Davis; and one man said he could organize
like Davitt. The applause pleased him. 'I did not examine
this applause,' he says in his autobiography,

nor the true thoughts of those I met, nor the general condition of
the country, but I examined myself a great deal, and was puzzled
at myself. I knew that I was shy and timid ... and yet here was
I delightedly talking to strange people every day. It was many
years before I understood that I had surrendered myself to the
chief temptation of the artist, creation without toil.

While Yeats was enjoying these successes in Ireland,
Rolleston and Sir Charles Gavan Duffy combined to persuade Fisher Unwin, or his reader, Edward Garnett, to

accept their series of Irish books. Edward Garnett, a personal friend of the poet, tried to make peace, writing as follows:

Now, my dear fellow, I'm not going to preach anything at all, but I do ask you to examine what the differences are between your view and the rival schemes and see whether it is for the good of the idea *you* are working for that you and your party should be irreconcilable. ... It seems to me absurd that Duffy should want to boss a national affair, but why not let him have the *figure-headship* so long as he isn't really *Dictator* ... the fact is the whole issue of the split lies between you and Rolleston – If you and he would join hands (you representing the Parnellite party, and Rolleston the London Irish Literary Society) you would find that you and he are practically of the same mind about the books and that your own ideas would be carried through. ...

Why not drop personal feeling, quiet the hornet's nest in your side, come over here first and see whether you cannot make a practical agreement? ...

O'Leary supported Yeats in this battle of the books, but thought him 'a young man in a hurry' and indiscreet, and recommended him to study Parnell's aloofness, and not live on terms of intimacy with those whom he wished to influence; advice which Yeats did not really find it very difficult to follow.

[Dublin] 8th Nov. 92

Dear Willie,

... You should write to Rolleston about these negotiations with F. U. but needn't tell him ('tis one of your faults that you often tell what not authorised to do) where you got the information. Indeed you should have written to R. long ago, as [I] urged you to do. They seem not to have been playing us quite fair, as they have not all along – Anyway if publishing scheme given up, we are quite at liberty to carry out our [library] scheme, or any similar one. ... B. O'B.* has put a little nationality into Miss Gonne, but 'twill do little good if tenants not in a measure put out of it. I shouldn't stir if I were you, till she comes here.

* Barry O'Brien, the biographer of Parnell and a leading member of the London Irish Literary Society.

I know you can't be kept away then. You're doing far better work
[in Sligo] and I hope in better health than you could be here.
We arranged at last meeting of com. of lit. soc. for a lecture a
month from end of November beginning with Hyde, and taking
you in, when and where the secretary to find out from you, and
we have names that will take us on till June. . . . As ever,

J. O'L.

    P.S. – You put neither Clontarf nor Dublin on your last letter.
You lick me into a cocked hat in this kind of thing.

The quarrel was political, because Yeats ranged the
Parnellites on his side, and literary, because what Duffy
wanted was not original literature, but simply repetition.
Duffy, to quote a contemporary chronicler, carried with him
'the large nondescript element which takes a patronizing
interest in literature, and to whom the voice of a poet is
nothing, and the word of an ex-Premier divine music'. When
Yeats or Johnson criticized verse, Davis's in particular, that
only owed its position to moral or political worth, people felt
that they were in some way wronging or throwing doubt on
the character of a patriot. When the opposition spread to the
general public, sectarian prejudice entered into it, and
writers of Protestant birth and upbringing, like Yeats, Standish O'Grady and George Russell, were made to feel that
they were separated by the vast gulf of the religious question
from the majority of their countrymen. Lionel Johnson
might tell the unlearned parish priests who thought good
literature or good criticism dangerous that they were 'all
heretics'. But Johnson was considered an Englishman, and
his words therefore carried little weight, nor was any novel
argument intelligible to those smooth smiling faces en-
countered in Dublin; faces, Yeats has said, that Velasquez
might have painted: 'the hungry, medieval speculation
vanished . . . and in its place a self-complacent certainty that
all had been arranged, all provided for, all set out in clear
type, in manual of devotion or in doctrine.' Yet if Yeats had
been content to remain simply a poet of Irish folk faiths or
the re-creator of pagan epics, he would not have been

attacked. He began to stir enmities and suspicions only when he began to introduce Christian symbols into his poetry and prose; his mysticism could no longer be regarded merely as a private affair, poetic licence, when theology mixed with it, as in his *Countess Cathleen* play.

The books that Gavan Duffy wished to publish were all books that by some mischance had failed to find publication in his youth, the works of political associates or of friends long dead. After long dispute Yeats arranged that Dr Hyde and Rolleston should be appointed editors under Duffy, and he sent in his own suggestions through these editors, or through an advisory Committee he had persuaded the London society to elect. In this way Dr Hyde's *History of Gaelic Literature* and O'Grady's *Bog of Stars* were published; lives of Swift and of Goldsmith were added to a series that, had it not been killed after a couple of years by the books chosen by its editors, would have done much for popular education. Sir Charles insisted on an excellent unpublished work, excellent, that is, for a learned Society, by Thomas Davis, and so successfully were plans laid that ten thousand copies were sold before anyone found time to read the work. Unhappily, when the public did read it, it made up its mind to have nothing further to do with the series.

Still, there was no limit to confidence. A few months after the first meeting of the Irish Literary Society a history of the movement was published in volume form, and Yeats had difficulty in preventing the Council from sending out a circular that began with the words, 'Ireland despite its dramatic genius has had no dramatist like Shakespeare, but a subcommittee of the Irish Literary Society has decided that the time has come ...'

5

Yeats's chief hopes were placed on Hyde and on George Russell. He believed that in Hyde, whom Henley and York Powell had declared to be the 'greatest of the folk-lorists', and in Russell, the religious genius, he would find powerful

allies against the rhetorical journalists and bad taste. As yet
Russell never spoke of politics, but he had begun to idealize
Celtic Ireland and to find curious correspondences between
the wisdom of ancient India and the spirit of Irish saga.
Yeats is quoted in E. A. Boyd's *Irish Literary Renaissance* as
having said (a little later, no doubt) that Russell and the
theosophists on the one hand, and Standish O'Grady on the
other, had done more for Irish literature than Trinity College in the course of three centuries. O'Grady was of an older
generation than Yeats and Russell, his *Bardic History*
having been published as long ago as 1875. It was a book of
high importance for modern Irish literature, considered as a
movement deriving its main nourishment from ancient
Gaelic sources. But O'Grady himself cherished an independence of judgement which made it impossible to enlist him
under any banner:

> Standish O' Grady supporting himself between the tables
> Speaking to a drunken audience high nonsensical words.*

A Unionist in politics, with a hatred of every form of democracy, he had given his heart to the smaller Protestant gentry
to whom he belonged, and mixed Carlylean apologies for
Cromwell with an attempt to make Fionn, Oisin and
Cuchulain a portion of the nation's soul.

The jovial Dubliner of the middle-nineteenth century
would have mocked at it all, or only half believed. The
patriots of '48 had sought a nation unified by political doctrine alone, creating through Davis and Duffy a method of
writing that took its style from English popular authors,
Campbell, Scott, Macaulay, and, in the case of Mitchel, from
Carlyle. Then came the scholars O'Donovan, Curry and their
German collaborators, who deciphered and translated the
great epics of the pagan Irish of the age of Christ. A country-
man – in the Sligo, for instance, of Yeats's childhood – would
have known nothing of the epic cycles, such as that of the
Red Branch tradition, Iliad and Odyssey of the Gael, written

* *Vide* 'Beautiful Lofty Things' in Yeats's *Last Poems*.

in a language more remote from modern Irish than is Anglo-Saxon from modern English and preserved by a literary caste that died out after the Tudor conquest. His memory would have been entirely oral and, unless, he had been exceptionally learned, would have carried only stories of the Fianna. When Yeats wrote *The Wanderings of Oisin*, the chief texts, interpreted by highly trained scholars and with translations, were available to men of letters in the publications of the Society for the Preservation of the Irish Language. But in his early work he sought little help from the scholars, unlike Ferguson, but symbolized and philosophized the grim originals, or, as in some of his lyrics, expressed the musical and plaintive strain of modern Irish, peculiar to Connaught, where the 'note' is primitive, passionate and tender, not classical and impersonal as in Munster, where Irish was best cultivated as a literary language in the eighteenth century.

Both the imaginative movement that will always be associated with Yeats's name, and the Gaelic League of Douglas Hyde, were de-Anglicizing movements, and the attention that they won from young men and women was largely due to the disillusionment and bitterness that followed the death of Parnell, when families were divided, son against father, brother against brother, and party politics became odious to sensitive minds. It was touching to see how writings like those of Peter O'Leary (the first author to use modern Irish with a literary object) enchanted old native-speakers as well as thousands of young men and women of the towns, who turned with enthusiasm to the study of what they imagined was the speech of their grandfathers. Gradually, however, it became apparent that Hyde was to create a great popular movement, far more important in its practical results than any movement Yeats could have made, and that the Gaelic League would conform to moral and educational enthusiasms alien alike to the folk spirit and to the aristocratic and critical nationalism which Yeats had learned at the feet of John O'Leary.

Mysticism in prose and verse

The Celtic Twilight and Symbolism – Production of
Land of Heart's Desire (1894) – a winter in Sligo; corre-
spondence with Mrs Shakespear and visit to Lissadell –
Publication of *Poems* (1895) – Arthur Symons and *The
Savoy* – 'Diana Vernon'

———

> *The host is riding from Knocknarea
> And over the grave of Clotoh-na-Bare;
> Caoilte tossing his burning hair,
> And Niamh calling* Away, come away:
> Empty your heart of its mortal dream ...

I

IN London Yeats was now a minor celebrity who attracted
occasional attention from the press. In March 1893 Katharine
Tynan, turned journalist, called at the house in Bedford
Park and reported to the *Sketch* that he was about to bring
out his *Celtic Twilight*, and was engaged upon a book of
'weird' stories of the Middle Ages in Ireland.

His study [she wrote] is at the back of a quaint and charming
house, in which, outside the poet's den, order reigns. It opens on
a little balcony, twined about and overhung with Virginia
creeper. He has generally a few plants there of which he is in-
ordinately jealous. ... The fireplace is littered with papers. The
mantelpiece is buried in layers of them. ... The books cover a
large range; but are mainly either poetry or books on occult subjects. ... Of books, papers, letters and proof sheets there is such a
confusion that one wonders how he came to disentangle anything.

The interview was illustrated with a photograph which
depicted the poet with the moustache worn by him for a time

after he had shaved his beard. A heavy Inverness cape, discarded by his father in the seventies and preserved by his mother, gave him a more burly and more out-of-doors appearance than he had worn in the early drawings by his father, where he is the complete aesthete. Katharine Tynan seems to have felt that some change was coming upon the 'delightful and easy Willie Yeats' of her girlhood in Dublin. He may have greeted her in the manner learned at the Rhymers' Club, where the custom was to be ceremonious, polite, but distant in manner. At all events she expressed a hope that he would soon be away again from 'London and literary coteries', and back in the country of faiths, where 'no dry-rot of cynicism or unbelief' would be likely to affect him.

Another poetess, Louise Imogen Guiney, wrote of him, on the occasion of the importation into Boston of a small edition of *The Countess Cathleen and Various Legends and Lyrics*. In her picture he is still remote and inconsequent, a creature of natural magic, whose playthings are the occult sciences.

He has no faith in them at all, but he has endless fun with them. He will give you an inspired monologue, like Hazlitt's, only on less material topics, over his thirty-first cup of tea, with the laugh in his eyes. ... He goes about, without a touch of conscious eccentricity ... to be met with now in the still aisles of the British Museum, now at the Cheshire Cheese ... anon in the middle of Holborn or the Strand, transfixed where a thought from on high has struck him. ... A gentle happy soul, and an out-of-door schoolman, if ever such were! No quarreller with the time, and yet by no possible evidence belonging to it.

The early work of the 'gentle happy soul', the 'out-of-door schoolman', culminated in *The Celtic Twilight* and in *The Land of Heart's Desire*. Neither tales nor play invited argument or opposition; it was as if someone had said, 'I ask you humbly to listen to the old people as they tell their stories'. 'The Crucifixion of the Outcast', first of a new set of stories to be gathered together a year or two later under the title *The Secret Rose*, appeared in Henley's *National Observer* in March 1894. It showed a new humour not so easy for all his readers to fall in with. Yeats was on the move from parochial prodigies to a scientific cosmopolitanism, from absorbed singing to symbolism. The only great prose in modern English for him, as for other members of the Rhymers' Club, was Pater's, and *The Secret Rose*, one might say, is Pater's style subdued to the matter of Villiers de L'Isle-Adam.

Arthur Symons was the channel in the Rhymers' Club between the new French influences and English literature. It was through Symons that Yeats made his acquaintance with the literary decadentism of France, recognizable in much of the poetry of the Symbolists as an aspect of that reaction against positivism and the scientific movement to which the Rhymers drank 'confusion'. Was it before, or after, Yeats's first visit to Paris that Symons read out to him his metrical translation of Herodiade's address to the Sibyl in Villiers de L'Isle-Adam's *Axël*? The visit, which took place in February 1894, enabled Yeats to witness the production of that dramatic masterpiece, Schopenhauer in fancy dress, and, with Maud Gonne accompanying him to the theatre, he was able to follow the play sufficiently well to write a notice of it for the London *Bookman*. He was enthusiastic: *Axël*, he confided to his readers, would take a place 'in the hierarchy of his recollections with a night-scene when the wind blew by a bed of roses by the borders of a little lake, with a line or two from Homer and with a Japanese picture of cranes flying through a blue sky'. As his article was not reprinted, some extracts from his account of a remarkable occasion may be given here.

. . . A crowded audience of artists and men of letters listened, and on the whole with enthusiasm, from two o'clock until ten minutes to seven to this drama, which is written in prose as elevated as poetry. . . .

One fat old critic who sat near me, so soon as a magician of the Rosy-Cross, who is the chief person in the third act, began to denounce the life of pleasure and to utter the ancient doctrine of the spirit, turned round with his back to the stage and looked at the pretty girls through his opera glass. . . . The lovers . . . drink poison and so complete the four-fold renunciation – of the cloister, of the active life of the world, of the labouring life of the intellect, of the passionate life of love. The infinite is alone worth attaining, and the infinite is in the possession of the dead. Such appears to be the moral. Seldom has utmost pessimism found a more magnificent expression.

Villiers's saying 'As for living, our servants will do that for us', was used as epigraph for the stories in *The Secret Rose*, and the pessimist's hope to break the circle (to be delivered from the crime of birth and death) was repeated in the dramatic poem, *The Shadowy Waters*, already begun at this time :

> . . . O ancient worm,
> Dragon that loved the world and held us to it,
> You are broken.

Axël became Yeats's guide and beacon in his theory and practice of a dramatic art where symbol replaces character, events are allegories and words keep more than half their secrets to themselves.

While in Paris Yeats stayed with the MacGregor Mathers, who were now conducting their cabalistic operations from a flat in the Champ de Mars, supported by a small allowance from one of the members of the Order. Bergson called, very courteous and well dressed; 'I have shown him all that magic can do,' Mathers said of his brother-in-law, 'and it has had no effect upon him.' The great mystagogue would come down to breakfast with a Horace in his hands or with Macpherson's *Ossian*, and become very angry if anyone cast doubt upon Macpherson's good faith. As a rule, though he evidently lived under a great strain, Mathers was a gay and companionable man. In the evenings he made his wife and Yeats play chess with him, a curious form of chess with four players. Yeats's partner was Mrs Mathers, Mathers's a spirit.

Mathers would shade his eyes with his hands and gaze at the empty chair at the opposite corner of the board before moving his partner's piece.

Arthur Symons arrived and took Yeats to call on Verlaine, who could speak English. No young man of letters at that time could be said to have seen Paris without climbing the stairs to the garret where the French poet nursed his ailing leg. The talk turned on Maeterlinck. 'Does he not touch the nerves sometimes when he should touch the heart?' asked Yeats. 'Ah, yes', Verlaine replied; 'he is a dear good fellow but a little bit of a mountebank.' Of the Tennyson of *In Memoriam* Verlaine said: 'When he should have been broken-hearted he had many reminiscences.'

2

The Land of Heart's Desire was produced on 29 March 1894, at the Avenue Theatre in London, as a curtain-raiser for John Todhunter's *Comedy of Sighs* and Bernard Shaw's *Arms and the Man.* Into this fairy play Yeats put the vague desire for an impossible life which he attributed to Maud Gonne, the dramatic conflict being between sentiment of home and kindred and the maddening and bewildering light from the old world of the Sidhe. Florence Farr had become manageress of the Avenue Theatre, and Yeats wrote the play on her suggestion in order that her niece, Dorothy Paget, might make a first stage appearance in the part of the fairy child. Miss Farr, always in revolt against her own musical gift, had tried when interviewed by the press to shock and startle, yet had feared to open her season with Shaw's play. Todhunter's *Comedy of Sighs* was a poor and pretentious piece, and the enemies of the intellectual drama, who crowded the gallery, derided the ominously entitled play with loud laughter, which even *The Times* critic thought excusable. The critic cut Todhunter to pieces, adding, however, that a mood of mocking protest might have been excited by the 'small piece on an Irish theme which preceded it', a measure of the author's eccentricity being offered by the strange line in the programme, 'The characters are supposed to speak in Gaelic'. It is doubtful if Yeats gained an advantage with an unpicked audience by believing in fairies. To be certain that fairies *are* fairies deprives them of some of their mystery.

The first night was a complete disaster. On his way to the theatre Yeats let his glasses fall into a grating in the Strand, and he saw the stage in a diminishing mist. The German poet Dauthendey, who came with him, fell asleep from heat and tiredness; he was unable to answer, when asked by Yeats whether he liked the play.* On another evening Oscar Wilde arrived just as the curtain fell on *The Land of Heart's Desire* and overwhelmed Yeats by his praise of the story 'The Crucifixion of the Outcast'. Todhunter's comedy was soon withdrawn, but Yeats's play was kept on the stage during the long run of *Arms and the Man* and was seen by the Prince of Wales and the Duke of Edinburgh. Yeats was in the theatre almost every night for several weeks, noting in the light of the performances the changes he might make in the monosyllabic verse, in which his interpreters were ill at ease. George Moore, flushed with the success of *Esther Waters*, had his first sight of him there, and has recorded in *Ave* of his famous trilogy of reminiscence that he was not taken with the poet's appearance:

It amused me to remember the amazement with which I watched Yeats marching around the dress circle after the performance of his little one-act play *The Land of Heart's Desire*. His play neither pleased nor displeased; it struck me as an inoffensive trifle, but he himself had provoked a violent antipathy

*Dauthendey met Yeats in London, introduced by American friends, who, like Yeats himself, belonged to some occult society. Later on, they used to see each other occasionally in Paris. Yeats mentions the German poet (spelling the name Douchenday) in *The Tragic Generation* as a friend of Strindberg who was looking for the Philosopher's Stone. The incident in the theatre is described in Dauthendey's *Gedankengut aus meinen Wanderjahren.*

as he strode to and forth at the back of the dress circle, a long black cloak drooping from his shoulders, a soft black sombrero on his head, a voluminous black silk tie flowing from his collar, loose black trousers dragging untidily over his long, heavy feet – a man of such excessive appearance that I could not do otherwise – could I? – than mistake him for an Irish parody of the poetry that I had seen all my life strutting its rhythmic way in the alleys of the Luxembourg gardens, preening its rhymes by the fountains, excessive in habit and gait.

Some months later J. T. Nettleship arranged a meeting between Moore and Yeats, and they argued about Blake. Moore was astonished at the rapidity with which Yeats's mind worked. ' "A dialectician", I muttered, "of the very first rank; one of a different kind from any I have met before"; and a few moments after I began to notice that Yeats was sparring beautifully, avoiding my rushes with great care, evidently playing to tire me, with the intention of killing me presently with a single spur stroke.' They parted without a presentiment that they would soon be literary associates.

3

The superior English periodicals now welcomed contributions from Yeats and he became a fairly regular writer in the *Speaker* and the *Bookman*. As a rule, he reviewed Irish writers, among others in this year: Larminie, George Russell, Aubrey de Vere, Nora Hopper, Emily Lawless, Lionel Johnson, John Eglinton. A note on *Brand* scarcely revealed a deep understanding of the Norwegian dramatist: Yeats was persistently prejudiced against Ibsen, perhaps on account of the insistence of Ibsen's English disciples on the 'social message', and he overlooked the great poet. Another work on which he was engaged in 1894 was *A Book of Irish Verse*, a modern anthology for Methuen. In reply to a request that he might quote 'Tread lightly, she is near, Under the snow', Oscar Wilde wrote to him:

With pleasure. I don't know that I think 'Requiescat' very typical of my work. Personally I would sooner you choose a sonnet on the sale of Keats' love letters, or the one beginning – 'Not that I love thy children' – with which the book opens – but the garden – such as it is – is yours to pluck from.

The anthology was put together in the midst of a battle provoked by certain remarks made by Dowden, Mahaffy and other spokesmen of the culture of Protestant Dublin, who disbelieved in the possibility of a distinctive Irish literature in English. There was an amazing controversy in the course of which Standish O'Grady treated Dowden like a pickpocket for daring to suggest that Ferguson was not in all essential qualities, except precedence, a greater poet than Homer. 'We should like', a *Saturday Reviewer* wrote, 'to get hold of Mr Yeats ... on some neutral shore, and there to press him as to the character and texture of the famous *Vengeance* ... we are tolerably sure that we would wring from him an admission that a vague and horrible story is incoherently told, though not, of course, without some passion.' In fact, though Ferguson took pride of place in the Irish anthology, Yeats had ceased to regard him as a star of magnitude in literature. He would have sacrificed most of Ferguson's volumes for a few pages of George Russell's *Homeward Songs*, which he thought might be immortal. He was to write in his autobiography that in looking back upon his Irish propaganda of early years he could 'see little but its bitterness'. He rarely met, or met but to quarrel with, his father's old family acquaintances, who had appointments at University or Castle, and this attitude he took by deliberate calculation, because if he had to belittle so much popular poetry that seemed sacred to Irish Nationalist opinion, he had to be sure that no man would suspect him of doing it to flatter the cultivated Unionist minority.

Dowden's attitude, condescending and aloof, towards the prospects of an Irish literary movement (he was generous in his appreciation of individuals) was a bitter disappointment. Yeats could never forgive him, and in a chapter of his autobiography (1914) Dowden is pictured as a little unreal, a specious moral image, set up for contrast beside the real image of O'Leary. Yeats had the long Irish memory for wrongs, and he was persuaded that Dowden, though always charming in private life, had fought him in ways that were not fair.

Not having solved the difficulty of living, Yeats went to Sligo in the autumn of 1894 and spent six months with his uncle at Thornhill. He wrote to his sister when Christmas came, 'A great many thanks for the handkerchiefs, and please convey my thanks to Lolly for the others – I am sorry I have sent you nothing, but I possess nothing but a 2/- piece and a half-penny borrowed – and will be no wealthier until Methuen chooses to publish *A Book of Irish Verse*.' George Pollexfen was now in the fifties, but appeared a much older man. His habits had become more and more fixed. Still, so long as one did not interfere with these, or cheat over a horse, there was freedom and peace in his companionship. He would go to his office in the morning, and then return for an afternoon walk with his nephew, for the benefit of health, along the Knocknarea road. The firm was doing well, but he attributed its success to an old and trustworthy clerk and was careful as ever of his money. The clairvoyant servant, Mary Battle, and a groom for a racehorse, comprised the staff at Thornhill. The horse ran second during the winter at Leopardstown, and George returned from the race, Yeats reported to his sister, 'in good spirits, but with a racing man under whose technical conversation I groan'.

Before Christmas Yeats rewrote *The Countess Cathleen*, helped in the revision by what he had learned from seeing *The Land of Heart's Desire* on the stage. He also wrote some more medieval stories for *The Secret Rose*. These were not mere fantasies, he said, but the signatures of things invisible and ideal. His environment favoured this work. George Pollexfen wore a scared look as if he saw ghosts no one else could see. He was a corresponding member of the Order of the Golden Dawn, but his chief passion was astrology; nephew and uncle studied the figures in the stars together. Yeats wrote to his sister in January 1895:

> Some friend sent him the birth date of a child and asked him for a horoscope. He made one but wrote – he did not know the child's name by-the-by – or whether it was boy or girl – that it was no use judging it, as the child, if it had not died at birth, could not outlive infancy, and that death would probably be caused by fits. He showed me the answer the other day. The friend had sent the birth date as a test. The child had died of fits ten or eleven days after birth.

Some doubt exists as to which it was, nephew or uncle, who introduced the other to astrology; but it is certain that Yeats's practice of this ancient science, as compared with George Pollexfen's, was somewhat meagre and occasional. Indeed Yeats never got further than the old-fashioned square figure, which the higher-grade astrologers have abandoned. He frequently made horary figures, but he shrank from the mathematical calculations for progressions.

During the winter there was an outbreak of smallpox in the vicinity of Sligo and both Yeats and his uncle were vaccinated. The vaccine was bad. Yeats made a slow recovery but had no serious illness, whereas Pollexfen became delirious and two doctors had to be called in. One night Yeats sat at the bedside and heard his uncle say, 'I see red dancing figures'. Without telling what he was doing, Yeats at once used his favourite symbol of water that is connected in the cabalistic system with the moon. Presently the sick man cried out that he saw a river flowing through the room and sweeping all the red figures away. Yeats then told him what he had done, and his uncle said, 'I think I can sleep now'. 'If the figures return', said Yeats, 'banish them in the name of Gabriel, who as moon archangel controls the waters.' The next morning the family doctor spoke to Yeats. 'I hear that you gave your uncle a secret word that cured his hallucination. I suppose it is a kind of hypnotism.' Then a young bank clerk, who sometimes came in for séances after dinner with

Lucy Middleton, saw the vision of the Garden of Eden, which Yeats later described in his essay on magic in *Ideas of Good and Evil*. The clerk refused to come to the house again, saying that he was in business and that he would not be able to do the queer things one has to do in business if he believed in the supernatural. Presently Yeats gained with the country people the reputation of being a magician. They said that he had been carried five miles in the winking of an eye, and that he had sent his cousin from her house at Rosses to Tory Island in a like eye-wink: he had seen these things in a vision. At the Middletons' one evening he made a water-evocation and his cousin saw mermaids during the night. The maid gave notice.

While in the reclusion of Sligo Yeats received many letters from Mrs Olivia Shakespear, to whom he had been introduced in London by Lionel Johnson, her cousin, at some literary dinner. Hers is the 'lovely face' of his later poem 'Memory'.* At the time Yeats met her Mrs Shakespear was a young woman of about his own age, well read in English, French and Italian literature; he admired her beauty and appreciated her apparent content to have no more in life than leisure and talk with her friends. She lived at 18 Porchester Square, Hyde Park, one of the houses perhaps of which he speaks in his autobiography, where he used to call on women friends, timid and abashed with them, apart from 'their intimate exchanges of thought'. Her husband was an elderly solicitor whom the poet saw but once.

She sent him the manuscript of a novel, *Beauty's Hour*, and he criticized it for her very carefully. Then he wrote of Lionel Johnson's recently published *Art of Thomas Hardy*. 'I think Lionel's work very wonderful and agree with you in caring more for his themes about literature than about Hardy in particular. ... I feel however that there is something wrong about praising Hardy in a style so much better

* *The Wild Swans at Coole*, 1919.
  One had a lovely face,
  And two or three had charm.

than Hardy's own.' His correspondent invited him to give an opinion on Maeterlinck and he replied: 'I feel about his things that they differ from really great work in lacking that ceaseless reverie that we call wisdom. In all the old dramatists, Greek and English, one feels that they are all the time thinking wonderful, and rather mournful things about their puppets, and every now and then they utter their thoughts in a sudden line or embody them in some unforeseen action.'

In the early letters to Mrs Shakespear there are passages which show that he was already feeling his way towards his doctrine of the self and anti-self, which was afterwards set out in *Per Amica Silentia Lunae* and expressed in his poetry, and finding confirmation of it in the marvels of psychic phenomena. He suggested that she should make one of the characters in her novel, a vigorous fair-haired athletic young man, wholly passive on the emotional and intellectual side. Had she not noticed the dramatic contradiction between Morris's table manners and the unfailing tact of the figures in his romances? He warned his correspondent against the use of some symbol, remarking that 'every influence has a shadow, as it were, an unbalanced – and the unbalanced is the cabalistic definition of evil – duplicate of itself'. Yeats had been familiarized by Jacob Boehme and by Blake with the idea of the coincidence of opposites: but whenever a philosophical idea interested him he wanted to trace it to images out of old time. George Russell used to say that the germ of the antithetical philosophy must have developed in Yeats as a boy, 'at the first decisive contact of soul and body'. While they were still at the art school together Yeats had been greatly moved by a drawing by Russell, in which a man on a mountain shrank from his own gigantic shadow in the mist. The preoccupation with the self and its shadow was in various lines of *The Wanderings of Oisin* and of other early poems:

But never with us where the wild fowl chases
Its shadow along in evening blaze.

But naught they heard, for they are always listening,
The dewdrops, for the sound of their own dropping.

A parrot sways upon a tree,
Raging at his own image in the enamelled sea.

The poet's winter with his uncle was pleasantly interrupted by two visits to Lissadell, where Sir Henry Gore-Booth, his wife and son and two daughters lived. In his childhood he had seen on clear days from the hill above his grandfather's house, or from a carriage if their drive was towards Ben Bulben, or from the smooth grass hill of Rosses, the grey stone walls of Lissadell among its trees. There was a strain of mutability in the Gore-Booths; and Sir Henry tiring of his beautiful demesne, as a county historian puts it, and of the timid hare and half domesticated pheasant, would from time to time seek his quarry in the polar bear and the arctic whale. The girls were famous for their nerve and dash riding to hounds. Constance, the rebel Countess Markievicz of 1916, had often passed Yeats in going to or coming from a hunt; she was acknowledged to be the loveliest girl in the county –

When long ago I saw her ride
Under Ben Bulben to the meet,
The beauty of her country-side
With all youth's lonely wildness stirred,
She seemed to have grown clean and sweet
Like any rock-bred, sea-borne bird.*

The long settled habit of Irish life had set up a wall between merchant families, however rich, and 'county' people. But Yeats had written books, and it was his business to write books; it was natural to wish to talk with those whose books one liked, and besides he was no longer of his grandfather's house. He was invited to lecture in the schoolhouse on the estate by the Rev. Fletcher Le Fanu, nephew of the Sweden-

* 'On a Political Prisoner', 1919.

borgian novelist, on Irish folk-lore before an audience of
Orangemen, who enjoyed his humorous tales but rejected
the folk-lore as some kind of Papist superstition. A Mr Jones,
who had been christened by his great-grandfather, said to
him, 'Now there must be another lecture to put your lecture
on a sound religious basis'.

He had not noticed it before; but now at Lissadell there
seemed to be some physical resemblance between Constance
Gore-Booth and Maud Gonne; both had then low and soft
voices. But it was with Eva, who was afterwards to lose
herself in philanthropic politics, that Yeats felt in closest
sympathy. For two happy weeks he was Eva's companion;
her gazelle-like beauty reflected a subtle and distinguished
mind. He told her of all his unhappiness in love and set her
to the study of Irish legend.* His elegant and lofty period
piece, 'In Memory of Eva Gore-Booth and Constance
Markievicz' (*The Winding Stair*, 1933), was to strike its note
in the rhyme 'Lissadell – gazelle'. The 'old Georgian man-
sion', 'that table and the talk of youth', the politics and
finally 'the great gazebo' that they built, conjure up a vivid
and beautiful family portrait.

By the end of the winter Yeats's friendship with his uncle
had become very close. It is true that he suffered irritation
because George Pollexfen never treated him quite as a grown
man; for instance, if there was only one kidney with the
bacon at breakfast his uncle always took it without apology.
But all the more he thought of Thornhill very much as one
thinks of home. In a sense Sligo always was his home.

4

He returned to London and found everyone excited by the
arrest of Oscar Wilde; his father said to him the moment he
arrived, 'You should go and see Wilde and ask if you can be

* Possibly he was the first to speak to the sisters of one in emulation
of whom perhaps Constance Gore-Booth was afterwards to earn a life
sentence from a British court-martial.

of any help. He was very kind to you.' George Russell and a few other Dublin friends had written letters of sympathy and Yeats went with these to Wilde's house in Oakley Street. He was ushered by a grave servant into the presence of William Wilde, Oscar's brother, who was in a maudlin condition, and said: 'Before I give him these letters, you must tell me what are in them. ... Oh yes, he could escape, there is a yacht anchored in the Thames, and £5000 to pay his bail – well, if not exactly anchored there, he can escape, even if I had to inflate a balloon in the back-garden myself, but he is resolved to face the music like Christ.' Then Mrs William Wilde came in; she had just seen Oscar, and said with an air of relief, 'It is all right now, he has resolved to go to jail if necessary'. William Wilde seemed grateful for Yeats's visit; letters from his countrymen would encourage Oscar, he said. 'He and I were not good friends. I need not say more, you will understand, but he came to me like a wounded stag and I took him in.' Yeats left, promising to get another bundle of letters, and these he carried to the court, but he never saw Oscar Wilde again.

Looking backwards, Yeats was inclined to find in Lionel Johnson rather than in Wilde the tragedy of a generation: 'souls turned from practical ends become contemplative but not yet ready for the impress of the divine will, an unendurable burden.' Johnson had been a powerful influence for a while in Yeats's Irish societies. His stately English, rich in the cadences of the eighteenth century, carried minds back to Grattan and the Irish Parliament of 1782; and yet the committees, lectures and public dinners to which he went with Yeats were all he ever saw of active life. He had given up the world for a library; he had refused rather than failed to live. Yeats would contrast him with Dowson, of whom the reverse could be said. With Yeats and T. W. Rolleston so often away, and with Lionel Johnson reading in the silence of the night, the Rhymers' Club began to fail. Only the so-called 'Celtic members' – Yeats, Rhys and Rolleston – had given it vitality.

What Yeats wished to preserve of his poetry as published to date was now brought out by Father Unwin in a volume entitled *Poems*, with a preface, dated Sligo, March 1895. Everything that was in this book, with the exception of a couple of lyrics and *The Land of Heart's Desire*, had already appeared in his two earlier volumes, *The Wanderings of Oisin, and Other Poems* and *The Countess Cathleen and Various Legends and Lyrics*. After the publication of the latter volume, either Unwin or Yeats had purchased unsold sheets of *The Wanderings of Oisin* from Kegan Paul, and re-issued that book with a stubbed title-page, the binding uniform with that of *The Countess Cathleen*, and with the addition of a dreadful frontispiece by Edwin J. Ellis, 'Cuchulain fighting the Waves'. The re-issue appears to have been overlooked by the poet's bibliographers.

The lyrics in the 1895 volume were divided into sections, one called 'Crossways', the other 'The Rose', titles which the poet retained until the end to distinguish between his earliest verse and that written between 1889 (the date of *The Wanderings of Oisin*) and 1892. At twenty-seven, with the publication of *The Countess Cathleen*, he came to unalterable decisions as to what he would preserve of his earliest verse; and he neither added to, nor subtracted from, the contents of 'Crossways' – sixteen poems – in any subsequent editions of his work. Revisions were another matter; like the she-bear to which Virgil was compared, he was for ever licking his cubs into shape. Already in 1895 some of his friends expressed their uneasiness over his refusal to leave things that they liked alone. 'I have not rewritten "Innisfree" or "The Two Trees"', he wrote to Mrs Shakespear.

The things I have re-written are *Wanderings of Oisin*, and practically all the lyrics which I care to preserve out of the same volume; and the end and the beginning of *The Countess Cathleen*. I am delighted at your liking 'The Two Trees', a favourite of mine, and you and one other person are the only people who have said they like it. The other person, by the way, is Miss Eva Gore-Booth.

Some slight changes were eventually introduced even into
'The Two Trees'; 'Innisfree' escaped presumably owing to
its popularity. A year or two later he would not have used
the conventional archaism 'arise and go' – nor permitted
himself the inversion in the last stanza.

Yeats made his most drastic revision of earlier lyrics quite
late in life. He was an elderly man when he turned 'The
Lamentation of the Old Pensioner' from 'early Yeats' into
'late Yeats', leaving nothing of the original except the title,
and yet allowing it to retain its place among the 'Rose' poems
of 1889–93, an outrage on history comparable to George
Moore's re-writing of the *Confessions of a Young Man* in
the style (the style is the man!) acquired in middle age. In
'The Sorrow of Love' every sentence was changed; in this
case, however, Yeats's claim that the revision was but an
attempt to express better what he thought and felt as a very
young man was more plausible. 'The curd-pale moon' became 'A climbing moon', the 'quarrel' of sparrows their
'brawling', 'Are shaken with earth's old and weary cry'
'Could but compose man's image and his cry'. Thus as an
expression of Yeats's wistful twilight period, the poem has
been emptied of its vital content; but the verses retain their
romantic, descriptive character, while now giving the impression of an active man speaking. These are the two readings
of the second stanza, the earlier italicized:

> A girl arose that had red mournful lips
> *And then you came with those red mournful lips,*
>
> And seemed the greatness of the world in tears,
> *And with you came the whole of the world's tears,*
>
> Doomed like Odysseus and the labouring ships
> *And all the trouble of her labouring ships,*
>
> And proud as Priam murdered with his peers;
> *And all the trouble of her myriad years.*

'Cuchulain fighting the Waves' in its original form was
perhaps somewhat passive. In this case Yeats did not make

a new poem, but contented himself with re-writing about half the lines. 'To Emer, raddling raiment in her dun' is better than 'Forgael's daughter, Emer, in her dun', but taken as a whole there is a good deal to be said for the first version. The case for a variorum edition of Yeats's work[*] is reinforced by a consideration of the two endings, which are as follows:

> In three days' time Cuchulain with a moan
> Stood up, and came to the long sand alone.
> For four days warred he with the bitter tide;
> And the waves flowed above him, and he died.

>   Cuchulain stirred,
> Stared on the horses of the sea, and heard
> The cars of battle and his own name cried;
> And fought with the invulnerable tide.

The second is fine too, but has not the same sense of water flowing on and on that is heard in the other. 'And the waves flowed above him and he died' holds the invulnerability of the sea, and the majesty, peace and finality of death. That it should be lost would be a tragedy.

5

Hitherto when in London Yeats had stayed with his family in Bedford Park, but now he was to live for some months in chambers in the Temple that opened into those of Arthur Symons. It has been found impossible to ascertain the exact date of the move. But Yeats says in his autobiography that he imagines he was already settled in Fountain Court when Leonard Smithers, a bookseller, Dowson's friend and Beardsley's, called and proposed that Symons should edit a successor to *The Yellow Book*; and the first number of *The Savoy* appeared in January 1896.

When Yeats had first known Symons he had accepted

[*] [*The Variorum Edition of the Poems of W. B. Yeats*, edited by Peter Allt and Russell K. Alspach, appeared in 1957.]

Lionel Johnson's characterization of him as 'an aesthete with a surfeit searching the music-halls sadly for commonplace pleasures'. He did not, like Johnson, who hated all thoughts of sex, despise a life of music-halls and amorous adventures. But he still cherished the hope of finding a sacred book in modern literature, and Symons's view of art and life as a series of impressions had discouraged him. Symons, however, possessed the faculty of experience, whereas Johnson repeated himself and had become, to tell the truth, a little bit of a bore. Moreover Johnson, after being advised to take stimulants for his insomnia, had turned into a solitary drunkard, and this embarrassed Yeats. The separation appears to have been gradual, as was the growth of the friendship with Symons. Finally Yeats discovered in Symons the sympathetic intelligence of a woman, whereas with Johnson there had always been a slight veil. He was the first man with whom Yeats formed a real intimacy, and their thoughts flowed side by side for many years. It was from Symons (who was making in these years his translations from Mallarmé, from Calderón and from St John of the Cross) that Yeats gained his first knowledge of Continental literature. They read much besides *Axël* together. The translations from Mallarmé, we are told in the autobiography, influenced the later poems in *The Wind among the Reeds*, while Villiers de L'Isle-Adam shaped whatever in the *Rosa Alchemica* Pater had not shaped.

It seemed to Yeats that, more than anyone he had ever known, Symons lived the temperate life recommended by Pater. One evening, comparing their habits with those of the unfortunate Dowson, they discussed some possible lack in themselves. They decided to have two whiskies every night at twelve to see if they could do without a third. When at the end of a fortnight they returned to their tumblers of hot water, Yeats said, half seriously, 'Symons, if we had felt a tendency to excess we would be better poets'.

The Rhymers had not been affected by the Wilde case. They all wrote for a small public which had knowledge and was undisturbed by popular feeling. There were, however, a number of novelists, essayists and artists (notably Aubrey Beardsley), whose contributions to *The Yellow Book* had caught and irritated the eye of the great public. At the time of the Wilde case Beardsley had been dismissed from the art editorship of *The Yellow Book* in circumstances that aroused his friends to fury. Calumnious accusations had been brought against Beardsley, and it was said that Mrs Humphry Ward wrote demanding his dismissal, saying that she owed it to her reputation with the British public to do so. William Watson certainly wrote and Beardsley went. When Smithers came to Fountain Court to discuss the new magazine, Symons made two conditions; the first, that Smithers should cease to traffic in *facetiae* the second, that Aubrey Beardsley should be appointed art editor. Both conditions were accepted, and *The Savoy* continued the warfare on Victorian convention which *The Yellow Book* had begun. Yeats felt that the publisher's name was against *The Savoy* and he gave Symons his help on the understanding that, at the supper given to celebrate the first number, he should not be asked to meet Smithers, nor ever be expected to enter his house. At the supper Yeats had in his pocket two letters remonstrating with him for associating himself with such a magazine; one from A E, the other from T. W. Rolleston. Symons borrowed the letters, and read them out in a spirit of mischief to the publisher and assembled company. 'Give me the letter, give me the letter', Smithers shouted out as Symons waved Rolleston's letter just beyond reach. Symons folded up the letter and began to read what George Russell had written. Russell's letter, which was far more violent than Rolleston's, reduced all to silence. He called *The Savoy* 'the organ of the incubi and the succubi' and besought Yeats not to sell his birthright for a mess of aesthete's pottage. 'I never see *The Savoy*', he wrote, 'nor do I intend to touch it. It is all mud from a muddy spring, and any pure thought that mingles must lose its purity. The gods', he went on, 'are filling Ireland with fire, mystics are arriving elsewhere, as

Blavatsky and H. P. Judge prophesied. What Emerson did for America we can do now with even greater effect.'

Presently Beardsley came up to Yeats and said: 'I agree with your friend. I have always been haunted by the spiritual life. When I was a child I saw the bleeding Christ over the mantelpiece. But after all I think there is a kind of morality in doing one's work when one wants to do other things more.' The supper over, Yeats wished to go home, but Symons persuaded him to break his resolution, and they went together to Smithers's flat. When they arrived they found Beardsley lying grey and exhausted on two chairs, and Smithers turning the handle of a hurdy-gurdy. Beardsley praised the beautiful tone, and the flattered publisher laboured on, the perspiration pouring from his brow.

Arthur Symons had always given Yeats his rightful place among the young poets, and Yeats's contributions to *The Savoy* during its short existence were considerable, both in prose and verse. The association with Beardsley kept people on the watch, and when Blake's design, *Antaeus setting Virgil and Dante upon the verge of Cocytus*, appeared the magazine was excluded from the station bookstalls. The design illustrated an article by Yeats, who relates that his casual acquaintance, and even his comfort in public places, began to be affected. But he enjoyed taking part in the battle against moral and academical prejudice. As he says: 'Being all young we delighted in enemies and in everything that had an heroic air'.

6

The elder Yeats suffered some moments of anxiety when his son left home. He feared that Willie might entangle himself with a ballet dancer, or become surprised by some fanciful love affair with a chorus girl he had never spoken to. Less had been heard of late of the hopeless infatuation for Maud Gonne. This had, in fact, been relieved, not by the charms of a chorus girl but by the warm attachment of a married

woman distinguished in looks and mind. In some autobiographical notes of much later date Yeats gives this lady
the imaginary name of Diana Vernon and mentions that
two of the slow-moving esoteric poems in *The Wind among
the Reeds*, 'The Shadowy Horses' and 'The Binding of the
Hair',* are addressed to her, as to one of those contemplative souls emptied of mortal dream; 'her still beauty had the
nobility of defeated things'. There was talk of flight together. She and a friend were to come to tea with him at
Fountain Court and make the decision; Symons was away,
and Yeats went out to buy the cake. Unfortunately he began
to think of Maud Gonne and forgot to take the key with
him. The thought was not interrupted until he found the
door locked on his return and his visitors standing at it. He
was off in a great fuss for a locksmith, and, instead, found a
man who climbed along the roof and let himself in at a
window. A day or two later he had a wild letter from Maud
Gonne: 'Was he ill? Had some accident happened?' The
letter was written on the day that he had lost the key. She
had seen him, she said, come into the room in Dublin where
she was sitting with some friends.

The affair with 'Diana Vernon' did not end in flight, but
it may have had something to do with a change of residence
from Fountain Court to two rooms in one of the little old
houses in Woburn Buildings, a stone-flagged alley or passage running eastward from the since obliterated Woburn
Place. One of Yeats's letters from the new address was to
John O'Leary:

I did not send the money before because Smithers, the publisher of *The Savoy*, was short of funds and asked me to wait, and
I now send only £3 : 5 : 0 because I am short in my turn. . . . You
shall have it almost at once, however; I have I believe definitely
turned the corner thanks partly to *The Savoy* which came in
the nick of time to let me raise my prices until I get the new
prices definitely established. *Rosa Alchemica*, the thing

* Their present titles are 'He bids his Beloved be at Peace' and 'He
gives his Beloved certain Rhymes'.

MacGrath * likes so much, is about to be translated into French and has drawn a wild eulogy from George Moore. I am now writing a rather elaborate series of essays on Blake.

He was still, however, very poor. In a note-book that he kept at the Temple there are figures of loans from Symons, evidence of his scrupulosity in money matters: the largest item is threepence for a bus fare. On the ground floor of his house, No. 18, lived a cobbler; on the first was a workman's family; the attic housed an old pedlar who painted in water-colours. Yeats brought with him a good many books and a few pictures, a little furniture lent by Symons, and in company with Diana Vernon he made some meagre purchases, chiefly of things which he could throw away without regret when he became more prosperous. Symons's charwoman at the Temple, Mrs Old, looked in two or three times a week. Later on, she became his regular and devoted servant. He was a pleasant master. As he once noted in a diary, the rages to which he was always liable had seldom to do with matters concerning his personal convenience. He had few of the domestic eccentricities of which men of genius are frequently accused.

The house on the north side of Woburn Buildings still stands, but is now No. 5 Woburn Walk. Yeats's rooms later extended from the second floor to take in most of the house.

* A member of the *United Ireland* staff.

[6]

Dramatis Personae:
Lady Gregory

Trip to Ireland with Symons – Yeats's perplexities at
Tulira; Meeting with Lady Gregory and Synge – *The
Secret Rose*; Robert Bridges's admiration – Coole; birth
of Irish National Theatre – Lady Gregory's influence

―――

In her life much artifice, in her nature much pride. . . .
Born to see the glory of the world in a peasant mirror.

I

SOON after the installation in Woburn Buildings Yeats
brought Arthur Symons on a trip to Ireland. They went first
to Sligo, lodging with people called Siberry* on the slopes
of Ben Bulben near the Glencar waterfall. It was Symons's
first visit to Ireland, and he sent an enchanting account to
The Savoy of days of soft rain mixed with sunshine on Ben
Bulben and of Rosses Point with its 'seafaring men who
know more of the coasts of Spain and of the Barbadoes than
of the other side of their mountains'. Symons was charmed
by George Pollexfen, and expressed the opinion that the
astrologer might in more favourable circumstances have
developed an excellent taste for literature. The fortnight in
Sligo was followed by a long stay, diversified by a visit to the
Aran islands, at Tulira Castle with Edward Martyn, a new
friend met in London through Symons's friend, George
Moore.† This was Yeats's first sight of that country of lime-

* Mr Siberry sent Yeats a telegram of congratulation on his seventieth birthday.
† Martyn at this time had rooms in the Temple, and was frequently
in London.

stone rock, storm-beaten trees and old towers, which lies
between Galway Bay and the Clare hills, and is the landscape of so much of his later poetry. George Moore was
expected to join Martyn's house party, and presently
arrived.

Moore had wearied of naturalism after his triumph with
Esther Waters and was looking for new fields to conquer on
the side of poetry. Recently he had frequently sought Yeats
out in London, for Yeats's talk stilled his cravings for
aggressive truth. He had begun a romantic novel, *Evelyn
Innes*, intertwining Mayfair and Bohemia, and Yeats was
sitting as model for the visionary musician in the story.
Moore was a Connaught squire, owner of a big house in
Mayo, who had gone to Paris straight from his father's
racing stables, and, as Yeats put it afterwards, 'acquired
copious inaccurate French, sat among art students, young
writers about to become famous, in some café; a man carved
out of a turnip, looking out on the world with astonished
eyes'. In the eighties he had written a book called *Parnell
and his Island*, a minor work, in which he had covered Irish
Catholicism and Irish Nationalism with sarcasm and contempt. He was by upbringing a Catholic, and his father had
been a leader of the patriotic party; the book, therefore, put
him in bad repute with his countrymen and gave him the
name of an apostate. But now in middle age he was inclined
to reconcile himself with Ireland, if it were possible, and
Yeats and Martyn were to act as mediators. This was just
the kind of task that Yeats liked and, although he could
have cared at this time for no book of Moore's, he undertook
it with zest. Between Martyn and Moore, on the other hand,
there had long been a familiar and grotesque friendship,
which Yeats was to describe many years later in a little play
called *The Cat and the Moon*; the speaker is a blind beggar
man, and Laban is the townland where Edward Martyn
went to church:

. . . Did you ever know a holy man but had a wicked man for his comrade and his heart's darling? There is not a more holy man in the barony than the man who has the big house at Laban, and he goes knocking about the roads day and night with that old lecher from the county of Mayo and he a woman-hater from the day of his birth. And well you know and all the neighbours know what they talk of by daylight and candlelight. The old lecher does be telling over all the sins he committed, or maybe never committed at all, and the man of Laban does be trying to head him off and quiet him down that he may quit telling them.

The Moores were Protestant by origin, but Martyn belonged to ancient 'quality' of Roman Catholic gentry, who had preserved their property in spite of penal laws and, though Martyn's father had married a woman but one generation from the peasant, he mixed on equal terms with 'ascendancy' landlords. He had been liberally educated but had refused the worldly marriage which his mother designed for him, being wholly devoted to his prayers and to art – to these he later added the Irish political cause. At the time of the Yeats and Symons visit he had finished *The Heather Field*, an Ibsenesque play with an Irish setting, which had been praised and refused in London, and he talked of having it produced in Germany, where he often travelled, for next to Ibsen among the moderns he loved Wagner.

2

Before setting out from London, on what proved indeed to be a momentous journey, Yeats had put Diana Vernon in a trance to question her. Diana Vernon was not a member of his Order, but could be powerfully affected by its symbols. The first sign he had of her feminine clairvoyance was certain Greek words. She explained 'endikon' as 'justified'. 'Justified' was applied in the Order (which made little use of Greek) to an Egyptian sun-god, but when Yeats consulted the Greek dictionary for 'endikon' he found it meant 'the harmonious'. He had for some time been troubled about his work. He had written the story called 'Rosa Alchemica', Pater become uncanny, and many of the more mystical poems in *The Wind among the Reeds*; he felt that he had wandered too far from the country emotions of his early poems and of *Countess Cathleen*, and that his new work would not contribute towards that spiritualization of the Irish imagination which was his lasting aim. He did not know what to do, and his anxiety was aggravated after the trip to the Aran islands, where men reaped with knives because of the stones, and a more beautiful English than any known in Sligo was spoken – the English of Irish-speaking districts, with its ancient vocabulary and its Gaelic idiom and metaphor. The party from Tulira landed from a fishing yawl among a group of islanders, who had gathered to watch the strangers' arrival. They were brought at once to the oldest man upon the island. He spoke but two sentences, speaking very distinctly, and with a look at Yeats's oblique eye, said: 'If any gentleman has done a crime, we'll hide him. There was a gentleman that killed his father, and I had him in my own house six months till he got away to America.' In 1896 visitors to the Aran islands were still a rarity, and the imagination of the inhabitants was not yet separated from life.

Diana Vernon, when consulted in London, had obtained some sentences unintelligible to herself: 'He is too much under solar influence. He is to live near water and to avoid woods, which concentrate the solar ray.' On his return to Tulira from Aran, with the sentences in mind, Yeats invoked the lunar moon, which he believed to be the chief source of his inspiration. He did this for nine evenings, with the result that on the ninth night, as he was going to sleep, he saw first a centaur and then a marvellous naked woman shooting an arrow at a star. By this time another guest had arrived at Tulira, the Comte de Basterot, descendant of an émigré family, a student of race and of history, who spent half the year on a little country estate called Duras, on the shore of Galway Bay, and the rest in Paris and Rome. Moore and Martyn were inclined to smile when Yeats told of his vision at the breakfast table, but Basterot was not only a pious Catholic, but a disciple of Gobineau,* the Aryan theorist, and became very serious. It was on this occasion that, as has already been related, Yeats was denounced as a Finnish sorcerer. Not to his face; Basterot took Martyn aside, and explained that he had himself dreamt a night or two before of Neptune and surging waves. Martyn returned from the interview to question Yeats, and it came out that Yeats had not confined his invocations to the bedroom, but had made some of them in the old Gothic tower of Tulira, where Martyn's chapel was. Martyn was very angry, for which Yeats was sorry, for he had thought at first there might be much in common between him and his host, who read St Chrysostom every night after the rest of the house had retired to bed. But it was useless to explain that his invocations were a form of prayer, accompanied by an active desire for a special result, a more conscious exercise of the human faculties. He was forbidden even to speak of magical practices so long as he remained under Martyn's roof.

Yeats's predilection was for an age like Chaucer's when the human mind was organic and art anonymous; and he felt that in his recent poetry and stories the images were too often arbitrary and picturesque – that his love of literature, his belief in nationality and his interest in mystical philosophy were ceasing to be a single conviction. His occult experiments had but added 'a multiplicity of images' to an already existing multiplicity of interests and opinions. 'Hammer your thoughts into unity': this sentence had formed itself in his head, without his writing it, when he was a young man of twenty-three or twenty-four. But now image called up image, and he could not choose among

* He wrote the biographical note attached to Gobineau's world-shaking book, *Essai sur L'Inégalité des Races Humaines*. His strange, attractive figure is described on a page of Arthur Symons's *Cities of Italy*.

them with any confidence; and when he did choose, 'the image lost the intensity, or changed into some other image. ... I was lost in that region a cabalistic manuscript shown me by MacGregor Mathers had warned me of; astray upon the path of the Chameleon.' He had begun a novel of contemporary life, partly descriptive of modern occultists, and he could neither introduce artistic unity into the narrative nor cease to write. 'My wretched novel', he used to call the book; which made his father indignant, for J. B. Y. held justly that his son had the story-teller's gift.*

3

As if in answer to his perplexities Lady Gregory, Edward Martyn's near neighbour, called at Tulira, and invited him and Arthur Symons to lunch at Coole. Lady Gregory was a little woman of forty-five, widowed for some years, with a son, her only child, at Harrow. 'La strega' (the witch) Symons called her. He disliked her on the instant and said afterwards that he had known at once from her 'terrible' eye that she would 'get Willie'. She had literary ambitions and was engaged upon editing her husband's autobiography and family papers, but she felt a desire for more creative work. Yeats had been but a few minutes in the library at Coole when she asked him if she could not help in the Irish movement; he said, 'If you get our books and watch what we are doing you will soon find your work.' Yeats and Symons lunched twice at Coole, and when Symons had returned to London, Yeats was asked to stay for a few days. All about this part of Galway lived a peasantry who told stories in that form of English, Gaelic in syntax, which was to make Lady Gregory's comedies so amusing, and she had

---

*Finally Yeats finished the novel, to which he gave the name of *The Speckled Bird*. But he could never make up his mind either to publish or to destroy the Mss. The title is taken from a verse in Jeremiah: 'Mine heritage is unto me as a speckled bird, the birds round about are against her.'

already begun to collect this folk-lore when Yeats arrived
for his visit. He felt that he was playing a part in a mystery
play. Her house was set among great woods, with a lake at
the edge of the woods. Coole took its name from the lake,
and he remembered the saying that he should live near
water. The common people are 'under the moon'. But why
the woods? He had invoked moon and water only. Lady
Gregory saw that he was ill and begged him to come again
to Coole, where he would have rest and comfort, the next
summer.

In Lady Gregory, in George Moore and in Edward
Martyn Yeats was now acquainted with three out of the
four persons who were to be his principal collaborators in
the early years of the Irish theatre. Three months later,
when in Paris, he met the fourth, J. M. Synge. Yeats was
staying in the Hôtel Corneille near the Luxembourg,
dividing his attentions between Maud Gonne and Mac-
Gregor Mathers. Someone told him that there lived at the
top of the house a young student, who had a private income
of about £50 a year which he supplemented by earning odd
guineas as a teacher of languages and as a journalist. Yeats
was interested, especially when it was added that Synge had
learnt some Irish at Trinity. Synge was introduced to Maud
Gonne and was also given literary advice. Yeats recommended him to make a thorough study of modern French
literature, to play, as it were, second fiddle to Arthur
Symons.* On subsequent visits to Paris Yeats sought out this
new acquaintance, whom finally he urged to give up France
and seek in the Aran islands a life that had never yet been
expressed in literature. He was far from divining a genius,
but he was attracted by Synge's sincerity and modesty, and

* I am aware that, according to his own account, Yeats, 'his imagination full of those grey islands', which he had just visited, at once
spoke to Synge about Aran. But correspondence passing between
Synge's relatives at the time shows that the facts are as here stated.
Nor was Synge so poor as Yeats supposed. His mother had a house
near Dublin where he spent a part of each year.

thought there might be a place for his scholarly mind in the Irish movement. Like Lady Gregory, Synge belonged to an old Irish Protestant family. There were five bishops among his ancestors, one that Edward Synge, friend of Berkeley, who wrote a treatise called *The Religion of a Gentleman* to explain how revelation could be accepted by thoughtful and educated persons.*

The business which brought Yeats to Paris in 1896 was the making of a ritual for an Order of Celtic Mysteries, a project which had the sympathies of both Maud Gonne and MacGregor Mathers, and by which he thought perhaps to find a way out of 'the path of the Chameleon'. He still hoped that instead of venerating Judea people would come to think of their own land as holy, and most holy when most beautiful. Unadulterated nature-worship robbed beauty of its sanctity, and he dreamed of initiating Young Ireland into a mystical philosophy which would combine the doctrines of Christianity with the faiths of a more ancient world, unite the perceptions of the spirit with those of natural beauty. He had a monachal solitude, a sanctuary for adepts, in mind, the Castle Rock on Lough Key, discovered on a recent visit to Douglas Hyde in Roscommon, when he went fishing with his host. It was this lake that aroused the enthusiasm of Arthur Young, who wrote of it in 1776 as 'one of the most delicious scenes I ever beheld'; a lake rich in islands and old ruins, a painted scene upon a drop curtain. Rock Castle, a former stronghold of the MacDermots, had been but lately lived in, and little money would be needed to make it habitable. The roof was sound, the windows unbroken, there was even a stone platform where meditative persons might pace to and fro. To Maud Gonne Yeats spoke of a Castle of the Heroes, a shrine of Irish tradition, where only those who had proved their devotion to Ireland should penetrate.

* It was another Synge, the Bishop of Elphin, who is said to have refused ordination to Oliver Goldsmith because Goldsmith wore red breeches.

Nobody ever felt certain about Yeats's faith in the occult. Did he really believe, or was it just a playing with fantastic images? The dull-witted were troubled by doubts, and forgot that even to be certain that magic is magic deprives it of all mysteriousness. Yeats felt mystery as a primary necessity of his soul. His poetic genius halted half-way between faith and smile, so as to preserve the sibylline quality of his own experience. He was never sure, therefore he could sing of it, uncertain whether the dim shapes surged from a deeper reality or were only a personal creation like that of a child tossing in the air balls painted by his own hand.

4

Back in London Yeats prepared his stories in *The Secret Rose* for publication, and continued his contributions to reviews and magazines. *The Savoy* had come to an untimely end; he printed new poems in the *Saturday*, the *Dome* and the *New Review*, and reviewed for the *Bookman* and the *Sketch*. O'Leary's *Recollections of Fenianism*, Symons's *Amoris Victima*, Fiona MacLeod's *Spiritual Tales*, Maeterlinck's *Treasure of the Humble*, were among the books that he noticed. An essay on Robert Bridges (*Bookman*, June 1897) was written after he had made the acquaintance of that poet. While in Ireland with Symons he had had an amiable note from Bridges about a reprint of his own early poems (the Fisher Unwin volume of 1895), written in such a way that he could answer or not as he liked. He did not answer until he went to Paris, by which time he had read some of his correspondent's work, which at once attracted him. Then came another letter from Bridges:

Your letter is as great a surprise as it is a pleasure to me this morning – and as you date from a hotel I answer by return. ... Had I said as much as I felt about your poetry you would have been constrained to thank me. As it was I was reconciling myself to the idea that you didn't care whether I liked your poetry or not. As a matter of fact I can read very little poetry so called –

and your book is a great exception. It has given me a great deal of delight, and I find magnificent things and very beautiful things in it. And it is most pleasant to me to hear that you have cared for my verse and will therefore welcome my admiration for your work . . .

I ought to say that your letter to me is unsigned – from which I hope I may conclude that you are in the middle of some piece of work which has got hold of you – I cannot make a mistake however in recognising in it an answer to the only letter which I have written in the required sense. . . . I should like to write to you some day about your poems or better talk with you. I think you have hit off one form (and really a new one as you do it) perfectly – in Cuchulain and the bag of dreams. By the way let bag stand in last line. Why did you alter it? but I liked most of your alterations. I saw the two editions.

In the spring following Yeats visited Robert Bridges and his family at Yattendon, near Newbury. The characters and opinions on general subjects of the two poets were extremely dissimilar, but they were happy together, and the visit laid the foundations of a most pleasant friendship, one without vicissitudes. Yeats was asked to come again, whenever he chose. There were few men whom Yeats liked for themselves alone, and Bridges was one of these. Nor did he ever cease to approve the delicate and scholarly art of the older poet, and some years later (at a moment, indeed, when he was feeling rather out of sorts), he decided that compared with Bridges, Wordsworth was 'a clumsy humbug'.

Yeats was consolidating his position in London. From George Moore, who seldom reviewed books, came a wonderful notice of *The Secret Rose*. Moore cited the following passage from the story called 'The Heart of the Spring' as 'a summer night equal to anything in literature, even in that ancient literature of which Mr Yeats' work seems to be a survival or a renaissance':

He went into the wood and began cutting green boughs from the hazels, and great bundles of rushes from the western border of the isle, where the small rocks gave place to gently sloping sand and clay. It was nightfall before he had cut enough for his purpose, and well-nigh midnight before he had carried the last bundle to its place, and gone back for the roses and the lilies. It was one of those warm, beautiful nights, when everything seems carved of precious stones. The woods of the Sleuth Hound away to the south looked as though cut out of green beryl, and the waters that mirrored them shone like opal. The roses he was gathering were like glowing rubies, and the lilies had the dull lustre of pearl. Everything had taken upon itself the look of something imperishable, except a glow-worm, whose faint flame burnt on steadily among the shadows, moving hither and thither, the only thing that seemed alive, the only thing that seemed perishable as mortal hope.

Robert Bridges wrote again (15 June 1897):

I was at Oxford on Friday and Saturday and on Sunday had two visitors here, one was Binyon, the other a man I had never met before who was quite enthusiastic about your work especially the two volumes of tales.* . . . I had read the two again with the intention of fulfilling my promise of writing to you about them, so I discussed with him the judgment that I had arrived at and found that he quite agreed with me and this I confess made me hesitate less in telling you the one criticism I have to make without further consideration. I think that the stories are artistically the worse for the apparent insistence on the part of the writer to have them taken otherwise (*i.e.* more seriously) than he suspects the reader would naturally take them. Of course I know that it is your intention that they should be so taken. Only I do not think that the intention should appear. The manner of presentation should be sufficient and I do not see you need distrust the power of your presentation. This is rather a subtle matter, because in looking again at the stories I don't quite see where I get my impression of this 'insistence' from, I fancy it lies chiefly in your sometimes just overstepping the mark, *e.g.* in 'Regina Pigmeorum' the sentence 'I asked the young girl, etc.' will not fail to make readers wonder at the personality of the writer – I should like to talk this over with you some day when we can refer to places in the stories. I should not have liked to offer the objection if my feeling about it had not been very strong, and if I had not found another admirer with exactly the same impression. Reading the stories again made me admire the workman-

* *The Secret Rose* and *The Celtic Twilight.*

ship more than ever. The gentleman in question said that he thought the prose style better than any that he knew and I am inclined to agree with him. – It is extremely beautiful. ... It seems to me that these stories are an excellent proof that English 'short stories' may be written in as good style as the best French ones. I hope you will do more short stories of Irish life – I am not in the least overstating my admiration of your style. I am *very grateful* to you for your presenting me with these two volumes – and I shall try and profit by them. The writing is too good for success in journalism – Is it not so? No one has ever told me of it – Perhaps the somewhat bizarre character of the subjects puts people off the mark.

Please come to see me again before long and be assured meanwhile of my blessing and high esteem.

Bridges admired most, he said in yet another letter, Yeats's gift of poetry and of humour. 'Poetry does not get stronger in a man as he gets older, whereas humour does. Therefore write poetry.' He did not care for the story 'Rosa Alchemica', finding in it perhaps something of the irony of the sacrilegious priest, and was glad that 'Michael Robartes' was 'dead'. In fact the report of the Irish riot in 'Rosa Alchemica' was greatly exaggerated and the alchemical mystic, 'something between a debauchee, a saint, and a peasant', had escaped with slight injuries. He reappeared twenty years later in the West of Ireland, to supply Yeats with further material for cabalistic narrative in verse and prose, having in the meantime lived in 'rooms ostentatious in their sordidness' with some dancer in Vienna.

In Red Hanrahan, the hero of a group of stories afterwards transferred to *The Celtic Twilight*, Yeats created a character liked by all. These stories and the lyrics interspersed in them, such as 'Oh, what to me the little room', convinced George Russell, to whom the book was dedicated, that the folk strain in Yeats had developed and strengthened, in despite of the dubious foreign influences – of Mallarmé, of Verlaine, and of Villiers de L'Isle-Adam – about which he theorized so freely. 'I must forgive you for many reasons', Russell wrote, mainly for the stories of the Red One. Many things which I used to think were due in your work to a perverted fancy for the grotesque I see now in another way. Your visionary faculty has an insight more tender than the moralist knows of. Just in the same way as O'Grady always seems to detect under the rude act the spirit of defiance and heroic manhood, so you unveil beneath excess and passion a love for spiritual beauty expressing itself pathetically in the life of this wayward outcast. That insight is indeed an ennobling thing to impart and I suppose just because the highest things are the most dangerous you will find a number of people, who have not got your mental balance, using your visionary revelation of a hidden spirit seeking for beauty as justification and defence of passions which have no justification except that they are the radiations of a spirit which can find no higher outlet. The Rosa Alchemica is a most wonderful piece of prose. Everything in it, thought and word, are so rich that they seem the gathering in the temple of the mind of thousands of pilgrim rays returning and leaving there their many experiences. A book sustained at that level throughout would be one of the greatest things in literature.

References to Robert Bridges's verse plays in his *Bookman* article contain, I think, Yeats's first public expression of his desire for the drama. Bridges had given little thought to getting his work performed; he would have been content to think his plays readable, amusing – in this again he differed much from Yeats. When Lady Gregory took a flat in Queen Anne's Mansions for the early months of 1897, Yeats called upon her 'full of playwriting', as she recorded in her diary,

and very keen with the aid of Florence Farr about taking or building a theatre somewhere in the suburbs to produce romantic plays, her own plays, Edward Martyn's, one of Bridges', and he is trying to stir up Standish O'Grady and Fiona Macleod to write some. He believes there will be a reaction from the realism of Ibsen and romance will have its turn. He has put a great deal of himself into his play *The Shadowy Waters* and rather startled me by saying that about half the characters have eagle faces.

Lady Gregory reminded Yeats that he must come again to Coole, and he spent much of the summer there, as he did much of his summers for years to come.

5

The unpretentious gates of Coole open on an avenue of
great trees, their leafy embracing branches a tunnel of twilight on the sunniest day.* The avenue curves through wood
and fields to a modest white-fronted house, rather like a
large Italian farm-house, which looks across a wide sloping
field to a great wood. On the left of the house are walled
pleasure-grounds, where may still be seen the catalpa tree
under which Yeats and George Moore quarrelled over their
play, *Diarmuid and Grania*, also a giant copper beech, its
trunk carved over with initials of many famous men:
W. B. Y., A E, G. B. S., Ian H. (Ian Hamilton), J. M. S.
(Synge), A. J. (Augustus John), J. M. (Masefield). More
woods spread out behind the house, the paths lost; at the
confines of the demesne, in a landscape of mysterious and
desolate beauty, as though one were at the world's end, lies
a grey lake with wild swans.

The Gregorys of Coole were known in Ireland as excellent landlords, in England as distinguished public servants.
An eighteenth-century ancestor had gained a large fortune
in the East India Company, which enabled him to cultivate
his Galway property in style and to give his part of the
country a much improved appearance. Lady Gregory was a
Galway Persse of Roxborough, and since her girlhood she
had been noted throughout Galway, where racing and hunting filled the lives of most, for her desire of education. In Sir
William Gregory, a former Governor of Ceylon, she had
found, when twenty-eight, a husband nearly forty years her
senior, who shared her love of books, pictures, architecture
and travel, and admired her nut-brown eyes, so appraising,
so observant, and also so full of fun behind their glasses.
She was not intellectually profound; but there was a rich
vein of poetry in her resolute nature and she had a great
capacity for service and devoted friendship.

Not Yeats's summers only were to be spent at Coole; in

* Coole stands no longer. See note on p. 487.

later years he came to know the edges of the lake better
than any spot on earth, 'to know it in all the changes of the
seasons, to find there always some new beauty'. He gave the
name of its swans to a volume which he published twenty
years after his first visit:

> The trees are in their autumn beauty,
> The woodland paths are dry,
> Under the October twilight the water
> Mirrors a still sky;
> Upon the brimming water among the stones
> Are nine-and-fifty swans.
>
> The nineteenth Autumn has come upon me
> Since I first made my count. . . .
>
> Unwearied still, lover by lover,
> They paddle in the cold
> Companionable streams or climb the air;
> Their hearts have not grown old;
> Passion or conquest, wander where they will,
> Attend upon them still.

At Coole Yeats found a life of order and of labour where
all outward things were the signatures of an inward life. In
his childhood, at his grandfather's, he had learned to love
an elaborate house, a garden and park, and those grey
country houses of Sligo – Lissadell, Hazelwood and the
more rarely seen towers of Markree – had always called to
his mind a life set amid natural beauty and the activities of
servants and labourers, who seemed themselves natural, as
birds and trees are natural. Many generations, and no un-
cultured generation, had left images of their service in the
outlines of wood and fields at Coole, in sculpture and pictures, in furniture, in a fine library with editions of the
classics and books on plants and agriculture. Her Galway
home was Lady Gregory's passion and that passion became
even greater when park and woods and lake, by their hold
on the imagination and the affection of the greatest poet of
the day, took a place in modern literature.

During the summer of 1897 Yeats again spoke to Lady Gregory of his ambition to found an Irish theatre. She had taken him over to Duras, Basterot's little country house, and it was in the garden at Duras that the Irish National Theatre, though not under that name, was born; for Lady Gregory at once expressed her disapproval of the London project, and offered to collect money for Irish performances of plays by himself and Martyn. The second version of *Countess Cathleen* was ready;* and either Lady Gregory or Yeats approached Edward Martyn, who gave up the proposed German performance of his *Heather Field* and (a little later) guaranteed the entire production. George Moore, about to renounce London as a centre of art because too large, too old and too wealthy to permit any new life, was almost equally excited. He wrote to Yeats:

Perhaps when I have said that you are the one person since Shakespeare who has succeeded in an actable blank verse play I have said enough. . . . I was at the Leeds festival and there I met Fauré – I half read, half told him the story of your *Countess Cathleen*. He thought the play most beautiful and I gave him the copy so that he might have a word for word translation made of it. The play is finer even than I thought it was. . . . I am your best advertiser, in all the houses I frequent I say, 'I am not the Lord. There is one greater than I, the latchet of whose shoes I am not worthy to unloose.'

At this time neither Yeats nor Martyn had any working knowledge of the theatre, and Lady Gregory had never given a thought to the stage – was not even much of a theatre-goer. Yeats at once realized that Moore, who had always been knocking about theatres and had produced a play of his own in London, would be essential to their rehearsals. But several prominent characters of the Irish Revival – George Russell among them – resented the introduction of Moore into the movement, on the ground of his political as well as his religious shortcomings. Yeats admitted that Moore was an embarrassing ally ('he must always

* There were those of 1892, 1895, 1899 and 1912.

be condemning or worshipping') but found his 'moral enthusiasm' inspiring. This advocacy came near to disrupting the Irish Literary Society. A famous lawyer, who had in the first instance invited Moore to become a member but had forgotten the fact, proposed to blackball him, at the instigation of another member. The dispute ended by Yeats withdrawing his candidate's name and resigning from the Committee himself, so as not to force the resignation of Barry O'Brien, who with himself had largely kept the Society alive.

Lady Gregory's social position and wide acquaintance enabled her to gain support for the dramatic project from distinguished men in the Unionist camp; and the list of patrons and guarantors of the Irish Literary Theatre included Dr Mahaffy and W. E. H. Lecky, Lord Dufferin and Aubrey de Vere, as well as John O'Leary and several Nationalist members of Parliament. Then an unforeseen difficulty arose. The two Dublin theatres had been granted patents, a system now obsolete everywhere else, whereby no performance, except for charity, could be given in Dublin but at these theatres. It was necessary to change the law, and this was done with the assistance of Lecky, the member for Trinity, but for many months Yeats, when in London, gave more hours than he cared to count putting the case before Irish M.P.s in the Lobby of the House of Commons.

6

He wrote little during his first two summers at Coole. His nervous system was worn out, and his sight was very bad – the doctor told him he had a conical cornea in his left eye and astigmatism in the right. The left eye was practically useless. Even the toil of dressing exhausted him; Lady Gregory sent him cups of soup when he was called in the morning. She saw that he ought not to work too much, and thinking that the open air would be beneficial, she took him from cottage to cottage collecting folk-lore and in the evenings she wrote out what she had heard in the dialect, vivid and sonorous, that she was to use in her *Cuchulain of Muirthemne* and her *Gods and Fighting Men*. She made him paint a little – a pastel which he did of Coole dates from this time – and she invited fellow-Celts down to Galway for his amusement and distraction. Douglas Hyde and George Russell came, also burly William Sharp, the inventor of the now almost forgotten Fiona Macleod*; Lady Gregory sympathized with Hyde's Gaelic projects, but realized that the substitution of Gaelic for English, in which all had come to write, would take many years, and that the theatre must seek support by putting Irish emotion into English. Hyde became a great favourite, but Russell – recently at Yeats's instigation become an organizer of Plunkett's co-operative movement – seemed morose and melancholy, and Sharp roused Martyn's derision by embracing an elm tree as the soul of the vaporous Fiona, and annoyed Lady Gregory by taking the best seat in the dog-cart and letting Yeats mount behind.

Two more stories in the rich prose of 'Rosa Alchemica' came from Yeats's pen in the course of 1897: 'The Tables of the Law' and 'The Adoration of the Magi'. They were privately printed; both came out of that *fin-de-siècle* mood which Mallarmé had described as 'the inquietude of the veil of the Temple'. Writing of these stories to John O'Leary, Yeats said that his aim was to found 'an aristocratic, esoteric literature' in Ireland: 'we have literature for the people but nothing for the few'. His view of Ireland, he told Miss Alice Milligan, had greatly changed in the last four years.

> I feel that the work of Irishmen of letters must be not so much to awaken or quicken or preserve the national idea among the mass of the people, but to convert the educated classes to it on the one hand ... and – this is more important – to fight for moderation, dignity and the rights of the intellect among their fellow Nationalists. Ireland is terribly demoralised. ... I am

*See note on p. 488.

doing what I can by writing my works with laborious care and studied moderation of style.

On the other hand he wanted to come closer to the folk, and so projected that version in peasant idiom of the Red Hanrahan stories, which he was to make a few years later in partnership with Lady Gregory. The two traditions, that of the folk and that of the *noblesse* in sentiment and taste, had this in common, that they were equally distant from the middle-class region of culture. That from these two sources came all beautiful things was a belief in which from now on Yeats never faltered: 'Dream of the noble and the beggarman'.

But at first he chiefly sought the cottages for evidence of the supernatural and proof of survival. 'I work from 11 to 2, chiefly at my novel', he wrote to his sister Lily in July 1898.

When reading I have to rest a minute or two every twenty minutes. . . . I have no news, for Galway is not the place for it, at least no news of this world – I have plenty of news of the other. For instance, a woman who came to mend chairs went a walk down the avenue with the housemaid last week and presently both came in in a fainting state. They had seen three fairies – tall figures with black hats ('Steeple-hats') and ruffs, evident Elizabethans. (I saw an Elizabethan woman here a year ago.) That night, later on, one of them was going upstairs to bed and saw a portrait of Mary Queen of Scots that is here, and fainted because she recognised the ruff. The way I saw my Elizabethan was I seemed to wake up in the middle of the night, not exactly to wake up but to see the room and the bed quite clearly – and I saw her pass through the room.

He began to have dreams of a curious and broken beauty, and one evening when crossing a little stream he had an emotion very strange to him. All his thought was pagan, but he felt a sudden dependence upon the Divine will. That night he seemed to wake in his bed and to hear a voice saying, 'The love of God is infinite, for every soul is unique, and no other soul can satisfy the same need in God'. At other times he received fragments of poems, part heard, part seen.

Often he would try to describe these things to Lady Gregory and fail, becoming inarticulate and confused. He remembered having read that mystics were not always able to speak; how they would stop in the middle of a word. Yet Lady Gregory was as sympathetic to this as to all his other preoccupations. She was prepared to accept without question his belief that high poetry could be brought back to life by finding dramatic themes in 'those old stories of the folk which were made by men who believed so much that they were never entirely certain that the earth was solid under their footsole'.

Twelve years after their first meeting, at a time when she was ill, he would write thus of Lady Gregory in his manuscript book: 'I cannot realise the world without her. She has been to me mother, friend, sister and brother. She brought to my wavering thoughts steadfast nobility – all day the thought of losing her is a conflagration in the rafters.'

[7]

Theatre and politics:
Maud Gonne

President of the Wolfe Tone Memorial Association – '98
Politics: tour with Maud Gonne – Mystical essays;
W. T. Horton – Commemoration activities; a proposal
in Westminster Abbey – The beginnings of a theatre;
attacks on Yeats – The Boer War – New Lyrics; *The
Shadowy Waters* – More alarms and excursions – Pro-
gress and setbacks of Irish literary theatre; the Fays;
James Joyce

———

Why should I blame her that she filled my days
With misery, or that she would of late
Have taught to ignorant men most violent ways,
Or hurled the little streets upon the great,
Had they but courage equal to desire?
What could have made her peaceful with a mind
That nobleness made simple as a fire,
With beauty like a tightened bow, a kind
That is not natural in an age like this ...

I

YEATS's early visits to Coole were interrupted by his work
on the '98 Commemoration Committee, which often took
him to Dublin. He had become President of the Wolfe Tone
Memorial Association; the story of how he reached this
high office is a curious one, and has never been told in
detail. Shortly before he moved into the rooms in Woburn
Buildings, he met T. W. Rolleston in a café in the Strand,
and Rolleston spoke to him of recent developments in the
Irish Republican Brotherhood, the secret organization of
'physical force' Nationalists which dated from the Fenian

rising in the Sixties. Yeats had always regarded himself as an I.R.B. man. It is true that he had never taken the oath, but neither had John O'Leary, by whom he had been admitted into the organization.* Nor probably had he ever attended any of its meetings, but he understood himself to be with the party on the major issues and wished to capture it for his imaginative movement, O'Leary having long ago said to him that 'in this country a man must have upon his side the Church or the Fenians, and you will never have the Church'.

The new development of which Rolleston spoke to him was an endeavour on the part of the I.R.B. to assume control not only of Fenian propaganda but of the Irish parliamentary party, which was still torn by internal dissensions. Yeats was interested, partly because he had long dreaded a revival of revolutionary action in Ireland, in which Maud Gonne might risk her life. People spoke of the swing of the pendulum in English politics; but in Ireland the swing brought defeat, death and long discouragement. When he had taken advantage of the swing away from the parliamentary party to found literary and patriotic clubs, he had hoped for a revival of Young Ireland politics, which, though ready as Davis would have been to take risks, would set itself against foolhardy adventure.

In accepting Rolleston's suggestion that he should help the 'new movement' Yeats acted at first without any thought of Maud Gonne, and he saw clearly that such a movement as was described might easily be swept from its path by ignorant men and involve all in some new conspiracy. He was introduced to Dr Mark Ryan, a chief of the I.R.B. in London, in whom he discovered a touching benevolence. Ryan was not an able man, but had great influence on

---

* On his last visit to America Yeats gave this piece of information to Dr Patrick MacCartan, saying that he always regarded himself as one of the party. O'Leary himself, when he was accepted as a young man into the Fenian organization, refused to take an oath and stipulated that he should not be asked to administer an oath to anyone else.

account of this benevolence; his indulgent nature even tolerated poets. His political associates were almost all London Irishmen in the medical profession, peasants or half-peasants in origin, but in Ireland it had seemed to Yeats that it was just such men who were most likely to understand his thought. The next news that Yeats heard was that Rolleston had resigned from the Brotherhood. Rolleston's handsome face had set a young Irish poetess dreaming; she dreamed one night that he was in danger of arrest. Rolleston had not much belief in dreams, but his belief in the cause seemed to be even fainter, and he asked Yeats to return to him all his letters – and they were innocent enough – lest the police might ransack Woburn Buildings and discover that he had written some seditious word.

Just as Yeats was beginning to forget all about the 'new movement', Maud Gonne, who had lately persuaded Mark Ryan to swear her into the Brotherhood, came to him to say that she wished to collect funds in America for a Wolfe Tone memorial, but could not get the necessary authorization from the Dublin body of which John O'Leary was chairman. Yeats offered to intervene, and called a meeting at Woburn Buildings which passed the necessary resolution. At this meeting he learned that the new movement represented one of two violently opposed sections into which Irish-American revolutionists had split. One was the Triangle, as it was called, and the other was that of John Devoy. They were split because Devoy's party accused the Triangle of the murder of a certain Dr Cronin. The Dublin Committee represented Devoy, and Yeats's friends the supposed murderers. It was years ago, and the court had acquitted Sullivan, the accused man. It occurred to Yeats that if he allowed his name to be put forward for the presidency of the English Committee for the memorial he could save the movement from dividing into its elements. His name was put forward and he was elected. Presently he formed a grandiose plan without considering the men he had to deal with, exactly as if he were writing something in a story. The Dublin Committee was a large body of two or three hundred members. It was soon to have a vast organization behind it, and the actual laying of the stone would be attended by 20,000 Irish-Americans. The Spanish-American war had not yet come to engage their thoughts elsewhere. Why, Yeats asked himself, could not this Council, or something like it, act as an Irish Parliament? There were four parties in Ireland: Parnellites, anti-Parnellites, the official Unionists and a new party of progressive landlords headed by Lord Castletown, which wished to secure fairer fiscal relations with England. Why not, after the laying of the stone, invite all the parties to present a statement to the Council? The first two dare not refuse; Lord Castletown, known to Yeats as a leader of pan-Celticism, had given a half promise. The Convention could then sit permanently, or appoint some Executive Committee to direct Irish policy and report from time to time. The total withdrawal of Irish members from Westminster had been proposed in the seventies, but the Convention could send them thither, not as an independent power, but as its delegation, and only when, and for what purpose, the Convention might decide. Yeats dreaded that Maud Gonne might be involved in some wild Fenian movement, and with literature more in his mind than politics, dreamed (he says) of 'a unity of culture which might begin with some few men controlling some form of administration'. He thought he had Maud Gonne's support, but when he overheard her conversation, she commonly urged the entire withdrawal of the Irish members, or if she did refer to his scheme, it was to suggest the despatch to Westminster of eighty ragged and drunken Dublin beggars or eighty pugilists 'to be paid by results'.

2

Eighteen-ninety-seven was the year of Queen Victoria's Jubilee, and the '98 Committee thought it important that the loyal shopkeepers of Dublin should not be allowed to decorate the fronts of their premises for the occasion. The police protected the shopkeepers, and Maud Gonne moved in the midst of street tumults, 'her laughing head thrown back'.

Lady Gregory knew of all these doings, as one political meeting followed another, and of Yeats's part in them. She had written a pamphlet against Gladstone's Home Rule, but she knew how and when to be indulgent. She had been moved by the story of Yeats's frustrated love; he had told her of the devotion that 'might as well have been offered to an image in a milliner's shop or to a statue in a museum'. In a letter to her, written from George Russell's lodgings, he said:

Maud Gonne was thrown from a car yesterday by a horse falling. Her arm is broken and her face scratched and bruised. I have not seen her. I was not at the demonstration when the accident happened. ... I did not know until a few minutes to nine to-day when a messenger came to tell me. ... I have just seen the doctor and on advice have taken the responsibility of writing to her sister. She is so self-reliant that she would probably ask no one to nurse her, if she could get on at all without. I cannot leave now – I am most anxious about the shock for she has been very ill this spring, with her old trouble in the lungs, and was looking pale and thin as it was.

One day, at Maud Gonne's hotel in Nassau Street, Yeats found a young labour leader who some nights before had headed a procession which threw a coffin inscribed 'British Empire' into the Liffey. He was a small man and looked very sad. Maud Gonne had promised him to speak at one of the regular meetings of his Society against the Queen, and he had placarded the streets with an announcement to that effect. She had now told him that she was not a Socialist, and could not attend the meeting. He went away saying that his career would be ruined, for no one would ever believe that he had had her promise. On Yeats's suggestion Maud Gonne followed him to the address which he had given. She came back to Yeats with a pathetic account of his tenement, and the next day she spoke at his meeting. The young man was James Connolly, who, with Padraic Pearse, was to make the insurrection of 1916 and to be executed.

A series of detached memories of his '98 politics floated up in Yeats's mind, when five-and-twenty years later he wrote that portion of his autobiography which is called *The Stirring of the Bones*. There was that elderly man who came in for a moment at the close of each of the weekly committee meetings and said something to the secretary and went out. Yeats asked who he was, and was told, 'a schoolmaster who early in life made a vow neither to smoke nor drink and to give up the money saved to the Irish cause.' There was that proposal for striking a silver medal which would contain on it the usual round tower, watch-dog, cross and harp. The Committee, all but Yeats good Catholics outside politics, decided that the cross had been so detrimental to nationalism – the fall of Parnell was a recent event – that it should be obliterated. Instructions to that effect were sent to the artist, who explained that the cross could not be left out as that would leave nothing for the harp to lean on. There was that intoxicated man coming to apologize for some rudeness, and then saying, 'No, I will not apologize, I care for nobody now but Venus and Adonis and the other planets of heaven.' There was that household of Protestant Republicans in Belfast to which he was taken by Maud Gonne. The old man kept explaining at great length how this man or that would break up the British Empire and his homely wife would say at intervals: 'Robert is so hopeful.' There was that visit to the office of the Dublin Committee, when he found the front door open, the room empty and eighteen pounds in gold on the shelf. Most vivid of all there was Maud Gonne herself:

> Although crowds gathered once if she but showed her face,
> And even old men's eyes grew dim, this hand alone,
> Like some last courtier at a gypsy camping-place
> Babbling of fallen majesty, records what's gone.

The Jubilee riots over, Yeats accompanied Maud Gonne, in his capacity as president of the '98 Association, on a tour among the Irish in England and in Scotland. This took place in the autumn. There were some stirring moments. 'We had a long and exciting meeting this morning', he wrote to Lady Gregory from Manchester,

and will have another tonight. After the meeting Miss Gonne and myself went to the picture gallery to see a Rossetti that is there. She is very kind and friendly but whether more than that I cannot tell. ... I told Miss Gonne what Lady Mayo said about her losing a lot of money at Aix les Bains and she says it is quite accurate except that she won instead of losing. This is a very feeble letter, the sort of thing one writes when one is ten years old ... but I have been chairman of a noisy meeting for three hours and am very done up. I have a speech to prepare for to-night. Everything went smoothly this morning in spite of anonymous letters warning me to keep a body-guard at the door. Perhaps the disturbance waits for to-night.

These months, Yeats has said, were the worst in his life. Yet for all his air of aloofness from everyday life he had a taste for affairs, and, however it may have been with him in early youth, he was now much more precise in his actions than many commonplace people. It is true that in private conversations, especially if the ideas of his own movement were implicated, he would sometimes lose his self-possession and be miserable afterwards for hours. But he never shirked the boredom of committee meetings, and here, when the technical forms gave him time to deliberate, he had great influence and was generally the governing mind. The experiences proved very useful to him later on, when he managed a theatre. His manner, if it had any defect, was too suave. Maud Gonne too could be surprisingly effective on questions of detail,* and she and Yeats were the best financial heads – it is not saying much – in the '98 Association.

* Stephen Gwynn says that she once drafted a parliamentary bill for meals for school children, and all he had to do was to persuade the Government to give time to a non-contentious measure.

3

Yeats spent the Christmas of 1897 with his family at Bedford
Park. His sister Lily remembers how he came down to breakfast one morning very much excited, and recounted the
dream which gave him that strange and symbolic love poem,
'The Cap and Bells', which is in *The Wind among the Reeds*.
A poem of which he said long afterwards at some lecture
that it was 'the way to win a lady', whereas the better known
'Embroidered Cloths' of the same period was the way to lose
one. Maud Gonne was in the States, and he had had (he told
Lady Gregory) some very nice letters from her; one began
'my dear friend', and ended 'affectionately your friend'.

Lady Gregory came to her flat in Queen Anne's Mansions
after Christmas. She looked after Yeats's comfort, and she
gave him a leather armchair and the blue curtains which
were the principal features of his room for twenty years. In
her collection of folklore he found the material for a number
of essays, all for the great English and American reviews,
with such titles as 'Prisoners of the Gods', 'Celtic Beliefs
about the Soul', 'Ireland Bewitched', 'The Broken Gates of
Death', 'The Celtic Element in Literature', each of which
brought him ten or fifteen pounds. He had never before
earned so much, but the articles offended certain Irish and
Catholic susceptibilities. A fairyland poet is one thing, a
psychologist with documents another. 'No nation in the
world', says *Hudibras* Butler, 'is more addicted to the occult
philosophy than the wild Irish, as appears from the whole
practice of their lives.' Yeats was accused of repeating a
traditional Saxon libel, of whittling down the spirituality of
the Irish until it could appear mere evidence of atavistic tendency or a parody of some Eastern cult. To one of the more
amiable of his critics he replied as follows:

A friendly paragraphist in *The Outlook* for 16 April regrets
that when I 'sit down to write for a prosaic world' I am unable
'always to separate the dreams and poetic fancies from the
realities' I have 'witnessed'; and wishes that I would be sure of

my facts. He says that when I wrote, in the *Fortnightly Review*,
'The most of the Irish country people believe that only people
who die of old age go straight to some distant Hell or Heaven
or Purgatory. All who are young enough for any use ... are
taken ... by the fairies; and live, until they die a second time, in
the green "forts" ', I wrote what is nearly altogether 'the dream
of a poetical folk-lorist'.

If your paragraphist will consult my article in the January
number of the *Nineteenth Century*, of which these sentences are
the summary, he will find that I have been very careful about
my facts and have quoted witness after witness. And if your
paragraphist, who is, perhaps, a Catholic, will wait until I have
completed the series of essays, of which the essay in the *Fortnightly* is but the third, he will find that the Irish peasant has
invented, or that somebody has invented for him, a vague,
though not altogether unphilosophical, reconciliation between his
Paganism and his Christianity.

'The Celtic Element in Literature' took its place in *Ideas of
Good and Evil*, Yeats's first book of prose criticism, published
five years later. Another early essay of 1897, also reprinted
in that volume, 'Symbolism in Painting', was suggested by
the work of W. T. Horton, a contributor to the queer magazines that publishers put out during the *Yellow Book–Savoy*
period. Horton's drawings were very obviously mystical, and
seemed to come from elsewhere than his brain. This odd
being, an Irvingite in religion, was truly devoted to Yeats's
spiritual welfare. Sometimes he would attend the social
'Monday evenings' at Woburn Buildings, but usually he
preferred to write what he had to say to the poet. Yeats was
most punctilious in his replies, and their correspondence,
which was carried on without a check for many years, was of
a truly extraordinary kind. This early letter to him from
Yeats about the Order of the Golden Dawn deserves a
biographic place:

... Nor is our order anti-Christian. That very pentagram
which I suggested your using is itself as you would have learned,
a symbol of Christ. I am convinced however that for you progress
lies not in dependence upon a Christ outside yourself but upon

the Christ in your own breast. . . . I do not mean that you cannot progress outside the G. D. but that you should read and study in some unemotional and difficult school. Jacob Boehme is certainly the greatest of the Christian mystics since the Middle Ages and none but an athletic student can get to the heart of his mystery. You would, I think, find him consonant with your temperament. But no matter what school you study in you must expect to find progress beset by false intuition and the persecution of phantoms. Our past and its elementals, masked often as angels of light, rise up always against our future. Of course my friendship has nothing to do with your going on or not going on in the G. D.

4

August was the month of the laying of the foundation stone of the Wolfe Tone monument. A procession passed through Dublin greater than any since the day of Parnell's funeral. At its head were the majority of the Council and their friends. Maud Gonne's waggonette came next, and with her were Yeats and Cipriani, a survivor of Garibaldi's Italy, a fire-eater who hated the peace of Victoria and of Bismarck, and used to make anti-clerical speeches in French to the Irish crowd. At the rear were the two Irish parliamentary parties, walking side by side like cattle in a storm. Yeats heard John Redmond say, 'I went up to the front of the procession just now, and one of the marshals said, "Your place is further back, Mr Redmond." I said, "I will stay where I am." "In that case," he said, "I will lead you back." ' At the unveiling ceremony, however, the parliament men managed to get on the platform, much to the disgust of the extremists; and to offset them Yeats was invited to speak for the I.R.B. He began: 'England had persuaded herself that Ireland discredited by disunion was about to submit – to accept a handful of alms. We have answered her today. She is no longer deceived. The people have made this movement. ...' There were calls from the crowd, 'No, no, it is Maud Gonne that has made it.'

Passion still ran high, the secret societies undermining all,

and yet so gracious was Maud Gonne, her voice ever sweet
and low, that she was applauded by friend and foe alike. In
prose as well as in verse Yeats has celebrated her as she was
at this time:

> When men and women did her bidding they did it not only
> because she was beautiful, but because that beauty suggested joy
> and freedom. Besides there was an element in her beauty that
> moved minds full of old Gaelic stories and poems, for she looked
> as though she lived in an ancient civilisation where all superiori-
> ties, whether of the mind or the body, were a part of public
> ceremonial. . . . Her beauty, backed by her great stature, could
> instantly affect an assembly, . . . for it was incredibly distin-
> guished, and if . . . her face, like the face of some Greek statue,
> showed little thought, her whole body seemed a master-work of
> long labouring thought, as though a Scopas had measured and
> calculated, consorted with Egyptian sages and mathematicians
> out of Babylon, that he might outface even Artemisia's sepul-
> chral image with a living norm.*

The commemoration ceremonies were on the whole disappointing, but Maud Gonne was not discouraged, for the
Fashoda crisis and then the Boer War revived hopes of continental coalition against England. A French officer, batoned
in the Dublin streets, reported to the French War Office that
Ireland was ready for insurrection; and perhaps through
Maud Gonne's influence with Millevoye, a famous orator
and the editor of *La Patrie*, a certain colonel of the French
military Intelligence travelled to London, carrying her
letters of introduction to members of the I.R.B., who (she
stated) were in a position to supply valuable information to
the French War Office, which at that time pursued a policy
opposed to that of Delcassé and the Ministry of Foreign
Affairs.

It is unlikely that Maud Gonne informed Yeats of the
plot; for one thing he was notoriously unable to keep a

---

* *The Stirring of the Bones*. Bernard Shaw has said (in conversation)
that she was 'outrageously beautiful'. He remembered in particular
coming on her and W. B. in Chancery Lane under the circle of light
thrown on the pavement by a street lamp.

secret. When he visited her in Paris at the beginning of 1899, it was to beg her to give up 'this life of hatred' (politics) and to marry him. He was fresh from some work with his uncle on rituals for the Celtic Order. Politics after all were only a means of meeting Maud Gonne. There was a deeper mind, he thought, a common memory of the race, which could be evoked by symbols, and he had believed that by practising these symbols with her, and by their search together for a new revelation, he might gain his heart's desire. The object of the visit to Paris was suspected by George Pollexfen, who wrote to him:

I have your letter and herewith I enclose the cheque £7 you request the loan of. I was in hopes you would have required more for another purpose but suppose affairs did not culminate favourably. When I told Mary [Battle] that you had gone to France she said you were in great form at present but added that something *you and I* had in mind would not come off this time. I made no remark in reply to this, but wondered whether her prognostication might refer to the Celtic rite or to another matter more immediately to do with your going to Paris. ... I am pleased to learn that MacGregor's vision and mine agree as to Aengus and it should give me some measure of confidence again.

Maud Gonne's resolution would not give way; Yeats's letters to Lady Gregory reflected deep distress, almost despair, because she refused to abandon the perilous and agitated life of a conspirator. 'It may be that Russell is right,' he wrote. ... 'I have little to set against what he says but a few omens. I would not so much lament but I am sure that if things remain as they are she will never leave this life, which a vision I made her see six years ago told her was her deepest hell, and contrasted with the life of labour from the divine love which was her deepest heaven.'

He had many opportunities of seeing her in the months following as she passed and repassed through London on her secret errands. An attractive page in her autobiography* tells how on one such occasion he found her with her sister

* *A Servant of the Queen.*

Mrs Pilcher, the wife of a British officer, at the latter's flat
in London. He arrived while they were at dinner, and all
went into the drawing-room for coffee. The sisters sat together on a big sofa amid piles of soft cushions. Miss Gonne
was tired and travel-stained. Yeats looked at her critically,
and then turned to Mrs Pilcher, who was in a lovely dinner
gown, to say that he liked her dress and that she was looking
younger than ever. It was Mrs Pilcher's reply, 'It's hard work
being beautiful,' which suggested some lines in 'Adam's
Curse', a poem written two or three years later:

> I said: 'It's certain there is no fine thing
> Since Adam's fall but needs much labouring.
> There have been lovers who thought love should be
> So much compounded of high courtesy
> That they would sigh and quote with learned looks
> Precedents out of beautiful old books;
> Yet now it seems an idle trade enough.'

The next day Yeats said: 'Oh, why do you not give up politics and live a peaceful life? I could make such a perfect
life for you among artists and writers who would appreciate
you. You don't take care of yourself as your sister does but
you will always be beautiful, more beautiful than anyone I
have ever known.' They were in Westminster Abbey together, examining the Lia Fail or Stone of Destiny, on
which is set the Coronation chair. Tradition says that the
stone belongs to Ireland, and that on it the kings of Ireland
used to be crowned; and so to change the subject Miss Gonne
made Yeats tell her once more of the four talismans of the
Tuatha de Danaan, the stone, the cauldron, the spear and
the sword, and of the ancient gods which old writings connect with them. 'It is very heavy,' she said, looking at the
iron clamps by which the chair is attached to the stone. 'It
would require several men to lift; we could scarcely steal it.
Have you no magic to get the spirit of the stone to Ireland –
to the Castle of the Heroes – in triumph, ceremony and
rejoicing?'

5

Details of the great dramatic project were now before the Irish public. A society called the Irish Literary Theatre, with Yeats, Martyn and Moore as directors, had been established, and a formal letter circulated. In this letter, in which Yeats's hand is evident, it was announced that there would be given in Dublin, for three years in the spring of every year, performances of certain Celtic and Irish plays which, whatever might be their degree of excellence, would be written with a high ambition for an 'uncorrupted and imaginative audience, trained to listen by its passion for oratory', plays which would aim at expressing 'the deeper thoughts and emotions' of Ireland and surpass dividing political opinions.

Even society people showed signs of interest. Lady Betty Balfour was good enough to assist by giving tableaux vivants of *The Countess Cathleen* at the Chief Secretary's Lodge. She asked Yeats to rehearse; he explained that he could not possibly enter an official house, but recommended her to employ the talents of T. W. Rolleston, the ex-Fenian. Rolleston made a very handsome demon, and Lady Constance Lytton played the part of the nurse.

Yeats chuckled over Rolleston's social advancement and retired in good spirits to his uncle's house in Sligo. He wrote from there to his sister Lily at the end of 1898:

All my Irish plays are going well. We have taken a hall for the plays in the week following May 8th. Meanwhile they are getting up at the Chief Secretary's Lodge 'living pictures' of *Countess Cathleen.* As I explained that I cannot possibly go near the Chief Secretary's Lodge, or take any part in the performances, Lady Fingall is trying to arrange for me to meet Lady Betty Balfour at her house (Lady Fingall's) that I may advise about costumes, etc. This may keep me a little while in Dublin. We are carrying on all manner of propaganda so as to prepare the public for the plays and expect a great success. Dublin is waking up in a number of things. Russell is doing a great part in the awakening. He is a most amazing person. He is at the moment busy over a scheme to settle the congested districts in a place of his own invention. Gerald Balfour has described it as the only practicable scheme yet thought of ...

Next came the rehearsals for the Dublin performances. These took place in London, as it was only there that a company could be gathered and rehearsed. Florence Farr was invited to find players for *The Countess Cathleen*, and Moore assumed control of the production of Martyn's play. Yeats wrote to Lady Gregory in March: 'Moore first got rid of practically the whole cast. —— ran at the chairs, kicked them and called them names, upon which the prompter threatened him with personal violence if he used such language in the presence of ladies.'

Then Moore descended upon Yeats's rehearsals also, Martyn having come to tell him that Yeats was explaining his method of speaking verse to the actors, while 'a lady in a long green cloak' (Miss Farr) gave illustrations of it on the psaltery. Moore had already found an experienced actress for the title part in place of the young girl who had played the fairy child in *The Land of Heart's Desire*. The experienced actress was at open feud with Florence Farr, and walked up and down the stage 'like a pantheress', while Florence Farr was 'invoking hell' by lying down on the floor and speaking through the chinks. Yeats suggested that she should stand on a chair and wave her hands. But it being 'always easy to do business with a clever man', Moore persuaded Yeats to go away for a fortnight and hand over the rehearsals to the husband of the experienced actress, who would also decide how the verses should be spoken.*

Suddenly all the plans for the theatre faced an hour of peril. A rumour against the orthodoxy of *The Countess Cathleen* began to wander to and fro. Edward Martyn, who invariably abided by the advice of the clergy, consulted an unnamed monk, who denounced the play. Lady Gregory and Yeats thought that two ecclesiastics might be found to outvote one, and they submitted the play to an Irish Jesuit and to Father Barry, a well-known Englishman of letters.

* This account of the rehearsals is Moore's in *Ave*.

Father Barry was emphatic in Yeats's favour. He quoted the text 'I must be anathema to the brethren' to justify the intention in the lines:

> The Light of Lights
> Looks always on the motive, not the deed,
> The Shadow of Shadows on the deed alone.

This failed to satisfy Martyn, who explained that it was not Yeats's intention, so mythical and undefined, that troubled his conscience, but certain stage directions and certain un-Catholic and heretical passages. 'I am quite ready', he wrote to Yeats, 'to abide by what Father Finlay says should come out ... but Barry does not seem to have realized that it is *my* difficulty not yours.' It was now Moore's turn to become restless; and he denounced Yeats's submission of a work of art to the judgement of theologians as an act unworthy of a man of letters. Yeats wrote to Lady Gregory (London, 11 April 1899):

> Last night I saw Moore. He lamented his lost row. He had hoped to write an article called 'Edward Martyn and his Soul'. He said, 'It was the best opportunity I ever had. What a sensation it would have made! Nobody has ever written that way about his most intimate friend. What a chance! It would have been heard of everywhere.'

A week or two later Yeats had a letter from Martyn which ran:

> I received this morning from Moore a most offensive letter which I will not stand. He attacks my most valued friend Dr Healy in a manner which disgusts me. ... After Moore's words I shall pay either to you, him or Lady Gregory the sum of £130 in aid of the Irish Literary Theatre (£100 my guarantee, £30 that of my late mother), withdraw my play, and leave the Irish Literary Theatre altogether. I do not wish to be mixed up in the concern any more. I have had too much trouble in various ways and cannot stand any more.

On the morning that this letter was received Florence Farr and Yeats were breakfasting together at the Nassau

Hotel in Dublin. The meal was interrupted by Edward
Martyn, who arrived to confirm his threat. The slow,
obstinate man had large drops of sweat on his forehead,
which he was wiping with his pocket-handkerchief. Yeats
applied some judicious flattery and by midday all was well
again, and the hall of the Antient Concert Rooms had been
engaged for the performance.

At about this time the course of the preparations was
diversified by another unexpected and sensational episode.
Some years before this Yeats had made the acquaintance of
a former member of the Irish party, named F. Hugh
O'Donnell, who had been expelled by Parnell and was now
trying to find his way back into politics through the 'new
movement'. O'Donnell was a very clever man but half mad
from vanity, long political contention and the strain of
impecuniosity. For a while he had amused Yeats. Then he
attacked Michael Davitt's reputation in a shameful manner,
which so shocked Maud Gonne and Yeats that they brought
the matter to the attention of John O'Leary, who proscribed
O'Donnell. The man now took a nice revenge upon Yeats by
publishing a pamphlet called *Souls for Gold*, which quoted
as Yeats's own words the words of the demon merchants, and
represented the scene where the women barter their souls as
an insult to Irish womanhood. The pamphlet was distributed
in letter-boxes all over residential Dublin, and the crusade
was elsewhere supported by a generous supply of porter. One
newspaper had long, violent leading articles; finally, Cardinal Logue, who had been stirred by some intrigue, issued
an artless letter to the effect that if the play were as the
pamphlet described it, no Catholic should go to the theatre.
Edward Martyn was not disturbed. The Cardinal had not
read the play, and that deprived his opinion of ecclesiastical
authority. Other Catholic friends, however, began to melt
away, and opinion at University College was profoundly
affected. There was nothing to be done. Letters to the press
only led to more misrepresentations. Arthur Griffith, then
the editor of a backstairs journal and afterwards first Presi-

dent of the Irish Free State, offered to bring 'a lot of men from the Quays', who would 'applaud anything the Church did not like'. But Yeats was reluctant to allow his play to degenerate into an anti-clerical demonstration; he preferred to risk his reputation with the political extremists and call in the police to protect the performance against riotous students in the gallery. The clamour was loud, but somehow or other unimpressive, and it ended in an anti-climax, when, as the audience was leaving the theatre, an Ulster malcontent squeaked out: 'One Boo for Yeets.'

Years later, in *Dramatis Personae*, Yeats admitted that the disturbances were in part his own fault:

In using ... traditional symbols I forgot that in Ireland they are not symbols but realities ... The play itself was ill-constructed, the dialogue turning aside at the lure of word or metaphor, very different, I hope, from what it is to-day after many alterations, every alteration tested by performance. It was not, nor is it now, more than a piece of tapestry. The Countess sells her soul, but she is not transformed. If I were to think out that scene to-day, she would at the moment her hand has signed burst into loud laughter, mock at all that she has held holy, horrify the peasants in the midst of their temptations. Nothing satisfied me but Florence Farr's performance in the part of Aleel ... and after five-and-thirty years, I keep among my unforgettable memories the sense of coming disaster she put into the words:

... But now
Two great horned owls hooted above our heads.

Martyn's *Heather Field* was entirely approved of, both by the English critics Max Beerbohm and A. B. Walkley, who came over to Dublin for the performances in the melancholy hall, and by the Dublin public. Edward Martyn was highly gratified, and not only paid all expenses – the guarantors were not called upon – but offered to take one of the large Dublin theatres for productions in the following year of Alice Milligan's *Last Feast of the Fianna* and two further plays by himself, *Maeve* and *The Tale of a Town*.

6

Even in their metaphysics the plays of the period were suspected of occasional political implications. When Martyn's mystical play, *Maeve*, was produced in February 1900, Yeats interpreted the criticism of the young men and women of the Gaelic League as a sign that the anti-English passion in Ireland might be transmuted into a passion of hatred against what Morris and Ruskin had denounced in English life. A young student named James Joyce, who had refused to sign the College manifesto against *The Countess Cathleen*, found this too much. 'Mr Yeats' treacherous instinct of adaptability', he wrote in *The Day of the Rabblement*, 'must be blamed for his recent association with a platform from which even self-respect should have urged him to refrain.'

All but Joyce were a little elated; Moore, Martyn and Yeats vied with each other in maledictions and accusations of the cold egoistic policy of England in South Africa. Edward Martyn resigned from his office of Deputy Lieutenant of County Galway as a mark of sympathy with the Boers, and Moore formed a project (in which he invited Yeats to join) of lecturing in America against Anglo-American alliance, and, as a protest against an impious war, took a house in Dublin from which to conduct his Irish operations. Already Moore had advised Yeats to shun politics as a pursuit dangerous to artistic interests (he recalled the case of Wagner), but now for a while he was as political as the rest. Even J. B. Y. was affected; his pleasure in the British reverses was such that he strained his friendship with the tender-hearted York Powell, a supporter of the Imperialist adventure. 'I don't contest your opinions with any controversial purpose', he would say to Powell, 'but merely to set a poor prisoner free. Your opinions – your jingoism, your materialism all stained and encrusted with Oxford cum Jew wickedness – are only a technique.' One evening the pair were arguing hotly in J. B. Y.'s house, when Yeats came in and expressed satisfaction that John Bull should be limp-

ing with a sore foot (another of de Wet's successes had been
reported). Powell could forgive J. B. Y. a great deal, but
Willie's caw was another story, and he dashed from the
room vowing he would never enter the house again. Jack
Yeats, who was staying with his father at the time, had gone
to bed early. He heard the door bang, a patter of slippered
footsteps following the Professor down the street, a whispered conversation and then the return together. A pact was
made; J. B. Y. promised not to speak of the war again. Separation from Powell would have broken his heart.

Lady Gregory suffered no temptations to become a political woman. But it is not the least of the proofs of her social
tact – 'in her life much artifice', as Yeats wrote – that she
was able, in spite of her new associations, to hold fast to her
moorings in county family. She kept all her old friends,
although Lecky and others protested to her against the line
on politics which the Irish literary leaders were following.
There was great indignation among the loyalists when, on
the occasion of the old Queen's visit to Dublin in the spring
of 1900, Maud Gonne's party organized counter-demon-
strations. The letters to the newspapers in which Yeats and
Martyn attacked the visit as a recruiting tour, caused Lecky
and some others to withdraw their support from the Irish
Literary Theatre. After the Queen's death George Wyndham was asked by Moore to use his influence for the production in London of *Diarmuid and Grania.* He had known
Yeats in Henley's circle and was an ardent admirer of his
poetry, some of which he had published in the *New Review.*
But he was forced to reply that he could do nothing unless
Yeats could draw a distinction between his views as a
Nationalist and his views of the Queen. 'The Queen,' he
reminded Moore, 'loved by many and by myself among the
number, is now dead.' Yeats, who had abandoned his
grandiose project of uniting Ireland – Lord Castletown's
fiscal reform party had disappointed him by lack of courage
– shrugged his shoulders and said: 'Then we must be baptized of the gutter.'

Lady Gregory chaffed him for the phrase, and yet she never repudiated it. On the other hand, she had to overcome a great deal of distrust in the Dublin circles to which Yeats introduced her. Here she was suspected, not only of some political afterthought, but of social condescension. John O'Leary of course rose superior to such pettiness. But J. F. Taylor sneered, and said she was turning Yeats from a revolutionary poet into a courtier – all images of service were, in fact, dear to Yeats, and he thought it his unhappiness that his analytic faculties should dissolve those things that invite service.* Maud Gonne's attitude was more complex. She had no reason to feel any social inferiority before Lady Gregory, and was glad that Yeats, who had led a comfortless enough life, should have found someone to pet and fuss over him. But she used to say that when writers returned from Coole they 'seemed less passionately interested in the national struggle than in their own lack of money'. On one of the first occasions that they met she found Lady Gregory in possession of the rooms in the Nassau Hotel which she herself always occupied when she came to Dublin. They had a little conversation and then Lady Gregory asked her what her intentions were in regard to Yeats. 'I am only doing for him,' she added, 'what I would do for my son. I feel for him as if he were my son.' Lady Gregory got the same reply that Yeats had had more than once, only delivered more shortly. 'I have more important things to think of than marriage and so has he.'

7

In picturesque apposition to his politics were Yeats's new lyrics, *The Wind among the Reeds*, and his new dramatic poem, *The Shadowy Waters*. On its publication in 1899, *The Wind among the Reeds* was highly praised by Arthur Symons and by a few critics, and this book still represents to

---

*Vide the line in a later poem, 'My medieval knees lack health and they bend'. In an essay on Yeats in old age Frank O'Connor went so far as to call him 'the born servant' – the Roman prelate, the secretary, the go-between.

some older readers – hardly to any of the young – the high-water mark of Yeats's lyricism. That he had advanced in technical accomplishment admitted of no doubt. There was far less of unnecessary beauty than in the earlier volume; he was no longer carried away by every fancy into the side images which marred the directness of the 'Rose' poems. The more characteristic, the dimmer and more esoteric poems in *The Wind among the Reeds* – those which bear the signature of what he afterwards called a dream-burdened will – create a curious effect of isolation in the whole body of the work; and it is significant that of all his books this was the one which he revised least for republication. These lyrics must be pre-Raphaelite or nothing.*

The plot of *The Shadowy Waters* had been told to George Russell when Yeats and he were still boys together at the Art School. Forgael was then a wanderer striving to escape from himself. He surprises a galley in the waters. There is a beautiful woman in the galley. He thinks that through love he can escape from himself, and casts a mystical spell upon Dectora. In the original version he finds the love created by the spell is but the empty echo of the shadow of himself, and he unrolls the spell and seeks the world of the immortals alone. But now Yeats was in love and did not relish the idea of going alone to the world of the immortals. George Moore came over from Tulira to Coole in the summer of 1900 in the hope of extricating the poet from his difficulties. But of all his suggestions the one that Yeats most resolutely rejected was that Dectora, instead of accompanying the metaphysical pirate on his quest for an immortality of love, should return 'somewhat diffidently and ashamed of herself' to the sailors quarrelling over their ale.

* Note, however, two major operations in the volume: 'O Beast of the wilderness, fowl of the air' for 'Although the rushes and the fowl of the air', and 'Till the attorney for lost souls' for 'Till Maurya of the wounded heart. . . .' As T. S. Eliot observes, Yeats in the nineties was not the least of the pre-Raphaelites. It was Bernard Shaw, by the way, who first noted the affinities between the Celtic movement and pre-Raphaelitism.

The Shadowy Waters was published in 1900, with a prologue, Yeats's first poem on Coole, written in the Seven
Woods:

> How shall I name you, immortal, mild, proud shadows?
> I only know that all we know comes from you,
> And that you come from Eden on flying feet.
> Is Eden far away, or do you hide
> From human thought, as hares and mice and coneys
> That run before the reaping-hook and lie
> In the last ridge of the barley? Do our woods
> And winds and ponds cover more quiet woods,
> More shining winds, more star-glimmering ponds?

Prompted by his father, who for some reason or other had
taken a violent dislike to Fisher Unwin, Yeats had changed
publishers. He gave *The Secret Rose* to A. H. Bullen, the
Elizabethan scholar and a friend of the family, and *The
Wind among the Reeds* to Elkin Mathews. While he was
finishing *The Shadowy Waters* at Coole, J. B. Yeats wrote to
him that

> Clement Shorter says he can make a 'good bargain' for your
> book [the *Poems*] by taking it away from Fisher Unwin and
> giving it to Nichols – These practical men are in their way good
> guides – not only will Nichols make a good bargain with you
> (I hear he offers £100 down and royalties) but he commands and
> influences a very large and important public. . . . I may add that
> *York Powell* told me on Sunday that you should certainly do
> it. . . . It would be delightful for you to have suddenly (with the
> suddenness of a Fairy gift) £100 in your pocket – you would
> then be free to write at your own work without thought of writing
> reviews, etc. . . . Don't despise the nonconformists – They *do*
> read and do *think* – at least large numbers of them do.

Unwin refused to part with the *Poems* of 1895, which was
fortunate, for he did very well by the book, reprinting it
time after time; there was never a year in which Yeats failed
to receive royalties on its account. But Yeats so far overcame
his prejudice against 'nonconformists' as to entrust *The
Shadowy Waters* to Hodder & Stoughton, of which firm

Robertson Nicoll, one of his firmest supporters in the press, was a director. Though the plot was not again altered, no play of Yeats's was more often revised than this; as first staged in 1904 it differed considerably from the 1900 version; it was rewritten in an acting version in 1911, and twice re-written later 'as a poem only'.

T. S. Eliot has described *The Shadowy Waters* as 'one of the most perfect expressions of the vague enchanted beauty of the pre-Raphaelite school', coming out of 'a phase of con-fusion' in which Yeats treated Irish legend in the manner of Rossetti or Morris. And Yeats's efforts whether to modernize this play or to render it theatrically effective must be cer-tainly considered ill-judged. 'The one thing for which we occasionally referred to the later version,' his friend Cecil French wrote to him in 1922, 'is spoiled.'

The lines: 'I am so lecherous with abstinence', etc., have aroused unlimited admiration among certain men of letters – they have been placed with the best and raciest of Shakespeare's lines. Your tinkering in that case will cause great indignation among certain of your readers. The first edition is rare. . . . Had I the wealth I should like to issue a reprint of it, and have lawsuits and quarrels with you.

8

For the third series of productions by the Irish Literary Theatre *The Twisting of the Rope* (from the Irish of Douglas Hyde), and *Diarmuid and Grania* by George Moore and Yeats, were announced. Delays ensued, owing to the vicissi-tudes of the Yeats–Moore collaboration, which has found its record in *Dramatis Personae* and in *Ave.* The finished work was shown to famous actors and actresses in London. 'Oh, Mr Yeats,' said Mrs Patrick Campbell, 'why did you not do the whole play yourself?' Yeats explained how essen-tial Moore had been; but Mrs Campbell went on, 'I am sure I know what part you have done . . . the words are sometimes so suitable and sometimes they are like a French play.' It was necessary to interest someone like Mrs Patrick Campbell

in the play, because Edward Martyn refused to open his
purse-strings any further, in consequence of the manner in
which his political satire, *The Tale of a Town*, had been
pulled to pieces by Yeats and by Moore.* The pleasure and
pride with which he had contemplated the early successes
of the Irish Literary Theatre had given way to very different
feelings.

It was at this difficult conjuncture that Yeats received
signals of distress which brought him rapidly to Maud
Gonne's side. She had a sad story to relate. The French
military spy, Colonel X., to whom she had given letters of
introduction to the I.R.B., had returned to Paris in disgrace,
under escort from the French Embassy in London. It
appeared that Colonel X., travelling as a half-blind invalid,
did not know English well, that he had gone to Dr Mark
Ryan to ask for a secretary or an interpreter, and that the
doctor in all innocence had brought him into contact with
Yeats's arch-enemy and hers, F. Hugh O'Donnell, author of
the pamphlet against *The Countess Cathleen*. The arrest of
the French Colonel had followed immediately. Nor was this
all. Maud Gonne had visited the Boer agent, Dr Leyds, in
Brussels in order to place before him a design for sending a
British troopship to the bottom by concealing in the bunkers
bombs disguised as lumps of coal. Leyds was reluctant to
adopt an unrecognized method of warfare, because he feared
the effect upon English liberal sentiment, but he had yielded
to the entreaties of the fair envoy to the extent of offering
to place £2000 at her disposal for unspecified revolutionary
action in Ireland. The sum had been intercepted by a gentleman who, calling upon Leyds after Maud Gonne had left
Brussels, declared that he was her friend and that it was
undesirable for a lady to be mixed in such dangerous transactions. It was suspected, though not certainly known, that
the gentleman in question was the mad rogue, as Yeats now
called O'Donnell. O'Donnell at all events had latterly

* 'Yeats behaved to the poor man', says Moore, 'like a Torquemada
of literature.'

appeared to be in better financial circumstances than usual, for he had subscribed £100 to the Irish parliamentary party in the hope presumably that he would be received back into its ranks.

Maud Gonne was in despair. After enduring so many vicissitudes – including an attempt of Clemenceau to poison her – all the political credit she had built up in France lay in ruins about her. Millevoye had come to her and upbraided the Irish revolutionists. 'Your Irish revolutionists are nothing', he said, 'but a set of comedians. You had better go back and join the Home Rule party.' Yeats comforted her as best he could; he interviewed John Dillon, who acted very honourably and at once handed over the mad rogue's £100 to its rightful owners. Then the I.R.B. got wind of the affair, and some young hotheads decided that O'Donnell's crime could be expiated only by death. Maud Gonne felt a scruple about being privy to the removal of an enemy by means which she would not employ herself, and for some weeks Yeats lived the life of a hero of a sensational novel, pleading with her for their enemy at meetings of the I.R.B. Their efforts were successful; O'Donnell escaped vengeance and a few years later produced another lively pamphlet against the Yeatsian literature.

9

Suddenly Yeats's attention was diverted from politics and the theatre by a great schism in the Order of the Golden Dawn. For some time past MacGregor's restless conduct and extreme spiritual pretensions had been a cause of grave scandal among the more serious hermetic students. Though often warned of the consequences, he persisted in the attempt to impose upon the Order his claim to be directed from the Temple of the Holy Spirit itself. All practical and legal argument urged to immediate action, but the clair-voyants advised patience until he should behave in a manner so outrageous that the waverers would waver no more. The

Order therefore waited, and, sure enough, MacGregor presently provided the pretext by seeking the support of a dreadful young man, who broke into the rooms of the Order and took possession of a book containing much secret matter. On being ejected he attempted to retake the rooms, wearing a black mask and in full Highland costume with a gilt dagger by his side. Yeats, who was on guard with some others, was greatly startled. The envoy then issued a summons against the Society.

– 4.00. *To Lady Gregory*

For a week I have been worried to death with meetings, law and watching to prevent a sudden attack on the rooms. For three nights I did not get more than 4¼ hours' sleep any night. The trouble is that my Cabalists are hopelessly unbusiness-like, and their minutes and the like are in complete confusion. I have had to take the whole responsibility for everything, and to decide on every step. I am hopeful of the result. Fortunately this wretched envoy has any number of false names and has signed the summons in one of them. He is also wanted for debt and a trade union representative is to attend court on Saturday. The envoy is, I believe, seeking vengeance for our refusal to initiate him. We did not admit him because we did not think that a mystical society was intended to be reformatory. I arraigned Mathers on Saturday last before a chapter of the Order. I was carefully polite and I am particularly pleased by the fact that in our correspondence and meetings not one word has been written or said, which forgot the past and the honour one owes to a fallen idol. Whatever happens the activities of the society will have nothing unworthy to pass down to posterity. We have barbed our arrows with compliments and regrets and to do him justice he has done little less . . .

A new Order, the Stella Matutina, arose out of the ruins of the old, all the members resolving not to tolerate false mystery or mystagogues of any kind. 'Everyone', Yeats wrote to Russell from London in July, 'is working as I have never seen them work, and we have fought out our fight without one discourteous phrase.' MacGregor Mathers remained in Paris, where he died at the close of the Great War. It was rumoured that the pernicious incantations of some rival magician sent him to his death, and by hinting at something of the sort in the first edition of *The Trembling of the Veil* (1924) Yeats caused great pain to the loyal widow, who accused him of repeating lying statements reported by enemies. He made amends and was forgiven by 'Vestigia'.

10

The task of producing *Diarmuid and Grania* was finally undertaken by the Benson Company, who presented the play at the Gaiety Theatre in October 1901. Hyde's Irish play was given at the same time by a company of amateurs. Synge, who had now taken Yeats's advice and left his Paris students' hotel for the Aran islands, was present in the audience and contributed an article on the performances to *L'Européen*. The cheap seats were filled, mostly by members of the Gaelic League. 'In spite of the importance of this Society,' Synge wrote,

one always feels in whatever manifestations it organises (and this is always true of profoundly popular movements) that the ridiculous jostles with the deepest sentiments. For example, at the opening of the first act one could not refrain from smiling at the sight of all the pretty girls of the League jabbering in very bad Irish to young clerks pale with enthusiasm. But during an interval of *Diarmuid and Grania* . . . the people in the gallery started to sing. They sang old folk-songs. It was the first time I had heard these melodies sung in chorus by young voices with the Irish words. I heard in the lingering notes an incredible melancholy, the agony of a nation.

To Yeats, writing at a distance of many years,* *Diarmuid and Grania* did not seem to fail. 'When Maud Gonne and I got into our cab to go to some supper-party after the performance, the crowd from the gallery wanted to take the horse out of the cab and drag us there, but Maud Gonne, weary of public demonstrations, refused.' Yeats kept a copy

* In *Dramatis Personae*.

of the MS., but neither he nor Moore ever wanted to print the play.

After the ignominious collapse of her French plans Maud Gonne resigned from the Irish Republican Brotherhood, an action which had the approval of her spiritual director (she had become a Roman Catholic) and also that of Yeats, who left the party at the same time. She took a little house in a Dublin suburb, and began to work with Arthur Griffith, who was opposed to underground conspiracy and was developing the new policy, very strong on the moral side, known as Sinn Fein. To keep the literary movement on the Nationalist path, she aimed at forming a link between Yeats and Griffith, who had some taste in letters. She established or rejuvenated 'Young Ireland' societies, one of these, the *Inghinnide na h'Eireann* (Daughters of Ireland), which described its aim as educating the children of the poor, or according to its enemies, teaching them a catechism which began with the question 'What is the origin of evil?' and the answer 'England'. Yeats assisted Maud Gonne in drawing up rules for this organization, though he had little belief in the new political programme. His experiences on the '98 Committee had convinced him that the Irish parliamentary parties, now reunited, were the only people in Ireland with the slightest political training. But the comic aspects of his '98 adventure – the contacts with grey-haired pub-crawling dreamers; with resolution-mongers wringing the last drop of juice out of the bones of the dead; with professional patriots notorious for lives of cynicism and treachery, in whose conversation there might yet be strange flashes of beauty and of romance – provided him with a rich store of anecdotes for his old age.

He rejoiced over Maud Gonne's renunciation of Fenian politics, but was full of misgivings about the future of his theatre and his literary movement. He longed for productions of his poetic plays by Gordon Craig, still young and unknown, but these would be impossible without some financial help from Martyn, who was more interested in per-

formances of intellectual plays of middle and upper class
life and in foreign masterpieces than in folk-plays or the
Yeatsian lyrical drama. The moneyed classes, whether
Catholic or Protestant, were hostile. Unionists were slow to
forget Yeats's attitude towards Queen Victoria's visit and his
criticisms of the culture of Trinity College, and the clerical
party disliked *The Shadowy Waters* even more than *The
Countess Cathleen.* When his publisher, A. H. Bullen, very
drunk, came to Dublin, the booksellers refused to look at his
wares.

With Lady Gregory's help he had finished his patriotic
one-act *Cathleen ni Houlihan*: 'a dream almost as distinct
as a vision of a cottage where there was well-being and fire-
light and talk of a marriage and into that cottage there came
an old woman in a long cloak. She was Ireland herself. ...'
'A silly little play', said Edward Martyn. But *Cathleen ni
Houlihan* was assured of success with the Gaelic League and
the young men and women of Griffith's following, and Maud
Gonne was disappointed because Yeats failed to hand it
over to the 'Daughters of Ireland', and gave it instead to
Frank and William Fay, the first a stage-struck accountant's
clerk, the other a working man who had toured Ireland in
farce and melodrama with a theatrical company managed
by a negro. The methods of the company were rough and
ready, the negro whitening his face when he played a white
man, but, so strong is stage convention, blackening it when
he played a black man. Both the Fays were men of remarkable talent and character. Frank had studied the English
and French stage of the seventeenth and eighteenth centuries and was an exquisite elocutionist. William was a
comedian of genius with an unrivalled gift of personal distinction in the midst of farce.

George Russell and Lady Gregory were also advocates of
the Fays, and the former offered them a play on the subject
of Deirdre, which he had published in Standish O'Grady's
All Ireland Review. Maud Gonne consented to act the old
woman in *Cathleen ni Houlihan*, and brought some of the

gifted 'Daughters of Ireland' into the company. Later some
of these girls, when praised in the English press, suffered
from a bad conscience, a feeling that the patriotic impulse
had gone, that they had given themselves up to ambition and
vanity. But 2, 3 and 4 April 1902, were dates memorable in
the history of the Irish Theatre, so crowded were the
audiences of working men and women at St Teresa's Hall,
and so fine was Maud Gonne's acting in the part of the old
woman who lures the young man from marriage to death
for Ireland. As Yeats wrote: 'She made Cathleen seem like
a divine being fallen into our mortal infirmity'. The formation of the Irish National Theatre followed the performances. There was little money, and at first little was needed,
twenty-five pounds given by Lady Gregory, twenty by Yeats,
and a few pounds picked up here and there. Padraic Colum,
Seumas O'Sullivan and other young poets rallied round the
Society, of which Yeats was president, with George Russell,
Douglas Hyde and Maud Gonne vice-presidents. James
Joyce was almost alone among his kind, Bohemian and
Nationalist, in his critical aloofness. Conscious perhaps of a
strange new power, Joyce looked forward to a reversion
which would amply repay him for a few years of patience.
He met Yeats during this year, or the next, the introduction
being effected by George Russell, whose letter to Yeats
recommending 'a young fellow named Joyce' to his notice is
extant. 'He has all the intellectual equipment, the culture
and education which our other clever friends here lack',
Russell wrote: 'I think he writes amazingly well in prose. . . .
Moore who saw an article of this boy's says it is prepos-
terously clever . . .' * Yeats must have been impressed, for it
was Joyce's approval of 'The Adoration of the Magi' and of
'The Tables of the Law' as 'work worthy of the great Russian
masters' that presently caused him to reprint these two
stories for all to see.

The theatrical organization was absurd, players and
authors all sitting together and settling by vote what play

* An article on Ibsen in the *Fortnightly Review*.

should be performed and who should play it. It took a series
of disturbances, months of argument, during which relations with George Russell sensibly deteriorated, before Yeats
was put in control with Synge and Lady Gregory. At the
same time political difficulties arose. When Lady Gregory
wrote her first play *Twenty-Five*, the company was at first
unwilling to produce it because to admit an emigrant's return with a hundred pounds would encourage emigration.
Yeats's *Pot of Broth* of December 1902, and his morality *The
Hour-Glass* of March 1903, pleased all, but he lost the confidence of the Gaelic and Sinn Fein public by his defence of
Synge's first play *The Shadow of the Glen*, in which a married peasant woman has a lover. Yeats published the old
Aran folk-tale upon which *The Shadow of the Glen* is
founded, but Arthur Griffith was convinced that such a tale
could only have reached Aran from some decadent author
of Pagan Rome.

Out of twilight

Woburn Buildings; letters to Lady Gregory – Return of
the Yeats family to Dublin; a quarrel with George Moore
– *Ideas of Good and Evil* – New love poetry and marriage
of Maud Gonne – Theatre of Beauty – Miss Horniman's
offer: 'I will give you a theatre' – Letters from America –
Yeats's successes in the States; Yeats as orator

———

Hurry to bless the hands that play,
The mouths that speak, the notes and strings,
O masters of the glittering town!
O! lay the shrilly trumpet down,
Though drunken with the flags that sway
Over the ramparts and the towers,
And with the waving of your wings.

I

EVEN in the years of the foundation of the Irish Theatre,
when business took him so often to Ireland, Yeats spent at
least half his time in London. Though he considered the
summer at Coole as the most productive period of his year,
at least in poetry, his life at Woburn Buildings was laborious
and ordered. Unless he was working at the British Museum,
he would be indoors writing until four, when he dressed,
and either received visitors or went out to seek literary
friends or his 'mystics'. When he had no evening engagements he would take long solitary walks, because his eyesight discouraged reading or writing by candlelight; and his
tall cloaked figure, seemingly oblivious of its surroundings,
was very familiar to the late home-comers of Bloomsbury.

To the humble folk of his immediate neighbourhood he
was known as 'the toff wot lives in the Buildings'. It is said
that he was the only person in the Buildings who ever

received a letter. He had added to his accommodation by taking the attic, formerly lived in by the pedlar, and this he turned into his bedroom, making the smaller room below into a kitchen, so that he would need no longer to go out for his meals. There was no carriage-way through the alley, and the carriage people who came to his Monday evening receptions had to seek his door beside the cobbler's shop on foot, children swarming around them. His visitors were led by him up creaking winding stairs into a large room hung with Blake engravings, some Beardsleys, a Rossetti and other pictures of a pre-Raphaelite character. The windows with blue curtains looked out on the little shops across the way and on a tree or two. Two candles in tall green candlesticks were set upon the table. On one side of the fireplace was a low settle, and on the other the leather armchair, Lady Gregory's gift, like the curtains. A bookcase held fine editions of Morris and Blake, and against one of the walls was a long chest in which the poet kept his manuscripts, his tarot cards and astrological calculations. Somehow or other, out of slender resources, he had managed to make the room an expression of his mystical doctrines.

Some years later another author, Dorothy Richardson, moved into lodgings exactly opposite to his. From above the cobbler's his window looked into hers, above a stonemason's. He never knew himself observed, she has told us,

neither in his daytime talks with the bent old cobbler, no mere passing of the time of day with a fellow tenant . . . but long confabulations, wherein the two stood obviously in an equality of communication, discussing, agreeing, disagreeing, never at a loss and frequently amused . . . nor at night when people gathered in the rooms from afar . . . shadowy forms seated in high-backed chairs, or standing clear in the window space; talking, talking, but in an inequality of communication, and chiefly being talked to, by the tall pervading figure, visible now here, now there, but always in speech.

Yeats's correspondence with Lady Gregory is an important source of information in regard to incidents of his life in

London during the first years of the century. That part of his autobiography which describes his English career and sheds light upon his relations with English contemporaries and upon other than Irish influences in his work and thought, closes with his account of the men of the aesthetic nineties in *The Tragic Generation*. A great change came over the scene with the deaths of Beardsley, Johnson and Dowson. The new gospel of action affected even those who had hated the Boer War and Kiplingese imperialism. Symons alone continued in the old tradition – 'like some last courtier at a gypsy camping-place'. As Yeats wrote many years later: 'Everybody got down off their stilts; henceforth nobody drank absinthe with his black coffee; nobody went mad; nobody committed suicide; nobody joined the Catholic Church of if they did I have forgotten.'

The correspondence contains allusions to new friendships formed and forming. Miss Horniman, John Masefield, William Rothenstein, Ricketts and Shannon are much in evidence. He says in his autobiography that a fanaticism for mythology delayed his friendship with Ricketts and Shannon, men 'in the great tradition', but now he saw them every three or four days. The two young artists, Pamela Coleman Smith and Althea Gyles (who designed his first bookplate), also find frequent mention in his letters. To Miss Horniman, his fellow Cabalist, he used to hand over cases of hard luck or of conscience that came to his notice. 'Miss Horniman', he writes to Lady Gregory on one such occasion, 'is taking care of B.'

She has left word that all bills are to be sent to her and will I think look after her until she gets well. ... My mystics will not bemoralise her, which her other friends seem to have been doing vigorously (especially Lady Colin Campbell) for their faith makes them look on everything in the world as so wrong that the conventional errors seem to them trivial and all defiances a little meritorious.

He goes on to tell of a Mr and Mrs C., a pair of sharks who infested occult waters.

A poor lady came to me yesterday in distress. They and their friends had planted themselves upon her and were running up bills in her name and she was in too great terror to send them away. I am not going to act in the matter myself, but my mystics are off to hunt them. The poor lady had been in some remote part of the world when the English reverses in Africa began. She explained to me yesterday with great naïveté, that she asked herself 'What could have caused them, how could the English be defeated unless by black art?' then suddenly she thought, 'It is MacGregor, MacGregor is doing it', and she came to England to get some mystics to stop him. In England she met the C.'s, fresh from rooking the terrible E. himself, and all went well until they told her that she was the woman clothed with the sun and that the world was not convex but concave with the sun in the middle – and then she doubted. She is a good soul and felt that the world might have what shape it liked but that she could not believe that St John had made all that fuss about her.

Then he writes of an encounter with Bernard Shaw at a Fellowship called 'The Three Kings'. 'He tells of a play on the contrast between Irish and English character which sounds amusing. ...'* I replied to a speech of his and pleased the Fellowship very much by proving that Shaw's point of view belonged to a bygone generation – to the scientific epoch – and was now reactionary! He has never been called "reactionary" before. I think I beat him. He was not in very good form however.'

There is a reference to a visit to Benson performances at Stratford-on-Avon (April 1901). He read from ten to six in the library of the Shakespeare Institute, spent his evenings at the theatre, where the historical plays were being given, and felt that he was getting 'deeper into the Shakespeare mystery than ever before'. It was his hope to rescue Shakespeare from the critics like Dowden, who saw in him an infallible judge of actions and a distributor of awards and of penalties. In his essay 'At Stratford-on-Avon' (*Ideas of Good and Evil*) he gave reason why Shakespeare should have preferred 'the sweet lovely Rose' to Henry V :

* *John Bull's Other Island.*

He saw indeed, as I think, in Richard II the defeat that awaits all, whether they be Artist or Saint, who find themselves where men ask of them a rough energy and have nothing to give but some contemplative virtue, whether lyrical phantasy, or sweetness of temper, or dreamy dignity, or love of God, or love of His creatures. He saw that such a man through sheer bewilderment and impatience can become as unjust or as violent as any common man, any Bolingbroke or Prince John, and yet remain 'that sweet lovely rose'.

'The more I read, the worse does the Shakespeare criticism become, and Dowden is about the climax of it.'

He laments the departure of Masefield for a post in the country: 'When he is gone I shall be gloomy enough.' Masefield was an even closer friend of W. B.'s brother Jack, whose love of the sea and delight in colourful character he shared. They were joint owners of a little fleet, a varied and original one, the story of which is told in a chapbook which they published together (*A Little Fleet*, London, 1909). Their first boat, *Moby Dick*, was 'supposed to be a Mississippi steamboat'. The *Theodore*, built out of a long cardboard box, had no masts ('we did not have time to make any for her'); as for the *Monte*, she had a stone tied underneath her to keep her upright and a piece of string tied amidships to keep on the stone. The *Monte* was unfortunate or ill-designed, for her keel sank her on her maiden voyage ('hit against oh! such a nasty rock!') that heaved her over until her stone keel was atop, and then the pirate poet wrote the elegy which echoes W. B.'s *Stolen Child* and begins:

> And now by Gara rushes
> When stars are blinking white
> And sleep has lulled the thrushes
> And sunset brings the night,
> There where the stones are gleamin'
> A passer-by can hark
> To the old drowned *Monte* sea-men
> A-singing through the dark.

2

The long illness of the poet's mother came to its close in January 1900, and two years later J. B. Yeats and his daughters gave up the house in Bedford Park and settled near Dublin. They took a house at Dundrum, near the headquarters of the Dun Emer Guild, lately established by Miss Evelyn Gleeson for the production of handwoven carpets, embroideries and hand-printed books. Miss Lily Yeats became the embroideress and her sister Elizabeth presided over the hand press, first called Dun Emer and then the Cuala Press, which in forty years has established a record unequalled in the history of hand presses by publishing over seventy books. The first book that Miss Yeats published contained her brother's Cuchulain play, *On Baile's Strand*, and the lyrics, not very many, which he had written since *The Wind among the Reeds*, and it bore the title *In the Seven Woods*.

In deciding to return to Dublin J. B. Y. may have been partly influenced by the fact that Lady Gregory's nephew, Hugh Lane, had begun to work and to plan for art in Ireland. W. B. first met Lane in 1901, when they were both fellow-guests of Lady Gregory. Lane was no lover of literature, and Yeats has recorded somewhere that his first impressions of the young picture-dealer, whom afterwards he was to exalt in verse, were unfavourable; the dislike was reciprocal. But before the year was out Lane had commissioned the elder Yeats to do a portrait of the poet for inclusion among a series of portraits of distinguished Irishmen which he proposed to present to Dublin.

Hugh Lane organized the exhibition of the paintings of J. B. Yeats and of Nathaniel Hone which was held in Dublin in 1901, under a note by George Moore, and it was after reading about this exhibition and about Jack Yeats's pictures that John Quinn, the most important of Irish-American patrons of Irish art and literature, made his first visit to Europe. The Yeatses were still in Bedford Park when Quinn arrived in London. 'He is', J. B. Y. wrote to his elder son, the nearest approach to an angel in my experience. He has bought ten of Jack's pictures and given me several commissions. He and Jack have been going about London together. Jack is just the man to guide a newly arrived American ... I was greatly delighted with him and to think he is a rising barrister! I introduced him to Miss Purser, who looked at him hungrily to paint him.

Quinn travelled to Ireland, and there attended a Gaelic ceremony at the tomb, newly erected by Lady Gregory, of the Connaught poet Raftery, where he first made the acquaintance of W. B. Yeats, Lady Gregory, Martyn and Douglas Hyde. Before leaving he commissioned J. B. Yeats to do a portrait of Hyde, promised to arrange for a lecture tour by W B. in the States, began his famous collection of Irish manuscripts and first editions, and in an overflow of energy and benevolence effected a partial reconciliation between George Moore and Yeats, who were at quarrel over another collaboration.

Yeats told Moore a fantastic plot for a play, suggested by stories about a Catholic mystic of George Russell's acquaintance, who had earned a reputation for craziness by adopting the gospel precepts as a guide to life. They discussed collaboration, but after throwing in his lot with the Fays, Yeats begged to be excused on the somewhat slender pretext that Moore was not a member of the National Theatre Society. Moore retorted by declaring that he would write a novel on 'the scenario we have composed together', and get an injunction against Yeats if he used it. Whereupon Yeats went to Coole, asked the assistance of Lady Gregory and of a friend, dictated straight off the five-act tragedy *Where there is Nothing*, and wrote to Russell, now Moore's intimate: 'Tell Moore to write his story and be hanged'.

Various accounts have been given of the episode, from which it would appear that both parties were at fault. Moore indeed never wrote a line of the novel, but Russell was helping him with a play; as Yeats was reputed a slow worker,

Russell and Moore felt sure of reaching the post first, and
were discomfited when Yeats suddenly published *Where
There is Nothing* in Griffith's *United Ireland*. All Moore
would say was: 'Has Yeats's hero got a brother?' 'Yes.'
'Then Yeats has stolen the spoons.' But the brother of Yeats's
hero was in a monastery, whereas Moore had proposed that
the hero's brother should be a man about town who seduced
a London housemaid. The play being an exaltation of
mystical nihilism, it could not be presented in Dublin for
religious reasons, and Yeats gave the script to the London
Stage Society, by whom it was produced in 1904, with
Thomas Hardy in the audience. Subsequently Yeats took a
dislike to the 'pacificist commonplace' of the principal
act, and with Lady Gregory's help transformed the five-act
prose tragedy into a folk play, *The Unicorn from the
Stars*.

From time to time after the partial reconciliation and
until Moore published the third volume of his Irish autobiography in 1914, Yeats used to meet Moore, but harmony
was never restored, and the sullen peace of a mutual distrust settled on the scene. Moore had served his purpose in
the Irish movement and could be cast aside. Thus commenced a duel which has made literature – is already a part
of English literature. 'I was young, vain, self-righteous,'
Yeats was to write in *Dramatis Personae*, his rejoinder to
Moore's autobiography, 'and bent on proving myself a man
of action.'

Yeats was changing. He now insisted on 'life' in a poet.
Byron, he said to H. W. Nevinson, though he wrote badly,
except in satire, was the last *man* who made poetry; and he
would quote the old Greek who said: 'I am a servant of the
Lord God of War and I know the lovely arts of the Muses'.
He found in some of his own early work – perhaps in *The
Rose* poems particularly – an 'unmanly' exaggeration of
sentiment and sentimental beauty, and he began to feel a
horror of the word 'Celtic', which the newspapers still continued to apply to his work. The collection of verses, *New*

Songs, the work of Padraic Colum, Seumas O'Sullivan, George Roberts and other young Irish poets, which George Russell edited, exasperated him because he was reminded by it of a weakness in himself. 'I have just been reading', he wrote to Russell when the book was published,

> some reviews of *New Songs*. Miss Gore-Booth's poem about the roads is charming and delights my conscience and I like the poem about the wise dead under grass and the strong gone over seas, but it leaves my conscience hungry. Some of the poems I will probably underrate (though I am certain I could recognise a masterpiece come out of any temperament) because the dominant mood is one I have fought in myself to put down. . . . This region of shadows is full of false images of the spirit and of the body. I have come to feel towards it as O'Grady feels towards it and even as some of my stupidest critics feel. As so often happens I am roused by it to a kind of frenzied hatred which is quite out of control. Beardsley exasperated some people in this way but he has never the form of decadence which tempted me, and so I am not unjust to him . . .

3

In his book of essays, *Ideas of Good and Evil*, published in 1903, Yeats still opposed the primitive to the popular, the subtleties and obscurities of ancient doctrine to the products of ratiocinating intellect, poetry as a craft with 'ancient technicalities' to poetry as a faithful mirror of manners and of life. Shelley's *Prometheus Unbound*, read lately again under Slieve Echtge, is treated not as a myth infused with modern thought, as Godwin's *Political Justice* put into verse, but as a poem, as a mysterious song setting its author beside Blake and other poets of mystic meanings, whose symbols are images transcending time and space and in a sense living souls. Poetry is regarded throughout the book as a positive truth and contrasted with the illusions of history and politics. It has 'descended a fatal stairway' since, with Goethe, Wordsworth and Browning in their various degrees, it has sought to affirm or define the meaning and value of human agitations. Yeats's culture was weak on the German and Italian sides, and he is inclined in *Ideas of Good and Evil* to announce as innovation commonplaces of European criticism. At this stage he was unacquainted with Vico's theory which he afterwards learned through Croce – that ancient wisdom is only due to a myth, to be supplanted in the course of history by prose and rational thinking – or with Vico's idea of recurring cycles which gives sanction to that opposition of primitive and popular posited in his essay 'What is "Popular Poetry"?'

One of the earliest essays in *Ideas of Good and Evil* was 'The Autumn of the Body' (1898), where Yeats wrote that

We are, it may be, at a crowning crisis of the world, at the moment when man is about to ascend, with the wealth he has been so long gathering, upon his shoulders, the stairway he has been descending from the first days. The first poets, if one may find their images in the *Kalevala*, had not Homer's pre-occupation with things, and he was not so full of their excitement as Virgil. ... Man has wooed and won the world and has fallen weary. ... The arts are, I believe, about to take upon their shoulders the burdens that have fallen from the shoulders of priests ...

Ideas of Good and Evil was, however, scarcely out before Yeats felt that he was about to leave the road on which he had been travelling with Mallarmé and Symons. Politics and men continually urged him on to new problems. He took them in his stride. Yet the eternal changing of things was the highest problem which confronted him always; and it would be a mistake to regard his phases as other than different manifestations of a single mind, more firm and assured than most. The great poet is indeed a child who is 'always remaking the world, not always in the same way, but always after his own heart'.

'I am no longer in sympathy', he wrote to Russell, 'with an essay like The Autumn of the Body, not that I think the essay untrue, but I think I mistook for a permanent phase of the world what was only a preparation. The close of the past century was full of a strange desire to get out of form.... I now feel an impulse to create form, to carry the realization of beauty as far as possible. ...' And to John Quinn: 'I have always felt that the soul has two movements primarily: one to transcend forms, and the other to create forms. Nietzsche, to whom you have been the first to introduce me, calls these the Dionysiac and the Apollonian respectively. I think I have to some extent got weary of the wild god Dionysus, and I am hoping that the Far-Darter will come in his place.'

He called Nietzsche 'that strong enchanter'; he had read him so much that his eyes were bad again, and had found a thought that 'runs but even in a more violent current in the bed Blake's thought has worn'. The influence was to declare itself in the lines given to the poet's pupils at the close of a new play, *The King's Threshold*:

> O silver trumpets, be you lifted up
> And cry to the great race that is to come.
> Long-throated swans upon the waves of time,
> Sing loudly, for beyond the wall of the world
> That race may hear our music and awake.

4

The resolve not to be content with repeating early triumphs was manifest in his new volume of verse *In the Seven Woods*, also of 1903, where, although he describes an intangible world, all is now seen in the daylight of clear thought without veiling twilight. His father singled out 'Baile and Aillinn' for especial praise:

It will delight your friends and baffle your enemies and turn them into friends. I should say it will at once become popular. It is so absolutely lucid and so *simple* – here I touch on an angry controversy; simple art is not for simple people but for deep revolving people. Yet great art is simple – It is where a great artist knows his own mind and says it, his words, how easy to read, how easy to remember – a child is attentive to their meaning and their charm – yet only here and there is there anyone to know the true sense.

He is still moved by opposing voices, and some lovely lines in 'Adam's Curse' seem to echo Baudelaire's 'Recueillement':

> We sat grown quiet at the name of love;
> We saw the last embers of daylight die,
> And in the trembling blue-green of the sky
> A moon, worn as if it had been a shell
> Washed by time's waters as they rose and fell
> About the stars and broke in days and years.

With 'Adam's Curse' Yeats began the series of poems in which he gave personal expression to early experience. They were love poems of a kind very different from those in *The Wind among the Reeds* to which his incapacity to take life easy had given a youthful nostalgic quality, as though he had learned from love only the impulse of escape. Now he is more pointed, epigrammatic and colloquial. The first, and perhaps the finest poem in the new 'middle-aged' group, was 'The Folly of being Comforted':

>   No,
> I have not a crumb of comfort, not a grain.
> Time can but make her beauty over again:
> Because of that great nobleness of hers
> The fire that stirs about her, when she stirs,
> Burns but more clearly. O she had not these ways
> When all the wild summer was in her gaze.
>
> O heart! O heart! if she'd but turn her head,
> You'd know the folly of being comforted.

Maud Gonne's marriage, which took place in Paris at about this time, hit Yeats very hard. Her choice fell upon a red-haired high-spirited Celt, John MacBride, who had led the Irish Brigade with the Boers and was now secretary of Laffan's Bureau in Paris at £2 a week. It was a patriotic wedding. Unquestionably MacBride was a gallant man, ready to risk his life in any fight against England, and no mere boaster. But he scarcely seemed suited to share the life of an unconventional and delicately nurtured woman. Yeats stood aghast, angry as well as very miserable, and Arthur Griffith, a great friend of MacBride's, and MacBride's relatives in Ireland also, were filled with dismay and misgivings when they heard of Maud Gonne's intention. 'I think of both your happiness', Griffith wrote to her; 'for your own sake and for the sake of Ireland to whom you both belong, don't get married.'

5

In May 1903 the Fays' company travelled to London where they played Yeats's morality, *The Hour-Glass*, his *Cathleen ni Houlihan*, and his *Pot of Broth*; with these were produced Lady Gregory's *Twenty-Five* and F. Ryan's *Laying the Foundations*. The visit to London was suggested and organized by Stephen Gwynn, who acted for the Irish Literary Society in the matter, and the Queen's Gate Hall was filled to its utmost capacity, the audience including A. B. Walkley and all London's foremost critics. Lady Gregory was unable to be present; Yeats wrote to her (4 May) from Woburn Buildings:

I have noticed that the young men, the men of my own generation, or younger, are the people who like us. It was a very distinguished audience. Blunt was there, but went away after your play as he is recovering from influenza. . . . Lady Aberdeen, Henry James, Michael Field – who has sent me an enthusiastic letter about the acting – Mrs Wyndham – the Chief Secretary's mother – Lord Monteagle, Mrs Thackeray Ritchie, and I don't know how many other notables were there, and all, I think, were moved. The evening audience was the more Irish and *Cathleen* and *The Pot of Broth* got a great reception. *The Foundations* went well, indeed everything went well.

Nevertheless it would appear that Yeats was not yet certain that he would succeed in realizing his Theatre of Beauty in Ireland, where finances must be extremely limited. In London he engaged with John Masefield, Gordon Bottomley and a few others in endeavours to establish the poetic drama as a working theatre form. The pioneers differed to some extent in method, but seemed to pursue ends similar enough to bring them together in the one movement. Yeats knew best what he wanted; and he received frequent invitations to speak, both in London and the provinces, on his poetic faith, practice and theory. Of all the rebels against the conventional theatre, with the possible exception of Gordon Craig, he was the most uncompromising. 'I think', he said in *Samhain* for 1903, 'the theatre must be reformed in its plays, its speaking, its acting and its scenery.' In notes for one of his English lectures he wrote:

We in Dublin are trying to do our part, and I want to talk to you about a theatre which some of us are trying to build up there. I have made a little model here of a stage where I have every reason to believe realism would be impossible (describe shape of theatre, reason of projecting platform, steps down toward audience, shallow stage, deep wings, etc., speak also of lighting). I then go on to describe the secularisation of the theatre caused by the fading of the sanctity of the legends it had once founded itself upon and from the daily life of man. These are two of the marks, shafts of death. The theatre becoming secular was on the high-road to become vulgar, to become merely amusing, to merely tickle the eye. Describe how in Ireland we have the remnants of the old sanctity of the land itself and so are seeing in the ordinary energies of life supernatural energies, are seeking to restore the ancient stage.

In acting he wanted to drive home a lesson already mastered by the French, namely, that of keeping the actors very quiet, often merely posing and speaking, as he had seen Fay's company do, with a curiously dream-like and gentle result, in Russell's *Deirdre*. Scenery might be no more than a curtain, or, at the most, a simple scene, indicating vaguely the picture in the poet's mind, and the cast should speak in such a way that their words would evoke the picture. In the case of lyrics they should be delivered in a certain pitched tone, so that the audience could hear every word and detect the metre without difficulty.

Sometimes he would preach his revolutionary doctrine, accompanied by Florence Farr; he would then take for subject the revival of the art of speaking verse to well-defined musical notes, and, beginning with Homer, continue through the centuries and the countries of the world with his tale of what he called Bardic poetry. When he had finished Miss Farr would recite selected pieces with strong rhythmical emphasis, intoning others and chanting a few to distinct musical phrases. The thrilling tones of her low voice when she rendered 'Impetuous Heart, be still, be still', and the way in which her voice melted into something light and unsubstantial when she reached 'the wandering moon', always left a lasting impression on the audiences. Arnold Dolmetsch writes:

The point was to find the 'time' to which the poet recited his own verse. I once spent a whole night listening to Yeats reciting, and I came to the conclusion that he did not recognise the inflexions of his own voice. In fact he had a short phrase of fairly indistinct tones which he employed to recite any of his poems. This did not interfere with the expression of his readings, which was very beautiful; but it was useless from my point of view. I then tried Florence Farr, whose golden voice harmonized perfectly with the notes of the instrument. I taught her to play. In my own room, with nobody but Yeats and myself present, it was delightful. But I got engagements for her in America, and it came out that in public she raised the pitch of her voice and was not capable of following it with the psaltery as I did myself. Result, the whole thing was discordant; she did not know it and it ended in failure. I never found a reciter with a sufficiently musical ear to *listen* to the instrument and make the voice and the instrument fit together. ... I had better results with Mrs Patrick Campbell, having tuned her psaltery to a vague drone which did not interfere much with her voice. ... The idea of reciting poetry to well-defined musical notes is sound; it may be revived some day given the right exponent. An experiment I made, the effect of which was most impressive, was with the 'Chorus' of *Samson Agonistes*, as performed under William Poel ...*

At a demonstration held in the now vanished Hall at Clifford's Inn Miss Farr guided the melodic line to the accompaniment of a psaltery made for the occasion by

* This note reached the biographer shortly before Arnold Dolmetsch's death.

Arnold Dolmetsch, and three out of the four poets present confessed to their total ignorance of music. Twenty-two pounds were collected at the door, and were added to the funds of a society called The Masquers, which was founded at a meeting held in Henrietta Street on 28 March 1903, with Walter Crane in the chair. This society proposed to give performances of 'plays, masques, ballets and ceremonies', with the object of bringing the stage back again to that beauty of appropriate simplicity in the presentation of a play which liberates the attention of an audience for the words of a writer and the movements of an actor. Translations of the classics and of contemporary foreign masterpieces were promised, as well as plays by Yeats, Robert Bridges, Laurence Irving and Douglas Hyde, and on the committee with Yeats were Symons, Gilbert Murray, T. Sturge Moore, Edith Craig and Pamela Coleman Smith. A few months later the society was dissolved in the circumstances set out by Gilbert Murray in a letter to Yeats:

You will hear with mixed feelings that the Masquers Society is no more! As you know, I have long been in favour of its decease, and some ten days ago Acton Bond (whom Miss Craig had put on the committee as an active theatrical person who could 'run' it) moved that the society should cease until such time as there might be a project of working with more success . . . *i.e.* principally when you and Symons and [Sturge] Moore and Miss Craig and himself should all be available for work. I promptly supported him, and told the committee that I had mentioned the point both to you and to Symons and that though I was not authorised to speak for you, I had had letters from you inclining in the direction of winding the society up. . . . We are returning subscriptions, and explaining that though we had enough money and members to justify us in starting, we found other circumstances unfavourable and thought the attempt at a 'Theatre of Beauty' should be postponed, though we still keep our faith in it. It is a great weight off my mind. We shall actually end our life without having swindled anybody, and I shall no longer shrink from the eye of a policeman. But what bad luck we have had, in the way of marriages and foreign travels . . .

6

The visit of the Irish players to London was repeated, and
with such success that the company was invited to form
a part in the Irish section of the International Exhibition at
St Louis. As nearly all the members held employments in
Dublin, the invitation had to be refused, but Dudley Digges,
who had played The Wise Man in *The Hour-Glass*, and one
or two others accepted. Digges, later a star at Hollywood,
was the only man then in the company who, from the point
of view of looks and stature, made a suitable impression in
heroic parts, so that with his departure the prospects of
Yeats's plays about 'Kings, helmets and swords, and half-
forgotten things' seemed to have suffered a serious blow, as
far as their production in Ireland went.

Miss Horniman now came forward as a bearer of gifts to
the Irish Theatre. She not only staged *The King's Threshold*
at her own expense, but she designed and made the costumes. The play was first performed on 7 October 1903,
Frank Fay being entrusted with the part of the poet who
brings the King to submission by fasting on the steps of the
palace. Neither suffragette nor patriot had yet (it is worthy
of remark) adopted the hunger strike nor had the hunger
strike, so far as Yeats knew, been used anywhere as a
political weapon.

Owing to his support of Synge, who was incapable of 'a
political thought',* Yeats had lost his confidence of Arthur

---

*This is a part of the legend which Yeats built about Synge. A
friend who knew Synge in Paris judged him 'intensely, though not
practically, national'. 'He couldn't endure the lies that gathered round
all political movements. . . . He gently loathed Maud Gonne for those
she launched or tolerated . . .' (vide *Memoir of Stephen MacKenna*, by
E. R. Dodds). Once he heard Maud Gonne speak in Paris to a French
audience on Queen Victoria's alleged complicity in the Irish Famine.
When she had finished his companion asked him in awestruck tones,
'*Est-ce-vrai?*' '*Je ne sais pas*,' Synge replied with a shrug of the
shoulders.

Griffith, and Maud Gonne had sided with his critics in the disputes on questions of theatrical organization. He set forth his views of the relation between art and propaganda in a significant passage of *Samhain,* an occasional publication in which he defended the work of the theatre during these years:

We have to write or find plays that will make the theatre a place of intellectual excitement – a place where the mind goes to be liberated, as it was liberated by the theatres of Greece and England and France at certain great moments of their history, and as it is liberated in Scandinavia today. If we are to do this we must learn that beauty and truth are always justified of themselves, and that their creation is a greater service to our country than writing that compromises either in the seeming service of a cause. We will doubtless come more easily to truth and beauty because we love some cause with all but all our heart; but we must remember when truth and beauty open their mouths to speak, that all other mouths should be as silent as Finn bade the son of Lugaidh be in the houses of the great. Truth and beauty judge and are above judgement. They justify and have no need of justification.

After one of the Dublin newspapers had printed a particularly vicious leading article on the Theatre, Yeats came before the curtain and appealed to the hundred people in the audience for 'life' against the desire which every political party has to substitute for life, which never does the same thing twice, a bundle of reliable principles and assertions. When he came down from the stage Miss Horniman, from whom he had been expecting a contribution of twenty pounds, said to him, 'I will give you a theatre'.

7

Miss Horniman's promise put Yeats in good spirits for the American lecture tour which had been arranged for him by John Quinn. He set out in November 1903, and was away from three to four months. He spoke before dozens of

societies, mostly Irish, and before more than thirty schools
and universities; he also penetrated into Canada. His hon-
orarium for college lectures was the modest one of $75, but
he returned with money in his purse, and his first thought
was to repay Lady Gregory, who had rendered him some
financial assistance at the time that she had persuaded him
to give up journalism. She said, 'Not until you have enough
to feel independent,' and it was only after his third American tour of 1914 that she would accept repayment of a debt
which then amounted to £500.

A selection of the poet's letters, chiefly to Lady Gregory,
may be used as a description of the tour:

16.11.03. *To Lady Gregory*

. . . I am now established at Quinn's. . . . I had a long struggle
with a woman reporter yesterday who wanted to print, and probably will, a number of indiscreet remarks of mine. Here is an
example. 'What do you think of Kipling?' 'I shall say nothing
whatever about Kipling if you please. I will say nothing about
any living poet. If he would have the goodness to die I would
have plenty to say. Good heavens, have you written that down?'
'Yes, it is the one Irish remark you have made.' 'You will please
rub it out again.' Thereon we had a struggle of ten minutes, and
in spite of her promise I expect to see printed in large black
letters 'Yeats desires Kipling's death.' I have sent an urgent
message demanding a proof. I had been painfully judicious for
days, as the reporters had been Irish and asked about Ireland,
but this woman asked about general literature and I was off my
guard . . .

I hear . . . that I am to lecture to the Pauline Fathers who say
they don't mind my heretical theology. I go to the Pacific coast
in January, a five-days journey . . .

The Deanery, Bryn Mawr

8.12.03. *To George Russell*

. . . This is the chief women's college in America, the one to
which the richer classes send their girls – I have just given my
second lecture. I write to tell you of my success. At first I did not
like my lecture at all. But last week I gave a lecture here which
was, I thought, the best that I have given. It was on the 'intellectual movement'. Last night I lectured again on heroic poetry

and there was not standing room in the house. Not only the girls were there but a number of people from the neighbourhood. . . . One of the professors told me that I was the most 'vital influence' that had come near the college 'for 15 years'. What has pleased me so much is getting this big audience by my own effort. . . . They are getting all our books here now. Do you know I have not met a single woman here who puts 'tin tacks in the soup'? and I find that the woman who does is recognised as an English type – One teacher explained to me the difference in this way: 'we prepare the girls to live their lives but in England they are making them all teachers.'

New York

18.12.03. *To Same*

Bryan has written to me as to selection from my poems in his proposed Irish Anthology. He asks me whether I or you are to make the selection. Now I have a very great objection to making a selection from my own poems. I don't think an author should authoritatively take out certain poems and give them a sort of special imprimatur. Besides I have another objection, I don't want to be connected with the advertising side of Mr ——'s book; he is a more enthusiastic advertiser than, I think, becomes my dignity. . . .

I am constantly lecturing and I think fairly well. I am just on my way to Canada, and go to the Pacific Coast in January. I bring your work into the greater number of my lectures. . . . When you write let me know how Colum's play has gone.*

2.1.04. *To Lady Gregory*

On Monday I go to St Louis, a long journey. . . . I will hardly be back in New York for another 3 weeks. . . . I lecture tonight somewhere in the neighbourhood of New York and tomorrow night in Carnegie Hall, my big lecture, the most important of the whole lot. . . .† I have been down practising my oratorical passages in the empty hall that I may not be put out if there are some empty benches. I got one compliment. I had just finished my peroration when I heard the clapping of hands in a dark corner. It was the Irish caretaker. You remember my old organ peroration, the one I wound up the speech with at the Horace

---

* *Broken Soil*, performed by the I.N.T.S. in December 1903.
† The subject was 'The Intellectual Revival in Ireland'.

Plunkett dinner? Well, there is a big organ on the platform at Carnegie Hall. I turn towards it meditatively and then, as if the thought suddenly struck me, speak that old peroration. It was this piece of extemporising that pleased the caretaker. I am working at this speech as I never worked at a speech before. . . . I have already dictated the whole speech once; indeed, I have already dictated some parts of it several times, and I am now going to go through it all again. Then I shall go down to the Hall and speak the whole lecture in the empty place. This is necessary, because I have found out that the larger the audience the more formal, rhythmical, oratorical must one's delivery be. My ordinary conversational happy-go-lucky, inspiration-of-the-moment kind of speaking gets all wrong when I get away from the small audiences I am accustomed to. Oratory does not exist, in any real sense, until one's got a crowd.

Chicago

18.1.04. *To Same*

I am on my way to a place called Indiana University and have just come from Notre Dame, a Catholic University, and before that I spoke here where I made a big success, and before that at an engineering University where I spoke my best and made a big failure – scientific students attentive and polite but like wet sand until I got to my poetry which they liked. I have been entirely delighted by the big merry priests of Notre Dame – all Irish and proud as Lucifer of their success in getting Jews and non-conformists to come to their college, and of the fact that they have no endowments. I did not succeed in my first lecture. I began of a sudden to think while I was lecturing that these Catholic students were so out of the world that my ideas must seem the thunder of a battle fought in some other star. The thought confused me and I spoke badly and so I asked if I might go to the literary classes and speak to the boys about poetry and read them some verses of my own. I did this both at Notre Dame and St Mary's, the girls' college near, and delighted them all. I gave four lectures in one day and sat up late telling ghost stories with the Fathers at night. . . . I think these big priests would be fair teachers, but I cannot think they would be more than that. They belong to an easy-going world that has passed away – more's the pity perhaps – but certainly I have been astonished at one thing, the general lack of religious prejudice I find on all sides here.

St Paul, Minn.

21.1.04. *To Miss Lily Yeats*

I am writing from St Paul where I am to lecture tonight,
dictating this to a stenographer in the office of one of the people
who have got up my lecture. I have been so busy running from
place to place that I have not had time to write. I am just about
beginning to think that when Stephenson invented the railway
he invented something that is very tedious and very disagreeable, I have just about enough of it. I had a charming time in
Chicago where I was entertained by a certain women's club,
lectured to it and also to another club – the Twentieth Century
Club. The lecture to this club was given in Mrs Pullman's house,
the widow of the man who made all the Pullman cars; and the
house was decorated right through in the style of a Pullman car.
One could see that the somewhat flamboyant woodwork of the
cars was an expression of his enthusiasm. I have seen a great
many charming places but I do not like the Pullman type. I
hear from Fay that Miss Quinn played 'Cathleen' at Dundrum
and that you have seen it. Write and tell me what kind of a
performance it was, addressing your letter care of John Quinn
of course . . .

In Pennsylvania I found Catholics going to school where the
Bible was read. One Bible reader, who was a Catholic, had given
one school nothing but the book of Proverbs for many years, as
he thought that quite safe. The man here who has most to do
with getting up my lecture, at any rate the man I have communicated with about it, knows Jack's name very well and asked a
lot of questions about him. I am growing a little tired of my
own voice and shall be glad when I am on the high seas. I am
keeping very well, however, not really feeling the fatigue of so
much travel at all.

San Francisco

31.1.04. *To Lady Gregory*

Yesterday Quinn wired asking if I could accept an engagement
for March 6th in New York to address Irish Societies on Emmet.
They offer very good terms, about £40. It means more than £40
for Quinn talks of two or three other lectures. . . . I wish I had
not to decide in a hurry. . . . The only thing to be said for this
new lecture is that with Toronto on the 14th and an inevitable
few days with Quinn I could hardly get away before end of
month. I shall be at least £70 the richer – but the boredom of

another month here my heart at home all the while – and I
have so much to tell you. I left St Paul last Friday, amid ice and
snow – 14 degrees below zero and the first thing I saw in the
railway station when I got here was a notice to say that for 11
dollars return people could take their children to see 'real ice
and snow'. Here there are palm trees and pepper trees and one
walks about without a coat. The bay is beautiful, all is beautiful.
I gave my first lecture here, at a university amid great trees,
great evergreens, in a huge gymnasium to some 2000 people. I
spoke on the theatre and didn't do well because I was hoarse and
a little deaf with a cold, and I gave my second to about 2000
people, Irish mostly, last night and did well I think.

8

During his absence Yeats was kept informed by his family
and friends of Irish affairs, such as the productions of *The
Shadowy Waters* and of Synge's tragic masterpiece *Riders
to the Sea*, and the discovery of a new 'peasant' dramatist in
Padraic Colum. His father wrote to him, 4 February 1904:

Lily is collecting all the criticisms that came out. You know
her magpie acquisitiveness. Your first speech when you come
back here will find us all on the lookout to see what novelties it
may display after your American experience. ... All the great
people, Sir Antony MacDonnell, Wyndhams, at once showed
themselves ready to sit – *because* as I knew at the time I was
your father. As time went on I discovered that they had a very
definite objection in contemplation – nothing less than to capture
you and the Irish National Theatre and to induce the latter to
play before the King when he arrives here next April – when it
gradually leaked out that was impossible, all interest subsided.
... It is doubtful whether Wyndham will ever sit. ... Lady
Grosvenor (Wyndham's wife) might sit, and she would make a
delightful subject – she is the warm summer sea into which that
shivering and over sensitive mortal her husband may dive. She
was in one day at the MacDonnells' and saw my portrait and
invited me over to tea to meet her husband. I was there about
two hours and there was a good deal of talk in which he pronounced cultivated opinions about you and Henley – he was
delighted to see you producing so much, having feared that you

would give yourself up to the producing merely of verse melodies ...

Some of the poet's friends had looked forward to the American trip with apprehension. They thought that he would be late for appointments, that he would fail to respond to the American warmth, and so on; Lady Gregory and John Quinn were alone in being entirely confident. 'Well,' said Quinn when the tour was over,

he got the chance, and made a great success. No Irishman since the time of Parnell's great trip here has made so grand an impression. . . . He was always on time and made the entire western tour alone and never missed a train, and did it all just as planned very successfully, Mrs Jack to the contrary notwithstanding. She felt he must have been so helpless. . . . I took care to assure her that he was always on time, and was eager and alert to do the correct and right things always.

Friends made for Irish literature by Yeats's tour included two famous men, William James and Theodore Roosevelt. 'His trip to Washington', Quinn wrote to Lady Gregory, 'was a pleasant experience.' Yeats found in Roosevelt the charm of men whose passions compel and illuminate their decisions. At Yale, where he was Professor Reed's guest, he made the remark, quoted and considered as perverse in London, that American humour differs from English in its good-nature; and he returned with glowing accounts of the intellectual alertness of American women. His most memorable aesthetic impression was Julia Marlowe's acting as Juliet, and he commemorated her art in a passage of a later poem: 'His Phoenix':

And there's a player in the States who gathers up her cloak
And flings herself out of the room when Juliet would be bride
With all a woman's passion, a child's imperious way,
And there are – but no matter if there are scores beside:
I knew a phoenix in my youth, so let them have their day.*

* Miss Marlowe was a friend of Arthur Symons, and of another of Yeats's friends, the Californian poetess Agnes Tobin, who often visited Ireland. There was a question a few years later of approaching her

As a rule the newspapers gave eulogistic accounts of a nimble and energetic intellect and an eagerness in controversy which surprised them in a mystic, a symbolist, a believer in fairies. In tête-à-tête conversation Yeats always gave of his best, rarely allowing an otiose remark to pass his lips; and this consideration sprang no less from an inborn courtesy than from a sense of his own dignity and what was due to others. Though sometimes pontifical, he saw the humorous side of things and of an adversary, and would press home an argument with gleeful nodding of the head and rubbing of his clasped hands. Looking over the press cuttings of the tour, one finds here and there a reference to absent-mindedness: 'Who met you at the station?' he was asked when he came back from Palo Alto to San Francisco. 'I don't know.' 'Where did you lunch?' 'The man who met me took me over to his house for lunch.' 'Did you meet Dr Jordan?' 'I don't know.' The man who met him at the station and with whom he lunched, was none other than the great Jordan himself. Yeats's air of boredom at some reception for men only in California was attributed by an acute reporter to the fact that 'Mr Yeats cares nothing at all for men but a great deal for women'.

The Irish-Americans were as yet undisturbed by the political misunderstanding that hampered Yeats's work in Ireland. They welcomed him as a patriot without stain; and, shortly before he sailed for home, he was offered a substantial sum for a lecture upon Emmet at a great rally of the Clan-na-Gael in New York. He was reluctant to mount a purely political platform, but he passed through the ordeal triumphantly. His speech was something of a sword dance, for he avoided questions of the day as far as possible, and left others to supply the political rant and proclaim Irish

with a view to her playing in *Deirdre*. 'Her Juliet has that look', Miss Tobin wrote to the poet, 'of being entirely consumed by *innocent* passion, that luminous pallor which is so touching. Sothern is very fine also and charming in voice and appearance.'

friendship for Russia.* He characterized the growth of the
Gaelic League as the most significant event in contemporary
Ireland, more important than anything the politicians could
accomplish, and made his audience quite happy by a description of a Kingdom of the Gael not entirely of this world.

A word may be here said of Yeats as a public speaker. He
had the powerful lower lip which reveals the born orator
and the born pugilist; a certain disdain, a certain pugnacity,
is necessary both to the pugilist and the orator. In addressing
large audiences he was sometimes uneasy at the start, and
would then stride up and down the platform in a rather surprising manner before he attained to his natural distinction
of bearing, his gravity of utterance and his rhythm. His
voice was musical, touched with melancholy, the tones
rising and falling in a continuous flow of sound. He lingered
on certain words to avoid as it were a hiatus, but the pauses
when they occurred were timed and still full of sound, like
the musical pauses in the execution of a master. This
cadenced utterance was most characteristic. When emphasis
was needed he would introduce a hard metallic note, and
this when passion intruded was like the clash of sword-
blades. His myopic gaze as he spoke was turned within, looking into the darkness, where, as he himself said, 'there is
always something'. He seemed indeed to be discoursing with
himself rather than to be persuading others, as his Miltonic
periods flowed in unbroken rhythm. There is a famous
utterance of Milton which always brings Yeats to mind as
an orator: 'A good book is the precious life-blood of a
master-spirit, embalmed and treasured up on purpose to a
life beyond life'. 'To a life beyond life' – in that lofty strain
is the very essence of Yeats at his peak. For so he was wont
to handle the great themes which were his constant preoccupation – his vision and renewal of the past – for his
thought was always spiritual rather than personal, national
in the highest sense, and among his countrymen he always
assumed the voice and air of leadership.

* The Dogger Bank incident had strained Anglo-Russian relations.

9

The Abbey Theatre

Miss Horniman – Opening of the Abbey Theatre; political and other disputes – Maud Gonne's troubles – *Deirdre* and the English actress – Production of *Deirdre*

━━━━━

All things can tempt me from this craft of verse . . .

I

ON Yeats's return from America Miss Horniman fulfilled her promise to provide the National Theatre Society with a small theatre to be at the Company's disposal. In a formal letter she explained that her gift was due to her great sympathy with Yeats's artistic and dramatic aims, as publicly explained by him on various occasions. 'I can only afford', she wrote, 'to make a very little theatre, and it must be quite simple, you all must do the rest to make a powerful and prosperous theatre with a high artistic ideal.' Before the Theatre was opened, however, she already asked herself whether she had not made a mistake in befriending an Irish movement. There seems to have been no one in Dublin who pleased her, except Yeats himself, her 'Demon',* and it was evident that even he paid far more deference to Lady Gregory's views than to hers. The mischief commenced, perhaps, when her designs for the costumes in *The King's Threshold* failed to meet with appreciation.† Henceforth Yeats had to listen to continual complaints about the

---

* Her letters to him start 'My dear Demon', his to her, 'My dear Annie'. His device in the Cabalistic Society was: *Daemon est deus inversus*.

† Lennox Robinson, after rummaging through the Abbey wardrobe, says they were 'incredibly graceless and ugly'.

manners of the town. George Moore uttered some unkind witticism at her expense, and she was much hurt when Yeats repeated it to her and astounded when George Russell expected her to meet Moore as if nothing had happened. Lady Gregory was polite, even gracious, but it was obvious that she disliked being under obligation to a middle-class Englishwoman for the production of her plays. Then there was the question of politics. Miss Horniman said that if the French were really to land in the West of Ireland, it would make no difference to her, except that she would buy two evening papers instead of one. Nevertheless, as soon as it was announced that there would be no sixpenny seats at the Abbey, Arthur Griffith and Maud Gonne began to treat her as a suspicious political character.

Her portrait, painted by J. B. Yeats in 1903 or thereabouts, shows a thin middle-aged woman of the aesthetic type, with delicate features and beautiful hands. Generous, eccentric and outspoken, incapable of intrigue and quick to take offence; the Tarot cards, which she consulted for propitious aspects before every enterprise, should have warned her at a first glance to keep away from Ireland.

She bought the lease of the old Mechanics' Institute in Abbey Street and reconstructed the building, a part of which had been latterly used as a morgue. In August 1904 Yeats, having come up from Coole to watch the work, reported to Lady Gregory that some human bones had been discovered in one of the proposed dressing-rooms. The workmen thought they had lit upon one murder at least but the caretaker said, 'Oh, I remember we lost a body about seven years ago. When the time for the inquest came it couldn't be found.' By November the theatre was ready for the rehearsals. 'It goes magnificently,' Yeats wrote of his Cuchulain play *On Baile's Strand*,

and the end is particularly impressive. When I got here I found that Frank Fay seemed to have a curious incapacity to understand the part. It now promises to be his finest part. ... I am waiting for Jack's designs for Synge's play. ... They should come

today or tomorrow. Failing this I shall get Pixie Smith, who
alone seems to understand what I want. ... I am extremely
anxious, now that I am here and for the moment at any rate
master of the situation, to get designs of a decorative kind,
which will set a standard.

2

Indignation rose when Yeats refused to yield in the matter
of the sixpenny seats, and Maud Gonne (now Madame
MacBride) came to him to say that in the opinion of the
Sinn Fein clubs he was 'lost to nationalism'. But on the day
of the opening the 'stars were quiet and fairly favourable',
and during the week the curiosity of all sections of the population filled the theatre. The play about Cuchulain and his
son went well. It was richer in the speech of the dramatist
than anything which Yeats had yet written, and he had
learned a great deal about stage-craft since he had been at
George Moore's mercy during the rehearsals of *The Countess Cathleen.** An innovation was the use of characters –
Fool and Blind Man – to describe a traditional story not
known to all the audience, and some minor experiments
were made, with the help of Robert Gregory, in modern
staging.

His father wrote to him :

I cannot tell you how much I enjoyed your play. As I lay
awake most of the night I had plenty of time to think about it.
The scene between father and son over the duel was the most
thrilling and enthralling experience I ever went through. You
touched at the same moment the fountain of joy and tears.

But I maintain that the end won't do – it is not true to nature
to suppose that the fool would not have had thoughts of dinner
driven out of his head by such a sight as a great knight gone mad

* To qualify himself as a man of the theatre he had even thought in
the previous year of finding employment as an actor in London under
an assumed name. When he was quite a young man Forbes-Robertson
had promised him a place in his company at any time that he cared
to join it.

and confronting himself with his own fury. Nor do I quite like
the hero's coming on after the fight 'in good spirits' as you say.
There would have been something more than this – as it stands
it rather suggests that the father killed the son as you would a
chicken –

I wondered that no one applauded at the end of that great
scene. But it is written – Where one or two Dublin men are
gathered together there shall I be amongst them, saith the
critic –

Two months later Synge's *Well of the Saints* was produced. It was likened by Arthur Griffith to a story in Pet-
ronius, and declared by George Moore to be a 'great play,
more remarkable than any original play produced in
England during our time'.

15.2.05. *To John Quinn*

We had rather thin audiences for Synge's play but they were
always sufficient to play to and make expenses and a little more.
Our first production left us £90 after we had paid expenses.
Synge's play left us £30. ... The audiences always seemed
friendly, but the general atmosphere has for all that been one
of intense hostility. Irish national literature, though it has produced many fine ballads and many novels written in the objective
spirit of a ballad, has never produced an artistic personality in
the modern sense of the word. Tom Moore was merely an incar-
nate social ambition. And Clarence Mangan differed merely
from the impersonal ballad writers in being miserable. ... We
will have a hard fight before we get the right of every man to see
the world in his own way admitted. Synge is invaluable to us
because he has that kind of intense narrow personality which
necessarily raises the whole issue. ...

Miss Horniman has undertaken to make the arrangements for
our London expedition this year. ... Synge is pretty sure of a big
success in London. We are to follow *Kincora* with a revival of
The King's Threshold (partly re-written), and a new play by
Boyle. We shall probably follow these a month later with Colum's
three-act play. He read me an act last Sunday; really very good;
simple and coherent and with a curious dialect. Unlike Synge's
and Lady Gregory's, his is the dialect of a non-Irish-speaking
district.

To its usual London visit the company added in 1905 excursions to Oxford and Cambridge. Yeats travelled with the players, and his appearance at Cambridge is recalled in the following letter, written by the late Professor N. Wedd to Mrs Llewelyn Davies at the time of the poet's death.

I met Yeats once, years ago, when he brought the Irish players to Cambridge. Evelyn Whitehead had me to lunch to meet them; but he was then in a sort of trance and found it hard to open his eyes or his mouth. I don't believe he ate or spoke; his followers, a dear simple crowd of hero-worshippers rather nervous at being in such a foreign land, looked and watched for their leader to speak some words of power; but the oracle was dumb. At night, Evelyn told me, he came out of his trance, and it was then the turn of the others to be entranced, for his talk held them all spell-bound. But I was unable to be there. When Goldie Dickinson (G. L. Dickinson), George Trevelyan and I helped to run the *Independent Review* (in which Crompton and Theodore helped us at every turn), Yeats sent us a poem on a scrap of paper, a charming song which haunts me still, but our editor – a lawyer, Edward Jenks – lost it!

At the start of the Abbey Theatre the work was its own reward. Both players and playwrights gave their time for nothing. Nevertheless Miss Horniman found that the first year was likely to cost her £4000, counting the purchase of the lease, the reconstruction of buildings and the expenses of the visit to England. She was prepared to live, and did live, very simply, that she might help art, but she was not a woman of great wealth. Therefore to put the enterprise on a business-like basis, it was decided to turn the National Theatre Society into a limited company, with Yeats, Lady Gregory and Synge as directors. 'I think', Yeats wrote to Quinn in September, 'we have seen the end of democracy in the theatre, which was Russell's doing, for I go to Dublin at the end of the week to preside at a meeting summoned to abolish it. If all goes well, Synge, Lady Gregory and I will have everything in our hands . . .'

Some of the players resented the change, which was not

easy to effect. Yeats denounced this 'old vague fluctuating incoherent Dublin', and declared that the new management would not be trifled with. He threatened one actress with an action for breach of contract. He would only ask, he said, for nominal damages, but it was necessary to show that the fundamental fact of all business was contract. The actress was young and pretty, and J. B. Y. intervened on her behalf. Might it not be better to have a horoscope cast by George Pollexfen before proceeding to the law courts? Apparently Yeats agreed to the suggestion, for there is a letter extant in which J. B. Y. describes a visit to the girl's mother, from whom he learned that Miss X. had been born when the Angelus was ringing – 'and that, I believe, is twelve o'clock'.

In the course of these troubles the poet raised yet more enemies. He had always kept a distance between himself and a small sect of hero-worshippers and now he used language which cut deeply. 'So-and-so should go back to his office-stool', he would say, and so on. George Russell's 'canary birds', as he called them, might have accepted his aesthetic doctrines but they represented in his mind that 'vague' Dublin to which in his present mood he refused to make the smallest concession, and he declined to seek their support against the political opposition. Synge would never have knit the issue, and Yeats and Lady Gregory stood very much alone at this time. Even J. B. Y. – no great admirer of Russell's – criticized his son not so much for anything that he said, or did, as for the theory upon which he was acting:

I hope you won't think your parent altogether too tedious but when I said a poet must be a man,* I didn't mean anything that the English philistine means, only that all poetry is woven out of humanity, and for this purpose Lamb or Goldsmith are better material than the masterful Dr Johnson, though he also was a man. The English admiration for strong will, etc. is really part of the gospel of materialism and money-making and Empire-building. ... You would be a *philosophe* and you are really a poet. The men whom Nietzsche's theory fits are only great men

* A statement provoked by the consideration of Swinburne.

of a sort, a sort of Yahoo greatness. The struggle is how to get rid of them. It is a few men like Paget and York Powell and Oliver Elton that prevent the Almighty from destroying England. You are haunted by the Goethe idea, interpreted by Dowden, that a man must be a complete man. It is a chimera, a man can only be a specialist.

A letter of violent reproach reached him from Russell:

What I think is wrong about your way of getting a movement to work is that all movements need volunteer aid. You cannot afford to pay everyone, and when you talk about 'singing canaries' and 'poultry farms' it all comes back to the people for whom it was intended, and with very rigid exaggerations . . . you are committing the great mistake about Ireland, 'the twenty years of resolute government' theory. Irish people will only be held by their affections. . . . You spoke once to me of two courts of appeal, the 'popular' and the 'intellectual'. Neither one nor the other have awarded you any other position than as a writer of beautiful verse, and I think it a mistake which later on you may regret that you should lose time managing a business, bringing endless annoyance with no added influence. As a poet you could and would exercise an immense influence on your contemporaries, as a dramatist you lose influence. The few dozen people who come to the Abbey Theatre are a poor compensation for the thousands who would read another *Wind among the Reeds* or another *Usheen* . . .

It was well that Yeats acted regardless of any criticism he might arouse, to judge from what happened to rival literary theatres – one was Edward Martyn's – which were run upon the easy-going lines advocated by the kindly Russell. There were secessions from the original Fay company, offset, however, by the discovery of a great comedian in Arthur Sinclair and of the two gifted sisters, Sarah Allgood and Maire O'Neill. 'I have gathered the strong and capable about me,' Yeats announced to Russell, 'and all who love work better than idle talk will support me. It is a long fight, but that is the sport of it.'

3

In the meantime his attitude towards the patriot party was
further embittered by considerations of a personal nature
arising out of Maud Gonne's affairs. She apprised him early
in 1905 that she was about to seek a separation from her
husband. He saw her at once, and was deeply moved by the
story she had to tell. 'You must keep out of this,' she said;
'I brought this trouble on myself, and must fight it alone.'
'Dear friend', he wrote to Lady Gregory from Paris, 'I turn
to you in every trouble. I cannot bear the burden of this
terrible case alone – I know nothing about lawyers and so
on. When you know the story you will feel that if she were
the uttermost stranger, or one's bitterest enemy, one would
have, even to the putting aside of all else, to help her. ...'
The judicial separation which Maud Gonne sought was
opposed and months of anxiety followed. MacBride had his
partisans in Dublin, in spite of the fact that a letter justify-
ing his wife's action was circulated by her French confessor
among the bishops and priests of Ireland. O'Leary, who
indeed was now rather feeble and wandering in his mind,
said: 'John has his weaknesses but I know him to be a *good*
man'; and when Maud Gonne appeared at a première at the
Abbey, a few people in the pit, MacBride's partisans, hissed
mildly. Yeats was enraged. He felt that never again could
he touch popular politics; he recalled his indignation in a
later poem where he makes his 'Phoenix' say

> The drunkards, pilferers of public funds,
> All the dishonest crowd I had driven away,
> When my luck changed and they dared meet my face,
> Crawled from obscurity, and set upon me
> Those I had served and some that I had fed ...

Some have said of Yeats that he had a cold heart and a warm
brain, but the agonies which he suffered at this time dis-
prove the specious characterization. Nor had he an ulterior
motive in assisting Maud Gonne, as there was no question

of her being enabled to marry again. After she had secured the decree she partially withdrew from Irish politics and devoted herself to the upbringing of her son and an adopted niece. Her opinions remained unchanged. In her frank demand for art as propaganda she was far more honest and innocuous than Yeats's critics of the school of Arthur Griffith. Miss Horniman, however, regarded her as a public danger, and never ceased to fear that Yeats would desert his principles in order to regain her approval. 'The greatest poet', she once warned the poet, 'is always helpless beside a beautiful woman screaming from a cart.' Maud Gonne was deeply grateful to Yeats for his assistance and sympathy during a tragic crisis, but she continued to reproach him for having forsaken Ireland, for she was utterly unable to perceive that the theatre could not become an organ of the expression of a people's consciousness merely by dramatizing political tracts. All she was sure of was that Yeats would never write another *Cathleen ni Houlihan*.

> My darling cannot understand
> What I have done, and what would do,
> In this blind bitter land.

4

So central was Yeats's preoccupation with the small unpopular theatre that for many years he wrote little poetry and no prose that did not arise out of its needs or out of events connected with it directly or indirectly.

In 1906 A. H. Bullen reprinted the little collection *In the Seven Woods* in a volume entitled *Poems*, which also contained the three plays, *The Shadowy Waters*, *The King's Threshold* and *On Baile's Strand*, and the two beautiful musicians' songs from a new play, *Deirdre*. As an appreciation of Yeats's poetry in early middle-age a passage from T. Sturge Moore's correspondence with him may be quoted.

I must write to thank you for your *Poems* which has given me far more pleasure than any of your other books. 'The Folly of

Being Comforted', 'Never Give all the Heart' are the best of their kind ever written, and I am deeply in love with 'Baile and Aillinn'. The tone of voice is exquisite and the rhythm and rhyme exquisitely suited to it. I could only make one tiny criticism, that is, I wish you could invent something a little more worthy than your 'Orchard' to come before your 'Glass Boat' on page sixty. I think 'fruit of precious stone' and 'apples of the sun and moon' the most loathsome upholstery that was ever invented to cushion poetry with, and would prefer plain wood. But those four lines in the poem are the only ones that are not intoxicating.

Of *Deirdre*, which was published in a separate volume, Sturge Moore wrote:

It is very beautiful and very original; the verse in its very texture is quite an invention of your own, and the construction admirable, though I think the mood one of the most difficult to present dramatically. How I should like to see it adequately rendered! I think it would produce the effect of a religious mystery by the perfection of its seclusion from the world and the rare distinction of its self-decreed limitations. 'I never heard a death so out of reach Of common hearts' is exquisite ... of course the song 'Love is an Immoderate Thing' is one of your best. You have made your new note perfectly clear and it delights me far more than the most sounding rhetoric run in the old moulds can do.

The chief event during the year at the Abbey was to be the production of Yeats's play on the legend which had already exercised a spell on the imagination of so many poets. He felt that he lacked an emotional actress who could adequately fill the principal part, grown more complex than he had at first expected it would be. Being slow to recognize the lyrical and subtle genius of Maire O'Neill, he gave more hours than he could afford to the search for a London-trained actress for his 'Deirdre'. He told his father that he was inclined to think that he had discovered the finest tragedienne on the English stage in Miss Darragh:

A new school of acting is growing up under the influence of the various attempts to create an intellectual drama and of changes deeper than that. The new school seizes upon what is distinguished, solitary, proud even. One always got a little of this in Mrs Emery when she was good, and one gets a great deal of it in Miss Darvagh. Both miss their climaxes as yet, for they are the reaction and the old school missed everything else at least in tragedy. Besides they are interested, the best of them anyway, in building up character bit by bit.

The summer went by quickly; the players made an extensive tour in the North of England and in Scotland; Miss Horniman and Yeats accompanied it for a part of the time, then Synge took charge. There was again a great deal of unrest in the company. Discipline became dangerously loose during the tour, especially when Synge, whose harsh imagination as a writer belied his soft heart, was in control. At Glasgow, an understudy, deputed to sell the book of the play, appeared in the lobby in a low-cut dress borrowed from a chorus girl, and asked an extra sixpence for her own autograph. One never knew, Yeats admitted, what 'those convent-bred young women would be up to next'. Miss Horniman's complaints of indiscipline were recorded in one of those terrible letters on yellow paper which made Synge say that he hated daffodils; she suggested that a new stage manager should replace W. G. Fay. Yeats was inclined to consent to her demand, but his persuasion of Lady Gregory was a process of considerable delicacy, as he knew that she knew that Miss Horniman was her persistent critic. Moreover, Lady Gregory's affections went out to the young people to whose original talents her comedies owed so much of their success. Synge was on the same side. He disapproved of Yeats's effort to find a professional actress for the part of Deirdre and said that he 'would rather go on trying out people for ten years than bring in this ready-made style of acting that is so likely to destroy the sort of distinction everyone recognises in our company'. 'Lady Gregory and Synge,' Miss Horniman had written to Yeats, 'grovel at Fay's feet. They sacrifice your work and keep you an abject slave to them. They only care to show themselves off to a small

set in Dublin *at my expense*. Try to put yourself in the place
of some decent person who cares for the drama and does not
care a rap for hole-and-corner Irish ideas.'

5

As Miss Horniman was prepared to offer the Abbey a subsidy of £800 a year up to the time of the expiry of the patent,
a period of several years, Lady Gregory wrote W. G. Fay a
diplomatic letter by which he was persuaded to agree to the
proposed reduction of his powers 'pending the good time
when we shall be independent'. At the same time Miss
Horniman made a rash promise to the Directors, 'since that
is what you wish', not to interfere in the future beyond
remembering the dates of the subsidy and seeing to the
condition of the building, which was her property.

Yeats's *Deirdre* was played first at the Abbey Theatre on
26 November 1906. With Miss Darragh in the principal part
and Frank Fay as Naoise, the heroic kingly youth, with
'voice melodious as the sound of the waves', who carries
away the foundling child from the house of King Conchu-
bar, it roused greater interest among the general theatre-
going public in Dublin than any of Yeats's verse plays since
The Countess Cathleen; partly because the characters were
more individualized than was usual in his tragedies,* and
partly because of the introduction of the London actress
whose rendering of the emotion left nothing to the imagination. In 1907 and in 1908 the part was taken by Mrs Patrick
Campbell and, until the beautiful performance by Maire
O'Neill some years later, it seemed as if Yeats was for once
influenced by the prevailing fashion of problem plays, his
contrasts the usual contrasts out of which problem plays are
woven – the struggle between man and the social constitution of his time, the pangs of a new morality evolving out of
an old one:

* His theory was that character is continually present in comedy
alone; *vide* 'The Tragic Theatre'.

> One woman and two men : that is a quarrel
> That knows no mending.

His difference lies in the elemental quality of the contrasts in the fact that they are not problems but mysteries. They are seen as an argument of poetry, not as an excuse for vain dialogizing and discussing. No victory, no defeat – there is no solution.

Deirdre was the last of Yeats's short poetical plays in the grand traditional manner. No doubt, with it and with *On Baile's Strand* and *The Countess Cathleen* he had written the best plays of his time; but no one was ever quite certain how pleased he was with these works, their performances and their receptions. It has been suggested by so good a critic as John Eglinton that, having dreamed of an Irish theatre, almost religious in character, to which his own contribution was to be the dramatic presentation of Cuchulain, he had now renounced the great ambition of his life.

The beautiful lines which drifted down to us, weighted with poetic imagery, the blank verse which rose out of the babble of the meaner personages, made one think of the Shakespearean rather than of any new drama. The heroic element seemed a little crest-fallen on the Abbey stage, and the Irish heroes impersonated by actors who had gained their renown in peasant parts, gave one the feeling that they had fallen on very evil times . . .

To be sure, Yeats owed much to his Irish theatre, not only to the players but, as he has reminded us, to 'a pit with an ear for verse' and to Synge and Lady Gregory because they drove home the lesson that the strength of poetic language is common idiom. But the Abbey Theatre was never to him, as it was to others, an essential means to fame and achievement, and the time he gave to its battles, even after it had obviously ceased to go his way, is a remarkable example of self-forgetfulness.

Plays and controversies

———

They must to keep their certainty accuse
All that are different of a base intent;
Pull down established honour; hawk for news
Whatever their loose phantasy invent
And murmur it with bated breath, as though
The abounding gutter had been Helicon
Or calumny a song. How can they know
Truth flourishes where the student's lamp has shone,
And there alone, that have no solitude?
So the crowd come they care not what may come.
They have loud music, hope every day renewed
And heartier loves; that lamp is from the tomb.

I

A YOUNG man arrives at a little public-house and tells the publican's daughter that he has murdered his father. He so tells the story that he wins all her sympathy, and every time he retells it, with fresh exaggerations and additions, he wins the sympathy of somebody or other, for it is the country-man's habit to be against the law. The countryman thinks the greater the crime the greater the provocation must have been. The young man himself, under the excitement of his own story, becomes gay, energetic and lucky. He prospers in love, comes in first at the local races and bankrupts the roulette tables afterwards. Then the father arrives with his head bandaged but very lively, and the people turn upon the impostor. To recover their esteem he takes up a spade to kill his father in earnest, but horrified by the threat of what had sounded so well in the story, they bind him to hand over to the police. The father releases him and father and son walk off together, the son, still buoyed up by his imagination, announcing that he will be master henceforth.

Such in bare outline was Synge's play produced at the Abbey Theatre on 26 January 1907, and followed by a week of rioting. Lady Gregory telegraphed after the first night to Yeats, who was lecturing in Scotland: 'Audience broke up in disorder at the word *shift*'. 'I would never have used such a word [as shift] myself', an employee of the theatre was heard saying a day or two later to the stage carpenter, 'Isn't Mr Synge the bloody old snot to write such a play?' There was a certain spontaneity in the first outburst of protest; on subsequent nights men were sent from political clubs for the express purpose of making the play inaudible. Synge sat it through with white face and left Lady Gregory to make the decisions. It was she who called in the police and asked a nephew to bring some friends from Trinity College to support the performance. The Trinity boys unfortunately intensified the animosity of the pit by singing 'God save the King', thereby encouraging the political aspect of the disturbances, while antagonizing the players who were prepared to defend the play from the *literary* point of view, but not as a Unionist demonstration. 'I am informed', Miss Horniman wrote a few days later, 'that low behaviour (I mean hissing) took place from the stage, and that the hissing was political. It must be absolutely understood that I will not allow my theatre to be used for any political purpose whatever, and the players must be informed that hissing the drunken vulgarity of the stalls is just as bad as the patriotic vulgarity of the pit.'

Back in Dublin, Yeats spoke in a tone of authority. He announced that neither the house nor the race that bred him had given him a pliant knee, and he was not going to

bend before the populace. Then he threw open the theatre
for a discussion of the play. The author stayed at home, and
Yeats's chief support upon the platform was his father.*
What followed may best be given in the words of an eye-
witness, Mary Colum, who sat in a group of ten or twelve
girl students, accustomed to worship the poet and follow him
from place to place:

A motley mixture of workmen, students and bourgeoisie in
evening dress filled the theatre, most of them with denunciatory
speeches ready to deliver. Yeats took the platform in full evening
dress and faced the crowd. Step by step he interpreted the play,
delivering in the process some of his most complex theories of
art, one moment cowing the audience, the next shouted down by
them. ... Even on the patriotics Yeats was equal to them. 'The
author of *Cathleen ni Houlihan* addresses you,' he said. The
audience, remembering that passionately patriotic play, forgot
its antagonism for a few moments and Yeats got his cheers. At
one moment a student supporter of his took the platform beside
Yeats and made a remark which caused nearly all of the few
women in the audience to walk out. Myself and another girl
student were the only members of the female sex in sight: we
were surrounded by a group of angry males ordering us, if we
were virtuous girls, to leave the theatre. We stood our ground,
and Yeats, who, in spite of his well-publicised dimness of vision,
could always see when it suited him, saw our difficulties from
the platform and sent a couple of theatre attendants to escort us
to the stalls among the men in evening dress, who, however, did
not regard us with a friendly eye either. I never witnessed a
human being fight as Yeats fought that night, nor knew another
with so many weapons in his armory.

Yeats had been preparing for some time for a clash with the
little clubs, and with Arthur Griffith, their Sinn Fein men-
tor. Synge gave him difficult ground to fight on, for distaste
of *The Playboy* was not confined to Griffith's party; Lady

---

* *Vide* 'Beautiful Lofty Things' in *Last Poems*:
'My father upon the Abbey stage, before him a raging crowd:
"This Land of Saints", and then as the applause died out,
"Of plaster Saints"; his beautiful mischievous head thrown back.'

Gregory herself had no great love for it, and a politician of note, John Dillon, who constantly went to the theatre, urged Yeats not to risk all for the sake of so unpopular a talent. The whole Nationalist press was hostile. Yet only a few can have been stupid enough to think that Synge wanted to hold up the West of Ireland people – among whom, as he expressed it, he had escaped from the nullity of the rich and the squalor of the poor – to ridicule and contempt for some propagandist Unionist purpose. The masterpiece of style and music was rather his tribute to their sense of life. The play, if it mocked at all, mocked at the smooth rhetoricians whose profession it was to make the virtues of the Irish peasant canonical. Yeats wrote to Quinn that 'the objection to Synge is not mainly that he makes the country people unpleasant and immoral, but that he has got a standard of morals and intellect. They never minded Boyle, whose people are a sordid lot ... but they shrink from Synge's harsh, heroical, clean, wind-swept view of things.'

2

Now came a change of scene and rest from controversy. In April 1907 Yeats joined Lady Gregory and her son at Venice for a few weeks' tour of Northern Italy. They visited Florence, Milan, Urbino, Ferrara and Ravenna, and Yeats enjoyed himself in leisurely tourist fashion, making his peace with the Renaissance, which hitherto he had distrusted as the period when unity gave way to multiplication. Lady Gregory directed his reading, and he found in Castiglione's *The Courtier* 'one of the great books of our civilization'. Those Italian despotisms, which founded their legitimacy on the allegiance of poets and of artists, fascinated him:

> I might have lived,
> And you know well how great the longing has been,
> Where every day my footfall should have lit
> In the green shadow of Ferrara wall;

Or climbed among the images of the past –
The unperturbed and courtly images –
Evening and morning, the steep street of Urbino.

The tour helped to give a further aristocratic turn to Yeats's mind, and he came home to lecture at the National Literary Society on the 'immoral Irish bourgeoisie' without past and without discipline, to which Ireland was surrendering her soul. John O'Leary died this year; it had been for a long time a most affecting and moving thing to see the old man among his books, sorting, or thinking that he was sorting, his papers. One was conscious of his lonely life deserted, or almost deserted, by all, but he was not. Yeats could not bring himself to go to the funeral because, as he wrote in 'Poetry and Tradition', he shrank from seeing about the grave so many whose nationalism was so different from anything he had taught.

Maud Gonne, who had watched with mild amusement the struggle for Yeats between Lady Gregory and Miss Horniman, dates Lady Gregory's triumph from the Italian trip: 'They should have been allies,' she says in her memoirs, 'for both stood for art's sake ... [but] they both liked Willie too well. ... Miss Horniman brought back Italian plaques to decorate the Abbey but Lady Gregory carried off Willie to visit the Italian towns where they were made.' Miss Horniman at this time had £10,000, an unexpected legacy, to invest, and she decided to found with it a Repertory Theatre in Manchester. When she asked Yeats to place his poetic work at her disposal, he refused. He was not young enough to change his nationality; acceptance would have amounted to that. 'I understand my own race,' he wrote, 'and in all my work, lyric or dramatic, I have thought of it. If the theatre fails I may or may not write plays, there is always lyric poetry to return to, but I shall write for my own people, whether in love or hate matters little, perhaps I shall not know which it is...'

There was a faint hope in Yeats's mind that Miss Horniman would reconsider the use of her £10,000, but on that she wrote to him in November 1907:

I think it is a sad waste of time for you to try to make yourself into a technically good stage manager; all the more that you will have to work with unwilling material and neglect the literary tasks which you can carry out as no one else living can do. But what are my words against the wooing of the vampire Kathleen ni Houlihan!

That Mrs Pat Campbell made such an offer ... and that you are most naturally delighted with it are merely details. I believe she admires your poetical powers, and very likely she has taken a fancy to you too although you are much too old for a woman of forty who might well go in for someone young. The root matter is whether Willie Fay will let the Directors and the Company consent to allow an Englishwoman to play at the Abbey. ... This is the whole gist of it all, but you will only be angry with me for putting it so clearly. But I will not see the rest of your life wasted without raising my voice even if it be useless. You *must* know that Fay would not permit a second company of actors at the Abbey, they would need to be paid and some would not be Irish and they could not be kept together to do proper work amongst the company. ... I shall indeed be glad to see you in London, my dear old friend; but you must bear in mind that your wish that I should trouble you less will be fulfilled. You will have no less kindness from me, but I will not waste the rest of my life on a Lost Cause.

Though she did not come again to Dublin, and considered herself henceforth as responsible only for the subsidy, Miss Horniman played a part at the end of the year in the re-organization of the Abbey's affairs, which resulted in the resignation of the brothers Fay. Meanwhile the company was playing to almost empty houses as the result of Yeats's championship of Synge. He was not reckless; he had the qualities of the 'Jesuit' and the 'revolutionary' which Baudelaire says are united in the 'true politician'. Thus he persuaded Synge to cut out of *The Playboy* certain phrases to which particular exception had been taken, and when the company went to England in the summer of 1907, Synge's work was, on his advice, not produced at Birmingham, where there is a large Irish population. He was afraid that the Irish, by making a commotion, might force the English censor to withdraw the licence.* Synge was displeased, but Yeats, more far-sighted, realized that at all costs *The Playboy* must reach London safely. London at once acclaimed *The Playboy*, and during the course of the next two or three years Synge was the most discussed of all Irish authors. A. H. Bullen, who had taken over Yeats's books, looked on in dismay while Yeats wrote eloquent prefaces placing Synge among the classics. 'This is a difficult matter,' Bullen wrote a few years later to Yeats, to excuse the decline in the latter's sales, 'but certain people (both in the press and public) were exalting Synge at your expense. The older critics were not gulled; nor those young men who kept their fine enthusiasm. But the unbaked and doughy youth, semi-educated people who had no standard of comparison, proclaimed Synge to be the master-spirit of the Irish movement.'

3

A work of exhaustive revision preparatory to the publication of Bullen's edition of his *Collected Works*, was begun in the autumn of 1907. Augustus John came to Galway to do one of the portraits. A wall at Coole was covered by John's etchings, brought by Robert Gregory from the Slade, but this was Yeats's first meeting with the artist.

Nassau Hotel, Dublin

4.10.07. *To John Quinn*

Synge has just had an operation on his throat and has come through it all right. I am to see him today for the first time. When he woke out of the ether sleep his first words, to the great delight of the doctor, who knew his plays, were: 'May God damn

---

* It may be remarked that even in those times of her ease and peace England too had her 'patriotics'. The English censor before passing the play cut out the sentence 'I wouldn't be fearing the loosèd khaki cut-throats.'

the English, they can't even swear without vulgarity.' This tale delights the company. ... Augustus John has been staying at Coole. ... I don't know what John will make of me. He made a lot of sketches with the brush and the pencil to work the etching from when he went home. I felt rather like a martyr going to him. The students consider him the greatest living draughtsman, the only modern who draws like an old master. He exaggerates every little hill and hollow of the face till one looks a gypsy grown old in wickedness and hardship. If one looked like any of his pictures the country women would take the clean clothes off the hedges when one passed, as they do at the sight of a tinker. He is himself a delight, the most innocent-wicked man I have ever met. He wears earrings, his hair down over his shoulders, a green velvet collar. He climbed to the top of the highest tree in Coole garden and carved a symbol there. Nobody else has been able to get up there to know what it is; even Robert stuck half way. He is a magnificent-looking person, and looks the wild creature he is. His best work is etching. He is certainly a great etcher with a savage imagination.

Shannon, Sargent and Mancini were the other artists to whom Yeats sat; Sargent and Shannon did full justice to his looks, Sargent in particular bringing out the youthful appearance which he retained for so long. He found Sargent good company. 'Not so much like an artist', he told Quinn, 'as like some wise, wealthy man of business who has lived with artists. He looks on at the enthusiasts with an ironical tolerance which is very engaging. ...' The Sargent drawing took the place of the Augustus John, and the fourth portrait in the edition was a sketch by J. B. Y. showing an emaciated son through a mist of domestic sentiment. When Yeats saw the John portrait, or rather the etching taken from it,* he tried to hide his feelings but shuddered inwardly. Always particular about his clothes, never dissipated, never un-shaven except during illness, he saw himself there an un-shaven drunkard, a melancholy English bohemian, and it was a long time before he began to feel that John had found something he liked in him, something closer than character

* Now in Birmingham.

and by that very transformation made it visible.* It is curious that while rejecting the John, Yeats should have accepted the Mancini, a portrait which caused his father to write to remind him that 'you are not a Caliban publishing a volume of decadent verse nor in any movement of revolution that you should wish to identify yourself in elaborate humility with the ugly and discontented.'

The production of the *Collected Works* was due in a large measure to Miss Horniman. She guaranteed £1500, Bullen's estimate for bringing out the edition at his recently established Shakespeare Head Press at Stratford-on-Avon. 'I do this', she wrote to the poet, 'to enforce your status, or rather to show people, especially your twittering imitators in Ireland, what your real status is.' To Bullen she wrote that she disliked a 'certain coarseness' in the new *Shadowy Waters* 'as much as you do', and certain of the lines from *In the Seven Woods* ('Tara uprooted, and new commonness Upon the throne, and crying about the streets …'); but 'that it would be useless to hope that her objections would carry any weight with the poet'.

Recent work in the collected edition included *Discoveries*, a short series of essays from the Dun Emer Press, and a prose play, *The Golden Helmet*, which was produced at the Abbey Theatre, and then, renamed *The Green Helmet*, turned into a heroic farce in irregular metrics. The play proved that Yeats's inventive skill could respond to the stride he had taken critically in *Discoveries*. In the first of these essays he is enraged by a play (George Russell's *Deirdre*), where every emotion is made 'dainty-footed and dainty-figured', and in the next he is asking how he can make his work speak to 'vigorous and simple men'. States of mind, lyrical moments, intellectual essences no longer interest him solely; he has found that he enters into himself and not into some essence when he is not seeking beauty deliberately, but merely wishing to lighten the mind of some burden

* 'He had found Anglo-Irish solitude', Yeats wrote in his manuscript book in 1930. 'I have made for myself an outlawed solitude.'

thrown upon it by the events of life. To realism in literature, and to the mechanical stultification of life of Darwin and the English thinkers, he has in no way modified his hostility. But he casts back to the 'swift and natural observation of a man as he is shaped by the events of life'. He wishes to come nearer earth, to the 'market carts', and there is a new emphasis on the physical side of beauty and energy. Dramatists should ascend out of common interests only in so far as they can carry the normal, passionate, reasoning self with them. The impression made upon him by Synge is evident in all of this.

4

The announcement of the *Collected Works* set the literary gossips of Dublin saying that Yeats would write no more, or very little. A page in George Moore's *Salve* reproduces to perfection the way in which he was now talked about in the Moore–A E circle. 'But if we were not really sorry that Yeats's inspiration was declining, we were quite genuinely interested to discover the cause of it. All his best poems, A E said, were written before he went to London. ... A E was certain that he would have written volume after volume if he had never sought a style, if he had been content to write simply.' Yeats was now forty-three, an age at which the output of artists often decreases, and Lady Gregory began to get anxious. When her kinsman, Sir Ian Hamilton, came to Coole in the summer of 1908, Yeats had started on a new poem, and it was considered an event.

Yeats and I [Sir Ian writes to me] were the only guests in the big house. Yeats unfortunately for my enjoyment was in the throes of composition and was being thoroughly spoilt. No one ever can have heard anyone play up to him like Lady Gregory. His bedroom was halfway down a passage on the first floor at the end of which was my room. All along the passage for some distance on either side of Yeats's door were laid thick rugs to prevent the slightest sound reaching the holy of holies – Yeats's bed. Down the passage every now and then would tiptoe a maid with a tray bearing (they told me) beef tea or arrowroot, though once I declare I distinctly smelt eggs and bacon. All suggestions that I could cheer him up a good deal if I went into his room and had a chat were met with horror. What I said about his groans and grumbles is hardly correct for they only came to me by hearsay through Lady Gregory and the servants. Actually I never once set eyes upon the aristocratic features of my friend Yeats on that occasion.

The poem to which Sir Ian refers was probably either 'Galway Races' or the lines, Yeats's first on a political occasion since Parnell's death, on the refusal of the Government to appoint Hugh Lane curator of the Dublin National Museum. Ricketts said of Lady Gregory's nephew that he 'joined the profession of a picture-dealer with the magnanimity of a Medici', and Yeats was furious with Lord Aberdeen and Mr Birrell for passing Lane over, but calmed down a little, as Lady Gregory has recorded, when the sight of a squirrel in the woods gave him a thought for the poem, 'On a Government Appointment':

> Nor the tame will, nor timid brain,
> Nor heavy knitting of the brow
> Bred that fierce tooth and cleanly limb . . .

A third poem of the summer was 'All Things Can Tempt Me', a composition on which he was engaged when I stayed at Coole in July. He was then in ordinary evidence at meals, but disappeared for the rest of the day, except for an hour or two in the afternoons, when he could be found on the lake catching trout. A good many guests, mostly Robert's and Mrs Gregory's, came and went – J. D. Innes, the painter, a few of Robert Gregory's cricketing friends and the daughter of a Cambridge clergyman. After dinner Lady Gregory would make him recite 'All Things Can Tempt Me', and I remember the charming and modest manner in which he sought the advice of the clergyman's daughter in regard to alternative versions of the last line:

> Deafer and dumber and colder than a fish.

What he called in another autobiographical poem 'theatre-business, management of men' had no doubt an effect in limiting his output of verse. Sometimes he would be engaged at the Abbey morning, afternoon and evening. There was no drudgery that he declined. A note of a typical day in Dublin runs as follows: 'Breakfast 10.45; 11–1.10 reading script for the theatre and letters; 2.30–3.40 at the Abbey; 4–7 letters; evening Abbey'. He did not confine himself to producing the plays of young dramatists and to reading their manuscripts, but kept an eye on everything, from balance-sheets to heating; he was even known to compose lovers' quarrels. In a *Journal* which he kept at this time there are occasional outcries against this servitude. 'I have sleepless nights thinking of the time I must take from my poetry. Last night I could not sleep – and yet perhaps I must do all these things that I may set myself to a life of action, so as to express not the traditional poet, but the forgotten thing, the normal active man.'

The reference to 'theatre-business, management of men' is extraordinarily apt. Yeats was one of the few poets with a born dramatic gift, not only in the effect and economy with which he could nail down a really dramatic theme on the barest of boards in the rarest of words – one remembers in his *Deirdre*, 'Eagles have gone into their cloudy bed' – but in the fact that he knew exactly what effect he wanted and how it should be obtained. Even the best prose dramatists are rarely able to produce their own work and coach the actors. All this Yeats could do. Very often a word from him illuminated the mind of a puzzled actor more than an hour's harangue from a professional producer. At the beginning of his career as a dramatist George Moore remarked on the assiduity of his attendances at his own play. A probable explanation lies in the fact that even at an early age Yeats realized that he must use the theatre as a workshop, as Miss Ellis-Fermor emphasizes in her book *The Irish Dramatic Movement*.

The *Journal*, at the head of which is the poem 'Why

should I blame her that she filled my days With misery ...',
was started after a visit to Maud Gonne in Paris in December 1908. It appears that Yeats kept it as an aid to the new
understanding of himself out of which was to come the love
poetry and political poetry of *The Green Helmet and other
Poems* (1910) and of *Responsibilities* (1914), the magnificent
retort to Synge's enemies in *The Cutting of an Agate* (1912),
and his theory of the mask which 'all artists must find for
themselves' in *Per Amica Silentia Lunae* (1918). The entries
are intermittent and often undated; many years later he
printed some pages from this diary with the title *Estrangement*. There are drafts for poems. Some are written out at
first in prose, this, for instance, for 'On a House Shaken by
the Land Agitation':

How should the world gain, if this house failed, even though
a hundred little houses were the better for it; for here power has
given poetry or legend, giving energy, precision, and it gave to
a far people beneficial rule, and still under its roof the living
intellect is sweetened by old memories of its descent from far
off. How should the world be better if the wren's nest flourish
and the Eagle's house be shattered! *

Yeats had come to Dublin at the beginning of 1909, and
was in sole charge of the Abbey for several weeks. There was
a probability that Synge would soon be in his grave, and
Lady Gregory's health obliged her to rest at Coole.

JOURNAL

Today the thought came to me that P.I.A.L.† never really
understands my plans, or nature or ideas. Then came the thought
– what matter? How much of the best I have done and still do is
but the attempt to explain myself to her? If she understood I
should lack a reason for writing, and one can never have too
many reasons for doing what is so laborious.

It seems to me that love if it is fine is essentially a discipline,
but it needs so much wisdom that the love of Sheba and of
Solomon must have lasted for all the silence of the Scriptures.

---

* The house was Coole, not the House of Lords, as George Moore
pretended to believe.   † Maud Gonne.

In wise love each divines the high secret self of the other, and refusing to believe in the mere daily self creates a mirror where the lover or the beloved sees an image to copy in daily life. Love also creates the mask.

One reason for the tendency of the Russell group to extreme political opinion is that a taste fed for long on milk diet thirsts for strong pleasure. In England the reaction would be vice, in Ireland it is politics.

In what toils, in what life, in what war of the Amazons did women whose beauty is more than the promise of physical pleasure and an easy path to get it, win their beauty? For Castiglione says, speaking the high Urbino thought, that all such beauty is the spoil and monument of the victory of the soul.

I often wonder if my talent will ever recover from the heterogeneous labour of these last few years. ... I cry out for liberty and have ever less and less inner life. Evil comes to us men of imagination wearing as its mask all the virtues.

Feb. 26.

I made the following poem about six months ago but write it here that it may not be lost:

'Some may have blamed you that you took away
The verses that they cared for on the day
When the ears being deafened, the sight of the eyes blind
With lightning, you went from me; and I could find
Nothing to make a song about but kings...'

I went to see Synge yesterday. ... If he dies it will set me wondering whether he could have lived if he had not had his long bitter misunderstanding with the wreckage of Young Ireland. ... In one thing he and Lady Gregory are the strongest souls I have ever known. He and she alike have never for even an instant spoken to me the thoughts of their inferiors as their own thoughts. ... Both Synge and Lady Gregory isolate themselves, Synge instinctively and Lady Gregory consciously, from all contagious opinions of poorer minds. Synge so instinctively – and naturally helped certainly by the habit of an invalid – that no one is conscious of rejection. Lady Gregory's life is too energetic and complex for her rejections to be other than deliberate. I do

neither one nor the other, being too talkative, too full of belief
in whatever thought lays hold on me, to reject people from my
company, and so I only keep from these invasions of the soul,
which in old days used to come upon me, by a series of angry
outbreaks which are pure folly. One must agree with the clown
or be silent, for he has in him the strength and confidence of
the multitudes.

Synge died on 24 March 1909, at the age of thirty-seven.
Living, he had been somewhat far off in his imaginative
self-sufficiency; dying, he became for Yeats one of the heroic
figures of literature. Except in their work at the Abbey they
had never been much together. Synge was shy of Yeats and
would never speak at large to him, and it came as a genuine
surprise to the poet when John Masefield told him, later, on
what a pinnacle he had been placed by the younger man.
As George Moore says, Synge received Yeats's faith in his
genius as a dying saint receives the Eucharist.*

5

The eight volumes of the *Collected Works* were a lovely
production in their pale vellum bindings, gold letters and
covers of grey. The margins were generous, the notes copious, and the last volume contained a bibliography by Allan
Wade; still the eight volumes represented a good deal of
work for a man not yet forty-five. On the whole, the English
press gave the edition a good reception, and meeting his
sister in the street on the morrow of Swinburne's death
(April 1909), Yeats stopped her to say: 'I am the King of the
Cats.' For many years the Irish press, Unionist and Nationalist alike, had damned his work with faint praise and inevitable reference to a 'Celtic' Maeterlinck, or attacked it
sharply. He could not believe his eyes when he found a
eulogy in the *Freeman's Journal*. It came from the pen of

* Yeats's portrait of Synge in the *Autobiographies* and elsewhere is
very one-sided.

Stephen MacKenna, Fenian and later author of a noble translation of Plotinus. The editor had intended a hostile review which would have brought the usual charges against Yeats of being affected and obscure; in fact un-Irish. Mac-Kenna, who was employed at the time on the *Freeman's Journal*, carried away the volumes. 'The editor', he wrote long afterwards, 'would have given it to a good fellow who, I don't know why, honestly thought W. B. raised up by the devil to corrupt Holy Ireland, and himself raised up by God and, I think, the Blessed Virgin to save and protect her.'

Nevertheless, Yeats felt that his estrangement from Dublin literary life, which he identified with George Russell's group, was complete. His leadership in the Irish intellectual movement was more important to him than anything else; but he was not prepared to save it by making concessions. He thought of Balzac's phrase, 'barren rascals', applied to critics, when he considered A E's Sunday evenings in Rathgar, or George Moore's Saturdays. He pronounced a hasty judgement, afterwards withdrawn, upon James Stephens, now rising to fame. 'Colum', he noted in his *Journal*, 'is the one victim of George Russell's misunderstanding of life I rage over. ... A sensitive naturally dreaming man like Colum, even if he does not share their ideas, is lost in a work like this where no technique is respected, no manly laborious achievement applauded, and the disappointed sit like crows...'

For company in Dublin Yeats depended chiefly on the Arts Club, which was not bookish or particularly intellectual. Here was held, organized by Mrs Duncan, an early exhibition of post-impressionist painters, and Thomas Bodkin recalls how Yeats, wandering about the premises, expatiated on the merits of Cézanne, Gauguin, Van Gogh and Matisse, a taste which can have had little support from Lane and was ridiculed by George Russell in the columns of the *Irish Times*. It was in the Arts Club that Yeats ate the two dinners in the one sitting. He was so absorbed in talking, 'casting his pearls before swine in an open-handed and haphazard way', that he believed the man who told him that he had not dined.*

It pleased him to find listeners among the young who were not slaves to paper and to books. One member of the club, all muscular force and ardour, reminded him of Ben Jonson's line, 'so rammed with life that he can but grow in life with being'. This was Edward Evans, known as 'The Bishop', who conducted a Bible class (not in the club) which Yeats used to attend, doing his utmost to follow a line of thought not only unfamiliar but in itself irregular. He took a hand in Evans's literary education, trying him rather high with Coventry Patmore's *Odes* for a start, and together they belittled the spiritual pretensions of the Dublin theosophists. 'In Christianity,' Yeats noted in his *Journal* after one of the Bible classes, 'what was philosophy in eastern Asia became biography, drama. Was the *Bhavagad Gita* the scenario from which the Gospels were made?'

Until he became a member of the Stephen's Green Club, Yeats stayed when in Dublin at the Nassau Hotel overlooking the College Park. The following reminiscences of a guest, Mr E. R. Walsh, whom he frequently received there in the evenings, are pertinent:

I well remember the excitement aroused in him by the reading of *Wilhelm Meister*, and I date from that event a desire to follow the great poet in the dual role of poet and philosopher. Plotinus and St Thomas Aquinas were studied later. ... Another book which influenced him in a lighter way was Castiglione's *Il Cortegiano*. His aspiration towards a life of easy, dignified urbanity was inevitably misunderstood by some people. Once he was rebuked for standing up when 'God save the King' was played at a public dinner, and he wrote a charming reply to his critics quoting Balzac's dictum. 'There are only three classes I respect,' he exclaimed, 'the aristocracy who are above fear; the poor who are beneath it, and the artists whom God has made reckless.'

Among the people whom I met at the hotel Captain Shawe-Taylor came nearest to Yeats's ideal gentleman of the Renais-

* The perfectly true story is told by Page Dickinson in *The Dublin of Yesterday*.

sance. Like Hugh Lane, he was a nephew of Lady Gregory, and his remarkable personal beauty and his exquisitely winning way, made him irresistible as a conciliator, and Yeats hoped that as he had been the means of bringing about a settlement at the Land Bill conference, so he might succeed in the larger political issue.* On the political side of his character Yeats, I think, resembled Parnell, and his mentality, unlike that of many fiery patriots, struck me as quite un-English. So strong a Nationalism as his excluded one at that time from ruling society. Lady Lyttelton, the wife of the Commander-in-Chief, used to invite him sometimes to dinner at the Royal Hospital, but she had to be careful about the guests she asked to meet him. He was therefore a rather lonely man, for the merely Bohemian company he might have joined, such as that led by Count and Countess Markievicz, held no attraction for him. Yet I think he was never so happy as in those days when he fought the great battles of the Abbey Theatre for *The Playboy* and in a lesser degree for Norreys Connell's *Piper* and Shaw's *Blanco Posnet*.

6

It was now Yeats's aim to win over the general rather than any special public to the Abbey Theatre. Bernard Shaw's *Blanco Posnet*, which had been banned by the English censor, appeared to be a godsend from that point of view. Yeats thought Shaw's theology 'absurd', but he pressed Shaw to give the Abbey the play. The English censor's writ did not run in Ireland, the theatrical law in that country having been made in the old Irish Parliament by a ruling caste which (as Yeats once put it) 'being itself free, left the theatre in freedom'. Then it was discovered that, owing to some flaw in the Abbey Theatre's patent, Lord Aberdeen could forbid the performance in Dublin, and he did, in fact, seek to persuade Lady Gregory not to embarrass him by producing it. 'The real offender is the King,' Yeats wrote to his father,

---

Vide Yeats's essay on Shawe-Taylor in *The Cutting of an Agate*. The Captain called a conference of landlords and tenants, laying down no principles and simply stating the place and hour of meeting, and neither side dared refuse the invitation.

'who is trying to make England moral and as a means is
supporting the Censor by calling actors before him and
getting them to speak at the Royal Commission in favour of
censorship. ... He was in communication with Lord Aberdeen.' Yeats and Lady Gregory appear to have persuaded
themselves that Dublin Castle might proceed to extremities
and take away their patent; but they went forward with
their plans, and presented *Blanco* on 26 August 1909, to a
crowded house, in which there was a large party from the
Castle. Miss Horniman was not particularly pleased. She
was no advocate of censorship, but it seemed to her that the
green flag had once again been hoisted over her theatre.

The publicity was immense, and no doubt greatly enlarged
Yeats's audiences, when later in the year he went to the
North of England to lecture on the theatre's behalf. At
Liverpool Professor Oliver Elton, old friend of Bedford Park
days, was in the audience, and said to him afterwards: 'I
heard the voice of J. B. Y.' Yeats had contrasted old writers
with new, saying that the former were busy with their own
sins, the latter (from Milton on) with the sins of other people.

From London he wrote to his father of a call on Mrs
Patrick Campbell. She had invited him to read his new play,
The Player Queen, to her. He went to her house and was
kept waiting in the drawing-room for several hours before
luncheon, while he received messages of apology saying Mrs
Campbell was not yet ready. After luncheon Mrs Campbell
listened with enthusiasm to Act I, as far as the interruptions
of a parrot allowed. Then a musician arrived, then a dress-
maker, and lastly relations. Yeats went home, came back at
six, and was still waiting in the drawing-room at midnight.
At half-past twelve Mrs Campbell came in so tired that she
had to lean on her daughter's arm for support. 'But this is
absurd,' Yeats cried, 'you must go to your bed and I must
go home.' 'No,' she replied, 'I must hear the end of the play
on the same day as I have the beginning.' He began to read,
but it was evident that Mrs Campbell could scarcely follow
a word. She started to quarrel with him, taking up certain

of the heroine's remarks as though she thought them meant for herself. At intervals, in an exasperated sleepy voice, she repeated, 'No, I am not a slut, and I do not like "fool".'

Then he told of a round of social engagements. At a men's dinner-party, given by Edmund Gosse, he sat next the Prime Minister.

Edmund Gosse whispered to me in the few minutes before dinner, 'Mind! no politics,' and then introduced me to Lord Cromer, and Lord Cromer's first sentence was, 'We had a very interesting debate in the House of Lords this afternoon.' I, being still wax under Gosse's finger, replied, 'Ah, I look at English politics as a child does at a racecourse, taking sides by the colour of the jockey's coats. And I often change sides in the middle of a race.' This rather chilled the conversation. . . . I got on better with Asquith; I found him an exceedingly well-read man, especially, curiously enough, in poetry. . . . Not a man of really fine culture, I think, but exceedingly charming. . . .

In another letter to J. B. Y. there is a reference to Sir Ian Hamilton, sought out in London after the fiasco at Coole. 'A man of the really finest culture', Yeats wrote. 'As fine as that of anybody I have ever met. A very gentle person. . . .' This note to Yeats from Sir Ian Hamilton throws a singular and specialized light on another famous soldier:

My Dear Yeats,
I hope you will permit me my omission of the ceremonious prefix in writing to thank you very much for your kind thought regarding your quotation from Heraclitus.* Lord Roberts was at breakfast with me when I opened your letter. I read it to him and somewhat to my dismay he pulled out a notebook and wrote it down, I suppose the little wretch means to rob me of my pearl. I thought when first I set my eye on your writing it was that of Andrew Lang. Almost identical, only you write with a thicker pen . . .

Yours sincerely,
Ian Hamilton

*Meaning William Cory's anthology piece, 'They told me, Heraclitus, they told me you were dead'.

Turning again to the *Journal*, one finds a reference to a meeting in London with Wyndham Lewis, the innovating artist from the Slade, whose *Time and Western Man* and other works were many years later destined to stimulate Yeats greatly. It was through Ezra Pound, however, that Yeats first gained an insight into the tendencies of the generation next to his own in point of time, in England and in America, afterwards to be led by T. S. Eliot. Pound, well grounded in his Yeats by his Professor at Columbia, had made the Irish poet's acquaintance on his first visit to Europe. He had edited a volume of Lionel Johnson's poems, and in 1909 he published his *Personae*. Yeats appears to have been at once attracted by the intrepidity of Ezra Pound, who altered his (Yeats's) poems before sending them to some American magazine for which he acted as correspondent. They had something obscure but strong in common, apart from the fact that Yeats was an influence on Pound's first poetry.* 'A headlong rugged nature, and he is always hurting people's feelings,' Yeats wrote of his new friend to Sir William Rothenstein, 'but he has, I think, some genius and great good-will.' It also suited Yeats very well to be in contact with a young man of learning, who did not annoy him by descending to accuracy in petty matters like grammar. Indeed, the outlook of Pound, who has steadily and energetically used Provençal and other languages for his own purposes, like a happy tyro attacking a Beethoven piano sonata, is not dissimilar to that of Yeats in *A Vision*, whose Hebrew has grown rusty.

7

Early in 1910 Yeats and Lady Gregory, sole directors of the Abbey Theatre since the death of Synge, accepted an offer from Miss Horniman to hand over the Abbey Theatre to

* 'The first strong influences upon Pound at the moment when his verse was taking direction, were those of Browning and Yeats. In the background are the Nineties in general', says T. S. Eliot in his Introduction to Ezra Pound's *Selected Poems*.

them on certain conditions. The completion of the purchase was to take place in the following December, and Miss Horniman undertook to pay the subsidy, as heretofore, up to that date, the price agreed upon being £1000. During the negotiations Yeats received friendly letters from Miss Horniman, but then came an interview between her and Bernard Shaw, which threw her into a state of internal ferment. It appears that Shaw gave her the impression that he sympathized with her in her grievances against the rude and inconsequent Irishry. Yeats became angry and charged Shaw with having done 'measureless mischief in this business'. 'He seems to have no practical sense', he wrote to Lady Gregory. 'He is a logician, and a logician is a fool when life, which is a thing of emotion, is in question; it is as if a watch were to try to understand a bullock.'

Matters were in this posture when Yeats went to Normandy at the beginning of May on a visit to Maud Gonne. He left Lennox Robinson (a newly discovered dramatist) installed as manager at the Abbey. Yeats admired Robinson's work, and had sent to Cork for the young man, to whom he had as yet scarcely spoken, and said to him very solemnly: 'I like your face. I believe you have a dramatic future. I am doing what that man did who took Ibsen from behind the counter in the chemist's shop and set him to manage the Norwegian theatre. He was no older than you, and like you was ignorant of the work he was sent to.'

Maud Gonne's house, 'Les Mouettes', stood above the sea-shore at Colville, near Calvados. It was a big ugly building which she shared with a friend, Mrs Clay. She had her little son with her, a troop of black dogs and dozens of caged birds of various descriptions. There was a haunted picture in one of the rooms. On this, the first of many visits to her in Normandy, Yeats composed the poem 'Against Unworthy Praise' –

> Yet she, singing upon her road,
> Half lion, half child, is at peace.

and the poem 'Peace' –

> Ah, but peace that comes at length,
> Came when Time had touched her form –

and commenced his essay, 'Synge and Ireland', reading a little of Milton's prose every morning before he began to work. 'Madame Gonne has been a great help,' he wrote to Lady Gregory, 'and partly by differing from her and partly by agreeing with her I have made it double the force it was. ... It seems to me as good prose as any I have written.' His *Journal* contains the following entry under the heading 'Calvados':

Thinking of her as I do as, in a sense, Ireland, a summing up in one's mind of what is best in the romantic, political Ireland of my youth, and of the youth of others for some years yet, I must see to it that I close the Synge essay with a statement of national literature as I would recreate it and of its purpose. All literature created out of a conscious political aim in the long run creates weakness by creating a habit of unthinking obedience. Literature created for its own sake, for some eternal spiritual need, can be used for politics. Dante is said to have unified Italy. The more unconscious the creation the more powerful. A great statesman, let us say, should keep his conscious purpose for practical things but he should have grown up to find about him always, most perhaps in the minds of women, the nobleness of emotion, created and associated with his country by its great poets.

Maud Gonne and Mrs Clay took him for excursions into the 'happy poplar land', of William Morris's poem and early architectural essays. He had a day at Mont St Michel and another at Caen, where Iseult Gonne was being educated in a convent. For her too he wrote a poem. She had moved him since as a child she had told him that she disliked plays in modern dress and preferred the *Iliad* to any other book. At Mont St Michel, before 'that seeming fantasy, seeming more of Egypt than of Christendom', he found the eloquent close for his essay upon Synge:

Synge, like all of the great Kin, sought for the race, not through the eyes, or in history, but where those monks found

God, in the depths of the mind, and in all art like his, although it does not command – indeed because it does not – may lie the root of far-branching events. ... It has no array of arguments and maxims, because the great and simple (and the Muses have never known which of the two pleases them most) need their deliberate thought for the day's work, and yet will do it worse if they have not grown into or found about them, most perhaps in the minds of women, the nobleness of emotion associated with the scenery and events of their country by those great poets who have dreamed in it solitude, and who to this day in Europe are creating indestructible spiritual races, like those religion has created in the East.

8

Being so far off, Yeats had no knowledge of the opening of the theatre on the occasion of Edward VII's death (7 May) when every other theatre in Britain and in the kingdom of Ireland closed.

On the 10th Miss Horniman telegraphed to the manager: 'Opening last Saturday was disgraceful. Performance on day of funeral would be political and would stop subsidy automatically.' Lennox Robinson's inclination had been to keep the theatre open; being very young, he supposed that a public event had no significance to the arts. However, when he learned that the other theatres were closing, he telegraphed to Lady Gregory to ask her what he should do. The messenger boy at Gort took three hours to cover the two miles to Coole and return to the post-office. Lady Gregory wired, 'Should close through courtesy', but by that time the matinée was proceeding.

On the 11th Miss Horniman sent a letter of protest to the Dublin papers and to the *Stage* and *Era*. On the same day she telegraphed to Lady Gregory: 'Subsidy ceases now unless Directors and Robinson express regret in Dublin press that decent example was not followed.' Lady Gregory's expression of regret ran as follows:

Harvest, a play in three acts by S. L. Robinson, will be produced for the first time next week. ... There will be no performance on Friday (the date of the King's funeral). The Directors and Manager regret that owing to accident the theatre remained open on Saturday last. Lady Gregory, who was in the country, had wired immediately on receipt of the news of the King's death and of a telegram asking for instructions, desiring it to be closed, but this was too late in the day, the matinée had already been put on, and it was considered too late to stop the evening performance.

Arthur Griffith chimed in. 'Mr Yeats', he wrote in the next issue of his weekly journal, 'is not in Ireland at present, and circumstances may have prevented him reading the insult which his co-directors have accepted in the spirit of whipped curs. Whether he will permit himself to be whipped in public in return for English money, remains to be seen. We hope not. We remember how Mr Yeats boasted that in his father's house he was never taught to bend the knee. That was when he was fighting Irish opinion.'

Miss Horniman, however, considered Lady Gregory's apology to be inadequate and intentionally obscure. She chose to think that it might be read as a regret that the opening was an accident, not deliberate, and raised a demand for the dismissal of Lennox Robinson on the ground that he had made her theatre political.

On the seventeenth Yeats wrote to Miss Horniman from Woburn Buildings:

On my return yesterday from France I heard for the first time of the trouble in Dublin. I have read many letters but cannot yet understand it. I am amazed that you should have published such a letter without even waiting for Robinson's explanation, and that, explanation or no explanation, you should have done so much injury to a movement you have helped and cared for. I am going to Dublin tonight to inquire into the whole thing.

The position was precarious. Since signing the agreement to purchase the theatre Lady Gregory had been seeking subscriptions for a new endowment among moneyed people in Ireland, most of them Unionists; and now an incident which might have passed with little notice and, at the worst, have

been made harmless by a few words of explanation, had been
magnified and given a political complexion by Miss Horniman and advertised in England and Ireland as an insult to
the Crown. Nevertheless Yeats refused to sacrifice Robinson,
or to make any further apologies,* and when the time came,
in December, to implement the agreement to purchase, he
caused his lawyer to challenge Miss Horniman's right to
have withheld the subsidy. He had avoided meeting her
while an unsettled dispute lay between them. He wanted to
save the friendship from dying of a misunderstanding; and
he was hurt when she now sent him a fierce, personal message
of reproach.

When the case was placed before C. P. Scott, the editor of
the *Manchester Guardian*, for arbitration, Yeats pointed out
that he had never, directly or indirectly, taken any political
action in connection with the theatre. At the same time, he
denied the existence of any ground agreement, such as Miss
Horniman alleged, to ignore Nationalist sentiment, and to
permit her to withdraw the subsidy because of what she
might consider political action. Had there been such an
agreement, he said, he would 'have been in little better position than an Irish patriot who had taken Government money
in obedience to some secret compact'. It was true that Miss
Horniman had been drawn in part to his work by his insistence on the right of the artist to ignore political considerations, and on the injury these had done in Ireland to
the emotion of beauty and wise sense of life – an insistence
for which he had suffered much unpopularity. But in Miss
Horniman's memory declarations that referred entirely to
the creation and reception of a work of art had been given
an application to such questions as the right of players to
perform at political meetings and the attitude which the
Directors should adopt on the death of a monarch. The
British National Anthem, although played in other Dublin
theatres, was never played by the orchestra of the Abbey,

---

* A complaint, however, was lodged against the Gort messenger boy,
and he was severely dealt with by the authorities of the Post Office.

for the reason that Nationalists regarded it as a party tune
of the Unionists. On the other side it was submitted that the
condition of 'no politics' had been well understood by all.
Miss Horniman quoted a passage from a letter to Lady
Gregory of 28 June 1907:

It must never be forgotten that if the Theatre be used politically I am free to close it at once and stop the subsidy. The
undignified negotiations with the company as to the number of
times they condescend to appear in London in *Playboy* and
their refusal to remain longer were very near political action.

She also recalled that after a recital by Miss Sara Allgood at
a conservative Suffragette meeting in London, organized by
the Hon. Mrs Alfred Lyttelton, she had told Yeats that
this was a transgression of the 'no politics' rule, and that
Yeats, while questioning the application in this instance,
had not denied her right to assert the principle or to stop
the subsidy in the event of a breach. The opening of the
Theatre on the day of the King's death was a gross and
flagrant violation of the condition.

C. P. Scott decided that 'in view of all the circumstances
and events', Miss Horniman, who had throughout acted
'with great generosity and perfect good faith', had not been
justified in discontinuing the subsidy. On hearing of the
verdict Yeats and Lady Gregory wrote to her: 'We wish at
once to say that remembering your generosity in the past it
was never our intention to press the legal point against you.
If with all the facts before you you still cannot accept the
integrity of our action, we cannot accept the money, and
the matter is at an end.'

Miss Horniman replied through her lawyers that she did
not accept the integrity of the Directors' action. As she had
spent over £10,000 on the Theatre, it was not unnatural that
she should have felt that she had been used badly, and,
though she subsequently met Yeats occasionally in London,
their old companionship was not resumed. In 1934, after he
had not seen her for years, he recalled an ancient friendship

on a sudden impulse and instructed his publishers to send her his *Collected Plays*. Her acknowledgement of the gift may be quoted as a fitting close to this chapter:

My dear old Friend,

Long ago you instructed your publishers to send me the fresh volume of your plays. I determined to read it through, as I well remember how years ago you told me that it was well to write to authors and to thank them for the anticipated pleasure of reading. But it took some time, especially as I have been more or less weak and ill for a long time. I was most interested in the book, especially in noticing alterations made in the plays with which I am so familiar. Thank you very much for thinking of sending it to me.

Being away from London for a time, I have not got your book of reminiscences. Have you not waited patiently so that you may be safe from actions for libel? That is in the case of some Dublin experiences. In a few years' time no one will believe the tales of the odd happenings near to the Liffey. Hoping you have quite recovered from the illness of which I read in the paper,

Yours sincerely,
A. E. F. Horniman

[11]

Variety (1910-12)

J. B. Yeats in New York; passages from his letters –
Death of George Pollexfen – Yeats's government pension;
Trinity College and the chair of literature – *The Player
Queen* – *The Playboy* in America and revival of *The
Countess Cathleen* – social life in England

———

What's riches to him
That has made a great peacock
With the pride of his eye?
The wind-beaten, stone-grey,
And desolate Three Rock
Would nourish his whim.
Live he or die
Amid wet rocks and heather,
His ghost will be gay
Adding feather to feather
For the pride of his eye.

I

J. B. YEATS was now in New York on a 'visit' which had
already lasted three years. Late in 1907, after having been
presented with a cheque by Hugh Lane, Andrew Jameson
and other Dublin friends who wished to show their appreciation of a wonderful personality and their sense of what art
in Ireland owed to the old painter, he had chosen to cross the
Atlantic with his daughter Lily, who was giving an exhibition of her Dun Emer embroideries in New York, rather
than visit Italian galleries, as had originally been proposed.
Such was his interest in the American scene and such his
delight in the reception accorded him by John Quinn – 'the
crossest man in the world and the kindest' – and by Quinn's
friends, that when the time came for his daughter to return

he could not make up his mind to board the boat with her. To leave New York, he said, would be to leave a huge fair where at any moment he might meet with a huge bit of luck. Moreover, he had at last found a place where people did not eat too much at dinner to talk afterwards.

His work was in Dublin public galleries, but even in Dublin he had more fame as a talker than as a painter, and always it had been a hard struggle to live. He had never lost his buoyancy, and up to the time that he left Dublin he was still confident that the Judges and their wives would find him out as a more subtle modeller than William Orpen and far less expensive.* Henry Lamb, A.R.A., has written to me of his great gifts:

I should be proud to help in the recognition of his genius which is quite scandalously unknown.... From the very first time I saw his work fourteen years ago I considered him by far the greatest painter that Ireland has produced. Even now, in Parnell Square, it is doubtful whether his pictures do not hang by virtue of their subjects: for about three years ago I asked after one of them and was told it was kept in the cellar. Those that do appear seem to have assumed good positions by virtue of their natural girth and gravity, qualities for a parallel to which one has to think of Courbet or Titian, which brings us to one of his strangely unIrish (?) characteristics, the absence of facility and disregard of all the usual graces of effectiveness. ... The fact that such a very great (and I should say ultimately important) painter should fail to interest modern European taste seems to lead to a fruitful topic for aestheticians and philosophers. But you know John shares my opinion and he has seen many more in America. Also Thomas Bodkin and Sarah Purser.

The last fourteen years of the old painter's life were spent in New York. He was past seventy, and his family constantly urged him to return. Occasionally he would fix the date of sailing, and then ask for a few weeks more. He wrote of his growing skill in oils, tried his hand at essays, autobiography and stories, lectured, philosophized. He never lost his naturalness and ability to treat his children as if they

* £25 was his price for a portrait.

were contemporaries, or his acute insight into W. B.'s
poetical motives. Sometimes he would write three times in
the one day to his elder son. These are characteristic excerpts
from this correspondence:

I see that the *Spectator* says that your poetry lacks plan. The
Spectator always says the obvious thing, but never the profound
thing. The profound thing is that oftener than anyone else you
touch the *very centre*, reach to the very *quintessence*. It's like a
mother talking of a child which she has nursed as well as brought
into the world – she does not praise or blame. She just *knows*,
and when she talks, you listen. Yet there is truth in this want of
plan, or rather – for there is plenty of intellectual plan – there is
foundation for the discontent that prompted the criticism –
your poetry wants a basis. Tennyson had England and his domestic life and his class feeling. Since you have given up Ireland * –
and you gave it up no doubt because it seemed to you to make
for oratory rather than poetry – you have no basis. The super-
man won't do. It is too nonsensical and of course you have not
tried it.

A few days ago I met Olga Nethersole and a young lady, Miss
Field, and they both together and separately told me the extra-
ordinary admiration for your poetry that possesses the young
Rostand. He knows English ... and translates his father's work.
They said he would read out your work to anyone who would
listen, and does it for hours together ...

A young lady with the sweet eyes of a violet in early spring
will tell me that she has a perfect right to do anything she likes
provided she does not injure herself – another equally endowed
with youth and innocence will maintain that the criminal is only
a man in•advance of his times. A most attractive lady told me
that she and a girl friend with her husband lived in the woods
and walked about naked. Absolutely naked? I asked. Yes absolutely, she replied. I asked the purpose of it all and she told me
it was so *convenient for bathing in the lake*. . . . Emma Goldmann
says Mrs Pankhurst's mistake is in trying to make men chaste.
She should direct her efforts to curing women of chastity. . . . Her
courage is undoubted – probably her heart is black with hatred
. . . like so many agitators.

* But, as has been shown, W. B. had never 'given up' Ireland.

I have read Swinburne's preface to Blake. In old days as I remember (Nettleship told me) Rossetti would never invite Swinburne without Whistler, who alone was able to keep him from drink. These two little men with aspiring souls – which taught the other the sacerdotal assumption? – up to then unknown to poets – and quite alien from Shakespeare as it was from Shelley and Browning. Their attack upon you would be nothing without the insolent airs of infallibility. Swinburne is surely the poet of the thinnest humanity ever known – the damned homunculus, as Whitman said, without sweetheart or wife or child or friend but for Watts-Dunton who, kind creature, doubtless toadies him. It takes goodness to be a flatterer.

Perhaps you would like to know something of my lecture. I said that Dowden, Todhunter, Armstrong became poets because they were literary men and admired Wordsworth and other poets – you because you had convictions of the kind that *could be best expressed in verse, i.e.* convictions that were *desires*, and such as could never be imprisoned in opinions. This gave me the opportunity of speaking of John O'Leary and Blavatsky, and the occultists and magic, etc. The lecture was given in a drawing-room, and once I discovered that I could sit down (I commenced standing up) everything went well. There was a very intellectual clergyman there who was enthusiastic. From the first I took to him because he was like the curate at Dundrum, Mr Kerr, of whom Lily will tell you.

A miser may have a poet for his son, a spendthrift never.

Has it ever occurred to you that the poetical and lyrical mind are distinct? Or perhaps they are different aspects of the same mind, but so distinct from each other that one may be cultivated at the expense of the other. Jack, for instance, seems to me to have the poetical mind, *i.e.* all nature and all life spreads out before him and excites so much affection that he cannot study them enough or reproduce them in sufficient detail ... and for that reason it is my belief that if he lives a few years longer Jack's fame will over-shadow all the other artists.[*]

[*] J. B. Y. once said: 'I shall be known one day as the father of a painter.'

2

The elder who had been of next importance to J. B. Y. in Yeats's early manhood, died in the autumn of 1910. George Pollexfen had been ailing for some time and had grown difficult in temper. Nephew and uncle had continued in correspondence on astrological matters, but they had seen little of each other during recent years. George would have liked to keep the applauded poet near him like a racehorse, and was perhaps a little hurt when Yeats exchanged Thornhill for Coole as a West of Ireland home.

On hearing that their uncle could not recover, Yeats wrote to his sister (Coole, September 1910):

... I wish he had had a better life. He has a strongly religious nature and that must give him courage and peace. . . . I have had the cloud of George's dying over me since you wrote, and know how heavy it must lie upon you who have him before your eyes. I wonder if the sickness has really been wasting his life for years. That would account for so much. Your letter came as I was writing the last words of my essay on Synge. In a few months I may have to write on Arthur Symons. He by the way knew George and liked and admired him and thought that he might have grown into good taste in literature. It is a strange thing that this year I had made up my mind to go to George, if he would have me for a time during the summer. It is almost the first time (thanks to Robinson being at the theatre) that I have been able to map my life a little.

'Lily,' said George when his niece arrived at Rosses Point, 'I think I'm going.' He was brought to Thornhill, and though he had passed his life in a panic about his health he did not again speak of death, but lay calmly reading novels until two days before the end, when he gave very careful directions as to how certain small sums, which would be found in his pockets, should be distributed. His niece, as well as the nurses, heard the banshee wail outside the house on the night before his death. He died the night after, at the same hour that the banshee had cried out, and was buried in St

John's Churchyard beside old William and Elizabeth Pollexfen. Jack Yeats's wreath in his uncle's racing colours was
much admired.

> And after twenty years they laid
> In that tomb by him and her
> His son George, the astrologer;
> And Masons drove from miles away
> To scatter the acacia spray
> Upon a melancholy man
> Who had ended where his breath began.

After the funeral Yeats wrote to Lady Gregory:

I am tired out with the strain. I found it hard to see George's
house again with every detail as it was when I stayed with him
and worked at astrology. The funeral was very touching – the
church full of working people, Catholics who had never been in
a Protestant church before and the man next me crying all the
time. I thought of Synge's funeral, none at that after some two
or three but enemies or conventional images of gloom. The
masons (there were eighty of them) had their own service and
one by one threw acacia leaves into the grave with the traditional
masonic good-bye, 'Alas my brother, so mote it be'. Then there
came two who threw each a white rose and that was because
they and he were 'Prime masons', a high degree of masonry. It
was as George would have wished it for he loved form and
ceremony.

George Pollexfen left shares in the Sligo Steamships to his
Yeats nephews and nieces, but the bulk of his considerable
fortune went to Pollexfen relations. The will was a disappointment to J. B. Y., who had lately written to his elder
son: 'How is George? He and I are now seventy years of age.
If he knew what enjoyment meant, he would write to me
and say, "Old friend of my schooldays who married my sister
and attached himself to me, would you like a hundred
pounds, because if so it is at your disposal!"'

3

A. H. Bullen was a dear charming man and a famous scholar, but somewhat irregular in habit. On this account Yeats had gone to him in some doubt, in spite of an assurance from the elder A. P. Watt, the famous literary agent, that 'the better they are the more they drink'. Watt presumably spoke from experience, but Bullen formed an exception to the general rule, and Yeats's publishing affairs were now in great confusion. Only two-thirds of the collected edition had been sold, and the Shakespeare Head Press from which it had come was on the point of dissolution. Bullen wrote: 'Scholarly books be hanged! What the booksellers want is bawdy (they cry with Martial "nulla mihi nuda puella satis"); and they shall have it, damn 'em.'

To raise the poet above material anxieties, efforts were set on foot by Lady Gregory and Edmund Gosse to find him a place on the Civil List. These came to a successful issue, Mr Birrell writing to 'My dear Mr Yeats' at the end of 1910 to say that he had had a very easy task. 'Indeed no task at all. The Prime Minister was at least as eager as I was. I know you don't much care about Dr Johnson but I always think *his* pension was the money best spent in England during the whole of my beloved eighteenth century. It is well that the Twentieth should follow suit.' Before permitting Lady Gregory and Gosse to proceed in the matter, Yeats had had some scruples to overcome, but Gosse advised him that acceptance of the grant (£150) would not commit him to political loyalties of any description. The Nationalist mosquito press, which henceforth nicknamed him Pensioner Yeats, might have found a more plausible reason for attacking him when (at about the same time that he took the pension) he accepted a seat on the newly formed Academic Committee of the Royal Society of Literature. His name was passed without discussion on the original list of twenty-eight members. The Royal Society of Literature was moribund, but it was hoped to make this Committee a body in

England corresponding in weight to the French Academy, and at the start Yeats and Gosse appear to have been the most active members. Yeats tried to secure Lady Gregory's election, but Gosse evaded the issue by saying that if they had women on the Committee it would be impossible to omit Mrs Humphry Ward without outraging public opinion. Yeats comforted Lady Gregory as best he could:

... Too many old men who don't know what's going on. Austin Dobson was half asleep, he woke up suddenly and murmured in my ear, 'What's that, is he proposing Lady Grove?' When he found it wasn't Lady Grove he sank back into sleepiness again. ... It will be ten or twenty years before the Academic Committee matters as far as anyone's public position is concerned, the one advantage of it is one gets to know writers and to find out one's friends and enemies. I never look at Prothero for five minutes without a desire to cut his throat. ... We are getting up a Browning celebration, he will probably deliver the oration. In the middle of the last meeting Maurice Hewlett said to Henry James (it was Sir Alfred Lyall's memorial meeting), 'This is dull', to which Henry James sternly replied, 'Hewlett, we are not here to amuse ourselves.'

In Dublin the interesting suggestion was thrown out that Yeats should succeed Edward Dowden, who was in poor health, in the chair of English Literature at Trinity College. Young Doctor Oliver Gogarty reported that the more lively of the Senior Fellows, such as Richard Yelverton Tyrrell, might favour an appointment so distinguished, and it was added that a word from Lord Dunsany, the new Abbey Theatre dramatist, or (better still) from Lord Iveagh, would influence the great Mahaffy in the right direction. As for Yeats's nationalist associations, Oliver Gogarty continued, these, in view of the recent establishment of the National University, ought now to be rather in the poet's favour than otherwise. The idea of a return to his own Protestant people offered attractions to Yeats. His disputes with Gaelic and Sinn Fein opinion made him feel that he had been a little hasty in his earlier judgements upon the university of Swift, Burke, Grattan, of his own father. Moreover, he fancied that

he would like to influence young minds, and he was sure
that he would like rooms in College. His father wrote to him
(29 November 1910):

The mere rumour of a chance of your getting Dowden's place
has caused me great *excitement*, though I can hardly believe it.
It would save you a world of anxiety – and I suppose you will
take care to keep yourself free so that these Trinity College
people (Mahaffy and such – I fancy they are a queer lot – probably Dowden could tell many strange things) don't get such a
tight hold over you that your freedom to write and say what
you like should be lost. A poet without his freedom would be a
poet lost and poetry is your best product and what people look
for. Of course if you got the post and had some time hence to
fight them, and the issue were a fine one, it would be very enjoy-
able, but they are a very astute people like the Vatican.*

Dowden rose to the occasion, and suggested that the Board
should make some arrangement whereby Yeats could be
excused from having to lecture on Early English and such
dry-as-dust matters, for which he would have had to read a
great deal.† It was a generous gesture on Dowden's part, in
view of the bitter words which had passed between him and
the poet in earlier days. The Professor's health, however,
improved, and he did not feel called upon to relinquish the
chair. When he died in 1913, the Board appointed Dr Wilbraham Trench, described by Yeats as 'a man of known
sobriety of manner and of mind'.‡

* And in another letter: 'It is easy to cage the poet bird. Tennyson
was caught and as for Browning he was born in a cage.'

† It may be mentioned that Yeats was deep in Chaucer at this time,
perhaps with a thought of the appointment. Asked what he thought
of a young poet, he said, 'I lent him a large volume of Chaucer. He
brought it back to me in one week saying he had read it. Now it would
have taken him several months to master it thoroughly. He will not
learn his craft . . .'

‡ 'I could wish', Yeats wrote in an introduction to Mr P. A. Ussher's
translation of the Irish poem *The Midnight Court*, 'that a Gaelic
scholar had been found or, failing that, a man of known sobriety of
manner and of mind – Professor Trench of Trinity College, let us say
– to introduce to the Irish reading public this vital, extravagant,
immoral, preposterous poem.'

4

In the critical period of Miss Horniman's withdrawal it became necessary to raise capital for the Abbey Theatre. In London Yeats pleaded for the younger generation of dramatists, Lennox Robinson, T. C. Murray, the Cork realists as he chose to call them, who would be 'driven into exile like Ibsen' if the Abbey were forced to close its doors. With Bernard Shaw, Edmund Gosse and Herbert Trench taking turns in the chair, he spoke before distinguished audiences on Synge and dialect work and on his memories of the Rhymers' Club. The proceeds of those lectures, added to the private donations, assured the Theatre of another lease of life.

He was encouraged by this success and resumed his efforts to establish the principles he had always asserted in face of the modern theatre. The first of these, the primacy of the dramatist over the actor, was well established, but his ideals of staging and of the speaking of verse had not yet been fulfilled. Early in 1911 Florence Farr was once more brought to Dublin; she spoke the musicians' songs in *Deirdre.* 'I am beginning to think,' Yeats wrote to Lady Gregory after the performance,

that Miss O'Neill will be a great tragic actress. The scenes between her and Mrs Emery [Florence Farr] are wonderful things – everyone else is blotted out. Mrs Emery thinks her finer than Mrs Campbell because of her natural emotion. . . . We have had one absurd difficulty at the last moment. Miss X. has been all smiles – we might know she was brooding some mischief. She has made off with the rubies. She has also, I understand, made off with the long mirror, so that Miss O'Neill will not be able to see herself.

In regard to staging, Yeats was in constant communication with Gordon Craig, and there was a moment when he was prepared to go to Florence to join the band of young men under that enthusiast. But Craig wrote to him: 'My school is not for the likes of you I fear. You could learn

nothing there. What you've learnt you've learnt already –
and how much you have learnt about the theatre is positively
appalling. Now we shall learn from you about fairies and
red dogs. My school will lead me and all of us in a place right
out of the theatre – right out and sprawl us on some queer
shore...'

Some of Craig's screens were at the Abbey, and on being
asked by Yeats whether they might be used as the scenery
for Lord Dunsany's fantasy *King Argimenes and the Unknown Warrior* he answered:

I don't understand a word of what you write about Dunsany.
Who is he – and why do you write me of him? It sounds a nice
name anyhow. And what will *he* do with my screens, grace or
disgrace them? The thought that his work (if he be a carpenter)
should go into my screens is pleasant enough – but Lord he
might be someone else – one never knows.

One of the least known of Yeats's plays, yet one of his
best, is *The Player Queen*. He had been at work upon this
verse tragedy for several years; he wrote of it to his father
in 1909: 'I think it will be my most stirring thing. ... There
is a dramatic contrast of character which can be philo-
sophically stated.' It was intended to be performed with
Craig's stage-lighting and the *dramatis personae* were without nationality because Craig's screens had no nationality.
It was first written as tragedy because Yeats was then deep
in the theory of his *Per Amica Silentia Lunae*, and he wasted
many months of several years in an attempt to make every
character an example of the antithetical, forgetful of his
own principle that passion, not thought, makes tragedy. The
play, later turned into prose, really belongs, therefore, to
the period of Yeats's *Vision* (1920–30), which is a clear picture of the poet's not-so-clear mode of thought – though
often considered obscure – and of his comic and sardonic
cast of mind, so much more in evidence in his later than in
his earlier life. Here we have the fairy-tale Queen of tradition – a virgin – suspected of coupling with the unicorn, a

beast so chaste that he can only be killed by a knife that
has been dipped in the blood of a serpent that has died
gazing upon an emerald. The remarks of the two old com-
mentators are an example of Yeats's best eerie manner
(about the tapster's dog: 'Yesterday he had a bone in his
mouth'). The drunken poet ('I saw the blessedest soul in the
world, and he nods a drunken head') abuses the bad popular
poets. The revitalized Queen puts tradition and chastity to
flight – a sort of saturnalia which seems almost prophetic
today.

5

In July 1911, after a few very successful weeks at the Court
Theatre, the Abbey Company received a proposal of an
American tour from Liebler and Co., the theatrical agents.
Liebler offered good terms, a guarantee of all expenses and
thirty-five per cent of the profits, but mentioned certain
plays as essential, among them *The Playboy of the Western
World*. Yeats shrank from the prospect of guiding the company for four months through the States, so before setting
out with Lennox Robinson and the players, he obtained a
promise from Lady Gregory that she would follow him by
the next boat and relieve him of the charge.

The tour opened at the Plymouth Theatre in Boston. At
first only a sprinkling of Irish came, but within a fortnight
the Gaelic societies met and denounced Lady Gregory and
Lennox Robinson as anti-Christian writers and conspirators
against Home Rule. Yeats interviewed the societies and discussed the matter with his usual patience. He had a letter
from his father in New York:

I am delighted with the Irish Society. . . . But the unco guid
have no chance, poor things, in America. We despise law and
order and civic duty and precedent and pardon our criminals or
try to make them happy in prison. We are going to bring in a
law to make judges give decisions, not according to law – which
is old-fashioned, but according to what people like, and 'people'
here always mean the ladies – God bless them – and the ladies

we know all have doctrinaire minds and talk like Lord Morley's
books or Herbert Spencer ...

Yeats was in haste to be home, and he did not wait for the
Irish-American reception of *The Playboy*. He spent a few
days with his father before sailing from New York on the
Lusitania. It was more than three years since he had seen
his parent, who had now settled at 317 West 29th Street, a
little French hotel kept by three Breton sisters who had
'black hair and grand health and laughed all day long'. The
ladies were kind to the old painter, and he brought custom
to their little restaurant. 'Petitpas', as the house was called,
had become famous as a place of good conversation, and
night after night J. B. Y. sat at the head of a table, sketch-
book in hand, surrounded by friends who came to hear him
talk. He was seventy-two, but his son found him little
changed, thin as a lath, brimful and overflowing with ideas,
and as hopeful as ever that fortune as well as recognition
would greet him round the next corner. He was about to
begin a self-portrait, a commission from John Quinn, which
was to be his masterpiece, and he was proud of his recent
essay, 'Back to the Home'.

Yeats felt a little ashamed afterwards when, safe in London or in Dublin, news reached him of the storms of the
tour. One performance of *The Playboy* was half wrecked in
New York; in Philadelphia the company was arrested, at
the instance of the Irish societies, and held to bail for five
days; and in Chicago Lady Gregory received a letter with
the familiar emblems of pistol and coffin, warning her that
she would never again 'gaze on the barren hilltops of Connemara'. She held out, but *The Playboy*, even on later tours,
was never played before an Irish audience for the first time
without something or other being flung at the players.
Yeats's reputation as man and poet among the Irish-
Americans suffered as a consequence of his connection with
Synge, and on his subsequent visits to the States it was in
places like Harvard rather than Irish centres that he was
acclaimed.

Upon his return to England Yeats spent a week at Norwich with Nugent Monck, the organizer of the Norwich players, who then came to Dublin to establish a school of acting at the Abbey Theatre. Monck's pupils played for a season in a cycle of mystery plays, in which were included *The Countess Cathleen* and a new acting version of *The Hour-Glass*, which was played in screens and costumes designed by Gordon Craig. The early version of 1902 had been, Yeats wrote, 'only too effective, converting a music-hall singer and sending him to mass for six weeks', and he now found a new end for the morality which was both closer to his thought and more dramatic. In this later version the Wise Man, whose faith has been undermined by his learning, no longer humbles his intellect before the Fool to receive salvation, but identifies the will of God with the call of the ideal – is prepared to 'perish into reality' – the theme of *Where there is Nothing*, and that of several old-age poems.

> The stream of the world has changed its course,
> And with the stream my thoughts have run
> Into some cloudy thunderous spring
> That is its mountain source –
> Aye to some frenzy of the mind,
> For all that we have done's undone,
> Our speculation but as the wind.*

During this winter Yeats was engaged upon a new piece of work, a translation of *Oedipus Rex*. Dr Rynd of the Norwich Cathedral Chapter, who was on a visit to Dublin, stood over him with the Greek text while he turned Jebb into speakable English with rough unrhymed verse for Chorus. It is interesting to note that seven years earlier Yeats had been advised by his fellow-member, Sir Gilbert Murray, of the ill-fated Masquers Society, not to put *Oedipus Rex* on the Irish stage. 'O man,' Sir Gilbert then wrote,

Vide in *Last Poems*, 'An Acre of Grass':

> 'Grant me an old man's frenzy . . .
> An old man's eagle mind.'

I will not translate Oedipus Rex for the Irish theatre. It has nothing Irish about it: no religion, not one beautiful action, hardly a stroke of poetry. Even the good things that have to be done in order to make the plot work are done through mere loss of temper. The spiritual tragedy is never faced or understood: all the stress is laid on the mere external uncleanness. Sophocles no doubt did many bad things in his life. I would not try to shield him from just blame. But in this case, I am sure, he was in a trance and his body was possessed by a series of devils – Sardou, the Lord Mayor of London, Aristotle, the judicious Hooker and all the Editors of the *Spectator* from its inception to the present day. It has splendid qualities as an acting play, but all of the most English – French – German sort: it is all construction and no spirit. ... It ought to be played not perhaps at His Majesty's by Tree, but by Irving at the Lyceum, with a lecture before ... and after. And a public dinner. With speeches. By Cabinet Ministers. ... Seriously, I rather hope you won't do the *Oedipus*. It is not the play for you to cast in your lot with. Do the *Prometheus* (Bevan's translation, not at all bad: or I might at a pinch attempt it, though I cannot promise without re-reading) or even the *Persae* with a seditious innuendo. Or the *Antigone*.

Yeats never used this version of *Oedipus Rex* of 1911–12. His *Sophocles' King Oedipus* of 1928 was an entirely new work, for which he consulted various translations, including one done in the meantime by Sir Gilbert Murray.

The Countess Cathleen, as played in 1912, was a final version intended to be performed as a series of lovely pictures, a tapestry for the stage. The first two scenes were almost wholly new, and the end after the exit of the merchants was also changed and was now less encumbered with Irish mythological detail. Early versions had been revived in New York by Miss Wycherley and in England by amateurs, but this was the first time that the play had been shown in Dublin since the disturbances occasioned by the famous production in 1899. No policemen were now required to preserve order, and in his inexhaustible optimism Yeats called upon that long-neglected figure of the Irish Revival, Edward Martyn, to have a talk about the possibility of a literary understanding with the Roman Catholic Church in

Ireland. Nugent Monck had staged an Annunciation, a Nativity and a Flight into Egypt; would the priests help, he asked Martyn, 'as they are doing in Paris', if the second Abbey company continued to specialize in religious drama? 'No,' said Martyn, 'they are too suspicious. They think that you are not only anti-Catholic but anti-Christian.' 'We are neither of these things,' Yeats replied, 'and it is the interest of your Church to encourage a distinguished intellectual life in Ireland, for the alternative will be atheism in a few years.' To this Martyn surprisingly assented, but said that the Church in Ireland was not clever enough to realize the danger.

Some people have wondered that Yeats, with his almost Confucian sense of custom and ceremony, should not have decided for purely aesthetic reasons to adopt some ancient and conventional creed. But ceremony was to him a kind of magic, not a thing ordained on grounds of reason and to establish a moral or a religious truth. Moreover, he was a born heretic; after poetry he loved heresy and dissension best. It was one of the most Irish sides of him – that passion for trailing his coat! He had a taste for the heterodox for its own sake; does not G. K. Chesterton rebuke him for not giving a traditional account of the fairies? So that it is not to be wondered at that the Church should have viewed him with extreme suspicion. Profoundly different has been its attitude towards James Joyce, who will always be, and rightly so, 'the Jesuit boy'. Joyce's whole work is instinct with the sense of original sin which Yeats in later life preached as an essential qualification of the poet ('What theme had Homer but original sin?') but which he himself never seems to have had. Yeats's mysticism, like that of Blake, is a kind of revolt against natural religion, and perhaps the words 'good' and 'evil' meant as little to his imagination as to that of any artist in history. If they meant anything, 'good' must have meant 'holy dread' in Coleridge's sense, the unknown force, 'the uncontrollable mystery on the bestial floor', 'evil' – dullness, generalized thought. There is even a touch of D. H.

Lawrence here and there in his writings, as in that passage
of a manifesto (meant to be provocative, it is true) in which
he speaks of the 'Holy Spirit' as an 'intellectual fountain'
and goes on to infer that good is richness '... the lust of the
Goat, even the abounding Horn'.

6

The absence of Lennox Robinson and of Lady Gregory in
the States obliged Yeats to be in Dublin for the greater part
of the winter of 1911–12. But he crossed to England for brief
periods, and during one of his visits his old friend, Mrs
Olivia Shakespear, brought him to Brighton to see her
brother, Mr Tucker, and his wife, formerly Mrs Hyde-Lees
of Pickhill Hall, Wrexham. Some months later Yeats revisited the Tuckers at Lynton in Devonshire, and there
made the acquaintance of Georgie Hyde-Lees, Mrs Tucker's
daughter by her first marriage, a young girl with musical
and literary interests, whom he met frequently during the
next five years, and whom he married in 1917.

After the American tour of the Abbey players had concluded, he was less seen in Dublin than formerly. Lennox
Robinson took over the practical work of the theatre, the
actual production of plays, most of which no longer led to
the villages, where nothing changes, or to the past of legend,
but concerned themselves with the actual, moving Ireland,
its comic figures, its popular abuses, bribery in local affairs,
subservience to the English Government, and so on. This
was the 'People's' theatre of which Yeats wrote in 1919 in a
'Letter to Lady Gregory'. 'Not the theatre we set out to
create ... but the first doing of something for which the
world is ripe, something that will be done all over the world
and done more and more perfectly: the making articulate
of all the dumb classes each with its own knowledge of the
world, its own dignity, but all objective with the objectivity
of the office and the workshop, of the newspaper and the
street, of mechanism and of politics. ...'

London was never attractive to Yeats for long periods, and he liked to be out of the town as much as possible. He had Maud Gonne's house in Normandy to go to now, as well as Coole; from time to time he accompanied Mrs Shakespear to hotels at English country places, where the Tuckers and their daughter, who moved about a great deal, were to be found. Occasionally he accepted invitations to important country houses for week-ends. At one such house among politicians he met Winston Churchill ('obviously the ablest man here,' he wrote to Lady Gregory, 'but I had not much opportunity to talk to him, as he preferred bridge'). Dame Edith Lyttelton (the Hon. Mrs Alfred Lyttelton) recalls him as a guest at Taplow Court. She had met him first at Hugh Lane's beautiful house in Cheyne Walk.

His hair was rather long and it seemed very grand and black, and to have a life of its own which he could not always control : it swayed when he spoke but often in a different rhythm from his speech, as if it were impatient of its owner's words. Then there were his eyes, burning with vehemence, smouldering with a deeper emotion than he was expressing, and finally a general sense that he did not belong to the life of London, or of England, or indeed perhaps to the life of the Earth itself. . . . I remember wondering if he would lead a revolt and be killed at a street barricade and only gradually I realised that his fight was not against anyone or anything, except in defence of what he conceived as Beauty and Spirit. . . . A year or two afterwards we were both fellow guests at one of Lady Desborough's famous week-end parties. I cannot remember who was there besides, but there were a great many, and it so happened that after dinner the whole company fitted into a pattern of whist tables in one or two different rooms and Yeats and I were the only ones left out, as neither he nor I played cards. . . . We sat side by side on a sofa and plunged into talk. I was tired, and rather fretful because I never seemed to have time enough to read or write. Politics, social service and society swallowed all my energies, and then came the duty of taking my daughter to her first round of balls and parties and I dreaded this interruption to the little spare time I had. I cannot think why I should have poured out all this to Yeats, but I did, and I am glad I did because he said something to me in that dimly-lit luxurious room which I have never forgotten. 'Whenever I have to do something,' he declared, 'like a dull bit of routine business, or enduring the talk of a bore, I always say to myself "Remember, this is an occupation which requires great skill." ' It is curious that a few words like these can reverberate in one's being for the whole of life. How often I have admonished myself when starting on some very distasteful job. 'Remember, this is an occupation which requires great skill' – at once the occasion is invested with dignity, and one's powers, whatever they may be, are called upon.

Sir Ian Hamilton's recollections of the social Yeats of the pre-war years fall into a series of mind-pictures:

Reigate Priory makes a very pretty one – Reigate when it was the abode of Somers Somerset and that beautiful daughter of the Duke of St Albans, now Lady Kitty Lambton. Young Lady Dufferin was one of our party and two other Rossetti damosels who looked as if they had just vaulted over that golden bar. Through the sylvan glades, blue as heaven with blue-bells, strolled Yeats followed by this bevy of beauties. In his eyes I felt I was at that time and place the one blot on the blue-bells, so when he perched himself on the root of a fallen tree and began to read out *Deirdre* or *Shadowy Waters*, I lay down at full length and was instantly swallowed up by the bracken. But I listened in and heard Yeats at his best. Some men might feel shy under that style of ordeal; as for me wild horses would not drag me to it though I can speak to thousands without being too frightened. Not so Yeats. His *milieu* was the centre of a small band of admirers. Lady Kitty still says of Yeats that he was 'the best conversationalist she ever met at a small [*sic*] party.' Oh, that I had jotted down the many pearls that fell so fast from his lips. But I thought that Yeats's sparkle was quenched before a big audience – that he was too self-conscious to carry away a crowd.

Years after, when a long interval had passed during which he had not seen Yeats, Sir Ian was suddenly again reminded of the speech of the poet. The occasion (he says) may arouse mixed feelings in the mind of English readers. It was during a two-hours' talk with Adolf Hitler in 1938, and as Sir Ian listened to that eager, nervy voice running up and down the gamut of the emotional scales – laughter, sorrow, pity – the thought kept rising at the back of his head like a question mark, 'Where ever have I heard someone speak like this?' Then, suddenly, as Hitler spoke of his nightingales, the mirror of memory flashed and there he was listening again to his old friend Yeats.

Responsibilities

Tagore – Hugh Lane; *Poems written in Discouragement* – Mabel Beardsley; correspondence on poetry with J. B. Y. – With Ezra Pound in Sussex – War on George Moore

======

> *Now all the truth is out,*
> *Be secret and take defeat*
> *From any brazen throat,*
> *For how can you compete,*
> *Being honour bred, with one*
> *Who, were it proved he lies,*
> *Were neither shamed in his own*
> *Nor in his neighbours' eyes?*

I

YEATS was now writing lyrics again at something like his old pace (never a very rapid one); the lovers' dialogue 'The Mask', which was made for *The Player Queen* and took its place in his next volume *Responsibilities*, is a beautiful example of his work at this time, masculine and astringent, freed from nostalgic yearnings:

> 'Put off that mask of burning gold,
>   With emerald eyes.'
> 'O, no, my dear, you make so bold
>   To find if hearts be wild and wise,
>   And yet not cold. . . .'

While with the Gonnes in Normandy in August 1912, he wrote his Rosicrucian 'Mountain Tomb' and a poem for Iseult Gonne, and worked at intervals on a preface for a book of Lord Dunsany's stories, and on an introduction to *Gitanjali*, Rabindranath Tagore's translations from his own

Bengali. He had already helped Tagore, who was visiting London for the first time, to revise and improve these translations; and Tagore was to write to him years later of the 'greater mastery of the English language' which he owed to 'intimate instruction in a quiet little room off Euston Road'. The poems deeply moved the heart of the young and lovely Iseult, who asked Yeats to get her a Bengali grammar and dictionary so that she might read Tagore in the original. If Yeats and she exaggerated the merits of *Gitanjali* (in English translation), so also did Robert Bridges, Henry Bradley and other English men of letters to whom Sir William Rothenstein, who acted as Tagore's cicerone in England, sent the manuscript. Bridges wrote to Yeats on receiving the book:

Binyon brought us Tagore's poems with your lovely preface. What a delight it was! Oh, most blessed one! There is no one but you who could write so. He told me that it was coming out in a cheap edition – and he promised to give you a message from me, the practical part of which was that I want you to alter one word in your master-piece. It is the expression 'four-fifths' or 'five-sixths' or something of that fractional quality. . . . It led me wondering what fractions could be admitted into that consummate style. A half is of course all right; and perhaps 'two-thirds', because 'three' is the mystic subdivision of all things, and 'two-thirds' might be called 'two-parts' but after that one falls into conversational meaninglessness. . . . Will you never come and see us again? You are always attended, I take it, by your company of players. . . . There are sympathetic souls who would be rejoiced to meet you: above all Walter Raleigh; and my house is retired on a hill and has a large room, library and music-room, where you could do what you liked. . . . Do come. . . . Don't feel obliged to write a letter – a postcard, or four-fifths of a postcard would tell me you will come.

Encouraged by the reception of *Gitanjali*, Tagore made further English translations of his own work, and presently Yeats produced his *Post Office* at the Abbey Theatre. It was not surprising that Yeats should have been attracted by a man who looked as if he had stepped out of the Vedic Age;

Tagore belonged to the Adi Bràhmo Samaj, a reformed religious minority, unaffected by English or Christian influences, and was a member of a distinguished and aristocratic family long associated with the national movement in India. His position, therefore, was not unlike that of Yeats in Ireland. Though Yeats had long held in contempt unlettered admiration for romantic exploitation of things Indian, he had never wholly ceased to await 'Light from the East'. Sarojini Naidu, the poetess and nationalist, was always welcome at his 'Monday evenings', and now he did not confine his inquiry into contemporary Indian culture to the poetry of Tagore or to the philosophical disquisitions of Tagore's brother, the saintly Dwijendranath Tagore. His attention was attracted to the life and work of Toru Dutt, another Bengali poet and essayist, and he placed before Mr Harihar Das a project for an annual gathering in India similar to the Welsh Eisteddfod, which, in his judgement, would prove of great value in bringing together Indian poets and act as a stimulus to existing literary societies.

There was a question of bringing Tagore to Ireland, and he was put in correspondence with P. H. Pearse, the Irish-speaking schoolmaster who was to lead the Rising of 1916. Tagore refrained from visiting Ireland, perhaps wisely, although Maud Gonne thought he might make himself useful there. Nevertheless, his transformation into a prophet with a practical message for the West may be said to have been started with the 'intimate instruction' in Woburn Buildings. One recalls how, at the height of the pacifist movement in the nineteen-twenties, Tagore – translated into every language (novels and essays as well as poems) – was received at Darmstadt, a visitor to Count Keyserling's 'School of Wisdom', by thousands who, in imitation of the Indian ceremonies, hung garlands about his neck and strewed the sunlit roads with flowers.

2

During the winter of 1912–13 Yeats was suddenly drawn back to Ireland and controversy. The collection of Hugh Lane's modern French pictures, a part of a Modern Art Gallery founded in Dublin in 1905, had become famous, and Lane insisted that they should be suitably housed by the Corporation. His desire for a bridge site across the Liffey to the design of Sir Edward Lutyens met with popular opposition, and Yeats took up the cause of the bridge site with the greater gusto because Lane's chief critic was the *Independent* newspaper, whose proprietor, William Martin Murphy, had been a prominent anti-Parnellite in the old days. Yeats chose to regard Martin Murphy, a man of distinguished character and appearance, to whose energy in industrial enterprise Dublin was under considerable debt, as a representative type and leader of the middle class which had begun to rise into power under the shadow of the Land League and kindred agitations. This Murphy certainly was not, even though he was ignorant of art and allowed his newspaper too much latitude in abuse.

Lane became the unnamed hero of a memorable series: *Poems written in Discouragement*. Money was needed from private subscribers as well as from the rate-payers for the new gallery, and the first poem in the series was addressed 'To a Rich Man who promises a Bigger Subscription than his First to the Dublin Municipal Gallery when the Amount Collected proves that there is a Popular Demand for the Pictures'. Thomas Bodkin, Lane's closest Dublin friend, has the corrected typescript of this poem, and in it the lines

> Indifferent how the rancour ran,
> He gave the hours they had set free
> To Michelozzo's latest plan
> For the San Marco Library

have been altered from

> Unknowing their predestined man,
> So much more time and thought had he
> For Michelozzo's latest plan
> Of the San Marco Library.

With the poem went a letter to Lane (1 January 1913) asking him if he thought it 'politic'. 'If it is not politic, tell me
so frankly. ... I have tried to meet the argument in Lady
Ardilaun's letter to somebody, her objection to giving because of Home Rule, and Lloyd George, and still more to
meet the general argument of people like Ardilaun that
they should not give unless there is public demand.'

The poem was obviously not politic, with its scathing
allusion to the possible slightness of 'little Paudeen's' desire
of art.

> You gave, but will not give again
> Until enough of Paudeen's pence
> By Biddy's halfpennies have lain
> To be 'some sort of evidence',
> Before you'll put your guineas down,
> That things it were a pride to give
> Are what the blind and ignorant town
> Imagines best to make it thrive.

Lady Gregory was again in America with the Abbey company and Yeats wrote to her there, telling of Hugh Lane's
increased impatience with Dublin and its Corporation. It had
become certain that Lane would fulfil his threat and take
away the loaned pictures to London if the money were not
quickly raised. Lady Gregory collected funds in America
but Lane continued to demand the bridge site, to which
others beside 'Paudeens' raised objections. The 'Paudeens',
however, held the floor; one man compared the pictures to
the Trojan horse which destroyed a city, and Lane and his
friends, rich and poor, were described as 'self-seekers', 'self-
advertisers', 'picture-dealers', 'log-rolling cranks and fana-
tics'. Someone asked instead of these eccentric Manets and
Monets, to be given pictures like 'those beautiful productions
displayed in the windows of our city shops'. It was all silly

enough, but Yeats gave offence by publishing his poem in a Unionist paper, and what with one thing and another the friends of art on the Corporation – and there were few – were put in a very difficult position. It was found impossible to induce a majority in the Corporation to swallow at one gulp bridge site and English architect; Lane carried the pictures away and lent them to the National Gallery in London, and Yeats enlarged the already rich body of his work by a number of fine political poems. In one of these, 'To a Shade', he gratified Lady Gregory by comparing Lane's fate to that of Parnell.

> ... A man
> Of your own passionate serving kind who had brought
> In his full hands what, had they only known,
> Had given their children's children loftier thought,
> Sweeter emotion, working in their veins
> Like gentle blood, has been driven from the place,
> And insult heaped upon him for his pains.

Writing of this great poem in his book on *Poetry and the Modern World*, Mr David Daiches has called it Yeats's finest expression of contrast between heroic and commonplace in his period as a disillusioned, realistic poet. 'The stately movement of the verse, the monumental phrasing, and the undulating movement of the poem, which comes to a temporary climax at the end of each of the first two verses and then to its overwhelming final climax at the end of the third and last stanza, show Yeats at his most impressive.'

> Go, unquiet wanderer,
> And gather the Glasnevin coverlet
> About your head till the dust stops your ear.
> The time for you to taste of that salt breath
> And listen at the corners has not come;
> You had enough of sorrow before death –
> Away, away! You are safer in the tomb.

The same mingling of the heroic and epigrammatic-satiric is heard in 'September 1913', lines which Catholic and Nationalist Ireland have found it hard to forgive:

What need you, being come to sense,
But fumble in a greasy till
And add the halfpence to the pence
And prayer to shivering prayer . . .

Was it for this the wild geese spread
The grey wing upon every tide;
For this that all that blood was shed,
For this Edward Fitzgerald died,
And Robert Emmet and Wolfe Tone,
All that delirium of the brave?
Romantic Ireland's dead and gone,
It's with O'Leary in the grave.

James Larkin, the celebrated labour agitator, had said some words in favour of Lane, and it may be surmised that Yeats was not actuated solely by humanitarian zeal when he intervened with a word for the workers during the great strike led by Larkin which paralysed the life of Dublin at the time of the bridge site controversy. Murphy led the employers and was denounced by all the intellectuals and Bohemians of the city as a cold-hearted tyrant who had without compunction turned thousands of men on the streets. George Russell, James Connolly of the '98 celebrations, Madame Markievicz – Constance Gore-Booth of Lissadell, Sligo, now no longer a particular friend to Yeats* – were in great prominence as supporters of the strike. Yeats's intervention took the form of an article in the *Irish Worker* rebuking the employers for 'misuse of religion', a charge based on the action of Dublin priests in preventing the children of strikers from being evacuated from the country by English and Protestant sympathizers. The article brought a letter of congratulation from George Russell, who wrote that 'all my old affection for you surges up again'.

* She was one of several who ran a rival dramatic company.

3

Singularly different in manner and matter from the Lane poems, but equally fine in workmanship, was another series with an unnamed heroine for subject. 'The Grey Rock', which commemorates Lionel Johnson, Dowson and other 'companions of the Cheshire Cheese', who, 'unrepenting faced their ends', appeared in the *Literary Digest* for November 1912; and in a letter to Lady Gregory, Yeats remarked upon the coincidence that he should so soon afterwards have been sitting by the bedside of Mabel Beardsley, whose brother had virtually formed one of the group. Mabel Beardsley was stricken with cancer, and Yeats was but one of many friends to admire the gay manner in which she rose superior to her sufferings. Her bright courage and daring wit are celebrated in the six pictorial poems 'On a Dying Lady'. The note, very much 'Beardsley period', is indicated in a letter to Lady Gregory:

Mabel Beardsley said to me on Sunday, 'I wonder who will introduce me in heaven. It should be my brother but then they might not appreciate the introduction. They may not have my good taste.' She said of her brother, 'He hated the people who denied the existence of evil and so being very young he filled his pictures with evil. He had a passion for reality.' She has the same passion and puts aside any attempt to suggest recovery, and yet I have never seen her in low spirits.

As Mabel Beardsley lingered on for several years, Yeats was unable to publish the poems in *Responsibilities*, his next considerable volume of verse. On the other hand, the Lane poems were at once printed in an edition of fifty copies, and subsequently in *Responsibilities*, the title of which they may have suggested. They led to an interesting exchange of letters between the poet and his father:

2.7.13. *From J. B. Yeats*

I hope you did not mind my saying that you were rather neglecting vision. In your first poems you were all *vision*, and it captured people. That was the time when Victor Hugo ruled the spheres. ... A poet should possess oratory but use it seldom – who so great an orator as Shakespeare! Victor Hugo also – yet only occasionally – mostly they were true solitaries. Poetry is the re-action of the imperfect from the perfect – to a perfect grief as in Synge's *Riders to the Sea*, or to a perfect joy as in your early poetry – the accompanying melody either of prose or verse, the effort to keep the heart soft and wakeful – portraiture in art or poetry, the effort to keep the pain alive and intensify it, since out of the heart of the pain comes the solace, as a monk scourges himself to bring on ecstasy. Some time ago I saw a young mother with a sick infant in her arms. ... I put question after question to her and was haunted by what I saw and heard for days and days. Why did I put these questions and why did I try constantly to recall and keep alive the incident? I regretted that I could not take my canvas and paint a portrait of her and her child. She was soft spoken, Irish and young and very pretty, from Donnybrook, and all her children had died in infancy. ... I could do nothing for her practically – misery beyond alleviation. I would fain scourge myself spiritually, and it pained me that the image should fade.

–.7.13. *To J. B. Yeats*

I thought your letter about portraiture being 'pain' most beautiful and profound ... of recent years instead of vision, meaning by vision the intense realisation of ecstatic emotion symbolised in a definite imagined region, I have tried for more self-portraiture, I have tried to make my work convincing with a speech so natural that the hearer would feel the presence of a man thinking and feeling. There are always the two types of poetry – Keats, the type of vision, Burns a very obvious type of the other, too obvious indeed. It is in dramatic lyrical expression that English poetry is most lacking as compared with French poetry. Villon always and Ronsard at times create marvellous drama out of their own lives.

20.7.13. *From J. B. Yeats*

I am afraid I sometimes take full advantage of your filial piety and write nonsense. I have just re-read some of your first plays and find you especially rich in *vision*, in splendid vision of great amplitude and detail. That at any rate is not where you are weak.

I have been trying lately to read American verse and it is good exercise as a preliminary to reading your verse. Your verse is so *packed with vision* and they're so charming and musical with everything that is *not* vision, that is the difference – and I fancy it is the difference between your work and that of most of the English poets nowadays.

I was quite right in insisting on the importance of vision – but wrong in fancying you deficient in it.

Having always urged Yeats to avoid the 'comparatively easy path of the lyrical writer', J. B. Y. was pleased with his son's return in 1913 to Irish heroic legend. He wrote of the narrative poem 'The Two Kings': 'It's about the only poem I can think of to which I would apply the word Homeric, by which I mean that it touches one at a thousand points. Had this poem been fifty pages instead of ten, it would rank with the three or four great poems of the world.' And again:

What the devil does Ezra Pound mean by comparing 'The Two Kings' with Tennyson's Idylls? 'The Two Kings' is immortal because of its *intensity* and *concentration*. In 'The Two Kings' there is another quality often sought for by Tennyson but never attained, and that is *Splendour of Imagination* – a liberating splendour cold as the sunrise. I do not agree with Ezra Pound. It is so full of the 'tears of things' that I could not read it aloud, and yet Ezra is the best of critics and writes with such lucid force, and I am only an amateur – but I have the advantage. I am no longer in the world and have travelled further, and *intensity* and *concentration* are not Tennysonian.

4

During the winter of 1912–13 a digestive disorder reduced Yeats to a milk diet for a long period; at other times his head ached and his eyes played the traitor. His life in Woburn Buildings was only rendered tolerable by the assiduous attentions of Ezra Pound, who would come to read to him in the evenings and also helped him to health by teaching him to fence.* It was during one bout of indigestion

* *Vide* – 'I thought no more was needed
　　　　Youth to prolong
　　　　Than dumbbell and foil
　　　　To keep the body young.'

that he worked himself into a fury against Wordsworth as a clumsy humbug and then cried over Robert Bridges. He decided, therefore, never to spend another complete winter in London; but he would have found solitude in the country impossible owing to his defective eyesight. In August 1913, when circumstances at Coole prevented him from going to Lady Gregory, he stayed for some weeks with the Tuckers and their daughter at 'The Prelude', a house in Ashdown Forest. As he enjoyed the walks in the woods, he searched for lodgings in this vicinity and found what he wanted at Stone Cottage, Coleman's Hatch, where tourists were not taken in. Here he settled down in the autumn with Ezra Pound. He felt that a new prospect had opened for his coming winters. 'Ezra', he wrote to Lady Gregory, 'never shrinks from work. ... A learned companion and a pleasant one. ... He is full of the Middle Ages and helps me to get back to the definite and concrete, away from modern abstractions, to talk over a poem with him is like getting you to put a sentence into dialect. All becomes clear and natural.'

Yeats left Sussex for London occasionally, once to make a speech on a compatriot's work at the Academic Committee, James Stephens having received the Polignac award for imaginative literature. His stay at the cottage was also interrupted by an excursion in company with Ezra Pound, Sturge Moore and a dozen or more other poets, to New Buildings to honour Wilfrid Blunt on his seventieth birthday. Lady Gregory as an old friend of Blunt desired that the event should be given publicity; but Pound said: 'Tell Lady Gregory we hate the newspapers as Blunt hates the British Empire'. Blunt's politics prevented Robert Bridges from travelling to New Buildings, but the day was a success and at its end the poets were photographed together, as if they were a shooting party. They were given peacock for luncheon,* and Yeats sent *The Times* an unsigned report of

---

* *Vide* (perhaps): 'What's riches to him
That has made a great peacock
With the pride of his eye?'

the proceedings as a 'record for posterity'. 'We presented our stone box,' he wrote to Lady Gregory. 'Ezra read out his poem. ... Blunt asked me to stay on with Belloc who came at 3.30, and finding himself in a company that could not be shocked, was, I think, a little bewildered. All the poets behaved well, except poor X. – the motor cost me £5, but it was the only thing to be done to avoid inflicting a whole day on Blunt ...'

During the first month in the cottage he had an exceptional amount of work on hand, as he had to prepare for a lecture tour in America fixed for the New Year. In the evenings Ezra Pound read to him.

11.11.13. *To Lady Gregory*

I want you to get from the Library Mrs Hinkson's* book *Twenty-five Years' Reminiscences*. It contains – without permission – pages of my letters written when I was twenty-one or two, to me very curious letters. I recognise the thought, but the personality seems to me someone else. The book contains a great deal that moves me, for it is a very vivid picture of the Dublin in my youth ...

I was surprised a few days ago by a cheque for £50 from *Poetry*, a little Chicago review which published 'The Grey Rock', a prize for the best poem published by them. After a few days of embarrassment I am sending back £40 and asking them to give it to some young writer and telling them I shall spend the rest on a book-plate. I hope I have done right. My first thought was to send it all back but that looked like pride, so much as to say I am too important to take a prize. I have written a formal letter to the editor suggesting Ezra for a part at any rate of the £40. I have asked Sturge Moore to do the book-plate and he says he will not take pay for it.

5

A memoir writer who pleased Yeats less than Katharine Tynan was George Moore, now completing his trilogy on the Irish Renaissance, *Hail and Farewell*. The earlier volumes

* Katharine Tynan.

had depicted Yeats as an 'old umbrella forgotten at a picnic-party', as a 'Torquemada of literature'; had made fun of his 'Order of the Golden Door [*sic*]', of his 'conspiracies with Maud Gonne in Kensington', of some statement he was alleged to have made regarding the Elizabethan character of the audience at the Antient Concert Rooms. Yeats had disparaged the first two volumes, calling them mere 'journalism', but it was only after the publication of certain chapters from *Vale* in the *English Review* that he declared war.* These dealt with his unhappy love affair and told how, on his return from America in 1904 in a fur coat, he 'began to thunder like Ben Tillett himself' against the middle classes.

We asked ourselves why Willie Yeats should feel himself called upon to denounce the class to which he himself belonged essentially . . . with so admirable a parentage it did not seem necessary that a man should look back for an ancestor, and we had laughed at the story . . . that on one occasion when Yeats was crooning over A E's fire he had said that if he had his rights he would be Duke of Ormonde, and that A E had answered, 'In any case, Willie, you are overlooking your father'.

His first step after reading the chapters was to persuade Lady Gregory to threaten to protect herself at law against a repetition of the suggestion that as a young woman she had gone amongst the cottages as a Bible reader – a statement calculated to damage Lady Gregory's prestige as a public figure in Ireland. Lady Gregory wrote to Moore, and he promised to amend the passage, which he did very dexterously. He assured the readers of *Vale* that Lady Gregory never brought the Bible into the cottages. 'In her own words, "early association has so much to do with that religion which is the secret of the heart with God". In saying as much she wins our hearts, but our intelligence warns us against seduction, and we remember that we may not acquiesce in what we believe to be error.'

* In *Dramatis Personae* he credited Moore with five great novels, but had no word of praise for *Hail and Farewell*.

The statements about himself, Yeats noted in his diary, were 'equally untrue but too indefinite for any action'. He had not referred to the middle classes in the speech which Moore described, but he had appealed to the Irish aristocracy to support Lane's Gallery. Moore had turned this into an attack on the middle classes, confusing it perhaps with a later speech at the National Literary Society when Yeats had used the word *bourgeois* not as a term of aristocratic reproach but like the older 'cit', a word of artistic usage found in Ben Jonson. 'Moore is the born demagogue,' he went on, 'and in nothing more than in his love for the wealthy. He has the mob's materialism and the mob's hatred of any privilege which is an incommunicable gift; also the demagogic virtues which are all bound up with logic.' There is some union of incompatibilities in his blood. Martyn and he were examples of 'the way Irish civilization is held back by the lack of education of Irish Catholic women. ... The women have checked again and again the rise of some refinement in Irish Catholic households. ... A long continuity of culture like that of Coole could not have arisen, and never has arisen, in a single Catholic family since the middle ages.'

Two poems followed, provoked by the incident. T. S. Eliot has spoken of 'that violent and terrible epistle dedicatory to *Responsibilities* ["Pardon, old fathers"], where is first fully evinced Yeats's power of speaking as a particular man to men – more than half a lifetime to arrive at this freedom of speech. It is a triumph.'

> Pardon that for a barren passion's sake,
> Although I have come close on forty-nine,
> I have no child, I have nothing but a book,
> Nothing but that to prove your blood and mine.*

The second poem, 'While I, from that reed-throated

---

* By making old William Pollexfen, trader and ship-owner, the hero of this poem Yeats thought to turn the tables on George Moore of Moore Hall.

whisperer', formed the epilogue of *Responsibilities*, and in this Yeats wrote of

> Those undreamt accidents that have made me –
> Seeing that Fame has perished this long while,
> Being but a part of ancient ceremony –
> Notorious, till all my priceless things
> Are but a post the passing dogs defile.

13

Nineteen-sixteen

A lecture tour in America – 'Immortality and survival';
a ghost story – Yeats's essay on Swedenborg; researches
with Everard Feilding – Japanese drama – Yeats during
the war; refusal of knighthood; Irish anxieties – Study
in Sussex; thoughts on Wordsworth, Browning and
Tennyson – Production of *Hawk's Well*; Keats and the
Queen; *Responsibilities* – Easter Week Rising – Thoughts
of marriage; a conditional proposal – Personal crisis

———

> *And what if excess of love*
> *Bewildered them till they died?*
> *I write it out in a verse –*
> *MacDonagh and MacBride*
> *And Connolly and Pearse*
> *Now and in time to be,*
> *Wherever green is worn,*
> *Are changed, changed utterly:*
> *A terrible beauty is born.*

I

THE voyage to America was villainous, and Yeats's ship was
several days at sea before he had an opportunity of picking
up acquaintances, as always he liked doing, among his fellow
passengers. The first day that he went on deck someone
recognized him and opened conversation by asking him
what he thought of George Moore's article in the *English
Review*. When others came out of their cabins, he found
himself at table with an American banker, an English boy
chiefly interested in horses and Gaiety girls, a handsome,
well-bred young German who talked of Mexico and sympathized with the rebels, and an American doctor, the head
of a great laboratory in New York. After the first meal he
was taken aside by the doctor and asked – 'because my wife

thinks you the greatest poet in the world' – to write something in a scrap-book. 'The German', he wrote to Lady Gregory,

does not display his personality and is therefore not amusing to a chance acquaintance. The Americans display their personalities at once. T —— talks American journalese and moral uplift and has the gestures of a public speaker. He sees the whole world as a war between all sorts of evil. He said, 'I do not publish my discoveries in the newspapers but in an obscure German review. If I published in newspapers my motives would cease to be pure. I would think of money and fame. The Greeks when they fought at Salamis did not think of fame and of Empire. We must become Greek.' I cannot remember his language – profound and incoherent and preposterous. ... He showed me his diary written for his wife – it was a collection of the most mechanical and even vulgar jokes except for a description of the rescue of certain sailors by the *Lusitania* on her journey to England. ... Matter-of-fact and well written, but the moment his science was off him he would break out into phrases such as 'O all-conquering power of love' and ejaculations about moral uplift. ... He is perhaps a man of genius but has no language. ... I find he knows Hugh Lane and so I have given him *Poems Written in Dejection*.

During his lecture tour, Yeats did not confine himself to Irish themes, but spoke on the 'theatre of beauty', on English and American contemporaries, on Lionel Johnson, Dowson and the aesthetic 'Nineties'. In his first lecture, which was in New York, he used many of his father's ideas, particularly that contrast drawn by J. B. Y. between pleasure which is personal and joy which is impersonal. He elicited two elements in poetry, one impersonal and generally sorrowful, and the other personal and pleasurable, and showed them existing side by side, the pleasurable element being the element of style, the conscious choice of words – all that remains of the ego in great work.

On 13 February he wrote to Lady Gregory from St Catherine's, Ontario:

I have been lecturing every night for a week, with long journeys in between, and today is Sunday and I am very tired. ... I am at St Catherine's, the guest of the hotel proprietor, and described last night the theatre of beauty and I think I puzzled the audience. I saw a great deal of my father in New York and found him happy but heavily in debt. I have just written to him that I will give him £50. He did not ask for it and seemed unwilling to talk over his affairs. He had a bad year last year, I expect. ... I think he is happy in his lodging-house where I spent three evenings and was taught dancing by several ladies.* Everybody makes a great deal of him . . .

23.2.14. *From J. B. Yeats*

Thanks indeed for the £40. You don't know how pleased it looks, as it lies there in all its fairness. Did I tell you that the Poetry Society, stirred by your speech at the luncheon, are to have at next meeting a debate on the question of uplift and whether it ought to be in poetry?

The whole land is crazy with rhetoric – the other night I happened to say to a lady near me, that a certain young lady was charming because in addition to good looks and a graceful manner she had a serious mind. 'You mean,' she asked, 'that she has a social conscience?' 'No,' I replied, 'she is a serious student of the Irish language.'

The poet has only one burthen, himself, and the human nature for which he stands – and it is enough. Jesus Christ was tempted in all things; the description which applies to *very very* few men applies to poets, and they, not being divine, have to do the best they can – hence poetry, hence music, hence art.

In Chicago Yeats met with a particularly brilliant reception, and on his last day in that town hundreds were unable to find a place in the hall where he spoke. Vachel Lindsay, writing to him years later, in 1928, recalled an address that he gave before the Poetry Society:

On March 1914, before the assembled poets, you did me the honour to speak well of one piece of my work in public, and by the magic of your name, everything that I have written since has been too much praised, whether you saw it or not, or whether it was worthy of your eyes. Before that time I was a Sangamon county poet, and would likely have remained so to the end of

* 'But never have I danced for joy' – vide *Last Poems.*

my days. That instant remains, as it appeared then, the literary transformation scene of my life.

Hearing of his successes his father wrote to him:

I dreamed that I was in a high house with many windows, and that through them I could see you bestride an immense black horse, stretched in a gallop and going at such a prodigious pace that though, as I was told, the course was fifteen miles, yet it seemed as if every few minutes you returned to pass the windows through which I watched for you; not a bad symbol, I fancy, of your lecture tour.

The picture of this father watching every move of his famous son, giving counsel to him from his earliest years, publicizing in whatsoever way he could his activities and work, always seeking to grant him what experience his extra years had taught, is not dissimilar to that of the two Mozarts where we find Wolfgang consulting his father over and over again; the father living a life inextricably bound up with that of the son.

After a stay at President's House, Amherst, Massachusetts, Yeats went south to Tennessee. He wrote to Lady Gregory from Memphis (4 March):

This is a southern town where everything is delectable except the climate. While I write a negro woman is doing up the room in spite of the fact that I have twice sent her out as I wanted to write letters. I had a stupid audience, very large and very ignorant. It has been a shock after Chicago where I had the most intelligent audiences. ... I am staying a couple of weeks longer than I intended as I want to clear £500 and a few more lectures will pay my travelling expenses which otherwise would have had to come out of my guaranteed £500. I am feeling the strain and have had a heavy cold but shall get through all right. I am furious with my father. ... He is a hopeless sentimentalist about practical life.

Yeats was upset because his father had suggested that the quarrel with George Moore should be composed. This liberality of J. B. Y. was interpreted by his son as due to lack of family pride. 'It is useless', W. B. wrote, 'to discuss it any further. We take a different view of the obligations of public life. I asked Lady Gregory's advice because a common work has given us the same view of public duty.'

'Live and let live' was the old man's motto. He ended the discussion by saying: 'I was chiefly concerned that you should write a good poem, and how can anyone write a poem of hate against Moore?'

2

It was noted that Yeats's recent poetry reflected comparatively little of his early effort to acquire a living faith in old mythologies, or of his preoccupation with ancient systems and beliefs. There had been a change in his peculiar interests, and though still a member of the Stella Matutina in London, he had latterly been moving from magic – charms and rites – to spiritualism properly so-called, and now he professed to be in possession of evidence of the kind (hardly to be found in the cottages about Coole!) that the Society of Psychical Research would value. As Mr Daiches remarks,* he did not long remain content to be a simple 'occasional' poet, but began to introduce into his work new devices for symbolizing experience, new systems and new myths. This movement of his imagination was encouraged greatly by an encounter, while he was in Boston in 1911, with a very remarkable American medium, the wife of a doctor named Crandon.

He had a strange experience with Mrs Alfred Lyttelton, in whose automatic script his name appeared several times. She sent him copies of her script but for a long time he failed to interpret the words. 'Yeats is a prince with an evil counsellor', and 'tell him to think of the double harness of Phaeton and the adverse principle'; these were among sentences which puzzled the poet. Then W. T. Horton, the visionary, called at Woburn Buildings and left the following message:

* *Poetry and the Modern World.*

The fight is still raging around you; whilst *you* are busy trying
to increase the speed and usefulness of your chariot by means
of a dark horse, you have parted with a winged white one which
so long has served you faithfully and well. Unless you give the
dark horse wings and subordinate it to the white one, the latter
will break away and leave you to the dark horse who will lead
your chariot into the enemies' camp where you will be made a
prisoner. Conquer and subordinate the dark horse to the white
one.

Yeats was greatly struck that Horton, of whom Mrs Lyttelton had never heard, should have conveyed a warning
similar to hers and made use of the same symbolism in
the image of Phaeton and the black and white horses.
He did not understand it, he said, because he knew of
no bad influence, but a long time afterwards he told Mrs
Lyttelton that the warning had been both real and
justified.*

In Yeats's manuscript book of the period before the Great
War and during it, are many notes of attendances at séances
in London. 'Have now proved spirit identity – in the E. R.
case final', he writes on one page. On another he sets himself
the problem why no sentence of literary or speculative pro-
fundity has been spoken by any medium in the last fifty
years or perhaps ever, for Plutarch speaks of the imperfect
expression of the Greek oracle, and he solves it on the
ground of the necessary objectivity of these messages which
come through the senses, as distinguished from those that
come through the apparently free action of the mind. He
discovers his familiar spirit, Leo Africanus, at a house in
Wimbledon. Leo is impatient. 'Why, man, I am Leo the
writer and explorer, you know – the writer; you will hear of
me in Rome.' Sometimes Sturge Moore and Ezra Pound
came with him to séances; but most of his friends were
frankly rather bored by this side of his activity. Yeats never
seems to have realized that immortality or survival is not

* The evil counsellor was not Ezra Pound, although this was Horton's opinion.

every man's subject,* and Desmond MacCarthy has recorded the disappointment which he experienced on more than one occasion at Woburn Buildings, when Yeats could not be persuaded to utter exquisite criticism of literature or poetry, but insisted on talking of magic and spiritualism. That Yeats was honest enough to acknowledge deceptions when they occurred is proved on another page of his manuscript book. 'Last Monday Madame —— said that she would die, (disappear was the word), between Dec. 2nd and Dec. 5th next. Pound and Sturge Moore present.' Immediately below this entry, fitted in between other matter, is one dated a year later: 'NO, Madame —— is in excellent health'.

On occasions Yeats could hold a company enthralled by a good ghost story. Mr Thomas Lowinsky, the artist, has furnished me with one told at a Ricketts 'Friday Evening'. It contains hints and suggestions of that strange play of his latter years, *Purgatory*.

Centuries ago there lived in a castle in Ireland a man and wife. To their abounding sorrow they remained childless despite prayers and pilgrimage. At last, when they had long given up all hope, the woman, to her joy, found herself pregnant. Her husband, who till then had been tender and trusting, became sullen and suspicious, often giving himself up to lonely bouts of drinking. Barely had the child been born when the man, roaring drunk, rushed into the upper chamber where his wife lay. With cries of 'Bastard, bastard' he wrested the baby from her breast, and with the screaming infant in his arms, strode raging from the room. Down the winding wooden stairs he ran into the hall where, all reason fled, he beat and beat the tiny thing against anything he could. From her bed the mother rose and followed ... to arrive too late. Her son was dead. Picking him up from where he had been flung, she turned and slowly climbed the spiral stairs that led to the threshold of her room. She moved as in a trance till, through the open door, the sight of the bed brought her to earth with a spasm of despair. Vehemently clasp-

*Myers's story of the London dinner-party is well known. 'Of course', said the host, 'I believe in immortality and all that, but need we talk any longer about disagreeable things?'

ing the child, in a flash she bent beneath the bar which fenced the stairs, and dropped, like a singed moth, to the stone floor below. The man, his frenzy spent, was overwhelmed with grief. He sought consolation in taking another wife by whom he had other sons. Thus a family was founded and generation followed generation, each living much the same uneventful bucolic lives as those whom they succeeded. Although they cared for their castle and husbanded its lands, each in turn from time to time abandoned himself to the same solitary bouts. The house as a rule was a happy place but, during those spells, when its master was saturated with drink, an ashen woman would drift past him, ascending the curved stairs. Transfixed, he would wait the tragedy that he knew he was doomed only to see when he was drunk. Always with the same simple gesture she would reach the topmost step; always in the same way, pause, then bend, to drop a fluttering mass. Yet when he peered down he could see nothing. With the years the family vice grew like a cancer until it ate away their entire fortune and they were reduced to poverty. To crown their misery fire gutted the castle. The descendant to whom it then belonged was without the money or the desire to re-build. Indolent and inane, he left with few regrets to live in far-distant Dublin. Thenceforth the family and its fount seemed after countless years to have severed every bond. But destinies and traditions are hard to break and one day the grandson of this deserter was drawn to the very spot. His boon companion, killed by the kick of a horse, was to be buried within sight of the crumbling towers. Moved partly by affection for his friend, partly by curiosity to see the place whence his stock had sprung, the survivor of this long line had journeyed to attend the funeral. He met many friends and tippled with them all and, drunk, he found himself at dusk before the sombre shell of a stronghold. There being no door, he walked straight into the empty well up the wall of which had twined the oaken stairs. As he gazed he saw a fragile dishevelled form glide past him up and round the walls as though the steps were still there. Almost at the top she stopped, then with a burst of emotion dived, to disappear. The man knew no surprise. He felt that he had watched this melancholy scene innumerable times before – and for an instant he dimly understood that neither his children nor yet his children's children could ever purge themselves of a crime that they had inherited with their blood.

During another evening at Ricketts's house he related how once, upon the road to a friend's house, he had passed a ghost standing by a tree. The apparition was pallid and vague, hardly more than a vapour, still he was sure it was there. As soon as he arrived he described his adventure and was questioned and cross-questioned and pressed for fuller details. Harassed and having nothing further to say, he answered recklessly, 'Oh, it looked like a monkey' – much to the vexation of his friend who counted the ghost as one of his ancestors.

3

In 1913 Yeats re-read Swedenborg after a long interval, and compared what he had learned of medieval tradition in his Order and of Irish country beliefs with the affirmations in *The Spiritual Diary*. Influenced by William Blake's revolt against the Illuminism of the eighteenth century he had been repelled as a young man by that experimentalist of natural religion, but he now realized with excitement that the generalizations of the Swede confirmed the beliefs of Aran and of the servant girls of Soho. In fact, in Swedenborg's conception of the future life the soul hardly knows that it has reached 'the next world', but inhabits that state, in Heaven or in Hell, for which it was always fitted. There is, one might almost say, for Swedenborg, as for the early races, no *other* world. 'The country man', Yeats wrote in his essay on 'Swedenborg, Mediums and the Desolate Places',

has need of but Swedenborg's keen ears and eagle sight to hear the noise of swords in the empty valley, or to meet the old master hunting with all his hounds upon the stroke of midnight among the moonlit fields. ... It was indeed Swedenborg who affirmed for the modern world, as against the abstract reasoning of the learned, the doctrine and practice of desolate places, of shepherds and of midwives, and discovered a world of spirits where there was a scenery like that of the earth, human forms grotesque or beautiful, senses that knew pleasure and pain, marriage and war, all that could be painted on canvas, or put into stories to make one's hair stand up.

Reading this passage, one remembers that Yeats's father once observed to him: 'Your interest is in *mundane* things, whether beyond the stars or not.'

The essay subsequently appeared as an epilogue to Lady Gregory's collection of *Visions and Beliefs in the West of Ireland*. It must certainly be the most lively exposition existing of an author who (as Yeats says) himself wrote 'a dry language', and 'considered the whole destiny of Man as if he were sitting before a large table in a Government office'.* With Yeats's permission Mrs Lyttelton sent the paper to Mr Gerald Balfour (the present Earl of Balfour), who was greatly interested in the acute analysis, but unfortunately a meeting arranged between him and the poet fell through owing to the outbreak of the war.

In the meantime Yeats made the acquaintance of another leading member of the Psychical Research Society, the Hon. Everard Feilding. Feilding possessed a sense of the picturesque and of drama, and Yeats and he were quickly friends. They went to Paris together in the June before the war, lured by 'the chance of a lifetime, a most sensational materializing medium', and from Paris they went on to Mirabeau, near Poitiers, to investigate a miracle, taking Maude Gonne with them. Oleographs of the Sacred Heart had begun to bleed, and spiritual voices to speak to a certain Abbé Vacher who had been condemned by his Bishop. Feilding, a member of a leading English Catholic family, possessed the proper ecclesiastical authority to investigate the miracle. One picture had already been delivered to Rome on the order of the Holy Office, but a replica had likewise begun to bleed. The three investigators saw nothing from which to draw a conclusion. Some of the drops were still fresh when the Abbé took them to the picture, but there was no fresh formation of blood before their eyes, either then or when they went alone. The Abbé had all the appearance of a simple and pious man, and his face suggested neither

* Swedenborg's system is 'as strictly logical as Newman's', says Mr Geoffrey Faber in *Oxford Apostles*.

saint nor medium; but Yeats and Feilding were impressed
by his evident sincerity. It was impossible to think that a
man who had been satisfied so many years with his garden
and his prayers should suddenly and consciously make a
false miracle. The Abbé brought his visitors to hear Mass
at his private chapel where there were already three devout
women; up to this Yeats had not found himself moved. The
miracle was to him a subject of investigation, but now he
realized its place in spiritual drama, and tested his own
beliefs by the intensity of those around him. He, too, had
his image of the divine man. He thought of the poetry full
of instinct and tenderness belief might enable him to write,
and then of the Cabala and of Swedenborg, who has
arranged the heavens as a vast man, the angels and the souls
making the members of the body. As they were going away
the next day the Abbé said: 'I had a message for Mr Yeats
at four this morning when I was at prayer. The voice said:
"He is to become an apostle; he must use his intelligence.
If he does not, our Lord will take away his intelligence and
leave him at the mercy of his heart" '; and turning to Maud
Gonne, the Abbé solemnly warned her to leave France,
where terrible events would presently take place. There was
more, and just at the moment of parting he said to Yeats:
'Learn some French and come again'.

When Yeats got back to Paris he dictated a long essay on
the miracle. This survives but was never published, and
neither he nor Maud Gonne visited Mirabeau again. The
Abbé went to Rome, and wrote from there to Feilding that
he had been able to refute many calumnies about himself.
Feilding returned to Mirabeau after the war, for he was
repelled by the orthodox explanation. He would never believe that the Abbé had perpetrated conscious frauds, and
writing of the case for the transactions of the Fourth International Congress for Psychical Research in Great Britain,*
he found that any conclusion whatever was unwarranted.

* Held at Athens in 1930.

4

On the outbreak of the Great War Feilding's continental investigations received a set-back. He had hoped that Yeats might accompany him to Transylvania in September in pursuit of a Hungarian poltergeist whose activities in the house of a lawyer were reported in marvellous terms. After the war Feilding travelled in Poland, Czechoslovakia and Hungary and wrote to Yeats from these countries, where mediums abounded, full accounts of his experiences. It seems a pity that Yeats never accompanied him on these expeditions. Once in the nineteen-twenties he spoke of joining forces, saying that he wanted to escape from Dublin politics for a while, but Feilding warned him that there were also politics in these countries.

Yeats was in London during the early months of the war. Everard Feilding supplied him with items of inside information which he sent to Lady Gregory in the solitude of Coole. Of his own feelings he wrote:

I wonder if history will ever know at what man's door to lay the crime of this inexplicable war? I suppose, like most wars, it is a big man's war, a sacrifice of the best for the worst. I feel, strangely enough, most for the young Germans who are being killed. The spectacled, dreamy faces, or so I pictured them, remind me more of men I have known than the strong-bodied young English footballers. ... Sturge Moore has a fine poem in *The Times* today.

The last pages of *Reveries over Childhood and Youth* were finished at Coole during the closing days of 1914. 'I go to Dublin Thursday', he wrote to his sister Lily on 29 December.

... if you can give me about four hours on Saturday morning or afternoon I will read you the memoir. I think Ruth had better leave us to ourselves, – I should not mind her hearing it but I would not like to read it to her husband. I would not feel at ease and it is necessary to talk it over 'in the family'. I may go to London that night. Please let me have a note at the club when

I arrive (Stephen's Green Club, Stephen's Green, Dublin). If you cannot give me the time I had better read it to Jack but I much prefer you. Lady Gregory praises the memoir very much, and indeed the few friends who have seen it foretell even a popular success. You and Lolly come in only slightly, Jack a little more definitely, but our father and mother occur again and again. I have written it as some sort of an 'apologia' for the Yeats family and to lead up to a selection of our father's letters (I now sometimes get three in one day, so I think he likes the idea). It is about 20,000 words and should think it would end with our grandfather's death. As Dowden and O'Leary were dealt with in some detail it should interest Dublin.

In the opening year of the war the Abbey Theatre suffered a loss of £500, and it became necessary to make further appeals to wealthy people in Ireland and in England on its behalf. Yeats did not spare himself in an effort which he found disagreeable. He gave a series of lectures for the Theatre in London, and these, together with some generous subscriptions, restored the finances of the enterprise for the time being. He was a little tired of theatre work, and would have liked at this time, had he been able to gain Lady Gregory's consent, to maintain but a slight connection with the Abbey, such as would enable him to carry out occasional experiments that interested him and belonged to his own art. Ezra Pound having introduced him to the Nōh drama of Japan, he was at work on the first of his 'Plays for Dancers', *At the Hawk's Well*, which substituted the folding and unfolding of a cloth for the rising of a curtain and was to be played to the accompaniment of drum and zither and flute. One of his collaborators was a Mr Ito (a traditional dancer of Japan), who attracted considerable notice at the London Zoo by prancing about outside the cages of the birds of prey, and behaving in such a weird way that people supposed he must be either mad or a follower of some unknown Eastern religion who worshipped birds. Presently Mr Ito was set to evolve a dance based on the movements of the hawks as they hopped about and stretched their wings, and Yeats was often seen beside him at the Zoo, all attention.

When completed, *The Hawk's Well*, based on the technique of classical Greek tragedy, admirably brought together
the mythologies of Ireland and of Japan. But in every later
phase of Yeats's personality some remote origin or impetus
can always be discerned, and it is doubtful whether his
adolescent instinct in regard to the theatre ever underwent
any radical change. As a young man he had imagined himself taking his plays around Ireland on a waggon, but he did
not then know of this art which at most needed a square
platform for a stage, and where the performers sitting before
a wall or patterned screen themselves describe the landscape.
He wrote in 1921 the following Apologia for his abandonment of the drama of the Elizabethans:

... When I first began to write poetical plays for an Irish
theatre I had to put away an ambition of helping to bring again
to certain places their old sanctity or their romance. ... I could
not, in *The King's Threshold*, find room, before I began the
ancient story, to call up the shallow river and a few trees and
rocky fields of modern Gort. But in the *Nishikigi*, the tale of the
modern lovers would lose its pathos if we did not see that forgotten tomb where 'the hiding fox' lives among 'the orchards
and chrysanthemum flowers'. The men who created that convention were more like ourselves than the Greeks and Romans, more
like us even than are Shakespeare and Corneille. Their emotion
was self-conscious and reminiscent, always associating itself with
pictures and poems. ... I have been elaborating my poem in
London where alone I can find the help I need – Mr Dulac's
mastery of design and Mr Ito's genius of movement; yet it pleases
me to think I am working for my own country. Perhaps some
day a play in the form I am adapting for European purposes
shall awake once more, whether in Gaelic or in English, under
the slope of Slieve-na-man or Croagh Patrick, ancient memories.*

5

Yeats accepted the view, which at first appeared to be that of
the great majority of his countrymen, that Irish Nationalists should co-operate with England in the European con-

* *Four Plays for Dancers.*

flagration. The lies of politicians did not humbug him. But the Home Rule Bill had been brought to the Statute Book; he had long been inclined to orthodoxy in Irish politics, and John Redmond, who was after all still the leader, had called upon the country to provide recruits for foreign service. Lady Gregory, whose son later enlisted in the Air Force, strongly favoured Irish participation in the war. Maud Gonne did not, though she nursed wounded in a French hospital. St John Ervine, who had temporarily replaced Lennox Robinson as manager of the Abbey Theatre, warned Yeats and Lady Gregory that 'the pit' was alive with the ancient suspicion of England – 'horn of a bull, hoof of a horse, smile of a Saxon'. Nevertheless, a production of Bernard Shaw's skit, *O'Flaherty, V.C.*, was postponed out of deference to the British garrison in Dublin, and Lady Gregory and Yeats discussed a project (which they thought better of at the last moment) of inviting the Viceroy to visit the Abbey Theatre in his official character. Yeats met Lord Wimborne at a luncheon party in London given by Lady Cunard, who at once raised the question of the viceregal visit. 'Lady Cunard is too hasty', Yeats said immediately. 'Personally I think that the declaration of Parnell should be considered at an end, but we must first find out what the Pit thinks of it.' Lord Wimborne inquired what the declaration of Parnell might be and Yeats gave him an exposition of modern Irish political history. The rest of the meal was a fencing match, Yeats trying to extract the Viceroy's promise that he would only come to the Abbey if invited, and the Viceroy trying to persuade Yeats to lift his voice in favour of recruiting. Neither was successful, but Lord Wimborne said afterwards: 'I really believe I could govern Ireland if I had Mr Yeats's assistance.'

The same hostess whispered to Yeats that the Prime Minister intended presently to be 'very gracious' to him. Upon this he wrote to his sister:

Here is a piece of very private information for you. I have just refused a Knighthood. Lady Cunard had already sounded the authorities and asked me about it. Please keep it to yourself as it would be very ungracious of me to let it get talked about in Dublin. It was very kindly meant. I said 'As I grow older I become more conservative and I do not know whether that is because my thoughts are deeper or my blood more chill but I do not wish anyone to say of me "only for a ribbon he left us" '.

Yeats declined to write a war poem. He said, because

> He has had enough of meddling who can please
> A young girl in the indolence of her youth,
> Or an old man upon a winter's night.

But it was really that he had no public objects out of Ireland. Yet certain of his poems, already written before 1914, on obscure Irish occasions can apply well enough to certain aspects of Europe at war; and it is curious that the author of (for example) 'The Leaders of the Crowd' should be reproached by the younger generation of today for finding no subject of moral significance in the world of his time.*

Robert Bridges had no difficulty in persuading the Irish poet to contribute to an anthology which people in distress might like to read. 'It is absolutely necessary', Bridges wrote,

that you should consent, and I believe that if you saw my book you would readily agree to my proposition. I can hardly give you a notion of it but I can tell you a few points. French is admitted equally with English. All other languages are translated, the authors who show most solid are Plato, Aristotle, Homer, Shelley. Other names are Spinoza, Augustine, Gregory the Great, Pascal, Descartes, Keats, Wordsworth, Milton, etc. Then oriental poems are set alongside of the Greek and English and the juxtaposition of extracts from Spinoza and Keats, Augustine and Shelley, you and Aristotle, etc. will show people what poetry means.

I find that very little modern poetry willl stand up among these people, but you are an exception and your 'Sad Shepherd' and 'The Man who dreamed of Faeryland' come by their own. I want these and 'Innisfree' and two other short pieces. . . . I am quite sure that the way in which I set your poems will do them

---

* *Vide* Stephen Spender in *The Destructive Element in Literature.*

a lot of good. For the people do not recognise the extreme beauty and mastery of the 'Shepherd' and the 'Faeryland Man'.

To the record of Yeats's life during the war should be added a mention of his support of James Joyce, then in a very unhappy condition in Zurich, where he was almost totally excluded from his ordinary means of livelihood, the teaching of languages. In latter years Yeats had heard a good deal of Joyce from Ezra Pound, who had sought contributions from the proud exile when he was compiling his first *Imagist Anthology* and acting as advisory editor to the *Egoist* in which T. S. Eliot and Wyndham Lewis appeared. Moreover, Joyce had been for some time past in correspondence with Yeats regarding the Italian translation of *The Countess Cathleen* and his difficulties with publishers. Ezra Pound procured that Yeats, Moore and Edmund Gosse should separately make representations to Mr Asquith, and these resulted in a royal bounty of £100 being granted to an almost entirely unpublished author. 'I have every reason to be grateful to the many friends who have helped me since I came here,' Joyce wrote to Yeats from Zurich, 'and I can never thank you enough for having brought me into relation with your friend Ezra Pound who is indeed a miracle worker.'

In Ireland Yeats unwittingly strayed into the controversial scene by consenting to speak at a commemoration of Thomas Davis's centenary organized by the Gaelic Society of Trinity College. The Society invited Patrick Pearse to deliver another of the orations, and Dr Mahaffy, who was now Provost, closed the gates of the College against this known author of sedition, and dissolved the Society. Whereupon the promoters of the commemoration announced that it would be held elsewhere in the city, and Yeats felt that he was placed in an awkward position. He did not wish to be associated with dark plots or inflammatory propaganda; on the other hand, it was tempting to defy Mahaffy, no particular friend, and he respected Pearse, who had lifted up his voice on behalf of Synge at the height of the Gaelic and

Sinn Fein clamour against *The Playboy*. Having decided to
fulfil his engagement, he made several drafts of his speech,
so that it would not touch the sore places of the public mind
and yet be useful and effective. He eulogized in Davis a
public character notable above all for magnanimity and
scrupulousness in controversy, and was pleased when his
speech (which paid no compliments to any party) met with
the approval not only of Pearse but also of T. M. Kettle, who
afterwards fell in Flanders. This man (he said of Davis),
who had not showy talent, neither wit nor oratory, who put
money into no man's pocket, whose only achievements were
of the moral nature, and yet who influenced so deeply the
generation he lived amongst, was mourned after his death as
only conquerors are mourned.

An event of 1915 which touched Yeats to the quick, both
on Ireland's account and Lady Gregory's, was the sinking
of the *Lusitania* with Hugh Lane on board. Latterly Lane
had been reconciled to Ireland, having become Director of
the Dublin National Gallery, and before sailing to America
in February he had added a codicil to his will bequeathing
his French pictures, then in the London National Gallery,
to the City of Dublin. The codicil was unwitnessed (and
therefore invalid), but there seemed to be no doubt from the
evidence of Lane's friends that it represented his last wishes.
A decision on the question of what it would be proper to
do in these circumstances was left over for the period of the
war, but in 1918 it became apparent that the Trustees of the
London National Gallery, or some of them, intended to
insist on their legal rights. As a leader in the campaign of
Irish protest which followed, Yeats often forgot 'the lesson
of Thomas Davis', which he had recommended to the attention of his countrymen in 1915. For instance, he thought fit
to taunt the English by saying in public that their willing-
ness to profit by the horror of the *Lusitania* made them*

* [Agreement was reached on 12 November 1959, between the
Trustees of the National Gallery and the Irish authorities on the Lane
bequest. The paintings were divided into two approximately equal

accessories after the fact; and, in answer to their plea that Lord Duveen had provided an extension to the Tate Gallery mainly for the purpose of housing the 'Lane pictures', he retorted that Ali Baba might, on the same reasoning, have advanced a claim for the retention of the stolen jewels because he had a cave in which to hide them. But, as he wrote:

> Out of Ireland have we come.
> Great hatred, little room,
> Maimed us at the start.
> I carry from my mother's womb
> A fanatic heart.

6

At the beginning of 1916, that year fateful for Ireland, Yeats was in Sussex with Ezra Pound, lately married to the daughter of Mrs Shakespear. There was room for all in the cottage on the edge of the forest, and Yeats was happy with the young people who kept him *au courant* with the new canons of criticism, the new models of style that were being disputed during the war years. Perhaps to demonstrate his independence of novelty, he started to read through the seven volumes of Dowden's edition of Wordsworth; of which he wrote to his father:

I have finished 'The Excursion' and begun 'The Prelude'. I want to get through all the heavy part that I may properly understand the famous things. At the same time I am not finding the long poems really heavy. Have you any impressions of him? He strikes me as always destroying his poetic experience, which was of course of incomparable value, by his reflective power. His intellect was commonplace, and unfortunately he had been taught to respect nothing else. He thinks of his poetic experience not as incomparable in itself but as an engine that may be yoked to his intellect. He is full of a sort of utilitarianism, and that is

groups, and each group is being lent to the Dublin National Gallery for four successive periods of five years. However, they still remain the property of the London National Gallery.]

perhaps the reason why in later life he is continually looking
back upon a lost vision, a lost happiness. I have just got your last
letters back from the typist; as always, they interest me very
much. I am thinking of a long poem, a conversation on philosophical subjects, between a duellist and a gambler. . . . My gambler is your American woman.

J. B. Y. had written that the poet seeks truth, not abstract
truth, but a kind of vision of reality which satisfies the whole
being. In support of his father Yeats cited Henry More, the
Platonist, who argues from the goodness and omnipotence
of God that all our deep desires must be satisfied, and that
we should reject a philosophy that does not satisfy them.
In regard to Cubism, another topic in the correspondence
between father and son at this time, W. B. was indisposed to
accept his parent's view that 'all art is imitation'. 'A pretty
woman has her rhythm ... to paint her and to miss her
rhythm is to fail in the art of imitation', wrote J. B. Y.
W. B. replied:

You ask for examples of 'imitation' in poetry. I suggest that
the corresponding things are drama and the pictorial element,
and that in poetry those who lack these are rhetoricians. I feel
in Wyndham Lewis's Cubist pictures an element corresponding
to rhetoric arising from his confusing the abstract with the
rhythmical. The rhythm implies a living body. . . . This rhythm
is not imitation. Impressionism, by leaving it out, brought all
the rhetoric of the abstract upon us. I have just been turning over
a book of Japanese paintings. Everywhere there is delight in
form, repeated yet varied, in curious patterns, lines, but their
lines are all an ordering of natural objects though they are certainly not imitation. In every case the artist, one feels, has had
to *consciously* and deliberately arrange his subject. It was the
impressionists' belief that this arrangement should be only unconscious and instinctive that brought the violent reaction. They
are right in believing that they should be conscious but wrong
in substituting abstract scientific thought for conscious feeling.
If I delight in rhythm I love nature though she is not rhythmical.
I express my love in rhythm. The more I express it the less can I
forget her. I think Keats perhaps greater than Shelley and

beyond words greater than Swinburne because he makes pictures one cannot forget and sees them as full of rhythm as a Chinese painting.

Either now, or a little later, he re-read large parts of two other old masters, Tennyson and Browning, and introduced some remarks concerning them into a manuscript-book. If a poem talks, he noted, we have the passionate syntax, the impression of the man who speaks, no abstract poet. Tennyson's syntax is seldom contorted, but it is perhaps never good speech. 'In Memoriam' is neither song nor any man's speech when moved. Browning wrote speech but in a language which he studied from outside, as if it were a dialect, and he gained his impressions of reality from ejaculations and suppressions, which are all an avoidance of the expressions of passion. When we get a passionate rhythmical syntax in Browning, he is often furthest from the natural order of words, as in the song about the 'aloe-balls' in *Paracelsus*.

7

In March, Yeats went up to London to supervise arrangements for the production of his *Hawk's Well* in Lady Cunard's drawing-room. To the first performance only those who cared for poetry were invited. The players came in by the same door as the audience and all were pleased by the quaint originality of the proceedings. A second performance a few days later in Lady Islington's larger drawing-room failed to create the same impression of distance from life. This second representation was for the benefit of a war charity, and Queen Alexandra's presence attracted three hundred fashionable people and a press photographer who was with difficulty ejected. Years earlier, during the reign of Edward VII, Yeats had met Queen Alexandra at a reception given by the Duchess of Sutherland, and in all innocence had spoken to her without constraint, disregarding the conventions. She knew his poems, but had not heard of his political manifestos, and had said that she would like to see

one of his plays on the stage.* At Lady Islington's, however,
she wearied of his preliminary explanation of Nōh drama,
and sent a message by her lady-in-waiting to ask for it to be
cut short, as she was growing hoarse.

The publication in 1916 by Macmillan of *Responsibilities*
gave the general reader his first opportunity of estimating
the distance which Yeats had travelled from 'Celtic Renaissance'. This edition included a reprint of poems from *The
Green Helmet*, and so was representative of what now can
be classified as Yeats's middle period. He would now 'Dine
at journey's end With Landor and with Donne', a curious
couple. However, side by side with the autobiographical and
political contents of *Responsibilities* were many evidences
that his old preoccupations with the unfamiliar and intangible survived, though now expressed with the same adjec-
tival economy as his poetical repudiations of the baser sides
of Irish patriotism. 'The Cold Heaven' and the strange and
solemn fancy 'That the Night Come' are among the flower
of Yeats's dream poetry in any period. In 'The Cold Heaven'
he suddenly achieves that fury of self-control, later proclaimed as a deliberate end, which aligns him with the turbulent Donne:

> Suddenly I saw the cold and rook-delighting heaven
> That seemed as though ice burned and was but the more ice,
> And thereupon imagination and heart were driven
> So wild that every casual thought of that and this
> Vanished, and left but memories, that should be out of season
> With the hot blood of youth, of love crossed long ago;
> And I took all the blame out of all sense and reason,
> Until I cried and trembled and rocked to and fro,
> Riddled with light. Ah! when the ghost begins to quicken,
> Confusion of the death-bed over, is it sent
> Out naked on the roads, as the books say, and stricken
> By the injustice of the skies for punishment?

Some extracts from a letter written by Yeats to a friend
who preferred his later to his earlier work should be quoted
here, because they confute the idea (prevalent in Dublin at

* *Vide* Ricketts's *Self-Portrait*, p. 112.

this time) that he was contemplating withdrawal from the Irish scene:

I wish to thank you for your most generous article. ... You quoted what I myself most care for and saw what I have tried to do. One great pleasure is that whereas I used to feel that the articles people wrote in praise of my early work were, with some exceptions, vague and a little sentimental, the very few who praise my later work (and you have been the most subtle) have praised it in words full of intellect and force. ... You have done me great service. ... I know that my work has been done in every detail with a deliberate Irish aim, but it is hard for those who know it in fragments to know that, especially if the most that they know of me is about some contest with Irish opinion. I am particularly glad [of what you say] just now because I am making some alterations in my publishing schemes and hope to make my work as a whole accessible. Up to this no Irishman as poor as I was when I was twenty could afford to read me.

8

Yeats was staying with the Rothensteins in Gloucestershire when the Easter Rising of 1916 broke out. The news took him with the same surprise as it took the general public in Ireland. The leader of the Rising whom he knew best was Thomas MacDonagh, whose book on Gaelic influences on English prosody he had admired; but Pearse and Joseph Plunkett were among his acquaintances, and James Connolly's name on the Proclamation of an Irish Republic sent his memory back to the days of his work on the '98 Memorial Committee. While his first thought was of the safety of Lady Gregory at Coole, his English friends noticed that at last he seemed to be moved by a public event. To Rothenstein he spoke of innocent and patriotic theorists carried away by the belief that they must sacrifice themselves to an abstraction. They would fail and pay the penalty for their failure. On 8 May, writing to Lady Gregory from London, he spoke of the 'heroic, tragic lunacy of Sinn Fein', and wondered whether his letter would reach Galway with Arthur Griffith as censor at the Post Office, – meaning that Griffith would regard him as a dubious political character.

Though some of the leaders of 1916, such as Pearse and MacDonagh, drew inspiration from ancient Irish literature and had been nurtured in the atmosphere of Celtic Renaissance, the Rising was chiefly promoted by the extreme Nationalists of the Irish Republican Brotherhood which had drawn into it many members of the Gaelic and Sinn Fein movements. A generation of Nationalists of whom Yeats really knew very little had arisen since the days when he and Maud Gonne had been 'in the party'. Arthur Griffith, whose influence upon the national mind Yeats had so long deplored, was not in the secrets of the physical force men, nor had he approved of the Rising. 'Those of us', says Dr Patrick MacCartan, speaking of the I.R.B., 'who were capable of understanding Yeats's work were then, and continued to be, his ardent admirers. He was not, of course, employed in our ranks ... but he had (in his own work) the support of the Fenians.' The most curious thing reported of Yeats's attitude on the occasion of the Rising is Sir William Rothenstein's statement that 'he fretted somewhat that he had not been consulted' as to what was afoot!

The country was against the Rising, but the execution, one by one, of the leaders lit a flame of popular resentment which assured the triumph of the separatist principles for which Pearse had died. Even the most moderate Nationalist opinion was shocked by the severity of the repression. 'Cosgrave,'* Yeats wrote to Lady Gregory,

whom I saw a few months ago in connection with the Municipal Gallery project and [in whom] I found our best support, has got many years' imprisonment, and today I see that an old friend, Henry Dixon – unless there are two of the name – who began with me the whole work of the literary movement, has been shot in a barrack yard without trial of any kind. I have little doubt there have been many miscarriages of justice. ... I am trying to write a poem on the men executed – 'terrible beauty has been

* W. T. Cosgrave, afterwards President of the Irish Free State.

born again'. If the English Conservative Party had made a declaration that they did not intend to rescind the Home Rule Bill, there would have been no rebellion. I had no idea that any public event could so deeply move me – and I am very despondent about the future. . . . Maud Gonne reminds me that she saw the ruined houses about O'Connell Street, and the wounded and dying lying about the streets in the first few days of the war. I perfectly remember the vision and my making light of it and saying that if a time vision at all it could only have a symbolical meaning. This is the only letter I have had from her since she knew of the rebellion. I have sent her the papers every day. . . . Her main thought seems to be 'tragic dignity has returned to Ireland' . . .

In his poem 'No Second Troy' he had taunted 'the little streets' with wanting 'courage equal to desire', and now he felt that some retraction would become him. His consultation with his muse had been correctly described by John Eglinton as 'somewhat hurried', for 'Easter, 1916', with the refrain 'A terrible beauty is born', was composed within a few weeks of the executions. He returned, however, in one passage to an old thought:

> Too long a sacrifice
> Can make a stone of the heart.
> Oh, when may it suffice?
> That is Heaven's part, our part
> To murmur name upon name,
> As a mother names her child
> When sleep at last has come
> On limbs that had run wild.

'Easter, 1916' was printed almost at once by Clement Shorter in an edition of twenty-five copies 'for distribution amongst friends'. Three other poems, instinct with the same tenderness, followed – 'Sixteen Dead Men'; 'The Rose Tree'; 'On a Political Prisoner'. Though politically non-committal – it was only in his late years that Yeats started to sing in a Fenian spirit of Pearse and Connolly – the series was withheld from the sight of the general public until 1920.

9

Thou art thy mother's glass, and she in thee
Gives back the lovely April of her prime. (*Shakespeare*)

When he was about forty-five Yeats had formed a liaison
with an unmarried woman past her first youth. The liaison,
after having been carried on for some years without great
conviction on either side, had suddenly threatened to land
him in difficulties. In the event it proved that the person
concerned harboured no embarrassing designs upon him.
The experience, nevertheless, had its effect, and a harsh note
of disillusionment in certain poems in *Responsibilities*, such
as 'Beggar to Beggar Cried', may perhaps be traced to it. The
unfounded suspicion that he had been ensnared by a
huntress was confided to Lady Gregory, who became convinced by the imagined crisis that he ought to 'settle down'.
She set her mind on match-making. A man of strong feeling for family memory and tradition, Yeats was not averse
to the idea of marriage, and now that he was more prosperous – up to the time that he was fifty his books seldom
brought him in more than £200 a year – his father and
sisters lived in great hopes of hearing that he was affianced.
Indeed, his father frequently consulted soothsayers in New
York about his chances of having grandchildren and the
probable looks of his daughter-in-law.

During one summer of the war, when Lady Gregory was
in London, Yeats being with Ezra Pound, she drove down
several times to Stone Cottage, each time accompanied by a
different young lady with means and looks; with one of these
charmers he was often seen in London. But of marriage he
only spoke, apparently, to Mrs Tucker's daughter, Miss
Hyde-Lees, set apart from the others by her keen sense of
criticism and humour, and a naturalness and practical
ability which would distinguish her from the conventional
'poet's wife'. Lady Gregory had spoken to Miss Hyde-Lees
but once – at some picture show where Yeats had introduced
her.

The whole question took a new turn in Yeats's eyes after the Easter Week executions, which left Maud Gonne a widow. Her husband, John MacBride, had, since the separation from her, eked out an obscure existence near Dublin. He was not in any secret councils, and yet, upon hearing of the seizure of the Post Office, he threw off the load which had so long oppressed his body and mind, and at once joined a contingent, which he helped to capture a factory. It is probable that he was the only man in the Rising who had ever been under fire before, and his candid and soldierly demeanour at the court-martial greatly impressed the officers who sentenced him to death.*

Soon after the suppression of the Rising, Iseult Gonne arrived in London from Paris with messages for Yeats from her mother. Maud Gonne was 'very sad', seemed 'lonely', and was 'sleeping badly'; she wished Yeats to find a lawyer for a Miss Moloney, one of the women prisoners, and then to bring Iseult back with him to Normandy. Yeats introduced the young girl to houses of his fashionable friends, and Lady Cunard said, 'Oh, who is she? Never in my life have I seen such a complexion.' He wrote to Lady Gregory: 'She looks very distinguished and is now full of self-possession. She is beautifully dressed, though very plainly. I said, "Why are you so pale?" and she said, "Too much responsibility". She makes me sad, for I think that if my life had been normal I might have had a daughter of her age. That means, I suppose, that I am beginning to get old.'

Yeats's first impulse was to ask Maud Gonne to marry him now that she was free, and yet before going to France he all but made a compact with Lady Gregory, for the sake of the Abbey Theatre (which at this time largely depended for its existence on the donation of rich Irish Unionists), and as 'a refuge from some weakness in myself', not to marry unless Maud Gonne renounced all politics, including amnesty for

* *Vide* 'Easter, 1916':

> 'He, too, has resigned his part
> In the casual comedy.'

the political prisoners. In August, after he had been for a while in Normandy, he wrote to Lady Gregory:

> I believe I was meant to be the father of an unruly family. I did not think that I liked little boys but I liked Shawn.* I am really managing Iseult very well. The other night she made a prolonged appeal for an extra cigarette. ... I have stayed on much longer than I intended but I think you will forgive me under the circumstances – as father, but as father only, I have been a great success.

He talked of marriage to Maud Gonne, but it was evident that she was far more interested in securing a passport to Ireland to work for the prisoners than in any such notion. No romance about the new situation created in Ireland by the Rising was too wild to be received with faith by her and she thought the mood of his poem, 'Easter, 1916' (read to her on the seashore in Normandy), wholly inadequate to the occasion. Yeats was left very uncertain of everything except that he was filled with fears for that fabulous household, with its dogs, cats and the monkey which interrupted the conversations on literature, religion and politics. He worked with Iseult Gonne; she acted as his secretary (he was writing a further instalment of his memoirs) and studied with him the new French Catholic poets. The thought that the lovely Iseult would 'civilise Dublin Catholics' by imparting to them an enthusiasm for Péguy, Claudel and Jammes almost reconciled him to Maud Gonne's project of getting back to Ireland. It was not long before Dublin learned of the new gleam which Yeats pursued, and George Moore, in correspondence with John Eglinton, made a withering comment:

> Yeats writes of having a new French book read aloud to him, and that he understood what was read to him seems implicit in the statement; he also says that he himself read a book in French. ... He talked of Francis Jammes' verses; but you have to read verses before you understand them, and I cannot believe that he has learned to read aloud a French sonnet – as difficult this as the Eucharist itself, of which he speaks in connection with some play. Oh land of dreams and dreamers.

*Seán MacBride.

10

Yeats returned to London and there finished a little book of philosophical essays, *Per Amica Silentia Lunae** (with the prologue to Iseult Gonne) and another play to be played with masks, *The Dreaming of the Bones*, on Dermot and Dervorgilla, Irish Paolo and Francesca, whose guilty love has been accused of facilitating the English conquest of Ireland. 'It is strong, too strong, politically', he wrote of the play to Lady Gregory. In *Per Amica Silentia Lunae* he outlined in terms of spiritism the doctrine of the antithetical self – or, as one might say, of philosophy as drama. 'Each daemon is drawn to whatever man or, if its nature is more general, to whatever nation it most differs from, and it shapes into its own image the antithetical dream of man or nation.' † He wrote to his father that

Much of your thought resembles mine . . . but mine is part of a religious system more or less logically worked out. A system which will, I hope, interest you as a form of poetry. I find the setting of it all in order has helped my verse, has given me a new framework and new patterns. One goes on year after year getting the disorder of one's own mind in order, and this is the real impulse to create.

In the summer of 1917 he was again in Normandy, where he found Maud Gonne as determined as ever to get back to Ireland. She grew angry at his suggesting that London might be a better place for Iseult. It was Iseult's prospects that now most afflicted his thoughts, and he repeated a proposal of marriage to the young girl. He was more heart-smitten than he quite realized. 'I don't think she will change her mind', he wrote to Lady Gregory; 'she has not the

* First called 'An Alphabet'.

† He cited the Jews 'If they had not been rapacious, lustful, narrow and persecuting beyond the people of their time, the Incarnation had been impossible.' Might he not also have cited his own Irish who cynically resist all efforts to be fused into a nation and yet have produced such great instances of devotion?

impulse to marry. We take long walks – she shows me many little signs of affection but otherwise things are as I wrote.' With some apprehension he used his influence to secure passports for the family, and all travelled to England early in September. At Southampton the ladies were taken into a shed and searched for secret codes, while he walked up and down the platform fuming under the drizzling rain and cursing the shame-faced and polite detectives. The train was held up for them, but no sooner had it reached London than Maud Gonne was served with a notice under the Defence of the Realm Act forbidding her to proceed to Ireland. At first it seemed that she would ignore the challenge; Yeats was much relieved when she said that she would take a flat in Chelsea for six months and study design at a London art school. He decided to go on with his former plan and marry Miss Hyde-Lees, if she were not 'tired of the idea', but he did not spare himself examination of conscience, for he feared that he had given pain to Maud Gonne by his proposal to Iseult, and made two women unhappy. 'Poor Iseult', he wrote, 'was very depressed on the journey, and at Havre went off by herself and cried because she was so ashamed "at being so selfish" in not wanting me to marry and so break her friendship with me.' And again: 'All night the darkness was full of writing, now on stone, now on paper, now on parchment, but I could not read it. Were spirits trying to communicate? I prayed a great deal and believe I am doing right.' He met Denison Ross at the Savile Club, who said that he could find Iseult (had she not read *Gitanjali*?) a post as assistant librarian in the School of Oriental Languages. The pay was small but the hours were short; she would be amongst educated men and women and be able to supplement her income with her own writing. When this had been arranged, Yeats burst into tears from sheer happiness.

14

Marriage

Beginning of the 'System' – Honeymoon in Ireland;
Ballylee – A fracas with Maud Gonne; Chesterton not a
'Garreteer' – *The Wild Swans at Coole*; 'A Prayer for
My Daughter' – Tour in America

———

> *I, the poet William Yeats,*
> *With old mill boards and sea-green slates,*
> *And smithy work from the Gort forge,*
> *Restored this tower for my wife George;*
> *And may these characters remain*
> *When all is ruin once again.*

I

YEATS and Miss Hyde-Lees were married at the Harrow
Road register office in London on 20 October 1917. Ezra
Pound was best man. Yeats wrote to his father a week or
two later from Stone Cottage where a part of the honeymoon
was spent:

I am dictating this to my wife. I call her George to avoid
Georgie which she has been called hitherto in spite of her pro-
tests. I enclose her photograph. She permits me to say that it
flatters her good looks at the expense of her character. She is not
so black and white, but has red-brown hair and a high colour
which she sets off by wearing dark green in her clothes and earrings, etc. You are right in saying that towns are bad for me and
my wife is ready to seem to dislike them too. I hope to see very
little of them henceforth . . .

A little later Lady Gregory had a letter from him headed
Woburn Buildings:

My wife is a perfect wife, kind, wise, and unselfish. I think you
were such another young girl once. She has made my life serene

and full of order. I wish you could see Woburn Buildings now – nothing changed in plan but little touches here and there, and my own bedroom (the old bathroom), with furniture of unpainted unpolished wood such as for years I have wished for. Then there is a dinner service of great purple plates for meat, and various earthenware bowls for other purposes. Then too all is very clean. Yet Mrs Old is most unhappy – she comes in the evening for better pay, and someone else does the rough-work in the mornings.

I have stopped work on my philosophic dialogue for the moment as it was keeping me awake at night, and am writing verse again. I have just all but finished another rebellion poem . . .

It was Yeats's intention to take his bride to Ireland with him after Christmas. They had invitations to Coole, and to Oliver Gogarty's recently acquired seventeenth-century house at Renvyle in Connemara. 'We shall both acquire certain country tastes', he wrote to his father. Robert Gregory's death in action in Italy and food difficulties in Connemara caused a postponement of the Irish visit. In the interval, 18 Woburn Buildings had been let to tenants and the married pair found themselves houseless. Oxford having suggested itself, Mrs Yeats succeeded in finding pleasant rooms at 45 Broad Street where they remained for two months or a little more after the New Year. Yeats thought to make Oxford a centre for Nōh plays, which required to be worked out with Edmund Dulac. 'Here,' he wrote to Lady Gregory,

I have so far only seen Walter Raleigh and Bridges. We are asking people for week-ends – Iseult next week, then Bessie Radcliffe and Aldington, a scholar and a poet. My work goes on well and before long I will send you the new Cuchulain play.* I have written two good lyrics for it. I then think of a narrative poem. I want to publish together the Macmillan edition of *Swans at Coole* and my four or five Nōh plays, and to follow in the autumn with 'Discoveries of Michael Robartes'.

He was delighted with the Bodleian Library, of which he wrote to Lady Gregory that 'One can leave one's book on

* *The Only Jealousy of Emer.*

one's table and read them at odd moments.... My table there is covered with such things as the etchings and wood-cuts of Palmer and Calvert. If you ever do any work that needs a library you must come and stay with us here, for it is well understood that the Bodleian is the most friendly comfortable library in the world and I suppose the most beautiful...'

'The Discoveries of Michael Robartes', embryo of *A Vision*, was first conceived as a philosophical dialogue to be written out as a series of conversations about a medieval book, the *Speculum Angelorum et Hominum* of Giraldus, and about a sect of the Arabs called the Judwalis (diagram-matists). Denison Ross helped in some references to Arabic manuscripts in the Bodleian Library. 'My Arabic has grown rusty', Yeats would say, and, though he smiled, he was con-vinced that many dreams and prophecies were reaching fufilment in a very profound, very exciting, mystical system. A strange sense of revelation was coming into his work, and he was astonished at the change (no doubt he would have taken to alcohol or hashish if he had thought it likely to benefit his particular style of creation). The manifestations began in a hotel at Ashdown Forest a few days after his marriage, when his wife surprised him by attempting automatic writing. What came in disjointed sentences was so remarkable that he persuaded her to give an hour or two day after day to the 'unknown communicators' and offered to spend what remained of life explaining and piecing the messages together.

It seems that Yeats, possibly fearing a scientific incredul-ity, sought to express himself in geometrical – or shall we say pseudo-geometrical? – terms. A month was given to an exposition of the 'twenty-eight typical incarnations', or phases, and to the movements of their 'Four Faculties', and then a 'cone or gyre was drawn, expressive of the soul's judgement after death'. The lunar phase is clearly indicated in a poem of the period, 'The Phases of the Moon':

Twenty-and-eight the phases of the moon,
The full and the moon's dark and all the crescents
Twenty-and-eight, and yet but six-and-twenty
The cradles that a man must needs be rocked in ...

whereas in *A Vision*, the Yeatsian *Anschauung*, he condes-
cended to mathematical formulae. He would look neither
further backward nor further forward – looking back: 'I
can but see bird and woman blotting out some corner of the
Babylonian mathematic starlight'; looking forward: 'What
discords will drive Europe to that artificial unity ... which
is the decadence of every civilization?' He was told by the
communicators that the system of symbolism which awaited
expression would take many years to become clear.*

2

When his tenants left, Yeats put 18 Woburn Buildings at the
disposal of Maud Gonne, still detained in England under the
Defence of the Realm Act, and crossed to Ireland with his
wife. As it was the first time that Mrs Yeats had been in
Ireland, there was much to show her. The first weeks were
spent between Dublin, Glendalough and Rosses Point. At
Glendalough he finished one of his several poems in memory
of Robert Gregory; 'Goatherd and Shepherd' it was called,
and he characterized it as a 'pastoral similar to what Spenser
wrote of Sydney'. 'My wife thinks it good', he wrote to Lady
Gregory. 'A goatherd and a shepherd are talking in some
vague place, perhaps on the Burren hills, in some remote
period of the world. It is a new form for me and I think for
modern poetry. I hope it may please Margaret [Mrs Robert
Gregory] also.'

Some months before his marriage Yeats had come into
possession of the Norman, river-encircled tower of Ballylee,
of which a description may be found in the chapter on the
blind poet Raftery in *The Celtic Twilight*. When Yeats, as
a young man, had first seen Ballylee, a farmer and his wife

---

* *A Packet for Ezra Pound* (1929).

inhabited the tower, and there was a mill with an old miller, and ash trees throwing green shadows upon a little river and great stepping-stones. He used to go there to chat with the miller about 'wise' Biddy Early. Ballylee occupied a part of the Gregory estate which was subsequently acquired for the purpose of redistribution among the people by the Congested Districts Board. No one wanted the tower and two attached cottages, one of which was in ruins, nor the tiny walled garden and a grove of trees across the road; and Yeats, after prolonged negotiations with the Board, succeeded in purchasing the little property for the sum of thirty-five pounds. Whether he would ever be able to live there was uncertain; but when he had talked the project over with Robert Gregory and an architect, it seemed to become possible.

Already he had been at some expense on the front cottage, and after his marriage he came to the decision that if his wife should like the place, they would restore the rest of the buildings and make Ballylee their summer home. Within the cottage there was space for a kitchen and bathroom, a sitting-room and two bedrooms. The Norman tower, with its winding stair, its four great apartments one above the other, wide stone fireplaces and mullioned windows, was the great attraction.

Lady Gregory lent Yeats and his wife Ballinamantane House, which was quite close to the castle, and also to Coole, and from which they could conveniently supervise the work. In June, Yeats wrote to his father from Ballinamantane House:

We hope to be in Ballylee by the end of July but building is slow and there is no certainty. George is at this moment at the Castle, where she has a man digging in front of the cottage that she may plant flowers. . . . Last week we had a fine dish of trout, grey trout and salmon trout, caught, though not by us, in the Ballylee river – the best place is almost under the castle walls.

Why do you call Bunyan a mystic? It is not possible to make a definition of mysticism to include him. The two great mystics of that epoch are Spinoza and Pascal. Nearly all our popular mysticism derives indirectly from the first or from a movement he was first to express. I remember hearing Madam Blavatsky explain the identity of predestination and freedom exactly as he explains the identity of the self-determination and the freedom of the self (in him God and self are one). Beside the intellect of Spinoza I do not think you will place the more merely professional intellect of the Victorians, even that of Mill. I only know Pascal slightly, but I do know that his influence has been as great on orthodox mysticism as that of Spinoza on heterodox and that his intellect is sufficient. You should not conclude that if a man does not give his reasons he has none. Remember Zarathustra's 'Am I a barrel of memories that I can give you my reasons?' All the great mystics have been great in intellect. In that they differ from great pietists like Bunyan. Certainly all the great mystics except some few (mainly Catholic) whose natures have been overmasteringly moral – St Francis perhaps – and perhaps we should call them pietists or visionaries, not mystics.

I do nothing but write verse. I have just finished a long poem on Robert Gregory, which is among my best work . . .

He had written 'In Memory of Major Robert Gregory', an elegy on lost friends, astonishing in the intricacy of its passion. Ballylee now for the first time takes a place in his verse:

> For all things the delighted eye now sees
> Were loved by him : the old storm-broken trees
> That cast their shadows upon road and bridge;
> The tower set on the stream's edge;
> The ford where drinking cattle make a stir
> Nightly, and startled by that sound
> The water-hen must change her ground . . .

> We dreamed that a great painter had been born
> To cold Clare rock and Galway rock and thorn,
> To that stern colour and that delicate line
> That are our secret discipline . . .

> What other could so well have counselled us
> In all lovely intricacies of a house . . .

3

Yeats wished his first child to be born in Ireland, and after a few weeks' picnic at Ballylee, his wife and he arrived in Dublin to search for a furnished flat where they could spend the winter. The town was crowded out with British military preparing to enforce conscription, but Maud Gonne heard of their difficulties and wrote to say that she would let them a house at a nominal rent in Stephen's Green, No. 73, which she had recently purchased and furnished. She had acquired this house in person, having visited Dublin in disguise and in contravention of the order prohibiting her entry into Ireland. She was now under arrest in London, not on account of this escapade but as one of the suspects of the 'German plot'. Yeats employed what influence he had to procure her release; but he was far from eager that she should find her way back to Ireland, which was evidently on the eve of a period of grave political disturbance. It would have been hard on her, however, if she had been away from Ireland during the election in December when her views triumphed and a new chapter of Irish history opened. Out of 105 candidates returned at the polls, 73 were Republicans or Sinn Feiners. The verdict for Connolly and Pearse and the 1916 men was decisive, and in January Dail Eireann ('The Assembly of Ireland') met as a parliament, and proclaimed the country's complete independence of England.

The intellectuals and wits of Dublin, George Russell, Oliver Gogarty, Stephen MacKenna, James Stephens and the rest, lived in a whirl of political talk. Yeats adopted an attitude of detachment, but a friend at the Arts Club induced him to send a communication to Lord Haldane putting the Irish case against conscription. On 16 October 1918, he wrote of these matters to Lady Gregory:

. . . I received a note from Lord Haldane, marked 'private', asking me to go to London. When I went to enquire about time of boats, etc., I heard of the *Leinster* disaster and that the port was 'closed'. I wired that I would come by the first boat when

port opened. He gave me an appointment for next Saturday. He
has now wired and written that he thinks danger of conscription
has passed. I was very much surprised by Balfour's speech saying
that the *Leinster* 'served no military purpose'. She carried hundreds of troops – 500 Berkshires returning to France – and was a
troopship. Balfour, one had always thought, was a most honour-
able man. One wonders how many statements in press or parliament are equally untrue.

We may have to give up our house to Maud Gonne, as we
hope for her release on grounds of health. Yesterday I got Gwynn
to apply to Shortt on the grounds that the abandonment of conscription would make her release safe.

Possibly as a result of Yeats's efforts, Maud Gonne was presently removed from her prison to a hospital. Here she
occupied her mind with plans for effecting a dramatic
appearance in Dublin; and on a dark December evening,
wearing nurse's uniform, she slipped past the two detectives
on guard in the street, and boarded the Irish mail at Euston.
Early next morning she knocked on the door of 73 Stephen's
Green expecting to be taken in. Yeats, without the knowledge of his wife, refused to have her in the house. It was
the period of the great influenza epidemic; Mrs Yeats, a
victim to the prevailing scourge, was hardly yet on the road
to recovery, and he could not risk the effect which a raid
by the police or military might have upon her health. He
had never failed Maud Gonne before, and there was a
stormy scene, followed by angry letters in which he was upbraided for lack of patriotism, if not for cowardice. The town
got wind of the incident and the wilder imaginations of the
Cumann na mBan (the women's organization of Sinn Fein),
accused the poet of having conspired with Mr Shortt, the
Chief Secretary, to shut Maud Gonne up in an English
sanatorium in order to keep possession of her house. Mr
Shortt did not interfere with Maud Gonne once she had
got to Dublin, and the Yeatses gave up No. 73 to her as soon
as possible and spent the weeks before and after Christmas
in various lodgings in the vicinity of Dublin. The quarrel
was quickly composed, and presently Yeats was seen as a

visitor to No. 73. 'It was at one of Madame's At Homes that I was first introduced to Yeats,' Cecil Salkeld writes.

There was then certainly no constraint between them. She received Yeats with the gay good-humour characteristic of her. I fancy the place she occupied in his verse had placed them both beyond possibility of any prolonged quarrel. Behind his aloofness I was soon to discover one of the most touching traits in his character : his instant recollection of, and unfailing courtesy to, anyone who was a friend or protégé, or even a dependant of Madame Gonne MacBride. Nor can I remember any exception to this rule.

I have often heard distinguished men and women regret Dr Yeats's 'short-sightedness', or 'forgetfulness', when they found themselves unrecognised in the street. Yet an ailing old servant, or a penniless young art-student (as I was at the time), were never passed by without a greeting and a kind inquiry – if they were friends of Madame Gonne MacBride.

This emotional quality, manifesting itself in courtesy to Madame MacBride's friends, was, I think, typically Irish, and more strongly developed in Yeats than in anybody I have ever met.

During this winter of 1918–19 Yeats organized a series of lectures at the Abbey Theatre and brought Bernard Shaw to Dublin to speak on Socialism. His own contribution was to act as chairman at a discussion on ghosts. G. K. Chesterton arrived to oppose Shaw, and the Arts Club arranged a dinner in his honour, which Yeats was asked to attend. Though he expressed a liking for the guest, he refused the invitation on the grounds that G. K. C. had never been a 'garreteer' and was therefore unknown, as Goethe would have said, to the Heavenly Powers. Chesterton had hardly finished his after-dinner speech, however, when, to the surprise of all, Yeats himself strode into the room and in answer to greeting cheers made a passionate speech, the event of the evening. Afterwards he invited the genial Catholic sophist to dine with him the following night and meet John Eglinton, the unencomiastic Protestant philosopher, thus exposing his own vehement imagination to fire from two sides at once. 'I speak in College (Trinity) to-morrow', he wrote to Lady Gregory on 20 January,

and then 'on the system' to a private audience at the United Arts on Friday night, and I debate with a Catholic Authority at the Abbey on Sunday. After that, at least when *Baile's Strand* has been played, I must take up my philosophic writing again. May I go to Coole about Feb. 12th? Ballylee is finished, I hope, for the present – ground floor castle and new room added to cottages and all castle windows in – and I want to find out if it is ready for George. I have 3 books coming out: (1) *Two Plays for Dancers* (Cuala), (2) *Cutting of Agate* (with new essays), (3) *Swans at Coole*, and the Stage Society are to do *Player Queen* and I am hoping that *Visions and Beliefs* will come to crown all. James Stephens is the first disciple of 'The System'.

4

In various poems at this time, which were included in the Macmillan edition of *The Wild Swans at Coole*,* Yeats wakened the dry astrological bones of 'the system' into breathing life. Never before had he invested the outlines of physical phenomena with such dramatic intensity as in 'The Double Vision of Michael Robartes'. In his later prose-work, *A Vision*, he speaks of 'two conjunctions' (Jupiter and Saturn), symbolic of a variety of 'phenomena', as being 'so to speak – Heraldic supporters guarding the mystery of the 15th phase'. The 'Heraldic' symbol is evident in the otherwise obscure poem 'The Double Vision', which Ezra Pound hated.

> On the grey rock of Cashel I suddenly saw
> A Sphinx with woman breast and lion paw,
> A Buddha, hand at rest,
> Hand lifted up that blest;
>
> And right between these two a girl at play
> That, it may be, had danced her life away,
> For now being dead it seemed
> That she of dancing dreamed.

* Not in the earlier Cuala Press book of the same name.

In February he received this letter from Sturge Moore:

I have received an early copy of *The Wild Swans at Coole* and
hope before they send you one they will put right a mistake
which originated on my drawing 'of Coole' instead of 'at Coole'.
The design is much less well printed than that for *Per Amica*
was and I have also remonstrated about that.

I have much enjoyed reading your poems many of which are
new. The Elegy on Robert Gregory is, I think, one of your best
things. Reading it again I liked it even better than at first, and
there are quite a number of others which I rank very high and
am glad to have at hand so that I can improve my acquaintance
with them.

Someone has suggested to me that you are thinking of the
quilt for a real baby and that that is why you are stopping in
Dublin this winter; the idea had never entered my head ... but
I hope the event has been brought to a happy termination and
that both mother and child are doing well. We are anxious to
learn whether the world is enriched by a boy or a girl.

Anne Butler Yeats was born on 26 February 1919. 'I think
a daughter (family ambition and disappointed relatives
apart) pleases me ...', Yeats confided to a friend: 'George
announces from the horoscope that the child will be good-
looking and lucky....' The ten-stanza poem, at once personal and mythological, in which he prays,

> May she become a flourishing hidden tree
> That all her thoughts may like the linnet be

and

> O may she live like some green laurel
> Rooted in one dear perpetual place

was begun a few weeks after Anne Yeats's birth, and completed in June at Ballylee, where the scene is set:

> I have walked and prayed for this young child an hour
> And heard the sea-wind scream upon the tower,
> And under the arches of the bridge, and scream
> In the elms above the flooded stream;

> Imagining in excited reverie
> That the future years had come,
> Dancing to a frenzied drum,
> Out of the murderous innocence of the sea.

In the lines of 'excited reverie ... murderous innocence of the sea' there is the first clear picture of the new 'murderous' music that was to come, 'to the beating of a drum' from Yeats's later verse. This magnificent poem is one of the few to remain untouched from its first draft. It appeared in Yeats's volume of 1920, *Michael Robartes and the Dancer*, and some surprise was felt at what may well have been a reference to feelings caused during the previous year by Maud Gonne's political activities and his refusal at 73 Stephen's Green to abet them. He hopes that his daughter may think opinions are accursed:

> Have I not seen the loveliest woman born
> Out of the mouth of Plenty's horn,
> Because of her opinionated mind
> Barter that horn and every good
> By quiet natures understood
> For an old bellows full of angry wind? ...
>
> And may her bridegroom bring her to a house
> Where all's accustomed, ceremonious;
> For arrogance and hatred are the wares
> Peddled in the thoroughfares.
> How but in custom and in ceremony
> Are innocence and beauty born?
> Ceremony's name for the rich horn,
> And custom for the spreading laurel tree.

J. B. Y., too, rose to the occasion; he was eighty and a grandfather at last. 'At first I was puzzled with "Anne Butler"', he wrote to his daughter Lily Yeats.

Who is Anne Butler? and then I realized that it was the little creature – the newly arrived. ... Tell George and Willie I am constantly thinking about my granddaughter, and hope that I shall arrive in some sphere from which I can look and see her grown up – perhaps she will be a brilliant woman. . . . Mrs Beattie when I first saw her and when she did not know who I was or my name, used these words, 'You once were important people, now you are all scattered, but you will again be important through another name'. What does that oracle mean? Is Anne Butler to marry a Duke or a Prime Minister and will she tell her friends that her family is illustrious, being descended from the Yeats and the Butlers of Ireland? – her complexion will be a lovely mixture of the dark with the fair. Her mind deeply revolving like her father's and yet alert, witty and gay like her mother's – and she will be a famous hostess in Mayfair . . .

The 'newly arrived' spent the first of her summers in the cottage attached to Ballylee Castle. The structural work on the tower still proceeded. Local craftsmen were employed to make heavy oak beds, chairs and tables suited to a Norman castle, and a smith from Gort supplied the iron-work. The ceilings of old mill boards were painted by Mrs Yeats. As yet the tower was roofless, the second and third floors open to all weathers. Later, when the second floor was completed for use as a bedroom, the first floor was converted into a study. The top or 'Ladies Room', the finest apartments in the castle, was never made habitable. In the summer of 1919 Yeats worked in the ground-floor room over the river. 'I have been driven by rain from the river bank', he wrote to his father, 16 July 1919,

where I have been writing and catching a distant glimpse of a young otter fishing, I suppose for trout. Probably an otter can catch them, even when there is rain overhead. We saw just his brown head and a long ripple on the water. Anne and George were there too, George sewing and Anne lying awake in her seventeenth-century cradle.

I am writing in the great ground floor of the castle – pleasantest room I have yet seen, a great wide window opening over the river and a round arched door leading to the thatched hall. [Drawing here as illustration].

A very bad drawing but I am put out by having the object in front of me, 'nature puts me out'. I could do it all right from memory. I mean to represent a great door, there is a stone floor and a stone-roofed entrance hall with the door to winding stair to left, and then a larger thatched hall, beyond which is a cottage and kitchen. In the thatched hall imagine a great copper hanging lanthorn (which is, however, not yet there but will be I hope next week). I am writing at a great trestle table which George keeps covered with wild flowers.

5

Yeats had now given up the rooms at Woburn Buildings which he had tenanted for twenty-four years. He did not wish to settle in London again; on the other hand, he had had enough of Dublin and its politics for the moment, and Ballylee was not possible in winter owing to the damp. It would be unfair, he thought, to ask his English wife to live out of England throughout the year; and for his part he wanted to escape the calls of the Abbey, and to leave Lennox Robinson as free a hand as possible. The young were in control of Irish politics, and he had warned Lady Gregory, who was more tenacious of power than he, that she must resign herself to the same thing happening in their theatre.

'Lennox Robinson,' he wrote to her, 'represents the Ireland that must sooner or later take the work over from us ... the sooner some young man, who feels that his own future is bound up with the Abbey, is put in charge the better.'

As the previous stay at Oxford had been a pleasant episode, Mrs Yeats returned there to take a house at No. 4 Broad Street, which had the advantage of a lease renewable every six months. The house (since pulled down to make room for a shop) was opposite Balliol, near the Cornmarket. The move was made in October 1919, but scarcely were they installed when Yeats decided that he must 'earn a roof for Thoor Ballylee' in America. There was no difficulty about finding a tenant for the Oxford house, and the poet's sisters were delighted to take charge of Anne. Consequently Mrs Yeats found it possible to accompany her husband.

The tour lasted well into May. After three weeks of it Yeats wrote to Lady Gregory from Pittsburgh:

George has stayed up till a few days ago in New York, only coming to Washington and Yale with me. This saves railway fares. We are travelling in much comfort. . . . In spite of all the expense and the high rate of living I hope to bring home more money than ever before. Pond promised to send last Tuesday £100 for the Ballylee roof for which we have bought beautiful slates of different colours and sizes. I am sorry Lord Gough is not there to see it for he seemed interested in what one did. George seems always thinking of Ballylee and of Anne. A week ago I thought she would go home – Anne had not been gaining weight, and then came a letter to say Anne had gained so many ounces. . . . My father has decided to stay in New York. He says his return would be 'to sink into the cradle of his second childhood' . . . he is as full of the future as when I was a child.

A new lecture, in which Yeats read poems of his own and told how he came to write them, hit the mark with every kind of audience. It was called 'My Own Poetry with Illustrative Readings' and dealt mainly with his early work, because (he said) 'everyone assures me that the older I grow the more unintelligible I become'. He would start off with 'The Lake Isle of Innisfree' – 'I like to get it over,' he would say; and then go on to 'The Fiddler of Dooney', 'Wandering Aengus', 'Cap and Bells' and 'Embroidered Cloths'. On one occasion a woman, whom afterwards he discovered to be an expert in voice production, challenged his method of reciting verse. 'Will you kindly tell me, Mr Yeats, why you read your poetry in that manner?' 'I read my poetry as all the great poets from Homer down have read their poetry', was the reply. 'Will Mr Yeats give me his authority for saying that Homer read his poetry in that manner?' 'The only authority I can give you is the authority that a Scotsman gave when he claimed Shakespeare for his own country, "The ability of the man justifies the assumption".'

From his love poetry he chose 'The Cap and Bells' and 'Had I the Heavens' Embroidered Cloths', the one telling 'how to win a lady, the other how to lose a lady'. He declined to read anything more personal, though invariably asked to do so. Once he was in a town which, he was told, had fallen from its former prosperity, save that it held many poets. These evidences of prosperity, all very old, came and sat beside him on the platform. At the end of the lecture the usual request was made, and the usual refusal given. But the request was repeated so many times that at last he lost his temper and announced: 'Under no circumstances will I read you a poem that may be taken as a personal utterance'. 'Quite right,' came in nasal tones from an elderly woman poet behind him. 'I will always say that in future.'

'Nothing ever alters in America,' he said in one of his letters home, 'at least outwardly.' And to Robert Bridges, speaking of a young American of their acquaintance: 'He has the American passion for ideas, combined, I judge, with the American intellectual indolence and physical energy. His mother, when with child with him, probably listened to fifteen lectures a week, two a day including Sundays, which is quite moderate.'

From Salt Lake City he wrote to Mrs Shakespear:

I lectured yesterday to a Mormon University in a wonderful little town among quiet mountains – like a Greek town. On Monday I lecture at a University that is Mormon in all but name. Tomorrow I am to meet some of the officials of their Church. I hope to ask questions about the doctrine of continuous inspiration. They claim that the miraculous has never ceased among them ... and now also pride themselves on never having more than one wife. They claim that their once generous plurality was a temporary measure after a great war ... so at least an enthusiast for the faith has been explaining to me. I told him that America and Germany had both made the mistake of standardizing life, the one in interest of monarchy, the other in interest of democracy, but both for the ultimate gain of a sterile devil. That once America and Germany had been infinitely abundant in variations from type to type, but now all was type.

Tell Ezra to come to America and found a paper devoted to the turning of the U.S.A. into a monarchy to balance Germany.

There was another notable Irishman in America at the same time as he – Eamonn de Valera, President (*de jure*) of the Irish Republic, who was enlisting support for Ireland's assertion of her rights to be an independent nation on the lines laid down by Wilson for the unfortunate European continent. De Valera wore the romantic halo of 1916, and Yeats had been impressed by a saying reported of him after the suppression of the Rising, 'If the people had only come out with knives and forks'. He now spoke to a syllogism, and Yeats recorded a slight feeling of disappointment when Quinn brought him to a big meeting in New York (11 May 1920):

A living argument rather than a living man. All propaganda, no human life, but not bitter or hysterical or unjust. I judged him persistent, being both patient and energetic, but that he will fail through not having enough human life as to judge the human life in others. He will ask too much of everyone and will ask it without charm. He will be pushed aside by others.*

Before leaving America Yeats addressed urgent inquiries to Lady Gregory as to conditions in Ireland, particularly beyond the Shannon. 'Will it be right', he asked in one letter,

to bring Anne to Ballylee? Has there been much cattle-driving, and if so is it enough to endanger the supply of milk? The papers here give very alarming accounts, and at Ballylee we are dependent on F.'s cows, and F. has enemies. ... If Ballylee is unwise we will give our tenant at Oxford notice. ... George and I would go to Ballylee for a short time to see how the work has gone and then fetch Anne to Oxford.

* When he met de Valera some years later he, like most others, found a charm in the personal contact that did not appear in the speeches.

[15]

Oxford

Oxford – Visit to Glenmalure; 'All Souls' Night', 1920 –
Speech at Oxford Union – Monday evenings at Broad
Street – Mysterious happenings at Shillingford and
Thame; birth of son – Plans to return to Ireland; death
of J. B. Yeats

———

Midnight has come, and the great Christ Church Bell
And many a lesser bell sound through the room;
And it is All Souls' Night,
And two long glasses brimmed with muscatel
Bubble upon the table. A ghost may come;
For it is a ghost's right,
His element is so fine
Being sharpened by his death,
To drink from the wine-breath
While our gross palates drink from the whole wine.

I

YEATS decided to speed up the work on Ballylee, and spend
what money he had earned in America on it without delay.
He would make it an efficient house where he could have a
guest. Two new luxuries only would he allow himself at
Oxford, where his house was chiefly furnished with things
from Woburn Buildings: pewter dinner plates and dishes
and a green parrot.

A transport strike was on, travelling difficult, and the nurse
on holiday in Ireland. Until the nurse's return Anne was sent
to an expensive home in Kensington where 'all the babies are
guaranteed born in wedlock'. Her parents, to be near her,
borrowed Ezra Pound's little flat in Church Street, and there
waited impatiently for news of the progress of work on
Ballylee. This came after a fortnight and was disheartening;

the workmen had not even begun. One hitch followed another, and it became apparent that it would be necessary to
give the tenant at 4 Broad Street notice, for Ballylee was not
likely to be ready before the winter, if then.

On 15 July 1920, Yeats wrote to Lady Gregory from
Oxford:

It is a great joy to be back in this house again after many
journeys and it looks very solemn and dignified to our eyes
wearied by many irrelevant things. . . . It is not 'arty', to use the
new word; there is no undue mark of present taste; all looks, I
think, as if it had some history behind it and yet there is unity.
I have many little pictures by my father, and of members of the
family, some of whom you have never seen, and all our furniture,
or nearly all, is old, and so suited to this seventeenth-century
house. . . . It all seems very peaceful, with a green parrot on a
landing, and Anne staggering about full of destructiveness –
they only heighten the sense of peace. If peace can ever come to
this world again it should be here.

With Robert Bridges and John Masefield resident at Boar's
Hill, Yeats at Oxford did not lack the company of old
friends. Bridges seldom came into town without calling at
4 Broad Street. He treated Yeats with affectionate nonchal-
ance. 'Don't think I have come to see you,' he would say
when the door was opened for him. 'I have come for luncheon.' The Sturge Moores and Edmund Dulac were invited
for week-ends, and another of Yeats's pleasures was to go to
Garsington, the beautiful manor-house of Lady Ottoline
and Philip Morrell, where undergraduates mixed with distinguished folk on Sunday afternoons. There is a poem by
Oliver Gogarty describing an afternoon there, which others
present remember very well. At about six or so the undergraduates would start to walk back to Cowley village, where
they could get a bus. On this occasion, a beautiful spring
evening, Yeats walked ahead with Lady Ottoline, and the
rest of the party walked behind with Gogarty. The two in
front made a marvellous pair, striking the villagers with
speechless amazement: Yeats tall and stately, gesticulating,
his hair ruffled in the wind, and Lady Ottoline, in period

lilac silk, large picture-hat and shoes with high red heels, listening to him and nodding, her long face alight with animation. They looked like beings from some pageant outside time.

2

The news of the world continued to be very disturbing, and caused Yeats to picture himself taking up a university post in Japan and returning to find London a grass-grown city and Sinn Fein in possession of Ballylee, or it stark and roof-less ('May these characters remain When all is ruin once again'). In September 1920, however, in spite of threats of railway strikes, he crossed to Dublin to have his tonsils re-moved by Oliver Gogarty. While awaiting the operation, he paid a flying visit to the water-filled silences of Glenmalure, twenty-five miles from the city, where Maud Gonne, her son and their friend Cecil Salkeld were on holiday in a lonely cottage. Mr Cecil Salkeld has been kind enough to oblige me with the following memory of the occasion:

The cottage is 'the last in the glen' – I put that in quotation marks because it is thus that it appears in the Stage Directions of *The Shadow of the Glen* by Synge, who wrote that play about that particular cottage. A day or two after I had been there, I saw, from half-way up Lugnaquilla, the tallest hill thereabouts, a jaunting car with a solitary passenger, approaching the cottage. The car had to stop on the far side of a little river which had to be crossed on stepping-stones. It was only then I saw that the arrival was Yeats, and hastened down to meet him. 'I hope you'll excuse my "country get-up" ', he said. I looked in vain for the 'country get-up'. Then I noticed that he had pulled his ordinary socks up outside his immaculate tweed trousers, as some cyclists do. He was tired by the journey and soon went to bed. I was up early the next morning, but not as early as Yeats. Coming down to breakfast, Madame Gonne MacBride smiled at me and said: 'Willie is booming and buzzing like a bumble bee . . . that means he is writing something. . . .' To my great surprise, Yeats, who appeared shortly, obviously preoccupied and absent-minded, asked me if I would walk up the glen with him. We walked, treading our way among boulders and small stones along the river bank for nearly half an hour in silence. By that I mean no word was spoken; but, all the while, Yeats kept up a persistent murmur – under his breath, as it were. Suddenly, he pulled up short at a big stone and said : 'Do you realize that eternity is not a long time but a *short* time . . . ?' I just said, I didn't quite understand. 'Eternity,' Yeats said, 'Eternity is in the glitter on the beetle's wing . . . it is something infinitely short. . . .' I said that I could well conceive 'Infinity' being excessively small as well as being excessively large. 'Yes,' he said, apparently irrelevantly, 'I was thinking of those Ephesian topers . . .'

He pulled out of his pocket a very small piece of paper on which he had written 8 lines which had been perhaps ten times corrected. It was almost impossible for me to read a line of it. I only saw one phrase which I knew was obsessing him at that time – for Yeats was at all times a man dominated – sometimes for weeks on end – by a single phrase : this one was 'Mummy wheat' – a phrase destined to appear in a much later poem – a phrase he never forgot.

That night I sat up late, long after the others had gone to bed, and finished a water-colour picture of a weird centaur at the edge of a dark wood : in the foreground, in the shade of the wood, lay the seven Ephesian 'topers' in a drunken stupor, while far behind on a sunny distant desert plain elephants and the glory of a great army passed away into the distance. Next day I showed the picture to Yeats. He looked at it so critically that I suddenly remembered that he had been an Art Student. He peered at me over the top of his glasses. 'Who is your teacher?' he asked. 'Has he told you about values?' 'What are values?' I asked. Yeats laughed his deep ferocious chuckle : 'Do you really tell me you don't know what "values" are?' I said 'No', and waited for instruction. 'Well, I'm certainly not going to tell you! Perhaps that is the beginning of a new Art. . . . "Values" were the bane of my youth.' When I walked out with him that day he made no reference to the poem, but talked continuously of the conception of the 'Daimon' which was particularly interesting him at the time : he also told me the history of his play *The Player Queen*, saying (perhaps with a faint reminiscence of Goethe's *Faust* in his head) that he had spent 20 years on the play.

Later that night, W.B. came down to supper with a perfectly

clear countenance; it was plain the poem was finished. He did not speak throughout the meal, yet I felt he would say something before the night was through. When the ladies had withdrawn, he produced a pigskin-covered brandy flask and a small beautifully written manuscript: 'Your picture made the thing clear', he said. 'I am going to dedicate the poem to you. I shall call it The Black Centaur.' ... It was then for the first time I heard those miraculous lines, one of which is:

> Stretch out your limbs and sleep a long Saturnian sleep.

I was impressed and gratified. But when printed in 1928, in *The Tower*, the poem was altered; it was corrected and it was entitled: 'On a Picture of a Black Centaur by Edmund Dulac'.

Oliver Gogarty removed his tonsils 'with exuberant gaiety', as Yeats wrote to John Quinn. While Yeats retained consciousness Gogarty discussed literature, and continued the discussion when the poet awoke. He came six times to the nursing home in the course of the afternoon to make suggestions as to the lines upon which the patient should conduct a dying speech.

While in Dublin, Yeats saw *Michael Robartes and the Dancer* through his sister's press: a slender volume which contained more poetry of dream prophecy, such as 'Demon and Beast' and 'The Second Coming', as well as the four 1916 poems and 'A Prayer for My Daughter'. 'It is quite strange,' Lady Gregory wrote to him when she received the book, 'a little sad too, seeing for the first time in print a poem of yours, not in your own writing.' In November, at Oxford, he wrote the grand stanzas 'All Souls' Night', commemorating Horton, Florence Farr and MacGregor Mathers, lost friends who had shared his love for strange thought.* After this the days went on with uniformity, while he worked at the chapters of his autobiography, which describe the basis and circumstances of his literary beginnings in London. 'I think', he wrote to Lady Gregory in December, 'you will

---

* Horton was recently dead. Mathers died in Paris just after the war, and Florence Farr during the war, in Ceylon, where she had gone to teach in a Buddhist school, 'away from neighbour or friend'.

find a curious change in me. A result of the ordered life of routine (now having lasted many months for the first time in my life) is that I have grown, without any effort, exceedingly tidy. I cannot bear a paper-knife crooked on my table. I sometimes feel as if all that time has left is routine – routine and waiting [writing?]'

The pacifist, humanitarian philosophy, which gained ground after the war, particularly at Oxford, seemed to Yeats to be artificial and unreal, at most good intentions. Witness his prophetic 'Second Coming':

> Things fall apart; the centre cannot hold;
> Mere anarchy is loosed upon the world,
>
> The best lack all conviction, while the worst
> Are full of passionate intensity.

And writing of the portraits in 'Four Years',* he said: 'Every analysis of character, of Wilde, Henley, Shaw and so on, builds up my philosophic nationalism – it is nationalism against internationalism, the rooted against the rootless peoples'. He had become President of the Irish Club in the hope of influencing members who might come to have importance in Ireland, and was even reading economics 'to some extent', in search for 'some sort of scheme to stir young minds'.

3

An incident of the winter of 1920–21 that should not go unrecorded was Yeats's appearance at the Oxford Union to denounce the exploits of the expert gunmen, Black and Tans and Auxiliaries, whom the British Government had let loose upon Ireland to track down the militants of the Irish Republican Army and terrorize the civil population. The poem 'Nineteen Hundred and Nineteen' was suggested by Lady Gregory's account of some horrors at Gort.

---

* Book I of *The Trembling of the Veil*.

> Now days are dragon-ridden, the nightmare
> Rides upon sleep : a drunken soldiery
> Can leave the mother, murdered at her door,
> To crawl in her own blood, and go scot-free;
> The night can sweat with terror as before
> We pieced our thoughts into philosophy,
> And planned to bring the world under a rule,
> Who are but weasels fighting in a hole.

Speaking to a motion of want of confidence in the Irish policy of the Government, Yeats stepped forward with some passionate exclamation of denial concerning something that had been said. Then with extraordinary vehemence he arraigned the English nation and scattered the speaker who had just resumed his seat. He gathered impetus from increasing rage, left the 'Treasury Box' and strode up and down the aisle between the Ayes and the Noes, waving his arms and shaking his fists at the audience, pouring out a sustained flow of eloquence. At first the house was changed into a theatre audience, but as he went on it became more and more beaten and subdued.... Eventually Yeats sat down amidst unexampled enthusiasm – the fourth speaker was completely disliked and the motion approved by an overwhelming majority. The occasion was considered unique in the history of the Union.*

When his name was published among a list of speakers at Drury Lane Theatre for 'Warriors' Day', he wrote to the organizer of the meeting that a tribute from him would lack all sincerity. He might try to think of men who served in France or Italy with a good conscience and who now perhaps needed help, but would think instead of certain ex-service men called 'Auxiliary police', who in his own country robbed and murdered without hindrance. He sent a poem to the *Nation* on Robert Gregory, with this thought in it, but cancelled the publication on learning that it would distress Robert's widow. Every day he expected to hear that Ballylee

---

*I am indebted for a description of the scene to Mr J. S. Collis, who proposed the motion.

had been raided and sacked. Lady Gregory, who remained at Coole throughout this miserable time, could tell him nothing for certain, but reported a rumour that the Auxiliaries intended to settle in the Castle, 'as it affords greater facilities than Drumbosna for hanging their prisoners from a bridge'. This particular alarm passed off, and though Ballylee when Mrs Yeats next visited it showed signs of having been entered – by whom no one ever knew – little or nothing was missing. The poet had been particularly concerned for the security of his 'sea-green slates', which had cost £70, and were stored in the 'Ladies Room' at the top of the tower. The slates were untouched, but (it may be said here) were never used, as the local builders advised that the elaborate roof, designed in Lutyen's office, would never hold against Atlantic gales. The tower, which was finally provided with a flat cement roof – and here he could sit and work on fine days behind the high parapet – remained 'half dead at the top'.*

4

The Yeatses spent the greater part of 1921 in Oxford or in its vicinity. They were making friends among the younger members of University society, and held Monday At Homes at 4 Broad Street to which only undergraduates were invited. One went up the stairs, the walls of which were covered with Blake drawings from Job, to a dimly-lit room on the first floor; later on, to a room at the top of the narrow house where Yeats kept his Kelmscott Chaucer open on a lectern, and had many little birds in large cages, whose habits he observed with care.†

Sometimes he would attend meetings of literary societies by request of undergraduates, as when L. A. G. Strong of

---

* 'Is every modern nation like the tower,
   Half dead at the top?'
                              ('Blood and the Moon', *The Winding Stair*, 1933).
† *Vide* 'Now that I am a settled man and have many birds . . .' in 'Hodos Chameliontos'. It was a return to his early interest in natural history, but he drew different deductions now.

Wadham called for him in a taxi and found him in evening clothes, although he was to be entertained – and this gave him great pleasure – in college at the ordinary table among undergraduates. On a second visit to Wadham, the meeting was held in the rooms of a classical don, Wade-Gery, and during the interval between Yeats's paper and the discussion, he was shown by Wade-Gery some photographs of recently discovered Greek sculptures. Wade-Gery hazarded a date. Yeats corrected him, and said that they must be at least thirty years later. He turned out to be right. His instinct in such matters was often remarkable.*

Mr Strong writes as follows of the 'Monday Evenings' in Broad Street:

On my visits to his house I was at first shy and awkward, and I remember, one day, breaking into a lull of the talk with the following question: 'Tell me, Mr Yeats,' I said, 'what is it about the writing of George Moore that makes one read on eagerly from page to page?' – 'I never did read on,' he replied, 'so I don't know.' Mrs Yeats grinned, Charles Morgan (up as an under-graduate after the war) smiled gently, and I felt that my ears were as big and as hot as crumpets. W. B. saw my embarrass-ment, and proceeded with real kindliness to soften the blow. I always noticed that, despite anything that was said about his aloofness, he was extraordinarily perceptive of and considerate to the feelings of young people . . .

In 1921, when my first small book of poems appeared, I sent W. B. a copy. He replied in a letter which I have always treasured, praising the poems highly, and asking me to go at once and see him. When I went he spoke in quite a different way. 'I have been confusing you with the schoolmaster',† he said. 'I now see that you have quite a different personality.' And the odd thing was that under this stimulus, from being tongue-tied and reverent, I was drawn out into a confidence which may not have survived the hours I was with him, but which helped slowly to build me up into something approaching an adult. From that time on he gave me a standing invitation to go in every Monday night, and would

* Sir Maurice Bowra, Warden of Wadham, became a great friend of his.

† Strong was teaching at a school near Oxford.

sometimes even ask me to go in early by myself, or stay on late afterwards. I seldom left the house till midnight or after, and would walk up the Banbury Road to the school where I was teaching, exhilarated, walking on air, upheld and inspired by the knowledge, which rapidly became incredible during the week, that life could be lived on such a plane of thought and at such a pitch.

A great interest at this time was the appraisal and classification of character, due to the twenty-eight phases of the moon. It was a kind of parlour game. Yeats and his wife had a rough division of objective and subjective, by which they set out to read the characters of the people they met both accurately and speedily. Both showed uncanny penetration. Yeats would watch the visitor privily from behind his glasses, listen for a couple of minutes, size him up, and then issue a question which went straight to the heart of a character, as often as not revealing a difficulty or a prepossession. It was not flattering to be placed in an objective 'phase', for, as he was to explain later, in a note to *The Only Jealousy of Emer*, 'objective natures are always ugly: hence the disagreeable appearance of politicians, philanthropists, reformers and men of science'.

Another regular visitor at the Monday At Homes was William Force Stead, American poet and student of theology, afterwards Chaplain at Worcester College.* Force Stead, as well as bringing his own problems, used often to bring his fellow undergraduates to discuss theirs. Yeats would accept these burdens eagerly: and it would be a nice subject for research to trace the influence of Yeats's quasi-Hegelian speculations, mixed with phases of the moon and mathematical symbols, upon the theological thought of certain years at Oxford. Force Stead had generally a dream or vision, apt to Yeats's teaching and beliefs, to record. On one occasion he arrived with theological comrades just as Yeats was recounting to Strong a long Rabelaisian anecdote. Yeats stopped as the bell rang. 'Remain behind after-

* Two of his poems are in Yeats's *Oxford Book of Modern Verse*.

wards,' he said. 'This will not be suitable'; and for two or
three hours weighty subjects were discussed till the theologians departed. Then Yeats came leaping up the stairs in
eagerness to resume his anecdote at the exact place where
he had broken off.

Minor phenomena took place in the house. One evening,
when the matter under discussion was India, the room was
filled with a strong smell of incense which one of those
present identified as being in use in certain Indian temples.
The room was well lit; there was no possibility of the scent
being produced by normal physical means. Another time,
Strong and he being alone, there was a discussion upon
'possession'; and Yeats went on, as if by way of illustration,
to tell about a house in Oxford where he had recently been
investigating certain phenomena. He began to describe these
phenomena, and at once seemed to behave like a man suffering from some mild form of stroke. He became rigid, the
veins swelled on his forehead, his jaws stiffened, he had to
force words from between them and the words that came
out were half of them at random. 'They are trying to stop
me', he got out. After a minute or two, he regained control,
and proceeded to describe the phenomena in question.
Neither he nor Strong could tell why 'they' should have
tried to stop him, for the phenomena were of a kind quite
well known to Strong already.

5

Between April and June of 1921, having let the house in
Broad Street for the summer months, the Yeatses rented a
two-storied cottage in the village of Shillingford, partly
from motives of economy. Already before his marriage the
sales of Yeats's books had taken an upward leap,* and his
wife had independent means, but their expenses were heavy.

---

*It was still his early work that was most popular. In February 1921
the royalties for his Unwin volume of poems (1895) were more than
double what he had received in any previous year.

The poet had now accepted liability for his father's support in New York.*

In this summer was begun 'Meditations in Time of Civil War', a series of poems all making up one poem, with a beginning which was somewhat in the mood of 'A Prayer for My Daughter', but wilder.† Another Nōh play was under consideration, in case the poems should turn out badly. Also there had come from Werner Laurie an offer of £500 for a limited edition of the autobiographies (*The Trembling of the Veil*); of which Yeats wrote to Mrs Shakespear:

My dear Olivia,

... Have you been reading me in the *London Mercury*? I am afraid Ezra will not forgive me for publishing there: he had recommended the *English Review*, but I have just as fierce a quarrel with that periodical as he has with the *Mercury*, so what could I do? Our canaries are now feeding four strapping but very ugly chicks – their third attempt – and I had hoped that young canaries were as engaging as chickens. Meanwhile Anne is as engaging as possible. The other day she asked me to put on her shoes (which she had pulled off). I put one on but could not get on the second. Then I found that she had screwed up her toes to prevent me. It was sheer coquetry and she has never been known to ask a woman to put her shoes on. In fact she cannot bear shoes. Next day when I went into the garden she pointed to the shoes, which were lying on the grass, where she had thrown them, but I was not to be snared or deceived thus.

He spent a month writing over and over again his account of the foundation of the National Literary Society, as the characterizations of Hyde, O'Grady, Russell and others still living gave him great trouble. The third part of *The Trembling of the Veil*, 'Hodos Chameliontos', on unity of being for man and nation conceived in terms of his theory of 'The

---

* Whereupon J. B. Y. wrote (he was eighty-one): 'At last I shall be able to put aside money-making and acquire skill, as a palmist advised me to do years ago'.

† The poem was finished at Ballylee two years later and then given its title.

Mask', filled him with excitement; but when it was finished he feared it might bore people.

From Shillingford they went on to Thame, where they stayed until September at Cuttlebrook House, in which John Hampden had lived. 'The kind of house', Yeats wrote,

that always pleases me (because of Sligo memories, I daresay). . . . All manner of old sporting guns on the top landing, old-fashioned landscapes, 1830 to 1890 in style, and old engravings everywhere and family portraits and on the piano a large silver cup having engraved upon it the name of a horse that won a hunt race, or some such thing, in 1827. I have tried to give our own house such a look, but there of course it is only drama – however old the things may be in themselves – except a few pictures, the deluge of impecuniosity having cut the generation in two. As I look at my Anne I get a touch of pleasure when I think that she will be so much further from the deluge, that she will hardly know of its existence, and, if old Isaac Yeats leaves mc his treasures, will be familiar with some house – her own or a brother's – that will show itself for the accredit of many generations.

He took a course of Trollope at Thame and at Shillingford, beginning with *The Warden* and *Barchester Towers*, books which 'have gained with time and not with any merit of their own, like Frith's Derby Day and his Railway Station'. Wonders never ceased, and Trollope and Jane Austen, whom also he dipped into, may have acted as useful sedatives at this time. At Shillingford, for two or three nights in succession, both he and his wife met with what seemed a sudden warm breath coming up from the same quarter of the road. Sweet smells were the most constant phenomena, but they also heard whistling, generally to warn them that some communication was at hand. During an indisposition at Thame some astringent smell like that of resinous wood filled the poet's room, and sometimes, though rarely, a bad smell.

The poet's son, William Michael, was born at Thame in August. There was such a smell of roses in the room, though

it was not their season, that even the nurse and doctor remarked upon it, 'and I have no doubt, though I did not
question them, the nurse and servants'.* Yeats was fond of
telling the story, and some years later when he met Bertrand
Russell (of all men) at Mrs Llewelyn Davies's house near
Dublin, he made it the climax of a discourse upon magic.
He said then that there were periods when he had only to
rub his hands (which he illustrated without effect) for the
room to be filled with the perfume of roses. Everybody
looked uncomfortable, but all the same the almost childish
pleasure with which he gave the information was disarming.

Usually Yeats was prepared to discuss sceptical theories
and to allow for somnambulistic cheating of mediums or
juggling that deceived the waking man, being content to
insist upon facts that did not fit into the orthodox framework
of science. Indeed he had been thrown out of more than one
séance in London on account of his scepticism. But now, for
a time, he let imagination become freely peopled with
daemons, fairies, discarnate spirits, wizards, or Rosicrucians
in cowls or shrouds, who filled the pockets of his coat with
handfuls of scented blossom in the depths of winter, and
filled his mind with marvels. He was perhaps a medium,
whatever that means, but he certainly was an actor playing
a part in a mystery play.

One afternoon his friend, Dr F. P. Sturm, poet and student
of oriental mysticisms, was walking with him through some
cloister when a shrill whistle sounded from the street. 'Did
you hear that?' said W. B. Y. 'Yes, some boy whistling.' 'Not
at all, Sturm, not at all. I was just on the point of revealing
to you a magical formula which would enable you to remember your past incarnations, when your daemon gave that
whistle to warn me not to do so. It would be dangerous for
you to know.'

Upon another occasion he drew Dr Sturm's attention to
steps on the stairs outside the room in which they sat. 'Do
you hear the daemons now?' 'I do not, Yeats, it is the maid

* Vide *A Packet for Ezra Pound.*

going to bed', and opening the door the doctor called: 'Is that you, Mary?' or whatever her name was, and Mary replied, 'Yes, sir, goodnight'. 'There are your daemons,' said Sturm. 'Do not be deceived,' said Yeats; 'remember that daemons may take any shape.'

6

Yeats was not a flower that could flourish on foreign soil. Oxford or any other place outside Ireland could only be a diversion for him, however long he might stay in it. His inspiration ultimately depended upon the roots he had formed in Ireland, and he expressed the hope and belief that the end of his life would be as full of Irish activities as the start of it.

He was always game for a trip. The project of a two-year Professorship in Japan met, however, with firm objections from his wife, when she learned that all his time would be occupied with lectures and that they would have to share a tea-house with a minor poet. He then toyed for a time with the idea of spending the winter in Cork, where he believed he might attract attention to his 'system'. Was it not in Cork that Thackeray had overheard two ragged boys talking about the Ptolemies, and talking very well too? 'I had suggested it half seriously,' he wrote to Lady Gregory, 'partly because George wants to be near Ballylee to look after it and partly because she hopes to get a house on the edge of Cork city, a town house, and yet with a garden. I had proposed Oxford as a place to live in because I thought it unfair to George to live wholly in Ireland. I now find she would have preferred Ireland from the start.'

Then there were the Nōh plays. Perhaps Cork would welcome these, and he could leave the Abbey Theatre in undisputed possession of the realists. His four plays on the Nōh model, *Plays for Dancers*, came out with Macmillan in October 1921. Two of them, *The Dreaming of the Bones* and *The Only Jealousy of Emer*, had been printed at Miss Yeats's hand press in a limited edition in 1919, whereas *At the Hawk's Well* had made a part of the edition of *The Wild Swans at Coole*, although not of the later edition of that book published by Macmillan. The fourth of the series was *Calvary*, and all were most subtly linked together by a sort of 'psychic' development, so that they could be suitably done as a sequence. When he had once allowed himself to be tempted 'from this craft of verse', it was evident that Yeats could not but follow his natural dramatic talent till he had achieved perfection. His main difficulty at first was that while gifted with a real 'stage sense' his craft was that of the lyric poet. In his earlier verse plays he overcame this handicap (as it then seemed) by loosening his texture into blank verse: traditional device of the poet who is willing to sacrifice something of his music to obtain a larger measure of dramatic freedom. Yet so great was his power of synthesis that after years of experiment he succeeded in fusing two modes of expression hitherto only defined as contrasts: lyrical and dramatic verse. In his *Four Plays for Dancers* this novel union is at once evident; inspired by the traditional limitations and conventions of the Eastern drama he set out to achieve his dramatic effects through a lyric medium, sublimating his action to the plane of the imagination.* It is possible that the many years of work on *The Player Queen* helped the poet to come to certain conclusions: (*a*) if a play is to be a drama of life, it cannot be too lifelike in technique even though such a drama be highly symbolic as *The Player Queen* is; (*b*) if, however, the drama is to be abstract, and functions by hypnotic compulsion, it cannot be too limited, formal and hence *lyrical*. Certainly no greater contrast could be imagined than that between the respective techniques of

* The ultra-modern Robot plays – or plays of types and forces rather than personalities and destinies – attempt to achieve what Yeats succeeded in doing so much earlier, but without the salutary formalism of poetry, a medium which Yeats realized was as essential to success as the lack of scenery and the masks; the clockwork motion to the tap of a drum.

The Player Queen and the *Four Plays for Dancers*, for the first is all abandon, and the second are all reserve.

Lady Gregory thought that the move to Cork would be very foolish as it would imply desertion of the Abbey Theatre. A house in Dublin was then spoken of. Yeats, however, felt rather frightened of Dublin, with Maud Gonne and her friends in their violent mood, and could not think that it would be a good place in which to bring up his children. In December 1921, when the British Cabinet achieved the discreditable 'Partition' settlement with Michael Collins and Arthur Griffith, Yeats remained pessimist, foreseeing that the opposition of de Valera, grounded on abstract principle, would prove a formidable obstacle to peace. He wrote to Mrs Shakespear from 4 Broad Street:

I am deep in gloom about Ireland, for though I expect a ratification of the treaty from a plebiscite I see no hope of escape from bitterness, and the extreme party may carry the country. When men are very bitter, death and ruin draw them on as a rabbit is supposed to be drawn on by the dancing of the fox. In the last week I have been planning to live in Dublin – George very urgent about this – but I feel now that all may be blood and misery. If that comes we may abandon Ballylee to the owls and rats and England too (where passion will rise and I shall find myself with no answer) and live in some far-off land. What else could one do for the children's sake, and one's own work? I could not bring them to Ireland where they would inherit bitterness, nor leave them in England where, being Irish by tradition and my family and fame, they would be in an unnatural condition of mind and grow as so many Irishmen who live here do, sour and argumentative.

After protracted discussion in Dublin, turning mainly on the question of the oath of allegiance, Collins and Griffith secured ratification of the settlement by a majority of seven. Yeats could consider the issue with more detachment than most Irishmen, because on the one hand he felt no sentimental attachment either to Crown or Empire, and on the other he disliked and distrusted Republican idealism. It was his view, however, that the Treaty conferred effective powers of freedom on the larger part of Ireland, and he rejoiced at the defeat of Madame Markievicz and other non-jurors, whose influence upon Irish affairs he had always dreaded. His comment, for Lady Gregory's ear, on the leader of the non-jurors was characteristic: 'De Valera has fulfilled, I think, what I wrote to you from America but keeps one's personal sympathy like the hero of our own *Unicorn from the Stars*'.

7

The period of hesitancy ended with the purchase of a Georgian house at 82 Merrion Square, Dublin. It was a stately house with immense rooms, which could be brought within their means by letting the stable and the top floor.

On 3 February, shortly before the purchase was made, the news of his father's death reached Yeats at Oxford. J. B. Y.'s illness was brought on by a long walk in the cold of a New York winter and lasted only a few hours. He awoke in the middle of the night to find his friends, Mrs Foster and John Quinn, sitting beside his bed, and after Quinn had gone he said to Mrs Foster, 'Did you see Quinn looking at my portrait?'* He then went to sleep and died in his sleep.

Quinn sent the family a note on the last days of the old painter:

He tried to go on as actively as he had gone on ten years before, keeping thoughts of death from him. He did not become bent with his age. His figure was erect and his stride was sturdy and vigorous. ... He even danced in those last evenings right up to the attack that brought on his end. ... He had great pride always in his children.

He was out shopping with Mrs Foster and myself on January 27 and we drove to see the Kelekian pictures. Five or six beautiful Cézannes hung on the walls. I said, 'There are some fine Courbets, I imagine you prefer them to the Cézannes'. To my

* The self-portrait, begun thirteen years before, which still stood on his easel.

surprise he said, 'No, Quinn, I do not. I like Cézanne very much. I do not think that everything by Cézanne is great, but I think he was a very great artist . . .'

It was difficult for Yeats to realize his father's death; he had been so long a mind to him, and that mind seemed to him still thinking and writing. 'I wish', he wrote, 'that he could have lived to see us in Dublin. I think constantly that my children will have that spacious home that I lacked after I left Sligo. I am longing to be back in Ireland, and I had not that longing till George found 82 Merrion Square, so I conclude I must have feared a house like that Rathgar villa where we all lived when I went to school.' And he quoted the ballad about the Duke of Wellington, which made him feel very grand:

> In Merrion Square
> This noble hero first drew breath
> Amid a nation's cheers.

But he felt upon leaving Oxford that he would miss the students of whom he had seen so many of all kinds, and at whose societies he had spoken so often, and that he would miss the buildings and his charming house in Broad Street.

[16]

Meditations in time of
civil war

Yeats in the Free State – Ballylee: summer 1922 –
Senator – Parliamentary work – Nobel Prize – The
'System' – Speech at Tailteann Games

———

Much did I rage when young,
Being by the world oppressed,
But now with flattering tongue
It speeds the parting guest.

I

THE new Ireland created by the 'Treaty' appeared to be
ready to honour Yeats. The Ard Fheis of Sinn Fein nominated him as a delegate to an Irish Race Congress which was
held in Paris during January 1922. To this he went and
spoke on the work of the Abbey, on Synge and on the poets
of 1916. Trinity College (which had thrown in its lot with
the 'Treaty' party) added a testimonial, and during the year
he received a welcome academic distinction when the degree
of Doctor of Letters in Dublin University was conferred
upon him.* Within two months *The Trembling of the Veil*,
Later Poems and *Plays in Prose and Verse* appeared, and
all three books were well received by the critics. These successes gratified him, but there were moments when he felt
tired. He could plan and think as never before; but he could
no longer hope to achieve all that he planned and thought;
he began to rage at the 'absurdity' of growing old:

* Yeats's first honorary degree from a university was from Belfast
(July 1922). Dublin followed in December.

> What shall I do with this absurdity –
> O heart, O troubled heart – this caricature,
> Decrepit age that has been tied to me
> As to a dog's tail?

Among other projects which he had in mind on his return to Ireland were a State Theatre, an Irish Academy of Letters, subsidized by Government, and the creation of a Ministry of Fine Arts. Arthur Griffith had formed a Provisional Government after the ratification of the Treaty and de Valera's resignation, and about this he felt some misgivings. But he hoped that Griffith, isolated among the hardheaded young men in his Cabinet, would prove more amenable to his purposes than of old. 'We have to be', he wrote to Lady Gregory, '"that old man eloquent" to the new governing generation. If we write our best, the spiritual part of the new Ireland will be in our books and the Free State's struggle with the impossiblists may even make some of our unpopular struggles shine with patriotic fire.'

It is to be observed that Yeats could never forgive Griffith for the strictures upon Synge and Hugh Lane or think of him as other than a fanatic. Griffith, on the contrary, was quite ready to let bygones be bygones, and had he lived, would have been the first to insist that Yeats's cultural work deserved the recognition of the State. Senator Desmond Fitzgerald informs me that at the time that he and Griffith had been interned in Gloucester Jail, Griffith, knowing his ardent admiration for the poet, said to him, 'What are you going to do about June 13?' Having drawn a confession of ignorance of the significance of that date, Griffith put on an air of pained surprise: 'Don't you know', he said, 'that June 13 is W. B.'s birthday?' They went together to the Governor and told him that the Irish in Gloucester Jail would require special facilities on 13 June, as it was the birthday of their national poet. The Governor consented, and asked whether the chaplain would be required to attend at the ceremony. Provisions were ordered in, and the dinner concluded with a speech in which Griffith proclaimed Yeats as the greatest poet who had come out of Ireland.

The weary, harassed nation acquiesced on the whole in the settlement, but the opponents of Griffith and Collins were indefatigable in provoking discontents, and when Yeats visited Dublin in March 1922 to look at his new house in Merrion Square, he found the bitterness on both sides appalling. Lady Gregory wanted him to make a political pronouncement, but he felt that he should say nothing until he found something to say that was his own thought. 'I will never', he wrote to her, 'like any position in life where I have to speak but half my mind, and I feel that both sides are responsible for this whirlpool of hate. Besides, only action counts or can count till there is some change.'

Action was not slow in coming. In April the leaders of the fighting men who refused to comply with the Treaty signified their contempt of the verdict of the electorate by seizing the Four Courts and other positions of importance in Dublin. The scene was set for civil war, as in the meantime Michael Collins had formed a new army loyal to the Provisional Government. Yeats was at Ballylee with his family, somewhat cut off from news when the fighting began. He wrote from there to Mrs Shakespear:

... All is quiet in this part of the world except that two weeks ago the commander of the — Irregulars robbed a neighbouring post-office of the dog tax, that he might pay his men, was hunted by the — Regulars, who shot at him and made him swim a river. He got off with the money and he and the Regulars are now the best of friends. The post-mistress says that he was so nice-mannered that when she found that the dog tax did not amount to quite £20 she made it up to that amount with her own money. I am not alarmed at anything but the murders of Protestants in Cork. The whole situation in Ireland interests me. We have here popular leaders representing a minority, but a considerable one, who mock at an appeal to the vote. ... One saw the same thing in Russia when the Communists dissolved the Constituent Assembly. On the other hand I hear that the Free State party will bring in a Constitution especially arranged to give power to the heads of departments as distinguished from the politicians, and with a second chamber so arranged as to put power into the hands of able men who could not expect election in the ordinary way. ... In other words, out of all this murder and rapine will come not a demagogic but an authoritarian Government.

... The tower is much nearer finishing so that we have a large bedroom with a fine wooden ceiling. George is very happy. ... What do you think of our new address – Thoor Ballylee? Thoor is Irish for a tower and it will keep people from suspecting us of modern Gothic and a deer park.

The older literary folk, led by George Russell, were mostly advocates of the Treaty, but younger men whose acquaintance Yeats had yet to make – Frank O'Connor, Francis Stuart, Seán O'Faoláin, Liam O'Flaherty – took the side of de Valera and the republicans.

2

Later Poems, which were prepared for the press during the summer at Ballylee, included *The Wind among the Reeds* and all the poems that Yeats had written since its date up to 1921. Some of the new versions startled his readers; for instance, 'Till the Attorney for Lost Souls cry her sweet cry' for 'Till Mary of the Wounded Heart cry a sweet cry'. There was a new 'Folly of Being Comforted', though this had been one of the most generally accepted of his lyrics and was lately widespread in a popular anthology. When *Later Poems* came out, a London friend, Cecil French, sent him a protest against a number of the alterations. 'You are the spoiled child of letters', he wrote. Yeats defended his revisions with obstinacy, but was at pains to give attention to Mr French's scrupulous criticism of the proof-reading and of certain obscurities of sense and syntax to be found in some of the more recent poems in the volume. In 'Solomon and the Witch' there was a line missing, 'three hundred years before the Fall' being without a rhyme sound, and in 'Friends' 'Heart and delighted heart' was similarly isolated.

These matters were put right when the *Collected Poems*
were published fifteen years later. The meaning of

> O little did they care who danced between,
> And little she by whom her dance was seen
> So that she danced, no thought,
> Body perfection brought,
>
> For what but eye and ear silence the mind . . .

in the 'Double Vision' seemed to be problematical. Was it
'So that she danced – she who had no thought, her body
being brought to perfection', or 'So that she danced. No
thought ever brought body to perfection. For what but eye
and ear, etc.'? In *Collected Poems* the lines became

> So she had outdanced thought.
> Body perfection brought, . . .

Yeats's reading at Ballylee included James Joyce's *Ulysses*,
Ossendowski's *Beasts, Men and Gods*, Laurence Binyon on
Blake, and two novels by George Sand. History in the present
vibrated for Yeats in George Sand. He relished her Hussites,
her eighteenth-century secret societies, her figures immersed
in politics and intrigues, who yet seemed to appertain to a
magical and transcendental universe: 'all that turmoil of
an imagined wisdom from which came the barricades'.
George Sand might be a child when she tried to philoso-
phize, but she seemed to know everything. Something of the
feeling in *Consuelo* and its sequel found its way into the
conclusion of 'Meditations in Time of Civil War':

> I, my wits astray
> Because of all that senseless tumult, all but cried
> For vengeance on the murderers of Jacques Molay.
>
> Their legs long, delicate and slender, aquamarine their eyes,
> Magical unicorns bear ladies on their backs.
> The ladies close their musing eyes. No prophecies,
> Remembered out of Babylonian almanacs,
> Have closed the ladies' eyes . . .

He commenced *Beasts, Men and Gods*, 'a strange vivid book with much supernatural incident', and liked the half-German, half-Russian Baron who would organize Asia under the rule of China to fight 'the depravity of revolution' in the world. In *Ulysses* he found 'our Irish cruelty, also our kind of strength'. 'The Martello Tower pages', he wrote, 'are full of beauty, a cruel playful mind like a great soft tiger cat.' He wished to recover Joyce for Dublin; but 'I will have to hide him,' he said, 'from our politicians, who are not yet ready for his doctrine'.

He was much better in body for having left Oxford for the storm-beaten Galway plain, and his letters continued in a cheerful strain:

5.6.22. To John Quinn

. . . It is a great pleasure to live in a place where George makes at every moment a fourteenth-century picture. And out of doors, with the hawthorn all in blossom all along the river banks, everything is so beautiful that to go elsewhere is to leave beauty behind.

It is no use writing you about politics, except perhaps that I have information from Dublin that the de Valera–Collins pact was caused by the fear of revolution. There is a great disorder, as the newspapers will have told you, and even a little of it reaches us and reaches Coole, but so far nothing serious.

The children are well, and your godson has eight teeth and nothing ails Anne but her theology. When she says the Lord's Prayer she makes such interjections as 'Father not in heaven – father in the study', or 'Dada gone to Coole'. Then again, finding Kingdom difficult to pronounce, she has been accustomed to say, 'Thine is the Kitten, the Power, and the Glory'. But owing to the growth of her intelligence has lately noticed that my cat Pangur is not a kitten, so the last form has been, 'Thine is the Cat, the Power, and the Glory'.

Lady Gregory is writing her memoirs and has read me about half. I have criticised a good deal the old political friends of her youth – Sir Alfred Lyall's bad poetry, and she is interjecting my criticisms into the text, like a Greek chorus. It will be a rich book, with some chapters of historical importance, but all objective, extracts from old letters, diaries, and the like; one chapter bringing back vividly to the imagination the dinner talk of the London season during the first Home Rule Bill debates. The reverse of my memoirs in every way, for I could not have quoted a letter or a diary without spoiling my effect.

Ballylee was visited by both parties of troops during the summer. First came the Republicans and then a small detachment of the National Army. The Republican leader 'cracked jokes of civil war', and the National Army lieutenant discussed the weather. Yeats felt a curious jealousy of these young men of action:

> I count those feathered balls of soot
> The moor-hen guides upon the stream,
> To silence the envy in my thought;
> And turn towards my chamber, caught
> In the cold snows of a dream.

The Republicans blew up the old bridge leading to the tower. Yeats asked permission to remove Anne and Michael to a place of safety during the operation. The request was politely refused, but time was granted to put the children in the upper room of the tower before the laying of the mine.

3

Arthur Griffith died of sheer exhaustion – or, as some said, of a broken heart – on 12 August, and ten days later Collins was killed in an ambush in a mountain pass. Griffith was succeeded by a man of equal determination and courage, W. T. Cosgrave, whom Yeats had known as a friendly member of the Corporation at the time of the controversy about the Lane pictures. Yet the Civil War went on, and was near its worst when the Yeatses settled in their Merrion Square house at the end of September. Yeats's sympathies were somewhat mixed. As he felt that the world was suffering from democracy, the fact that the Republicans refused to admit the verdict of the majority did not stir his indignation.* 'The situation here is very curious – a revolt against democracy by a small section', he wrote to Mrs Shakespear. 'I always knew that it would come, but not that it would come in this tragic way.' On the other hand, some of the Ministers (though they justified themselves on the ground of democratic principle) pleased him by their courage, conservatism and energy.

The Constitution which the Free State adopted with English approval provided little check upon whatever group of politicians might catch a majority by appeals to the confused passions of the mass, and the Senate, or Upper House, was entrusted with virtually no legislative powers. Special provision, however, was made for the composition of the first Senate, which was to consist of thirty nominated Senators representing minorities and distinguished aspects of the nation's life, as well as of thirty chosen by the Dail. Oliver Gogarty had been an intimate friend of the late Arthur Griffith, and his views therefore carried some weight with the Government. He pressed Yeats's claims to represent a distinguished aspect of the nation's life, also those of AE. Yeats at the time was on a visit to London, and when Gogarty called at No. 82 one evening to report the success of his endeavours, Mrs Yeats was out, so he chalked 'Senator W. B. Yeats' on the letter-box, and went his way. The next day he told Mrs Yeats on the telephone that her husband owed his election neither to his poetry nor to his work at the Abbey Theatre, but to the fact that he had once been a member of the Irish Republican Brotherhood. The I.R.B. (not to be confused with the I.R.A., or Republican Army) had in the main used its influence to get the Treaty accepted, and many of its members received their rewards in the new State. No one could have been more communicative about his past than Yeats, but this was the first time his wife had

* 'The concern you feel', Ricketts wrote to him at this time, 'is of common application. . . . We are all suffering from democracy, and I read every morning whatever news there is from Italy *re* Mussolini and his incomparable Fascisti. Are they the counter revolution?'

heard of his connection with the I.R.B. 'You kept that dark', she said to him when he came home, and he replied, 'Never say again that I can't keep a secret'.

On 27 January he wrote to Robert Bridges:

I have just found a letter of yours dated Dec. 2 stuffed into the hollow place between the arms and the cushions of a leather armchair. I wonder if I ever answered. . . . When I got back here I found myself a senator, and the senate, though it did not break in upon my morning hours when I write verse, etc., took away a large part of those afternoon hours when I write letters. I wish very much I could have gone to you, and heaven knows when I shall be in England – probably not until peace has been made. Life here is interesting, but restless and unsafe – I have two bullet holes through my windows – as it must always be when the sheep endeavour to control the goats who are by nature so much the more enterprising race.

The war upon the Free State now assumed much the same forms as the war upon the British. An officer in the Army was shot, and the Government retaliated by executing prisoners. On Yeats's first attendance in the Senate he had for neighbour the owner of a Government newspaper who was under sentence of death from the I.R.A. A little later Gogarty was kidnapped, and the burning of the houses of Senators began.* There was no reason to think that Yeats would be molested,† but, like the other Senators, he was afforded the protection of an armed guard. One night one of the guards challenged him while he was walking up his own stairs. He used to lend the men detective stories (of which

---

* *Vide* for Gogarty's adventure Yeats's preface to *An Offering of Swans*. On a week-end visit to Sir Horace Plunkett's quite modern house near Dublin Yeats smelt the presence of an 'elemental' and told Lady Fingall that the house would most certainly be destroyed. This was before the burning of the houses of Senators had started.

† The 'aspects' for Yeats, at the hour of his entry into the Senate, were very favourable, money and travel being promised. There were, however, in the figure signs of rising trouble in the country, and he applied to Mr Fagan, President of the Irish Astrological Society, for Mr de Valera's horoscope.

he had become a great reader), in order (he said) to train them in the highest traditions of their profession.

4

There were other spokesmen of Irish cultural and literary interests in the Senate, such as the Celtic historian Alice Stopford Green, Dr Sigerson, an ancient Bard, the various personages who had been identified with the early work of the Gaelic League. George Russell preferred to edit the *Irish Statesman*, a weekly newspaper, founded by Sir Horace Plunkett, which gave philosophical support to the Government. It was reported that on receiving the offer of a seat in the Senate, George Russell said, 'I must consult the Gods', and that Mr Cosgrave's emissary replied, 'Joking apart, Mr Russell, what answer shall I bring back to the President?'; whereas Yeats in accepting nomination may have remembered that Swedenborg, at sixty, with visions crowding upon him, discussed finance and politics in the Swedish Senate like a man of the world. However that may have been, Yeats was not long in the Senate before he attached himself to the practical men and avoided the littérateurs. He voted as a rule with a group of nominated Senators (peers, bankers, lawyers and business men), who expressed the views of that part of the Protestant and Unionist minority which wished to assist the new order. The group was led by Andrew Jameson, his father's old friend, and its ablest members frequently consulted him, and he them. He joined the famous landlords' Club in Kildare Street, where many of his new associates were to be found. More folklore clung to Kildare Street than to the Whiggish Club in Stephen's Green, from which he now resigned.

Some of the young Ministers used to come to his house, and he described them in a letter as 'honest and modern-minded men swimming still in conspiracies not of their own making'. His acquaintance even included officers in the Free State Army. Thomas MacGreevy called one evening at No.

82 Merrion Square, and saw two military overcoats in the hall. This was not his company, and so he asked Bridget when the officers would be gone. She advised him to call back again in an hour. He called back in an hour and found Yeats alone. Yeats, who had heard of his previous call, looked at him in a melancholy way, and said, 'It's difficult to like men of action'; a remark which MacGreevy put in his poem, 'Homage to Louis IX'.

> W. B. turned man of action, said,
> 'MacGreevy, it's difficult to like men of action'.

In the eyes of Maud Gonne, Yeats was now politically past redemption. Yet when she got into trouble with the Government he intervened on her behalf with Mr Cosgrave. It would not (he said) do Madame Markievicz any harm to be kept in prison, but Madame Gonne had always been delicate. He was surprised when Mr Cosgrave observed in the course of their conversation that women, doctors and clergy ought to keep out of politics, as their business is with the sick.

With a view to ending the Civil War, Yeats suggested to Ministers that some endeavour should be made to revise the Treaty so as to enable Mr de Valera to enter the Dail without loss of principle. He even offered to make private inquiries in London as to the removal by negotiation of the oath of allegiance, which appeared to be the chief obstacle to peace. To the journalists he would say that if the British Empire became a voluntary Federation of Free Nations, all would be well; but if it remained, as in the past, a domination of one, the Irish question was not yet settled. This done with, he would talk of the work of his generation in Ireland, the creation of a literature to express national character and feeling, but with no deliberate political aim.

22.3.23. To Mrs Shakespear

I think things are mending here – my own project in that matter postponed but not abandoned. In spite of all that has happened, I find constant evidence of ability or intensity which makes one hopeful. I was on a committee of the Senate the other day, which is considering legislation based on a series of blue-books, with elaborate maps of coal-fields, etc. issued by the revolutionary government at the start of the war with England . . .

One strange thing is the absence of personal bitterness. Senators whose houses have been burned (one man has lost archives going back to, I think, the 16th century) speak as if it were some impersonal tragedy, some event caused by storm or earthquake. Our debates are without emotion, dull, businesslike and well attended. We have just legalised after detailed discussion and approved changes in local government and in the poor law made in the midst of the revolutionary war, changes that have meant considerable economy and better treatment of the poor . . .

My plans are still Government policy but are postponed till peace has come by other means. They will be used not to bring peace but to lay war's ghost. At least so I am told officially. Unofficially I hear that the war party has carried the day (this all very private). . . . One is sure of nothing.*

Later in 1923 Yeats went to London, not on a high political mission, but to put the case for the return of the Lane pictures to Ireland before the Trustees of the National Gallery in Trafalgar Square.

He wrote to Thomas Bodkin: 'I have only one object in public life at present and this is to give what help I can to certain learned bodies. Nothing else would have justified me in taking time from my artistic work.' With Mrs J. R. Green he was the author of a scheme for the editing, indexing and publication of Irish manuscripts in the Royal Irish Academy and elsewhere, for the scientific investigation of the living dialects, and for the compiling and publication of an adequate dictionary of old Irish. At the same time he upheld the right of Senators to deal in statecraft and in matters in

* If Mr Cosgrave's Government had adopted Yeats's suggestion it might still be in power. Its opponents subsequently gained a great deal of support from people who believed that negotiations could easily be started with the Imperial Government which would result in the elimination of the oath. *Vide* Denis Gwynn, *The Irish Free State*, pp. 14–15.

which public feeling was engaged. When Mr Cosgrave told Senators that they should confine themselves to special subjects, he indignantly refused his assent. 'I think', he said, 'it is ... very important to this Senate, because of the very nature of its Constitution, that we should show ourselves as interested as the Dail is in every person in this country. We do not represent constituencies; we are drawn together to represent certain forms of special knowledge, certain special interests, but we are just as much passionately concerned in these great questions as the Dail.' * One of his first speeches dealt with the contentious policy of treating Irish as though it were, in fact, the mother tongue of the people. When a Bill to amalgamate railways was passing through the Senate, one of the Gaelic Senators introduced an amendment making it mandatory on the companies to replace all public notices and signs in Irish and to print railway tickets in both languages. Yeats denounced the amendment as a piece of make-believe that would tend to bring Gaelic into contempt with honest minds. Yet he gave careful consideration to the ideal of an Irish culture relying on its own resources. Years later he wrote:

Translate into modern Irish all that is most beautiful in old and middle Irish, what Frank O'Connor and Augusta Gregory, let us say, have translated into English; let every schoolmaster point out where in his neighbourhood this or that thing happened, or is said to have happened, but teach Irish and Greek together, make the pupil translate Greek into Irish, Irish into Greek. ... If Irish is to become the national tongue the change must come slowly, almost imperceptibly; a sudden or forced change of language may be the ruin of the soul. England forced English upon the schools and colleges of India, and now after generations of teaching no Indian can write or speak animated English and his mother tongue is despised and corrupted. Catholic Ireland is but slowly recovering from its change of language in the eighteenth century. Irishmen learn English at their mother's

*Vide *A Packet for Ezra Pound*: 'We writers are public opinion's children though we defy our mother'.

knee, English is now their mother-tongue, and a sudden change would bring a long barren epoch.*

In the summer of 1923, de Valera, while still refusing to enter the Dail, issued his 'Cease Fire' order to Republican troops. Guards were removed from the houses of Senators and Deputies, and a period of quiet progress appeared to lie ahead. It had been a real satisfaction to Yeats to have had a modest share in what he called in one of his letters 'the slow exciting work of creating institutions – all coral insects but with some design of the ultimate island'. He counted his first year as Senator one of the most satisfactory in his life, and it ended with his being accorded a mark of universal recognition: the Nobel Prize for Literature. On the evening after he received the news of the award, he gave a dinner party at the Shelbourne Hotel. During dinner the first telegram of congratulation arrived. It was (to his immense gratification) from James Joyce.

5

The Diploma and Medal were given by the King of Sweden on the afternoon of 10 December in the Hall of the Swedish Academy. Yeats has described the brilliant scene, which was followed by a week's stay in Stockholm, in *The Bounty of Sweden*:

In the body of the Hall every seat is full, and all there are in evening dress, and in the front row of seats are the King, Princess Ingeborg, wife of the King's brother, Prince Wilhelm, Princess Margaretha, and I think another Royalty. The President of the Swedish Academy speaks in English, and I see from the way he stands, from his self-possession, and from his rhythmical utterance, that he is an experienced orator. I study the face of the old King, intelligent and friendly, like some country gentlemen who can quote Horace and Catullus, and the face of the Princess Margaretha, full of subtle beauty, emotional and precise and impassive . . .

On the Boiler.

On the night of the presentation there was a banquet, and when his turn came he spoke of Swedenborg, Strindberg and Ibsen. The next day he watched the entrance of the new Crown Princess from the hotel window, and then went with his wife to a reception at the Palace, his first sight of a Court. Two days were given to seeing Stockholm, the picture galleries and the great Town Hall, described by him as the most important building of modern Europe, and an evening to the Swedish Royal Academy, when Yeats chose the Irish Theatre as his subject. He said:

When your King gave me medal and diploma, two forms should have stood, one at either side of me, an old woman sinking into the infirmity of age, and a young man's ghost. I think when Lady Gregory and John Synge's name are spoken by future generations, my name, if remembered, will come up in the talk, and that if my name is spoken first their names will come in their turn because of the years we worked together . . .

Some years later Yeats heard that the Swedish Royal Family 'liked him better than any previous Nobel Prize winner'. They said he had the manners of a courtier.

The award of the Nobel Prize to Yeats met with some criticism in England. Recollections of the Irish Rebellion made it difficult to call him an English poet. Furthermore, it is much to be doubted whether the objectors had ever read anything of Yeats later than 'Innisfree'. In reviewing *The Bounty of Sweden* Edmund Gosse did not disguise his disappointment; he spoke for a small but almost fanatical group of the supporters of Thomas Hardy. Yeats himself was modest on the subject, saying that he had no doubt that he had received the award owing to the interest then being taken in resurgent Irish nationality.

Stockholm brought with it an immense correspondence. People wrote to Yeats from all over the world, not only strangers but people he had known long ago. One of the first English men of letters to express pleasure at the award was A. C. Benson, who said:

I don't think that an honour could be better deserved. ... I believe I have read most if not all your books, and one, *Ideas of Good and Evil*, many times; and I am sure you differ from all writers of the time in having the best sort of detachment – the detachment from the urgent *present* which ends by bringing an artist, if he is a great artist, into line with the great spirits of the past and future.

The most unexpected missive was that of a Count Stephen Butler in Budapest; the Count, who claimed that his ancestor had murdered Wallenstein, hailed Yeats as a relative and asked for a photograph. 'This', Yeats commented, 'seems a recognized form of distinction. We may have seen the foundation of several noble houses in Ireland recently. If I remember Coleridge's translation of *Wallenstein* rightly, a certain Butler was rather the villain of the piece.'

The Irish Senate appreciated the award as a fitting European recognition of its most distinguished member. 'We take the greater pride in it', said Lord Glenavy, 'on account of the courage and patriotism which induced Senator Yeats twelve months ago to cast in his lot with his own people under conditions then very critical.'

The Nobel honour has the almost unique distinction of being directly and materially useful to the recipient, and Yeats did not disguise his satisfaction at getting the cheque for £7500. At first he was not sure, as he put it, 'whether to spend the money and be rich or to invest it and be substantial'. After adding a number of expensive books to his library, chiefly encyclopedias of various kinds and histories, he took the more prudent course. He wrote to John Quinn (29 January 1924):

I sometimes dictate seventeen or eighteen letters in an afternoon, and I am only just beginning to get through the flood. You needn't fear that we shall spend any of that money on Ballylee. I put aside the proceeds of my last lecturing tour for that purpose and I have still a substantial sum left, intended in part for the concrete roof, for we still live, when there, protected not very perfectly by the floors alone. We are not in a mood to spend much on it at present, for, with Cuala and the Senate, neither of us can be long away from Dublin. Its chief use for some time to come will be to house the children, my wife and I going down for but a few days at a time . . .

I am glad indeed to have my father's portrait . . .

6

The completion of his philosophy (or of his 'system', as sometimes he called it) was the chief work to which Yeats addressed himself in 1924. Two symbols have permeated his spiritual life, circle and straight line; in their opposition he expresses his sense of the ultimate mystery of the universe: Time against Eternity, unity against the variety of the world, the centrifugal versus the centripetal, immortality against the slow coming on of old age and the return to the dust. Now he understands that the hope to break the circle is vain. Progress in the infinite, 'as we understand it', is never to be attained – 'either with the soul from the myth to the union with the source of all, the breaking of the circle, or from the myth to reflection, the circle renewed for better or worse'. It is old-age wisdom.

But the book would not be merely theoretical. It was being written, he told Seán O'Faoláin, to be of serviceable information to those who live with sufficient intensity to make any misunderstanding of their personalities dangerous. This was a remembrance of the nineties, of the 'tragic generation', among whom, because of this misunderstanding, there died so many of his nearest friends. He said to this young in- quirer: 'Some have kindled their philosophy like a lamp or candle in their own dark rooms, but I would go out into the world' – he swung his arms – 'carrying mine like a lantern'. Asked why *A Vision* was so called, he replied, with a gesture of reverence, 'I am not permitted to tell'.

This is one of the aspects of Yeats which might seem part of his humorous self-dramatization. Yet what he really strove for above all was to speak with authority, and this makes it all the stranger that he was so successful in his resistance to even the greatest of the doctrines. It is as though he wished (in *A Vision*) to turn his heresy into a new orthodoxy. If his mediums would not tell him what he wanted, he would become his own medium. And here comes the subtle significance of the above remark. He probably felt a dim psychological conviction that 'telling' – *i.e.* partial crystallization – would shatter that power of becoming his own medium, as Mohammedans (and Irish peasants before the films came) felt it dangerous to be photographed : some part of their image and being might be thus sequestered and even destroyed.

Some insight into this conception may be gained by the following passage from *The Bounty of Sweden*, which is in-valuable as a record of the poet's half-mystical, half-dramatical methods of composing :

Every now and then, when something has stirred my imagin-ation, I begin talking to myself. I speak in my own person and dramatize myself, very much as I have seen a mad old woman do upon the Dublin quays, and sometimes detect myself speaking and moving as if I were still young, or walking perhaps like an old man with fumbling steps. Occasionally I write out what I have said in verse, and generally for no better reason than because I remember that I have written no verse for a long time. I do not think of my soliloquies as having different literary qualities. They stir my interest by their appropriateness to the men I imagine myself to be, or by their accurate description of some emotional circumstance, more than by any aesthetic value. When I begin to write I have no object but to find for them some natural speech, rhythm and syntax, and to set it out in some pattern, so seeming old that it may seem all men's speech, and though the labour is very great, I seem to have used no faculty peculiar to myself, certainly no special gift.

In 1924 he printed 'Meditations in Time of Civil War', 'The Gift of Harun al-Rashid', and one or two other pieces, in a Cuala volume which took its title from *The Cat and the Moon*, a play of occult character which incidentally satirized the friendship between George Moore and Edward Martyn.

It was the start of his 'Tower' period, the equivalent of Beethoven's third period in Yeats's work. He wrote many great poems later, but in the volume *The Tower* (1928), which is dominated by 'Meditations', he reaches the peak of his endeavours in 'cold passion'. Perhaps some of the classic quality in these poems, so noticeable in 'The Wheel'* –

> Through winter-time we call on spring,
> And through the spring on summer call,
> And when abounding hedges ring
> Declare that winter's best of all;
> And after that there's nothing good
> Because the spring-time has not come –
> Nor know that what disturbs our blood
> Is but its longing for the tomb –

is broken up, just as Yeats's life is broken up, by the actual fact of physical war raging around him; but the breaking seems to renew Yeats's interest in the world and to encourage him in theories and dreams about Ireland's future. In 'Meditations' there is a characteristic touch. Describing 'My Table' he refers to 'Sato's sword' that had been forged before Chaucer had drawn breath. One got the impression from Yeats's conversational references to Sato that he was possibly a crony of Confucius. But in his will he directs that the sword shall be given back to Sato, who was in 1939 an official in the League of Nations in Geneva. Yeats met Sato in America.

The fact that he was working on *A Vision*, either in its first or second form, is reflected in many passages in *The Tower*. The 'Primum Mobile' and 'Magnus Annus', Plotinus (many times), Byzantium, 'I saw a staring virgin stand', are unmistakable evidence of his 'Ledaean' thought at this time.

The title of one part of *A Vision*, 'Dove or Swan', suggests that he was concerned to attempt a mythological parallel

---

* 'The Wheel' is exceptional among his poems in that it was written on the instant of thought. His wife and he were on Euston platform half an hour before the Irish mail train was due to start. He disappeared suddenly and came back in good time for the train with the poem as it stands written out on a sheet of Euston Hotel notepaper.

between Grecian legend and Christian doctrine – a thought
he had harped on much. Moreover, it was while he was at
work on 'Dove or Swan' that he stimulated the publication
of a monthly magazine in Dublin, about which he wrote as
follows to Mrs Shakespear (21 June 1924):

I am in high spirits this morning seeing my way to a most
admirable row. I heard that a group of Dublin poets, a man
called Higgins,* and the Stuarts and another, whose name I do
not know, were about to publish a review. I said to them, 'Why
not found yourself on the doctrine of the immortality of the
soul, most bishops and all bad writers being obviously atheists'.
I heard no more till last night when I received a kind of deputation. They had adopted my suggestion and been suppressed by
the priests for blasphemy. I got a bottle of sparkling Moselle
which I hope youthful ignorance mistook for champagne and
we swore alliance. . . . My dream is a wild paper for the young,
which will make enemies everywhere and suffer suppression, I
hope a number of times, for the logical assertion, with all fitting
deductions, of the immortality of the soul.

He contributed the poem 'Leda and the Swan' to the
periodical in question, which was immediately suppressed
(though not on account of the poem). 'Leda', which his
typist refused in tears to copy, had been originally intended
for the *Irish Statesman*. Russell asked for a poem, and (the
Irish Statesman being primarily a political journal) Yeats
thought, 'After the individualistic, demagogue movement,
founded by Hobbes and popularised by the Encyclopaedists
and the French Revolution, we have a soil so exhausted that
we cannot grow that crop again for centuries.' Then he
thought, 'Nothing is now possible but some movement or
birth from above.' His fancy began to play with Leda and
the swan as metaphor, and he began the poem; but as he
wrote, bird and lady took such possession of the scene that
all politics went out of it.† He was rather annoyed, however,

---

*F. R. Higgins, afterwards Yeats's chief protégé among the poets
of the younger generation in Ireland.
†*Vide* note to *The Cat and the Moon*.

when AE told him that conservative readers would misunderstand the poem. What a chance for an 'admirable row'
would have been the suppression of that blameless man.
AE's editorial office was in Merrion Square, a few doors
away from No. 82, and Yeats dropped in frequently to see
him and to discuss the policy of the paper. 'Scenes' between
them were not uncommon, as Russell had no intention of
getting the *Irish Statesman* into trouble for Yeats's enter-
tainment.

7

The Free State Government, having reached more tranquil
waters and anxious perhaps to keep alert the heroic ardour
that quickens all national movements until they are successful, had conceived the idea of reviving the Tailteann Games,
an ancient Celtic festival. These took place in August 1924,
immediately after Horse Show week, when there is always
a great influx of visitors into Dublin. Either because the
original games had been accompanied by bardic contests, or
else because Pindar now seems as much a part of the glory
of Olympia as its charioteers or boxers, Yeats persuaded the
Royal Irish Academy to take part in the occasion by 'crowning' such recently published Irish work as could be said to
have conferred 'honour and dignity upon Ireland'. The
principal award, a gold medal, was made to Stephen
MacKenna for his translation of Plotinus.* MacKenna was
in England, and G. K. Chesterton, who was one of the distinguished guests of the Irish Government at the Festival,
took it for him. Cecil Salkeld writes:

I was present at the solemn crowning with laurel wreaths of
Oliver Gogarty, Francis Stuart, James Stephens (for his *Deirdre*)
and Chesterton. W. B. described MacKenna's *Plotinus* as worthy
at its best to take its place among the masterpieces of English
prose. His speech was very amusing, and among other things he

* Austin Clarke has drawn attention to the effect upon Yeats's later
work of 'the sombre yet glittering eloquence' of this translation.

spoke of the days 'when God came down to Danae in a Shower of Gold'. The daily press reported this as, 'when the god,' etc.

At an informal lunch afterwards I met G. K. C., who told me *sotto voce* how surprised he was that Yeats was such a sporting man. I suppose I must have looked puzzled, for he went on to tell me of W. B.'s appearance at the racecourse in top-hat, and binoculars, and of his knowledge of horseflesh. 'But then,' he said humbly, 'all you Irish are so horsy.'

Yeats had an eye for horseflesh, possibly from 'melan-choly George Pollexfen'. Hence his delight at Lady Gerald Wellesley's phrase, 'moderate ears', in the opening passage of her poem 'Horses'.*

Stephen MacKenna refused to accept the gold medal for political reasons, writing to Yeats as follows:

. . . I'm a mere hack and haven't the words to utter my feelings for your loveliness but I can't bear to think that it should be thought that what was mere ugly (though to me quite essentially necessary) politics should be taken by idiots and animals to imply any disrespect to so exquisite an inspiration, so lofty a soul. To everyone that has written to me in that ignoble style I have administered the severest castigation or in more appropriate language I have swotten them one and have been rejoiced to hear a whimper or two in proof of the efficacy of my blows. It's a horrible thing that in Ireland we haven't yet learned to resist an opinion, on politics, to all extremes that may seem necessary and yet with full admission of all that is not politics in the enemy: here as in so many things the English have much to teach us – tho' I hasten to add it is not from them that I wish to learn it, or to learn anything, but from the great body of civilised principle and from the habit of all the intellectual world.†

An assembly as oddly assorted as ever met together in the one room gathered at the banquet given during the gala

---

* He should have been familiar with this use of the word 'moderate' from the time that he lived with George Pollexfen. Still, one has a suspicion that he thought it 'Chinese'.

† Stephen MacKenna was never in doubt about Yeats's feeling for Ireland. 'If W. B.', he once said, 'were in the desert of Gobi and some-one mentioned Ireland, he would be all aquiver.'

fortnight to the distinguished guests. A Swedish ambassador to the Court of St James, a Persian grandee, an ancient dynamiter from the States, Augustus John and two famous cricketers, C. B. Fry and K. S. Ranjitsinhji, listened to Yeats's speech, which struck an ominous note. The Governor-General, His Excellency Timothy Healy, who spoke after him, twitted 'our Bard' for not taking the advice, 'She bid me take life easy', given in an early poem. What Yeats had said was this:

We do not believe that war is passing away, and we do not believe that the world is growing better and better. We even tell ourselves that the idea of progress is quite modern, that it has been in the world but two hundred years; nor are we quite as stalwart as we used to be in our democratic politics. Psychologists and statisticians in Europe and America have all challenged the foundations, and a great popular leader has announced to an applauding multitude, 'We will trample on the decomposing body of the goddess of liberty'. It is impossible not to ask ourselves to what great task of the nations we have been called in this transformed world, where there is so much that is obscure and terrible. The world can never be the same. The stream has turned backwards, and generations to come will have for their task, not the widening of liberty, but recovery from its errors – the building up of authority, the restoration of discipline, the discovery of a life sufficiently heroic to live without the opium dream.*

* It was a remarkable feat to quote Lenin and Mussolini in one breath, remarkable in the Ireland of 1924.

A sixty-year-old smiling
public man

═══════

The people of Burke and of Grattan
That gave, though free to refuse –
Pride, like that of the morn,
When the headlong light is loose,
Or that of the fabulous horn,
Or that of the sudden shower
When all streams are dry,
Or that of the hour
When the swan must fix his eye
Upon a fading gleam,
Float out upon a long
Last reach of glittering stream
And there sing his last song.

I

As Yeats approached his sixtieth year, the measure of his
comfort became apparent in the cheerful broadening of his
outlines. This but added importance to his signally remarkable appearance. Visiting him one evening in his aristocratic
eighteenth-century house, Mlle Simone Téry, the gifted
French journalist, was impressed by his style and care in
dress. Twenty years before, Yeats had been tall and thin,
and George Moore's wicked tongue then compared his
cloaked figure to a folded umbrella, point in air, left behind

by some picnic party. But now his ampler lines moulded his black velvet coat for evening wear. There was a search for elegance in his silver-buckled shoes, in the wide black riband, attached to his tortoise-shell-rimmed glasses, which fell like a bar across his face; and in the gold ring worn on his little finger. But more marked than these accessories was the elegance of his bearing, the noble carriage of his head, the harmony of his gestures; something of the ease and grace of a *grand seigneur* in his manners.

To Yeats, however, his increasing weight was a matter of concern. Always a very moderate eater and drinker, he now complained of scantiness of breath when he took the regular walks, substituted for Swedish exercises. It was found that his blood-pressure was too high. The doctor asked if he had had any over-excitement of late, and he replied, 'I have lived a life of excitement'. He was advised to give up work for a time; but for that he had to seek new surroundings. In November 1924 his wife brought him to Sicily, the attraction there being, besides the sunlight, the presence of Ezra Pound on the island, and the Byzantine mosaics of Monreale and the Capella Palatina at Palermo.

I met him in Rome in February 1925. He had had a week of beautiful weather in Capri following two months of clear skies in Sicily. This was the longest complete holiday he had ever taken, and he was much better for it. He felt that he could write as he pleased; he was able to walk long distances (I saw him refuse a lift in the Borghese Palace and dash up two flights of stairs). There was a week of sightseeing, and as in Sicily, he followed the enchantment of mosaics and glass, which he compared with the 'hammered gold and gold enamelling' that he had seen at Ravenna seventeen years before, when visiting Italy with Lady Gregory. Byzantium represented Rome approached from the East, and would therefore have been of great significance to Yeats.*

He viewed the Vatican Galleries more than once and the

* *Vide* the poems 'Sailing to Byzantium' (1926) and 'Byzantium' (1930).

Sistine Chapel often. He came home with great rolls of photographs of Michelangelo's 'fabulous' ceiling which, later, he spread out before the Minister of Justice as an argument against the Irish Censor's ban on Bernard Shaw's book *The Black Girl in Search of God*. The book had been banned on account of the illustrations, and Yeats hoped to have the decision reversed by showing that a Pope had not withheld approval of the naked human form. Shaw suggested that the Minister should be asked to consider a special edition for Ireland with the negress depicted in long skirts. The Irish objection stood because it was the portrayal of God that caused uneasiness.

My memory goes back to a morning in Rome spent in searching the book-shops with Mrs Yeats for works dealing with the spiritual antecedents of the Fascist revolution, an event which Yeats considered (justly as events have shown) as at least equal in importance to the proletarian conquest of Russia. Having attended the lectures given in London by Douglas Ainslie on Croce's *Estetica*, he already knew something of the new original thought of Italy. In 1924 he read and annotated Croce's *Philosophy of Vico* and now some phrase used by me about Gentile had caught his ear and one of the books he wanted was *La Riforma dell' Educazione*, a work which ensured for that metaphysician the post of Minister of Education in one of Mussolini's early cabinets. As he could not read Italian, his wife made summaries for him of this and other examples of Fascist literature for his easy reference. A little later, through Wildon Carr's translation, he acquainted himself with, and admired for its concentrated logic (its 'intensity of thought which is beauty'), Gentile's *Teoria generale dello Spirito come Atto puro*. Thus, his philosophic as opposed to his occult background was formed by the modern Italians, with a foundation of Plato and Plotinus, Boehme and Swedenborg. He read Croce's *Philosophy of the Practical* (annotated) in 1926, and in the same year his *Hegel*; Bergson's *Matter and Memory* and *Creative Evolution* in 1927; McTaggart's

Studies in Hegelian Cosmology in 1928; Kant's *Prolegomena* in 1929; and, much later, Husserl's *Ideas.*.

2

News reached him in Rome that the Senate would be presently invited to concur in a Government resolution prohibiting the introduction of Bills into the Free State legislature for divorce *a vinculo matrimonii.* This matter was very much upon Yeats's mind; in fact it was his chief topic of conversation, as he was already preparing the speech in which he proposed to accuse the Government of an assault upon Protestant liberties. When we met a young Italian woman of a princely family, he sought information in regard to 'educated' Italian opinion about divorce. She told him it was not a question which excited Italians. The easy divorce of America, being founded upon a Puritan ideal, could never commend itself to Italians as a means of mitigating marriage. I could see that Yeats had got the answer he wanted, and was not surprised when presently he informed the readers of the *Irish Statesman* that American public opinion on illicit relations between the sexes was considered extremely harsh in Italy, and was explained by the easy divorce, which made such relations seem inexcusable. In his article he quoted 'an Italian of an illustrious Catholic house from which have come Cardinals and, I believe, one Pope', side by side with Balzac and G. K. Chesterton, as evidence that the Catholic view of marriage was founded upon the family and upon the family only.

The speech with which he opened the debate on 11 June 1925, was a very considerable performance, perhaps the most remarkable witnessed in the Irish Senate during its existence. It had been carefully prepared. 'I think it tragic', he said towards its close, 'that within three years of this country gaining its independence, we should be discussing a measure which the minority considers grossly oppressive'. His audience was very restive. One or two of the Roman Catholic

Senators, a majority in the House, got up and went out; others interrupted. Inside as well as outside the Senate he was charged with having shown himself at last in his true Cromwellian colours. But if sectarian animosity entered into the debate, it was not introduced by him. He criticized Catholic and Anglican ecclesiastics impartially. He did not ask to control any man's conscience; all he asked for was individual liberty.

It was not a politic speech. In one passage he referred to the Gospels as devotional not historical documents. In another he directed the attention of moralists to the private lives of Nelson, Parnell and O'Connell, whose statues adorn the principal thoroughfare of Dublin. Was it intended to remove these monuments? * Lord Glenavy interrupted him: 'Do you not think we might leave the dead alone?' 'I would hate to leave the dead alone', he retorted. Such indiscretions were not helpful to members on his own side of the house, whose endeavours had been directed towards posing the concrete problem and its solution. Yet Yeats had not come to the Senate just to trail his coat. He was always a controversialist, but this was certainly an occasion when he spoke with conviction. Even in his attack on the censorship of books he was not so deeply stirred. He had been extremely nervous while rehearsing his oration at home; he was deathly white when he rose, and when he had finished the sweat was pouring from his brow.

One Senator asked good-naturedly whether Yeats wished the Senate to spend their afternoons listening to tales of the domestic infelicities of married couples; another, whether he would regard the thieving confraternity as entitled to have laws of its own. It is difficult to think that Yeats was excited over such an unphilosophic legal compromise as divorce.

---

* *Vide* the poem, presently written, called 'The Three Monuments':
    'They hold their public meetings where
    Our most renownèd patriots stand,
            .   .   .
    The three old rascals laugh aloud.'

How could a poet be? His passionate protest was on behalf
of that small Protestant band which had so often proved
itself the chivalry of Ireland.* All led up to the proud and
justifiable peroration. 'We against whom you have done this
thing are no petty people. We are one of the great stocks of
Europe. We are the people of Burke; we are the people of
Grattan; we are the people of Swift, the people of Parnell.
We have created the most of the modern literature of this
country. We have created the best of its political intelligence.'

3

In the autumn of 1925, after lecturing at Mürren with Lennox Robinson for Sir Henry Lunn, Yeats was again in Italy,
at Milan. To this town he had taken a great dislike during
his first Italian visit of 1907, and the dismal impression
remained. He called the Cathedral 'Nottingham Lace', and
left his wife to do the sightseeing with Lennox Robinson
and Thomas MacGreevy, who had joined the tour; he read
The Times in the hotel. He was in deep dejection. 'We'll go
to Verona,' he pleaded, 'we will go to Lugano, *or we'll go
home*.' Of *The Times* he remarked: 'Whether one reads it
in London or in Milan, it is invariably successful in saying
nothing in a thousand words'. Lennox Robinson turned the
conversation one evening to contemporary English poets
and made him admit that Hardy had his 'moments'. And
Kipling? Yeats raised his hand episcopally. 'That, no.' He
then brightened a little and related that Charles Doughty,
on being informed by a deputation from the Academic
Committee that he was on the list for the Order of Merit,
had replied, 'I don't want the bloody thing'.

At the end of the year Werner Laurie printed *A Vision* in
a private edition. The dedication 'To Vestigia' (MacGregor
Mathers's widow), dated Capri, February 1925, announced

* 'Ireland is not more theirs than ours', he declared in the *Irish
Statesman*. 'We must glory in our difference, be as proud of it as they
are of theirs.'

that the author, having now put the book out of reach, hoped to write the poems of 'a new simplicity' it seemed to have made possible, rather than texts for exposition.

4.3.26. *To Mrs Shakespear*

... When you are well again I want you to read the part of my work called 'The Gates of Pluto' – it is overloaded with detail and not as bold in thought as it should have been, but does, I think, reconcile spiritist fact with credible philosophy ...

A Vision reminds one of the stones I used to drop as a child into a certain very deep well. The splash is very far off and very faint. Not a review except one by A E, and no response of any kind except from a very learned doctor in the north of England who sends me profound and curious extracts from ancient philosophies on the subject of gyres.*

Spring found him at Ballylee, writing poetry, as indeed he always did there; only now, no matter how he began, it invariably ended as love poetry: 'One feels at moments as if one could with a touch convey a vision – that the mystic vision and sexual love are the same means – opposed yet parallel existences ...'

An old beggar, formerly a wandering piper, stopped at Coole and then made his way to Ballylee. He opened the conversation at Coole by saying to Lady Gregory, 'My Lady, you are in the winter of your age'. With Yeats he began by lamenting the great houses, burned or empty, and his courtly device did not fail of its effect. 'The gentry', he said, 'have kept the shoes on my feet, and the coat on my back, and the shilling in my pocket – never once in all these forty and five years that I have been upon the road have I asked a penny of a farmer.' Yeats gave him five shillings, and he went off gaily to drink the money at the nearest town.

Yeats's poem of this year included the famous 'Sailing to Byzantium', 'Among School Children' and 'A Woman Young and Old'. When he went to London in the autumn, with the Byzantium poem in his pocket, he called upon a

*F. P. Sturm, presumably.

medium who gave him a book test: 'Third book from right bottom shelf, page 48 or 84, study'. On his return to Dublin he sought out the place. The book in question was a complete set of Blake's designs for Dante with numbered plates. On plate 84 he found 'Dante entering the Holy Fire'; on plate 48, 'The Serpent attacking Vanni Fucci'. When he referred to Dante he read that the serpent's sting is burned to ashes and that this symbolizes the 'temporal fire'. In 'Sailing to Byzantium' the medieval poet beseeches the sages in the 'holy fire' to send death or their ecstasy.

He wrote to Mrs Shakespear:

After this and all that has gone before I must capitulate if the dark mind lets me. Certainly we suck always at the eternal dugs. How well too it puts my own mood between spiritual excitement and the sexual torture and the knowledge that these are somehow inseparable! It is the eyes of the earthly Beatrice – she has not yet put on her divinity – that make Dante risk the fire 'like a child that is offered an apple'. Immediately after comes the Earthly Paradise and the Heavenly Beatrice. Yesterday, as if my soul already foresaw today's discovery, I re-wrote a poor threadbare poem of my youth called 'The Dream of a Blessed Spirit' and named it 'The Countess Cathleen in Paradise'.*

In 'Among School Children' the topic was school children and the thought that perhaps no possible life can fulfil our dream, or even our teachers' hope. This poem originated in an incident of his life as a 'smiling public man'. He had formed an intellectual bond with Joseph O'Neill, a man of letters and now Secretary of the Department of Education, and with Mrs Joseph O'Neill, both of whom had been at more pains than most to discover what he was driving at in *A Vision*. From Joseph O'Neill he learned a great deal about the educational system in Ireland, and equipped with this information and with Gentile's theories in his head, he felt competent to take part in a tour of inspection of the primary

*He was correcting a new edition of *Poems* 1895, still in Fisher Unwin's hands.

schools, proposed by certain of his Senatorial colleagues. 'I went', he wrote to Lady Gregory after his tour, 'to study a very remarkable convent school. Waterford is becoming the centre of Irish school reform and will remain so if it can be protected from the old-fashioned ideas of the inspectors. It is having the fight we have all had. Our work is being embodied in the programme and I was amused in one class when a child, on being asked to give the "narratives" last learned (my visit was unexpected), repeated my biography "out of *Who's Who*" – poor intellectual diet – and another child, Sigerson's – disgusting diet. The children had no idea who I was. This however was not typical. The literary work, prose and verse, was very remarkable . . .'

But 'Among School Children' became in part love poetry, in part a curse on old age.

> I dream of a Ledaean body, bent
> Above a sinking fire, . . .
>
> Her present image floats into the mind –
> Did Quattrocento finger fashion it
> Hollow of cheek as though it drank the wind
> And took a mess of shadows for its meat? . . .
>
> Labour is blossoming or dancing where
> The body is not bruised to pleasure soul,
> Nor beauty born out of its own despair,
> Nor blear-eyed wisdom out of midnight oil . . .

In 'The Old Countryman' he had written the wild regrets for youth and love of an old man; 'A Woman Young and Old' was its companion poem. In this series he makes a woman speak, first in youth, then in age. The opening passage was suggested by a remark of his daughter's. 'I don't like So-and-so,' said Mrs Yeats of a little boy whom Anne had met at a party, 'he is a very nasty child.' Anne answered: 'Yes, but he has such lovely hair, and his eyes are cold as a March wind'. 'The cry', said Yeats, 'of every woman who loves a blackguard.'

She hears me strike the board and say
That she is under ban
Of all good men and women,
Being mentioned with a man
That has the worst of all bad names;
And thereupon replies
That his hair is beautiful,
Cold as the March wind his eyes.

4

While he wrote love poetry he read philosophy. He was endeavouring to find some scientific, rational syllogism with which to buttress those large statements of his own, which, being inspired, he knew to be true, such as 'Sex and the Dead are the only things that can interest a serious mind'. Since he had placed the manuscript of *A Vision* in his publishers' hands he had read nothing but philosophy and an occasional detective story. He related, as certain passages of his manuscript-book testify, the terminology of his authors to the definitions in *A Vision*. What, for instance, was the One of Plotinus but Benedetto Croce's General Will and his own *Celestial Body*? His own *Spirit* was all forms of abstract thought, not only the Pure Concept of Croce, but, when in contact with the *Will*, all general ideas. His own *Passionate Body* was reflected in the Imagination or Pure Intuition of Croce and in Plotinus' Soul of the World. His *Husk* was what Plotinus calls Nature. 'So far', he noted,

my thought has been that of Plotinus but there is a fundamental difference. . . . Plotinus gives the real existence no antagonist but matter, and that is neither form, nor being, a phantasm as he calls it. . . . Before Plato there was a tense antagonist but with primary religion the need of a solitary, unassailed object of contemplation arose. Our religious thought is antithetical, so must insist on an antagonist, a black gyre, and it is antagonism that I must weave into my description of the origin of Principles and Faculties.

The path of Yeats's readings in philosophy can be followed in a long series of letters to T. Sturge Moore. These letters provoked animated replies, as Sturge Moore's sympathies went out strongly to the contemporary British Realists, who doubt whether any philosophical question can be answered absolutely, and insist upon the reality of what we call nature as distinct from man.

Yeats accuses this school of being mainly concerned, in its criticism of classical Idealism, to assert the prestige of science as a blind deity, invested with an infallible and objective authority. It has, he says, resuscitated the doctrine which thinks that primary and secondary qualities are both independent of consciousness because it finds no other way to 'get science down from Berkeley's roasting-spit'. He quotes Gentile with satisfaction: 'The external world is so improbable that we go along touching it with our hands to convince ourselves that it exists'; and adds that after reading Gentile he must abandon an essay on the 'real existence of gorgons and chimaeras' which he had proposed to dedicate to G. E. Moore of Cambridge (his correspondent's brother and leader with Bertrand Russell of the British School). 'I go back to Calderon. Not only things, but dreams themselves are a dream.' To all this Sturge Moore replies that not only is Yeats apt to hug conclusions and let the proof look after itself, but that he has omitted to notice, or conveniently forgets, that his own system proceeds from scientific or pseudo-scientific sources (astrology, spiritism). But Yeats's prejudice against the prudent style of conducting thought, the unaesthetic view of the world, the hostility to achieved systems, characteristic of the British tradition in philosophy, was deep-seated. His attitude recalls Nietzsche's pages on Hume and Locke, Darwin and Herbert Spencer. 'They are not a philosophical race – the English. ... There are truths which are best recognized by mediocre minds because they are best adapted to them.' He was particularly exasperated by Bertrand Russell, seen in his non-mathematical, utilitarian significance as the supreme representative of the Anglomania of 'modern ideas' and of 'politics', which Nietzsche accused of having twice brought about a general depression of the European intelligence.* Here are extracts from two letters to T. Sturge Moore, one of which is undated:

You speak of the difficulty which you feel in reconciling perspective with any system which sees reality as being and the world as thought created. You will find perspective fully discussed in Berkeley – New Theory of Vision and elsewhere – and that one of his principal arguments for immaterialism is founded upon it. It is a very abstract and technical argument. You have listened too much to B. Russell in his electioneering moods – the Plain Man has nothing to do with the matter. The Plain Man, even when magnified into a man of science, would be very little content with your brother's last conception [of the world] as a bundle of the 'possibilities of sensation' (possibilities are immaterial, by the way, till they are transformed into something else). To your brother and B. Russell alike the sense data – the only thing the Plain Man cares for – are mainly created by the mind. That is to say, the world in which the possibilities become real – the only reality – does not exist until it has been thought. You say 'idealism has to explain science'. But that has nothing to do with the matter (we are not compelled to write in the younger liberal reviews). Read Eddington's essay in 'Science, Religion and Reality'. He shows exactly why the discoveries of science can never affect reality.

[Thoor Ballylee.]

27.5.26

／ ... The statement that sensations – or 'sense data' – have underlying them 'a possibility' is Plotinus. He shows that matter has neither colour, scent nor magnitude, and finally defines it as the 'indeterminate' which possesses, however, the possibility of being shaped. He also defines it as 'the alien', which is Croce's position – an idealist position as distinct from your brother's realism – for Croce describes matter as created by 'intellect' from the mental images by its imposing upon those images the abstract conception of the external. My quarrel is not with your brother

---

* As already related, however, when Yeats met Bertrand Russell, he confined himself to speaking of his occult experiences, and avoided philosophical debate.

but with Bert Russell, who seems to accept your brother's position and yet discusses the 'possibilities' as 'physical objects' –
which is nonsense. I call that electioneering because it is an
attempt to get the support of 'the physical substratum' people,
and he knows quite well that their theory is dead. In the 17th
century people said our senses are responsible for colour, scent
and sound, that colour, scent and sound are 'appearances', but
that mass and movement really exist. In the 18th century one or
two men pointed out that mass and movement are just as much
'appearance', because the invention of our senses, as colour, scent
and sound.

Then a little later, it was discovered that the organs themselves
– the organs as observed as objects of science – are part of the
'appearance' – we see the eye through the eye. From that moment
we were back in ancient philosophy and must deduce all from
the premises known to Plato.

. . . Read Whitehead and from that go to Stephen MacKenna's
Plotinus and to the *Timaeus*. What Whitehead calls 'the three
provincial centuries' are over – wisdom and poetry return.*

He read Berkeley because a revolutionary soldier who was
living a very dangerous life said to him, 'All the philosophy
a man needs is in Berkeley', and because Lennox Robinson,
hearing him quote the soldier, bought him an old copy of
Berkeley's works on the Dublin quays. He discovered a
'humbug' in the 'good Bishop', as he has come down to us
in tradition. On the other hand, as an Irish Protestant and
Nationalist, he took delight in 'the fierce young man' who,
in the opening years of the eighteenth century, at the start
of Protestant ascendancy, formed a 'secret society' of Dublin
students to discuss the philosophy of 'a neighbouring nation'.
He proclaimed this Berkeley – the Berkeley who wrote in
The Commonplace Book, 'We Irishmen think otherwise'
(than Locke and Newton), and, 'I must publish to find if
men elsewhere agree with Irishmen'; who brought back to us
the world that only exists because it shines and sounds – to
be the founder with Swift and Burke, of modern Ireland, 'so

* Whitehead's *Science and the Modern World* was another philosophical book which Yeats closely annotated.

far as modern Ireland has expressed itself in the intellect'.
From these thoughts, and from his political experience in
the Senate, came the fine Dying Swan passage in 'The Tower'
beginning, 'It is time that I wrote my will . . .'

When Yeats was a young man the eighteenth century lay
all about him. O'Leary and Taylor praised it and seemed of
it, and at his school in Dublin Pope was the only poet since
Shakespeare. Then later, because his Unionist opponents
used to cry down Irish literature that sought audience in
Ireland, he hated it. Now (he noted) he was like the woman
in Balzac who after a rich marriage made in her old age the
jokes of the concierge's lodge where she was born. But the
Irish movements of the nineteenth century had become past
history, whereas the questions asked by Berkeley, Swift,
Burke, and the solutions they offered, lay in the forefront
of modern problems.

Yet it was impossible to ignore the masses. From now
onwards Yeats's mind was haunted by the question: how to
bring the aristocratic and Protestant tradition of Swift,
Berkeley, Burke into line with the modern 'Gaelic' nationalism? On this blending depended the prospects of an original
literature in enfranchised Ireland. His judgements were
always those of the poet. 'When I try to make a practical
rule', he wrote on a page of his diary,

I come once more to a truism – serve nothing from the heart that
is not its own evidence, what Blake called 'naked beauty displayed'. Recognise that the rest is machinery and should be used
as such. . . . Preserve that which is living, help the two Irelands,
Gaelic Ireland and Anglo-Ireland, so to unite that neither shall
shed its pride. Study the great problems of the world, as they
have been lived in our own scenery, the rebirth of European
spirituality in the mind of Berkeley, the restoration of European
order in the mind of Burke. Every nation is the whole world in
a mirror, and our mirror has twice been very bright and clear.
Do not be afraid to boast so long as the boast lays burdens on

* Quoted at the head of this chapter. Here he echoed, as he acknowledged, one of the loveliest modern lyrics, Sturge Moore's 'Dying
Swan.'

the boaster, as that did about the toga and race. Study the educational system of Italy, the creation of the philosopher Gentile, where even religion is studied not in the abstract but in the minds and lives of Italian saints.

5

The composition of the Senate was renewable by stages on a complicated system, designed to turn it gradually into a typical elected body. When vacancies occurred there was keen competition among party men for the seats, which had a salary attached of £360, free of income-tax.

Yeats and a number of other nominated Senators were due to retire in 1928. He could seek re-election, but after his speech upon Divorce, was unlikely to secure it. However, he made the best of the time that remained to him; he was, for instance, a very useful member of the Joint Committee which held sittings under the chairmanship of his friend, S. L. Brown, K.C., to recast an impossible Bill on Patent and Copyright Law. Some of the Dublin printers wanted to insert a clause restricting Irish copyright to such Free State authors as printed their books in Ireland.

Ezra Pound wrote to him: 'President of the Howly Synod; William by the grace of God; Butler by descent uterine; on the male side Yeats. ... Can you be persuaded to stop reviving the ancient art of oratory – long enough to revive the ancient and more respectable art of literary correspondence?'

[Dublin]

13.3.27. *To Mrs Shakespear*

I made a long impassioned speech and have now a wonderful sense of repose and am back at *Oedipus at Colonus*. The strength behind the printers was the dislike of the more ignorant Catholics for our school. Which reminds me, have you read O'Flaherty's *Informer* or his *Mr Gilhooley*? I think they are great novels and too full of abounding natural life to be terrible despite their subjects. They are full of that tragic farce we have invented. I imagine that part of the desire for censorship here is the desire to keep him out.

... I am in quite good spirits, impersonal, active, enjoying public admiration, etc. etc., and so I cannot write a good letter. Presently somebody will call me names, I will remember that I am old, that 'we go no more a-roaming by the light of the moon', and that then I will write you beautiful letters. However, as a consolation for this hateful cheerful man, here are two stanzas from a Sophocles chorus:

Down the long echoing street the laughing dancers throng;
The Bride is carried to the Bridegroom's chamber through
   torchlight and tumultuous song;
I celebrate that silent kiss that ends short life or long.

Never to have lived is best, ancient writers say;
Never to have drawn the breath of life, never to have looked into
   the eye of day;
The second best's a gay goodnight and quickly turn away.

The last line is very bad Grecian but very good Elizabethan and so it must stay.

When there was some talk of a change being made in the apparel of the Irish Judiciary, to mark contrariety to the English tradition, Yeats went to London to ask Charles Shannon to make the designs. The robes now worn by District Justices in Southern Ireland were designed by Shannon as a result of Yeats's initiative. It was a great vexation when the Government rejected the same artist's beautiful and impressive designs for the robes of Judges of the High and Supreme Courts. On the Rules of the High Court and Supreme Court being brought before the Senate for approval, he moved an amendment dealing with this matter, but his eloquent plea for Shannon's work failed to convince the majority that there was any need for a change.

He was a regular attendant at the private meetings of the 'Jameson group' of Senators and was much impressed by the 'unperturbed lucidity' with which the 'old bankers, old lawyers, old business men', who dominated these, dealt with affairs. It was said by a banker that he would have made an eminent lawyer, and by a lawyer that he would have made an admirable banker. At the time of the Army mutiny no member of the group was so profluent of inner political information as he. His authorities were unnamed, but they were usually young men, and always dark in complexion, who called upon him late at night. The group included some of the most disinterested and ablest men in the Senate, and had nothing to be ashamed of, but its address was not communicated to the general public. This atmosphere of mystery was, of course, extremely congenial to Yeats, and even when he had left the Senate, he would often appear after hours at the 'unknown office' for a talk with the secretary, or for dictation to her of a poem or piece of prose.*

Among the Ministers Kevin O'Higgins, at once liberal-minded and authoritarian, who refused to flatter the instincts of the masses, had all his admiration. He regarded O'Higgins as Parnell's successor and the strongest political intellect produced by Catholic Ireland in his time, perhaps since its recovery from the Penal Laws.

Not only did O'Higgins reciprocate Yeats's sympathy, but there can be little doubt that his powerful influence in the Cabinet would have been used – if not openly, at least secretly – on Yeats's side in such matters as Censorship, etc., had he lived. Yeats's admiration for O'Higgins sprang more from his 'authoritarian' leanings than from anything else; his reverence for strength is clear:

> A great man in his pride
> Confronting murderous men . . .

The assassination of this young statesman on a Sunday morning in July 1927 was no mere public event to Yeats, for both he and his wife had been for some time on friendly terms of social intercourse with Kevin O'Higgins and Mrs O'Higgins. Yeats did not hear the news until the evening, when he went out with his wife to dine at a hotel. He refused

---

* This young lady received his dictation of a long English manuscript by the Shri Purohit Swami. 'It is a remarkable thing,' he said to her one day, 'but whenever I read the Swami to my wife she falls asleep.'

to eat, and they spent the evening together walking about
the streets until bedtime. He often told how, the night
before the tragedy, as he and his wife entered their door,
both heard bursts of music and voices singing together; and
how at the Mass for the dead he recognized the music as
that of the choir which — just before the elevation of the
Host – sang in just such short bursts of song.*

He wrote of this to Mrs Shakespear:

You will remember the part the motor-car had in the murder.
Had we seen more he might have been saved, for recent evidence
seems to show that these things are fate unless foreseen by clairvoyance and so brought within the range of free will. A French
man of science thinks that we all — including murderers and
victims – will and so create the future. I would bring in the dead.
Are we, that foreknow, the actual or potential traitors of the race-
process? Do we, as it were, forbid the bands [sic] when the event
is struggling to be born? Is that why — even if what we foresee
is not some trivial thing — we foresee too little to understand?

The two poems in *The Winding Stair*, 'Death' and 'Blood
and the Moon', were commenced at the time of the shock
of the assassination, and in his last prose writing, *On the
Boiler*, he was to place O'Higgins in his Irish 'saga' with
Berkeley, Swift, Burke, Grattan, Synge, Lady Gregory.
'There is nothing too hard for such as these', he wrote. 'If
the Catholic names are few on the list, history will soon fill
the gap. My imagination goes back to those exiled Catholic
gentlemen of whom Swift said that their bravery exceeded
that of all nations.' In 'Blood and the Moon' he makes the
tower at Ballylee a symbol of those arrogant conquerors, the
Normans; starting in simple short lines, and in the second
section breaking into a cataract of multi-syllabic verse. Goldsmith and the Dean, Berkeley and 'haughtier-headed' Burke
are obsessing him. In the third and fourth section he returns
to a twelve-line classical form.

* Yeats being tone deaf, his recognition of the music is in itself
miraculous.

6

Not many honours can have given Yeats greater pleasure than his appointment to be Chairman of the Committee set up in 1926 to advise the Ministry of Finance on the new coinage. He made a characteristic effort to secure the appointment of colleagues agreeable to himself, writing to Thomas Bodkin that 'Father Browne of Maynooth consents to go on the Advisory Board [which] will put us right with all Gaels and ultra-Nationalists'. The Committee, however, were not 'put right' with this section of opinion, and there was bitter comment, in which his old friend Maud Gonne joined, upon the designs ultimately adopted, which were those of an Englishman.

Dr Bodkin writes:

When our Committee was in session, at a crucial stage of the deliberations, I had occasion to consult him in his bedroom at Merrion Square where he was confined with a chill. Never have I seen an invalid more cosseted. He was sitting wrapped in a thick Jaeger jacket, propped up with several pillows under a heavy down quilt. The big anthracite stove was almost red-hot. Half a bottle of champagne stood at his elbow. I could hardly breathe in the atmosphere. But he was full of plans for the dis-comfiture of the Ministry of Finance. He told me then that when he was engaged to attend any dinner of importance, private or public, it was his habit to spend the afternoon in bed so that he should be at his best, mentally and physically, for the enter-tainment.

The Committee sat at intervals over a period of nearly two years and Yeats never missed a meeting, except when abroad. One of the Committee's first resolutions, aimed at him and proposed by Thomas Bodkin, bound the members to make no disclosure of their proceedings until the final report had been presented. It was hardly expected that Yeats would observe the agreement strictly, and the Committee soon found that he was discussing matters in the lobbies of the Senate and elsewhere. When taxed with his fault, he admitted it coyly like a child caught stealing sugar, and he promised to amend his ways.

He had seen and greatly admired, when in Stockholm, Carl Milles's work, and Milles was his candidate for the designs on the coinage. He may have made his project a little too plain, for, though Milles was invited to compete, the set of designs he sent were too slight to get serious consideration. The following letter to Bodkin (29 December 1926) shows that he was in direct communication with Milles:

I have just heard from Milles. He writes, 'I have already made sketches for all the coins. I must now have them cast in plaster and hope to be able to send them in the beginning of January. I have followed the program pretty closely but have taken certain liberties I shall explain the meaning of.'

The designs chosen were by an artist from Yorkshire, Mr Percy Metcalfe. Yeats was abroad when the coins were first issued; Bodkin lectured upon the coins (bird, beast and fish were selected for portrayal) and sent Yeats a typescript of what he had said. In reply Yeats wrote:

I have read that full, lucid and gracious lecture of yours and thank you for sending it. I see an occasional Irish newspaper and noticed some letter or speech which said we were under the influence of the Freemasons who wanted to drive out of Ireland all traces of the Christian Religion. I wish they would tell us what coinage seems to them most charged with piety . . .

I have not heard of anything in music, art and literature that has had better treatment in Ireland. . . . 'The bust outlives' – who was it? – the coin of Tiberius [*sic*].

When, on the resignation of Mr Lucius O'Callaghan from the Directorship of the National Gallery, Dr Bodkin decided to stand for the post, Yeats put forward Thomas MacGreevy as candidate. Bodkin was unanimously elected, and found, though hitherto their relations had never been entirely unembarrassed, a firm and most whole-hearted supporter among the Governors in Yeats, who was extremely conscientious in his attendance at the Board meetings. One afternoon he came unexpectedly to Bodkin's house and suddenly said, 'I have for a long time entertained and spread prejudices against you, which I have lately felt to be quite unfounded. With your consent I will go to certain members of the Government and explain my altered views.' Needless to say, Bodkin hastily dissuaded him from putting this quaint but generous impulse into effect.

7

The days when Yeats had been largely employed in managing the Abbey Theatre, and writing for it, were long over. But he still read, or had read to him, every new play before its production, he attended all the Board meetings, and exercised, when he wished to do so, the decisive influence upon policy.

At the end of the Civil War the Theatre was virtually bankrupt. Time and time again Lady Gregory and he had had to go to their rich friends, mostly English or of English political sympathies, to save the Irish dramatic movement. Up to the time that he left Oxford, Yeats constantly lectured in London to raise funds sufficient to carry on the work for a year or two. Then, when the Treaty was signed, both felt that it would no longer become Irish dignity to seek support outside Ireland. Though the new Government could not afford to set up a State theatre, it did what it could; chiefly through the good offices of the Minister of Finance, Ernest Blythe, a connoisseur of dramatic art, it gave the little Theatre an annual subsidy, in the first year (1925) £800, and in subsequent years £1000. The directorate, which henceforth included a nominee of the Government, carried on the tradition of years of willing, unpaid service.

Yeats's latter-day contributions to the stage of the Abbey Theatre were in this order: *The Cat and the Moon*, two translations from Sophocles, *King Oedipus* and *Oedipus at Colonus*, certain *Plays for Dancers*, *The Words upon the Window-Pane*, *The King of the Great Clock Tower*, *Resur-*

*rection, Purgatory.** He did not actually produce these plays, but took an active part in their rehearsal, being now not so much concerned, as Lennox Robinson has recorded, with the speaking of the verse as with emotion, movement, scenery, dress and lighting. The first of the translations, *King Oedipus*, was played at the end of 1926.

7.12.26. To Mrs Shakespear

I have not written as life has been rather broken since I returned – writing a couple of poems and so in a dream, entertaining a great Swedish architect, giving up my study to a Cuala sale . . .

My version of Oedipus comes on tonight. I think my shaping of the speech will prove powerful on the stage, for I have made it hard, bare and natural like a Saga, and that it will be well, though not greatly acted – it is all too new to our people. I am more anxious about the audience, who will have to sustain an hour and a half's tension. The actor who plays Oedipus felt the strain at dress rehearsal so much that he could hardly act in the last great moments – a good audience will give him life, but how will the Catholics take it? In rehearsal I had but one overwhelming emotion, a sense of the actual presence in a terrible sacrament of the God. But I have got this always, though never so strongly before, from Greek Drama.

The next day he reported: 'A very great success, both papers and the audience enthusiastic. . . . MacCormick has now established himself in the minds of our audience as a great tragedian. He has certainly magnificent moments.'

Even before the subsidy came, another spin was given to the Theatre's wheel of fortune by the discovery of a new dramatist in Sean O'Casey. O'Casey's *Shadow of a Gunman* and *Juno and the Paycock*, set in the Dublin slums in time

---

* His early work, apart from *Cathleen ni Houlihan*, was too seldom revived. It had its readers, however; the first of his work to have been put upon the stage, *The Land of Heart's Desire*, was particularly popular. Brought out as a separate edition, at two and sixpence, the play sold 10,000 copies in 1925. 'It brought me £100, I think', Yeats wrote to Lady Gregory. 'It amazes me, as if I saw the mango trick – so much from so little – for it's a vague sentimental trifle.'

of revolution, reached the Abbey at the moment of its greatest depression. They helped it to greater publicity than it had enjoyed since Synge and to a greater popularity than it had ever enjoyed. *Juno and the Paycock*, with Juno superbly played by Miss Allgood, was taken to London, and O'Casey was at once placed by the critics in the first rank of modern English-speaking dramatists. Yeats found himself at one with the crowd and critics in his admiration of O'Casey's work, writing of *The Plough and the Stars*, after its first production in February 1926, that it was 'a great play like a Russian novel'.

The Plough and the Stars, a more obvious censure of methods of revolution, angered the diehard Republicans. A small number of men attempted to rush the stage, and police protection had to be sought for the players. Yeats thought the row 'horrible' yet showed his old determination to see things through. In this case he had the support of pit and gallery. The play had its week's run and was quickly revived. Before the revival one of those 'dark young men' who provided Yeats with his political information under cover of night, warned him that the anti-Casey Republicans intended to blow up the Abbey. He did not tell the company but advised Lennox Robinson to see to the fire-extinguishers and have the house well guarded.

A quarrel with O'Casey himself once more plunged Yeats deep into Abbey affairs. His refusal, with the concurrence of Lady Gregory and Lennox Robinson, of *The Silver Tassie* created a sensation. In some letters that were published about the occurrence, O'Casey threw scorn upon Yeats for a suggestion, passed on to him by Lady Gregory, that he should let it be known that he himself had become dissatisfied with the play and wished to withdraw it for revision. The Directors thought *The Silver Tassie* a bad play, and one that would mar the fame and popularity of the author, but, as the Abbey had latterly produced many poor plays, the public felt that, with a man of O'Casey's stature, it was entitled to form a judgement. There were more reasons behind Yeats's rejection of *The Silver Tassie* than the simple fact of its defective construction. Some time later, on the production of the play in London, he commented in his manuscript-book on his distaste for O'Casey's approach to certain special subjects, which he considered spiritually unprofitable:

It would seem from its failure in London that we were right, upon the other hand Mr Shaw's and Mr Augustus John's admiration suggest that it was at least better than we thought it, and yet I am certain that if any of our other dramatists sent us a similar play we would reject it. We were biased, we are biased by the Irish Salamis. The war as O'Casey has conceived it is an equivalent for those primary qualities brought down by Berkeley's secret society, it stands outside the characters, it is not part of their expression, it is that very attempt denounced by Mallarmé to build as if with brick and mortar with the pages of a book. The English critics feel differently. To them a theme that 'bulks largely in the news' gives dignity to human nature, even raises it to international importance. We on the other hand are certain that nothing can give dignity to human nature but the character and energy of its expression. We do not even ask that it shall have dignity so long as it can burn away all that is not itself.

The thought in this bears a close resemblance to the much criticized section of the Introduction to the *Oxford Book of Modern Verse*, where Yeats explains his exclusion of the work of Wilfred Owen and of other English war poets, on the ground that 'When man has withdrawn into the quicksilver at the back of the mirror no great event becomes luminous to the mind'.*

8

In October 1927, soon after the production of the second translation of Sophocles, Yeats contracted a cold which developed into congestion of the lungs. This was the first

* Later on, the Abbey Directors accepted the verdict of London, and *The Silver Tassie* was produced in all its revolting integrity, to quote newspaper comment.

definite illness he had had apart from measles and scarlatina in his childhood and an attack of rheumatic fever one summer at Coole.

He ran a high temperature and was for a time delirious. One day, during the delirium, he sat up in bed: 'George Moore should eat more salt', he began (salt is the cabalistic emblem for immortality), and then he tried to dictate some sentences for his projected chapter of autobiography, *Dramatis Personae*, which could not be published while George Moore was alive.

As soon as his strength permitted, the doctors advised him to go in search of the sun. His wife made rapid arrangements for a voyage to Spain. They were first at Algeciras. Here through the early days of November he sat in the garden of the Hotel Reina Cristina, correcting proofs of *The Tower*, making notes for new poems and watching the butterflies light upon the roses. With sunset came the first white herons, flying from beyond Gibraltar, to sleep in the dark trees. Watching them, he wrote 'At Algeciras – a Meditation upon Death', which commences:

> The heron-billed pale cattle-birds.

His lung was not yet healed, and at Seville, where they went for the greater heat, it began to bleed. Some of the doctors subsequently consulted attributed the haemorrhages less to the condition of the lung than to blood-pressure and exhaustion. But it is possible that he was afflicted with tuberculosis, or that an early tendency towards this disease now revived. Lady Gerald Wellesley, writing of him as he was some years later, noted that he had all the symptoms: 'the feverish cerebral excitement, often the bodily excitement, the sudden rise in vitality, the sudden fall'.

A few weeks before leaving Ireland he had been offered £400 by W. E. Rudge, the proprietor of a private press in New York, for six months' use of sixteen pages of new verse. 'It is like one of my family mottoes "God cares for the ravens"', he wrote to Lady Gregory in reference to a windfall which enabled him to contemplate without anxiety the expenses that illness abroad involves. He gave Mr Rudge 'A Woman Young and Old' and 'Blood and the Moon' (which for that reason did not appear in *The Tower*), and agreed to write one hundred and fifty lines in two months. Notwithstanding illness and bad convalescence, he was able to carry out the contract.* The six lines 'Oil and Blood' – about St Teresa – were completed at Seville, and it was there that his wife with a shiver of excitement heard him read his 'In Memory of Eva Gore-Booth and Con Markievicz':

> Dear shadows, now you know it all,
> All the folly of a fight
> With a common wrong or right.
> The innocent and the beautiful
> Have no enemy but time;
> Arise and bid me strike a match
> And strike another till time catch; . . .

After ten days of Seville his wife decided to take him to the French Riviera for its better medical facilities. They travelled by slow stages; both were glad to see the last of Spain. But ill-luck pursued them, and at Cannes, where they stayed at the Hôtel St Georges on the Fréjus road, Yeats was twice assailed by influenza. He was told that the real trouble was exhaustion from the overwork of years. The doctors advised him to withdraw from public life and live far from crowded places, and one of them said that he must walk slowly, even move his head slowly, that his thoughts might become slow also. The same man added: 'If I had met you when this was beginning, five years ago, I could have saved you it all by sending you off on a bout of dissipation – all the great creators of the past were devils. Drink and women have saved many a man from death and madness.'†

To keep his thoughts 'slow', he was forbidden for a time to read serious books, but the rule was honoured more in

* *The Winding Stair* (Fountain Press, N.Y.). The six poems in this volume were reprinted four years later.

† An Irish doctor.

the breach than in the observance. When he heard the doctor's step he would hide Macran's *Logic of Hegel* under his pillow and appear to be immersed in a detective story. As soon as he was up he defied medical opinion openly by reading Browning's *Paracelsus*, St Teresa's autobiography and, worst of all from the doctor's point of view, Wyndham Lewis's aggressive *Time and Western Man* had been sent him in all innocence by Sturge Moore as a prophylactic against dogmatism. The book attacked time-philosophies, in which category were strangely placed together the Italian anti-naturalist school, Bertrand Russell and Whitehead, and works revolving as closely round the history of science as Spengler's *Decline of the West*. Though Yeats would not abandon the rich pastures, the abundant historical speculations of time-philosophy, he was greatly excited by Wyndham Lewis's hard-hitting criticism. 'I have read *Time and Western Man* with gratitude', he wrote to Sturge Moore.

The last chapters again and again. It has given what I could not, a coherent root to my hatred. You are wrong to think Lewis attacks the conclusions of men like Alexander and Russell because he thinks them 'uncertain'. He thinks them false. To admit uncertainty into philosophy, necessary uncertainty, would seem to him to wrong the sovereignty of intellect, or worse, to accept the hypocritical humility of the scientific propagandists which is, he declares, their 'cloak for dogma'. He is Kantian with some mixture of older thought, Catholic or Greek – and has the vast Kantian argument behind him, the most powerful in philosophy. He considers that both 'space and time are mere appearances', whereas his opponents think that time is real though space is a construction of the mind . . .

He makes metaphors in the most preposterous way, but he can write, he has intellectual passion, and of that there has been very little for thirty years. His last book is among other things Plotinus or some Buddhist monk answering the astrologers (the only believers ever persecuted by the Buddhists). I do not always hate what he hates and yet I am always glad that he hates. There are always men like that. Schopenhauer can do no wrong in my eyes – I no more quarrel with him than I do with a mountain cataract. Error is but the abyss into which he precipitates his truths.

While Yeats was still at Cannes the 'unknown communicators' made an attempt to reassert their prestige by drawing 'in a few minutes', the Kantian distinction between the human perception and understanding and the practical reason. Yet they had, it appears, no more than tolerated Yeats's readings in philosophy proper, and were inclined to pick quarrels with him for a use (which was not theirs) of 'School terminology'. They had offered no objection, however, to his reading history in relation to their historical logic, and biography in relation to their twenty-eight typical incarnations, and on the appearance of the first English translation of Spengler, Yeats had found in it whole metaphors that were also in his *Vision*, and many of the same dates as well. He was also acquainted with the previous attempt of Henry Adams to interpret and predict the future through the concepts and relationships of physical science.* He could never resist the attraction of these prophetic constructions, where error preserves a value, and that belong perhaps to the sphere of art (verisimilitude) and of symbol rather than to that of absolute truth.

9

Yeats remained at Cannes until the middle of February; before he left for Rapallo he was well enough to dictate to his wife a vigorous prose version of his *Fighting the Waves* (originally *The Only Jealousy of Emer*), arranged for stage dancing: 'as we hope', he wrote to Lady Gregory, 'that Miss de Valois and her Dublin representative will be able soon to dance in those Dutch masks'.†

* Adams, like Yeats in *A Vision*, predicted the breakdown of human reason, making the date 1921.

† The Dutch masks were made by Hildo Krop for a performance in Holland. Yeats had first seen Miss de Valois in a performance of his *Player Queen* at the Cambridge Festival Theatre. An Irishwoman, who was an original member of Diaghilev's famous Russian ballet, she came to Dublin to found a school of dancing at the Abbey.

The doctors said that he should winter abroad, and Yeats was ready to accept their views upon this point, not so much because he believed in climate as because he thought that a new environment would take the bitterness out of his verse. Ezra Pound now lived at Rapallo, and Mrs Yeats planned to take a flat there, remove to a smaller house in Dublin, put the children into a Swiss school, while Yeats retired from the Senate. 'We shall have to change our way of life at home', he wrote to Lady Gregory. 'We have put 82 [Merrion Square] in the hands of an agent. ... The only activity I shall keep on is my work as Abbey Director.'

At Rapallo, in February 1928, Yeats spent sunny afternoons on the roof-garden, into which Ezra Pound's rooms opened, and walked at night with his friend through the little streets. He was better; and satisfied that he was safe near such good friends, Mrs Yeats left him at the Albergo Rapallo and went to Switzerland to place little Michael in a home school. He wrote her letters about the cats of Rapallo. Ezra Pound's passion for cats seemed to equal Maud Gonne's. They came out of the houses as he passed, knowing that his pockets were full of meat and chicken bones. 'Cats', Yeats remarked, 'belong to the oppressed races.' 'Ezra has most of Maud Gonne's opinions (political and economic), being what Lewis calls "a revolutionary simpleton". The chief difference is that he hates Palgrave's *Golden Treasury*, as she hates the Irish Free State Government, and thinks even worse of its editor than she does of President Cosgrave.'

Moved thereto by Wyndham Lewis's criticisms of Joyce, Gertrude Stein, Picasso and 'all the gods', Yeats started during the first weeks at Rapallo his *Packet for Ezra Pound*. Lewis's *Time and Western Man* made him wish to say something about typical books, such as *Ulysses*, some of Pound's *Cantos*, Virginia Woolf's *Waves*, in which he found a philosophy automatic and abstract like the *Sankhara* school of ancient India, perhaps like that of G. E. Moore and the English neo-Realists, making all we perceive exist in the external world, all a stream extraneous to the contemplator – the tragedy that there is no tragedy. At the same time he resumed his philosophical contentions with Sturge Moore; his first long letter since his illness (27 February 1928) being another vicious thrust at Bertrand Russell and the scientists.

Why should you get caught in the scientific mousetrap which is baited with British sentimentalism? You say Bertrand Russell says that Kant smashed his own philosophy by the doctrine of practical reason. So he does say, and what more can you expect? ... He merely repeats a common electioneering nonsense, which writers have copied for generations. The men who invented it had as much to do with philosophy as an Orange brass band has to do with religion ...

To this Sturge Moore replied: 'My brother's first exploits were the absolute smashing of philosophies raised on science. The European tradition to which he belongs begins with Socrates and Zeno and ends with Hume, Kant, Wittgenstein.'

On his wife's return from Switzerland they searched for flats in Rapallo, and found the rooms which they took for the following winter: Via Americhe 12–8.

12.3.28. To Lady Gregory

We shall have a guest-room always and two when the children are at school so I shall hope that you will come in reality and not but dream of it as you say. We have large balconies and an incomparable view. I am longing to be settled there for the centre of all my hopes is to be back in my study, and not in Dublin where there is much besides my study. I am working on alternate days, that is to say writing on alternate days some paragraphs for the *Vision* or for a little book I am writing for Lolly, an account of this place, and Ezra and his work and things that arise out of that. After my day's, or rather morning's work, I am tired, and need the whole of next day to get back my freshness. It is not so much that the morning tires me as that it excites me and I go on thinking all day. My effort is always now to break off the stream of thought when its permitted hour is at an end. I am not my old self but am wonderfully better than when I came here a month ago.

I am well satisfied to think that Anne and Michael will get their schooling in Switzerland instead of Dublin. They will know Ireland from Ballylee and Coole (and they very naturally much prefer Coole to Ballylee), and then they will come here for Xmas and as they grow older will see Rome and Florence, and the few people they meet will be intellectual persons. I would not have liked London for them, or anywhere that would bring them in contact with people much richer than themselves, and I dreaded Dublin because people much poorer are even worse. Then too they will grow up with perfect French and Italian.

I am delighted that you like the pictures in *Red Hanrahan** – I wanted and have got something that suggests a carving on a stone in some little ruined chapel (say) on Insula Trinitatis in Lough Gara. Two Irish Catholic papers – one in Belfast and one in Glasgow – have given the pictures great praise, so I think they are what I wanted.

The coins are all struck now, I think except the pig. The artist had given the pig rather a large cheek, and as there is no suffi-cient market for pigs' cheeks it has had to be reduced and that upset the general balance of the design.

On their way home the Yeatses stopped for a few days at Villiers-sur-Bax to see their boy, who – choice being offered him – decided to stay in Switzerland.† They were back in Merrion Square on 18 April.

25.4.28. To Mrs Shakespear

Two Dublin doctors have sat upon me; the Cannes man said 'Lungs and nervous breakdown can be neglected, nothing mat-ters but blood pressure', and gave me a white pill. The Monte Carlo man said 'Blood pressure and lungs can be neglected, nothing matters but nervous breakdown', and gave me a brown pill. The Dublin men say 'Blood pressure and nervous breakdown can be neglected, nothing matters but the lungs', and have given me a black pill, and as a sort of postscript I am to have a vaccine injection once a week for the next three months. However I shall

---

* *Stories of Red Hanrahan and The Secret Rose.* Illustrated and decorated by Norah McGuinness. (Macmillan, 1927.)

† Extract from letter: 'We asked him if he would like to lunch with us on Easter day, and he said he was not sure as he did not know what the school would have for lunch.'

cut out one week in order to spend ten days in London in June. We came direct from Cherbourg to Queenstown, so I have seen nobody.

The Tower is a great success, two thousand copies in the first month, much the largest sale I have ever had. I do nothing at present but potter over a new edition of *A Vision* which should be ready some time next year. When I get back to Rapallo I hope to write verse again, but no more bitter passion I think. Rereading *The Tower* I am astonished at its bitterness and long to live out of Ireland that I may find some new vintage. Yet that bitterness gave the book its power and it is the best book I have written …

A month later they succeeded in disposing of 82 Merrion Square to a professor of architecture. Yeats was sad at parting from the noble double drawing-room, the fine Georgian woodwork and marble fireplaces, the tall windows. The family spent a week or two at Ballylee, merely on picnic, and for July took a furnished house in Howth; in August they were settled in a flat at the top of 42 Fitzwilliam Square, overlooking the garden admired by Thackeray for its flowers and fresh foliage. Yeats's study was a pretty room, with blue walls and ceilings, painted by Mrs Yeats, and gold-coloured curtains.

He made his last speech in the Senate on 18 July. The subject was the Constitutional Amendment Bill, and he remarked upon the simple fact that it would be more desirable and important to have able men than representative men in the House. A little speech, three sentences, and it was followed by a minute of great pain at the back of his neck. That comforted him, for he had been told that after all he might have been re-elected, and the giving up of £360 a year was on his conscience – it was a good deal of money to take from his family. Lord Glenavy, the Chairman of the Senate, stopped him coming out of the Senate one day to say 'The Senate will re-elect you whenever you like'. 'He meant', Yeats wrote to Lady Gregory, 'that they would co-opt me when there was a vacancy. I doubt it, but I am pleased that he should think it.'

Three years later, when Lord Glenavy died, Yeats wrote as follows to his son, the Hon. Gordon Campbell:

I read of your father's death with great regret. He was the best Chairman I have ever come across and as Chairman of the Senate he impressed upon that body a dignity that should outlast our time. Handsome, watchful, vigorous, dominating, courteous, he seemed like some figure from an historical painting. I remember with a personal satisfaction that when at a first private meeting of the Senate, convened to choose a chairman, another candidate was proposed I spoke in your father's favour and with some energy. I am certain that none who voted for him that day ever regretted their vote. My wife joins with me in sending you sympathy in your grief.

He had this reply:

In his heart I think my father would have treasured your tribute more than any other. Although he would affect suspicion and an undervaluation of the artist, something in him did acknowledge a superior claim in the imagination. He would not have explained it to himself in that way. But I have heard him puzzling aloud about the sway you asserted over the Senate on some occasions and thus admitting a quality which he could not himself command but did not undervalue.

If he had known that you approved him as the Chairman I think that he would have been quite content. Yours sincerely, Glenavy.*

* The first Lord Glenavy had been leader at the Irish Bar, and Unionist M.P. at Westminster, then Lord Chancellor of Ireland during the last years of the English regime. He retired from the Senate in the same year as Yeats.

18

Wheels and butterflies

Rapallo – 'Words for Music Perhaps' – *A Packet for Ezra Pound* – Summer of 1929; Ballylee abandoned – Illness and convalescence in Italy – Play about Swift – The garrets and cellars – Degree at Oxford; Rossi – The last of Coole – The Irish Academy of Letters – Last American tour.

═══

To Garret or Cellar a wheel I send,
But every butterfly to a friend.

The Primum Mobile that fashioned us
Has made the very owls in circles move.

I

RAPALLO appeared to be all that could be desired.

Mountains that shelter the bay from all but the south wind, bare brown branches of low vines and of tall trees blurring their outline as though with a soft mist; houses mirrored in an almost motionless sea; a verandahed gable a couple of miles away bringing to mind some Chinese painting. Rapallo's thin line of broken mother-of-pearl along the water's edge. The little town described in the Ode on a Grecian Urn. In what better place could I, forbidden Dublin winters, and all excited crowded places, spend what winters yet remain? *

In the flat in the Via Americhe, with his own books and furniture around him, Yeats felt so well disposed towards all the world that (he confided this to Lady Gregory, herself a churchgoer) he considered going to church and making

---

* *A Packet for Ezra Pound.* Nevertheless Rapallo has been considerably modernized since as a little fishing village it enchanted the Emperor Frederick III and cradled Zarathustra.

friends with the English in their villas. Then one day, as he sat in a café by the sea – the anecdote is in *A Packet for Ezra Pound* – he heard an English voice say: 'Our new Devil-dodger is not so bad. I have been practising with his choir all the afternoon. We sang hymns and then God Save the King, more hymns and He's a jolly good Fellow. We were at the hotel at the end of the esplanade where they have the best beer.' He decided that he was 'too anaemic for so British a faith', and that such leisure as he had should be reserved for the study of local memories of Nietzsche, the conversation of Ezra Pound and that of his own friends or Ezra's, who might pass through Rapallo.

Among the latter came George Antheil, the musician, who stayed for a while and was set to write some strange and dramatic music for *Fighting the Waves*; there was also 'one of Ezra's more savage disciples', a poet and writer of Balkan scenarios. 'He got into jail as a pacifist and then for assaulting the police and carrying concealed weapons', Yeats reported of this visitor. '... He is now writing up Antheil's music. ... I have no doubt that just such as he surrounded Shakespeare's theatre, when it was denounced by the first Puritans.' In conversation with Antheil, Yeats, the tone-deaf, rapidly and characteristically persuaded himself that his old theories of half-tones in verse-speaking were the dogmas of modern composers, and felt confident that he would be supplied in future with all the music he needed for his plays from this source. 'He is about 28', he wrote of Antheil, 'and looks 18 and has a face of indescribable innocence. His wife, a first violinist from somewhere or other, looks equally young and innocent. Both are persons of impulse and he may or may not get through his month of toil upon the three plays'.*

2

When he dedicated *The Winding Stair* to Edmund Dulac in 1933, he recalled 'exultant weeks' at Rapallo four years

*Mr Antheil did the musical setting for the one play only.

earlier, the date of several of that group of poems called
'Words for Music Perhaps'. It was a new phase of imaginative excitement; the poems came as follows:

'The heron-billed pale cattle-birds'	re-written. Feb. 4
'Mohini Chatterjee'	Feb. 9
'Mad as the Mist and Snow'	Feb. 12
'Three Things'	Feb. 14–24
'Cracked Mary's Vision' (an unpublished poem, with the refrain 'May the Devil take King George')*	Feb. 24
'The Nineteenth Century and After'	March 2
'Cracked Mary and the Dancers' (she became Crazy Jane later)	March 6
'Those Dancing Days are Gone'	March 8
'Lullaby'	March 20
'I care not what the sailors say' (afterwards 'Crazy Jane Reproved')	March 27
'Cracked Mary and the Bishop' (after this poem Cracked Mary became Crazy Jane for obvious reasons . . .)	undated, but March
'Girl's Song' ('I went out alone')	March 29

His principal correspondence was still with Lady Gregory,
Sturge Moore and Mrs Shakespear. Here are extracts from
letters to one or other of these – something in them about
the new and 'more amiable' poetry ('Turning Butterfly in
Old Age') which followed the publication of *The Tower*, and
the withdrawal from the Senate.

21.1.29. *To Lady Gregory*

You may have heard that I gave £50 to the *Irish Statesman*
fund. I hated giving so much, as you can imagine, but Russell
had written that the directors had decided to end the paper
before the end of the month . . . and I felt that the whole move-

---

*'Cracked Mary's Vision' was probably provoked by the King's
opening of the new wing of the Tate Gallery, in which were the 'stolen'
Lane pictures. The British monarch is contrasted unfavourably with a
Tuatha de Danaan king. Yeats did not think the poem good enough
to include in his *Collected Works*, but he tried to get A E to print the
incendiary lines in the *Irish Statesman*

ment would suffer if it did. I did not feel that I could write to Shaw and Plunkett unless I was obviously giving the utmost I could afford ..

Now that the philosophy is finished I am writing prose drafts for poems. I have a series of dramatic poems – very short – of Christ coming out of the tomb,* and am trying to make a draft for a series of impersonal lyrics. But the start after a long interval – this time more than a year – is very difficult. Here the weather is bright and cold, one of the coldest winters almost anybody can remember but almost always dry, which suits my complaint. I was knocked up in Rome for a few days (constant fatigue) but am now very well. We see almost as much as you do of Americans, celebrities occasionally. I see Ezra daily. We disagree about everything, but if we have not met for 24 hours he calls full of gloomy and almost dumb oppression.

2.3.39 *To Mrs Shakespear*

I am writing 'Twelve Poems for Music' † – have done three of them (and two other poems) – not so much that they may be sung as that I may define their kind of emotion to myself. I want them to be all emotion and all impersonal. ... They are the opposite of my recent work and all praise of joyous life, though in the best of them it is a dry bone upon the shore that sings the praise ...

To-night we dine with Ezra to meet Hauptmann. ... Auntille – how do you spell him? – and his lady will be there ...

I have turned from Browning – to me a dangerous influence — to Morris, and read things in *Defence of Guenevere* and some unfinished prose fragments with great wonder. I have come to feel that the world's great poetical period is over. ...‡ The young do not feel like that – George does not nor Ezra – but men far off feel it – in Japan, for instance.

Gerhard Hauptmann's grand appearance and physique, reminiscent of William Morris, at once created a favourable impression upon Yeats. He lived in a fine villa on the Zoagli Road, and gave big dinner parties to which Yeats and his

---

*Lyrics for the play *Resurrection*.

†Later on about twenty-five – 'For Music Perhaps'.

‡*Vide* 'The Nineteenth Century and After' in *The Winding Stair and Other Poems*, 'Though the great song return no more'.

wife were often asked. German and Irish dramatist grew fond and at the same time a little envious of each other, Hauptmann because Yeats was the younger man by two years, Yeats because Hauptmann could drink three bottles of champagne a day and bathe in the sea. Hauptmann would say, looking sadly at Yeats, '*Er hat zwei Jahre mehr zu leben als ich*'. Unfortunately, there could be no real conversation between the two, for Hauptmann, although he understood English, could not speak it with ease.*

24.3.29. *To Lady Gregory*

I am dictating this to George because I have tired myself over the proof-sheets for my new Cuala book, and then just before that I had the return journey from Monte Carlo where we had been staying with Mrs Phillimore. A wondrous land of the rich with no side-walks upon the roads which are intended only for murderous motor cars. . . . On Thursday George goes to Switzerland to see the children for Easter. They both are well, Michael working hard but Anne refusing to work at anything but French. Michael has perfect French and will never speak a sentence unless he is quite sure it is correct, but Anne talks helter-skelter as it comes, which is all very pleasing as it is in their horoscopes, and confirms our science.

29.3.29. *To Mrs Shakespear*

. . . I am filling up my time by sitting in the sun when not reading or writing. I have written eleven lyrics in the last two months – nine of them 'words for music', these last unlike my past work – wilder and perhaps slighter – Here is a 'Lullaby' that I like, A mother sings to her child

> Beloved may your sleep be sound
> That have found it where you fed;
> What were all the world's alarms
> To that great Paris when he found
> Sleep upon a golden bed
> That first dawn in Helen's arms?

* It may be mentioned here, although Hauptmann had nothing to do with the mattter, that in 1934 Yeats quite unexpectedly, as author of *The Countess Cathleen*, received the Goethe Plakette from the Oberbürgermeister of Frankfurt.

II

Sleep beloved such a sleep
As did that wild Tristram know
When, the potion's work being done,
Stags could run and hares could leap,
The beech-bough sway by the oak-bough
And the world begin again.

III

Beloved such a sleep as fell
Upon Eurotas' grassy bank
When the holy bird that there
Accomplished his predestined will,
From the limbs of Leda sank
But not from her protecting care.*

I have done two or three others that seem to me lucky and that does not often happen. Yet I am full of doubt. I am writing more easily than I ever wrote and I am happy. Whereas I have always been unhappy when I wrote and worked with great difficulty. I feel like one of those Japanese who in the middle ages retired from the world at 50 or so – not like an Indian of that age to live in jungle but to devote himself 'to art and letters' which were considered sacred.

If this new work do not seem as good as the old to my friends then I can take to some lesser task and live more contentedly – the happiness of finding idleness a duty – no more opinions, no more politics, no more practical tasks.

17.4.29. *To T. Sturge Moore*

No, I never compared your brother to Herbert Spencer nor did I accuse him of an adulterous commerce with physical science. However we belong to different troups. I can no more expect you

---

* Of this lovely poem Yeats wrote in some later letter that he would not be surprised if it should become as popular as 'Innisfree'. He changed 'that great Paris' to 'mighty Paris'; 'Stags could run and hares could leap' to 'Roe could run or doe could leap'; 'The beech-bough sway by the oak-bough' to 'Under oak and beechen bough'; 'And the world begin again' to 'Roe could leap or doe could run'; 'Beloved such a sleep as fell' to 'Such a sleep and sound as fell'. And added punctuation.

to acknowledge virtue in Hegel than Ezra Pound to acknowledge it in Tennyson. I give up your ebullient generation, and turn to The Bright Young People who never even quarrel with a marriage partner unless they have seen somebody they like better. Ezra Pound has just been in. He says 'Spengler is a Wells who has founded himself on German scholarship instead of English journalism'. He is sunk in Frobenius, Spengler's German source, and finds him a most interesting person. Frobenius suggested the idea that cultures (including arts and sciences) arise out of races, express those races as if they were fruit and leaves in a preordained order and perish with them. . . . He proved from his logic – some German told Ezra – that a certain civilization must have once existed at a certain spot in Africa and then went and dug it up. He proved his case all through by African research. I cannot read German and so must get him second hand. He has confirmed a conception I have had for years, a conception that has freed me from British Liberalism and all its dreams. The one heroic sanction is that of the last battle of the Norse gods, of a gay struggle without hope. Long ago I used to puzzle poor Maud Gonne by always avowing ultimate defeat as a test – our literary movement would be worthless but for its defeat. Science is the criticism of myths, there would be no Darwin had there been no Book of Genesis, no electrons but for the Greek atomic myth, and when the criticism is finished there is not even a drift of ashes on the pyre. Sexual desire dies because every touch consumed becomes a spectre.* I am reading William Morris with great delight and what a protection to my delight it is to know that in spite of all his loose writing I need not be jealous for him. He is the end, as Chaucer was the end in his day, Dante in his, incoherent Blake in his. There is no improvement, only a series of sudden fires each though fainter as necessary as that before it. We free ourselves from obsession that we may be nothing. The last kiss is given to the void.

It is interesting to place the assertions at the close of this letter side by side with Lady Gerald Wellesley's statement

---

* *Vide* the lines in *Resurrection*:

> 'The herald's cry, the soldier's tread
> Exhaust his glory and his might:
> Whatever flames upon the night
> Man's own resinous heart has fed.'

that, during her friendship with Yeats in the last five years of his life, he would never speak of the dead accepted poets about whom she so much desired his opinion. 'Sex, Philosophy, and the Occult preoccupy him. He strangely intermingles the three.'* And was it because of his belief that 'the Great Song returns no more' that he proposed the young 'realistic' novelists as Ireland's future literary leaders?

3

Besides writing these poems of a new simplicity, Yeats finished while at Rapallo a prose piece of purest English, his *Packet for Ezra Pound*. Owing to his having gained Mrs Yeats's consent for her share in an 'incredible experience' to be made known, the essay underwent a transformation in the course of composition. As published by Miss Elizabeth Yeats in June 1929, the *Packet* had added to it the 'Introduction to the Great Wheel', which was the first public disclosure of the psychic state in which *A Vision* had originated.

It would appear that upon receiving the manuscript Miss Yeats had a momentary suspicion that Willie's wits were astray; she consulted AE's wisdom, and he replied:

My opinion is that *anything* Willie writes will be of interest now or later on, and a book like this, which does not excite me or you, may be, possibly will be, studied later on when the psychology of the poet is considered by critics and biographers. ... Some will dislike it or think it fantastic nonsense, others will study it closely. As it is intimate and personal more than anything he has written it is of importance. ... If any change at all in W. B. Y.'s MMS. might be suggested it would be to lessen the references to the 'odours' which occur perhaps too often to be valuable to the psychologist and are too numerous from the purely literary point of view.

The 'Introduction to the Great Wheel' would serve as a Preface to a new edition of *A Vision*. But this new edition

* *Letters on Poetry to Dorothy Wellesley* (Oxford University Press).

would be a new book; 'all, I hope', he wrote to a friend, 'as clear and simple as the subject permits. Four or five years' reading has given me some knowledge of metaphysics and time to clear up endless errors in my understanding of script. My conviction of the truth of it all has grown also.'

But though he spoke of *A Vision* as finished, several years were to pass before he consented to hand over the manuscript of the new edition to the printers. He kept touching it up here and there, sharpening definitions and enriching descriptions, amidst correspondence with learned men, classical scholars and orientalists such as F. P. Sturm and Louis Claude Purser of Trinity College, Dublin. Apart from his ignorance of philosophy at the time (which had caused him to misunderstand distinctions upon which the coherence of the whole depended), there had been a shocking number of errors in the first edition, some of which a small schoolboy would have noticed. For instance, the frontispiece portrait of the bearded and cabala-eyed Giraldus, who bears a remarkable likeness to Yeats himself, was described as being from the *Speculum Angelorum et Hominorum*, and it was impossible to pretend that Giraldus wrote dog-Latin, for he was the most learned of twelfth-century translators from the Arabic. There was one way out. Yeats might assert Hominorum to be a misprint for Homunculorum or Homullorum, thus giving a satiric twist to Giraldus, as it would make the title of his book *The Mirror of Angels and Mannikins*, and Homunculus was a word that would come easily to the pen of Giraldus as the name given to the artificial man whom the alchemists were for ever trying to concoct in their stewpans.

F. P. Sturm wrote to him that he should get some friend who knows Latin to read the proofs this time:

I know that I am a pedant, but pedants read you. We cough in the ink till the world's end, as you cruelly said, but the least of us would save you from the errors which spoil the *Vision* as it is now. Personally I think your philosophy smells of the fagot. Some dead or damned Chaldean mathematikoi have got hold of your wife and are trying to revive a dead system. All these gyres and cones and wheels are parts of a machine that was thrown on the scrap-heap when Ptolemy died. It won't go. There is no petrol for such. The ghosts of the mathematikoi are weeping over their broken toy universe: the Primum Mobile no longer moves, the seven planetary spheres of crystal are dull as a steamy cookshop window – so they are trying to speak through your wife and are using much that she has read in the past. However, all that you write is letters. No doubt many an Inquisitor has sighed as he condemned some author to the flames. You would not have escaped. ... My new book, when I write it, is to be called *Seven Fagots for the Burning of the Great Heretic Yeats*, or *The Wheel Dismantled* – printed for the author by Michael Paleologus, and is to be purchased at the Sign of the Screaming Seraph in Byzantium.

4

Keeping clear of politics, Yeats passed a quiet summer in Ireland. For most of the time he was in his flat in Fitzwilliam Square, but he made a few trips to the country – Glenda-lough, Coole, Ballylee – and in May spent a fortnight in England calling on friends. His older friends there were a small circle now – Sturge Moore, Ricketts, Dulac, Lady Ottoline Morrell, Mrs Shakespear – Ricketts and Mrs Shake-spear his last links with the nineties. On his return he wrote to Lady Gregory:

In London I went to the Round Pond to see what sort of boat I should buy for Michael. I had a talk on the subject with a regular Round Pond Old Tar – a man of seventy.

I went out to Jack's this afternoon and saw there much of the new work – very strange and beautiful in a wild way. James Joyce says that he and Jack have the same method. He bought one of Jack's pictures of the Liffey.*

During his stay at Coole he promised Lady Gregory the poem on the well-loved house she would soon leave for ever.

---

* Jack B. Yeats, his brother, from whom, while a Senator, he had been separated by political difference.

It was a reversion to the deliberate manner of his mytholo-gizing elegies:

> I meditate upon a swallow's flight,
> Upon an aged woman and her house . . .*

'I think I shall "live on" ', he wrote to Mrs Shakespear. 'When Lady Gregory goes, and she is very frail now, I shall have but one old friend left (M. G. has been estranged by politics this long while).'

The visit to Glendalough, where Iseult Gonne and her husband Francis Stuart ran a chicken farm, was in July. 'I was not well', he wrote to Lady Gregory from that romantic spot,

and George thought I wanted quiet, so brought me here which has put me right. I have been to see Iseult Stuart and her husband. . . . Iseult says she preferred Glenmalure where they used to be – I imagine because the solitude there was greater. Her little boy is now about three, very fair haired and strong-looking. Her husband is silent unless one brings the conversation round to St John of the Cross or a kindred theme. They dined with me here and are convinced that they ate one of their own chickens.

He writes from Fitzwilliam Square to a very young ad-mirer of his verse, Miss Ruth Watt:

Your father has been a very good friend of mine for many years and it gives me pleasure to think that you have this book [*Poems*: 1895] and sometimes read it. When I was your age I did not think about poetry at all though I began to write it when I was two years older. Please don't think 'The Lake Isle of Innis-free' is better than all the rest, for I don't.

So the summer of 1929 went by, with for its most notable events a farewell to Thoor Ballylee, and a delightful pro-duction (15 August) by Miss de Valois of *Fighting the Waves* at the Abbey. Ballylee had served as a permanent symbol of Yeats's later, more outward-looking work, and was plainly visible to the passer-by in the rich, grave and beautiful design

---

* 'Coole Park, 1929', in *The Winding Stair and Other Poems*.

which Sturge Moore did for the book to which it gave its name, *The Tower*.

> I declare this tower in my symbol; I declare
> This winding, gyring, spiring treadmill of a stair is my
>   ancestral stair;
> That Goldsmith and the Dean, Berkeley and Burke have
>   travelled there.
> Swift beating on his breast in sibylline frenzy blind . . .*

'I am sending you some photographs', Yeats wrote to Sturge Moore when *The Tower* was coming out. '. . . I need not make any suggestions except that the Tower should not be too unlike the real object, or rather that it should suggest the real object. . . . As you know, all my art theories depend upon just this – rooting of mythology in the earth.'

In the material sense there were good reasons for abandoning Ballylee: the damp, a contributory to Yeats's rheumatism; the isolation and general inconvenience in bad weather. In early days Mrs Yeats used to bicycle the four miles to Gort for provisions in all kinds of weather, but she could not go on doing that for ever. Such a residence was never a practical proposition for an aging man, accustomed to comfort, who was not rich. At first it was hoped that the buildings might be kept in some repair, even when uninhabited. But this proved impossible without personal supervision; after a time no further effort was made to keep up the place. There is scarcely a sign today of Mrs Yeats's once pretty garden, and the rats and the winds have claimed the thatch of the cottages. The tower defies the gales, as it has done for centuries, and as it is well roofed the rains do not penetrate into the poet's chamber, which still contains the heavy oak furniture made on the spot for it, impossible to remove down the narrow winding stair.

Though he had been giving care to his health, Yeats started the winter of 1929–30 in bad style. 'I can't at present do a great deal', he wrote from London in November.

* 'Blood and the Moon', really a *Tower* poem, but first found in *The Winding Stair*.

I overtired myself yesterday – a lunch with Mrs Hall and a tea with Gerald Heard – and today I have coughed up blood again. . . . I caught the cold that undid me at *The Apple Cart*, and perhaps it was the cold coming on, but I hated the play. The second act was theatrical in the worst sense of the word in writing and in acting, and the theme just rich enough to show the superficiality of the treatment. It was the Shaw who writes letters to the papers and gives interviews, not the man who creates.

When he reached Rapallo he complained of sleepiness, but was vigorous enough to finish another poem for 'Words for Music' ('Speech after long silence . . .') and to make prose notes for 'Veronica's Napkin', aphoristic contrasts like his 'Oil and Blood', with the parallel between astrology and Christian dogma on already familiar lines. Then for a period he was an invalid, with temperature rising as the sun fell and signs of nervous prostration. The doctors were at a loss to find a name for his condition. He wrote three lines of a will on 21 December, and had it witnessed by Ezra Pound and Basil Bunting; then suddenly he collapsed, and lay for a time between life and death in a raging fever, with a nurse in attendance. The nature of his illness remained undiscovered until Dr Pende of Genoa, an expert in tropical diseases, was called in. A short examination convinced Dr Pende that Yeats had mysteriously contracted Malta fever; the proper injections were ordered, and the danger passed. The cure comprised among other things a half bottle of champagne every day, and Hauptmann, who had said from the first that what Yeats needed was champagne, supplied the wine from his villa. Yet after nine weeks Yeats was still obliged to spend the greater part of each day in bed; he had by then exhausted the detective literature of the world. 'I have just started upon the Wild West', he writes to Mrs Shakespear on 4 March. 'To-day I met Ezra for the first time . . . he admired my beard and decided I shall be sent by the Free State as Minister to Austria, that Austria would alone perfectly appreciate my beard. Certainly I cannot recognize myself in the mirror ... if Pirandello is right my friends will launch me into something reckless and dashing.'

A pleasant incident of his convalescence was a visit from John Masefield, who came from Florence for a day and a night on purpose to see him. To cheer him up Masefield not only promised him a model boat but made the designs for it while with him. The splendid brigantine 'The George and Willie', built at Oxford, soon reached Dublin and was thereafter one of the most attractive objects in the poet's study.

April came and Yeats could still neither work nor walk out alone; even when accompanied to the little café by the sea he was liable to stage-fright. Then his wife took him to the hotel at Portofino Vetta, fifteen hundred feet above the Gulf of Genoa, and here, no longer shut in by mountains, he made more rapid strides towards real health than the doctors had expected. Within a week he was able to give a little time each morning to the new version of *A Vision*. He opened a new manuscript-book with remarks on Swift's letters and political essays, suggested by F. S. Oliver's *Endless Adventure*.

Oliver, like all modern historians, sees history as a reasoned conflict of mechanical interests intelligible to all. I think of Swift's account of Marlborough's demand to be made general for life, of the Queen's fear that he had designs against the throne, of Argyle's boast that he would fetch him from the midst of his army dead or alive. These men put next one another, suspected one another and planned we do not know what. History seems to me a human drama, keeping the classical unities by the clear division of its epochs, turning one way or the other because this man hates or that man loves. Had any trade question at the opening of the eighteenth century as great an effect on subsequent history as Bolingbroke's impotence, and Harley's slowness and secrecy?

When first he had started his chapter on 'The Great Year' in *A Vision*, all the history he knew was what he remembered of English and classical history from his school-days and what was in the pages of Dumas and the plays of Shakespeare. Having obtained his dates and diagrams, he studied modern writers who have approached history as theory and system, as a sort of speculative science, and read Henry Adams, Sir Charles Petrie, Spengler, Gerald Heard, Arnold Toynbee; for the rest he relied chiefly upon encyclopedias and obvious authorities. Sometimes the more vivid the fact the less could he remember where it came from. Where did he learn that to anoint one's body ensured the favour of a king? And pick up that story of the Bishop of Emessa who, with a watchful eye on the Yeatsian *Anschauung*, warned 'certain Christians' that the Resurrection could not happen more than once, thereby nipping in the bud earlier efforts to identify the Doctrine of the Resurrection with recurrent cycles?

Mixing with the entries upon Swift in his manuscript-book are notes upon a 'change of control'. 'D—— came first, more anxious to speak than I to listen – for I am not yet ready. He confirmed the accounts I am about to give of the state after Beatitude, at least in principle, but was vague and uncertain. . . .' And on 30 April: 'new spirit touched the cat which lay in bed and said "soft, soft" and then that D—— was soft but he was rough. He touched my beard more than once and said, "rough, rough", a "dog".'

He was again 'astraddle on the dolphin's mire and blood'. The second of his 'Byzantium' poems was sketched out before he came down from the hill which overlooks the bay of Santa Margherita to Portofino. 'Describe Byzantium as it is in the system towards the end of the first Christian millennium. A walking mummy, flames in the street corners where the soul is purified, birds of hammered gold singing in the golden trees.'

> The unpurged images of day recede;
> The Emperor's drunken soldiery are abed;
> Night resonance recedes, night-walkers' song
> After great cathedral gong;

> A starlit or a moonlit dome disdains
> All that man is,
> All mere complexities,
> The fury and the mire of human veins.

It was thought wise not to let him go north until summer; through June days he lay on the balcony of Via Americhe with some book of Swift's, and in the evening read to his children and taught them chess. '... We are all brown like old meerschaum pipes ... and oh how intolerable *The Lay of the Last Minstrel,* and yet the magic book of Melrose makes them put up their faces side by side at the edge of my bed ...' he wrote to Mrs Shakespear.

His first portrait since his hair had turned from brindled grey to white was painted by Augustus John soon after he got home. Gogarty brought poet and painter together at Renvyle in Connemara, and John expressed the desire to do a 'serious portrait'. 'And today', Yeats noted in his diary (21 June),

I have been standing in front of the hotel mirror, noticing certain lines about my mouth and chin ... and have wondered if John would not select those very lines. ... In those lines I see the marks of recent illness, marks of time, growing irresolution, perhaps some faults that I have long dreaded, but then my character is so little myself that all my life it has thwarted me. It has affected my poems, my true self, no more than the character of a dancer affects the movements of a dance.*

5

He sat in the open air for the portrait with his feet in a fur bag and his magnificent hair blown over his forehead by the wind. John then decamped to the Galway races, leaving him at the mercy of a rich Socialist lady, who despised Spengler and thought that the world must become better, mainly because the English Labour Party was there. 'Mrs ——', he

---

* He drew this distinction between his 'practical' and 'poetical' personality in a much earlier note-book; it was therefore not suggested to him by his reading of Croce.

wrote, 'has turned up, which makes me curse all expensive hotels, you never know whom you will meet. ... Peace has gone from the sunset and a new turbulence come upon the sea.' These lines were found on his blotting-paper:

> I learned to think in a man's way
> And women's toys forget.
> None learned like you that think today
> Like the first man you met.

He went on from Renvyle to Coole, and in an interval joined his family on an excursion to Rosses Point. Henry Middleton was still living, but this time Yeats did not call at Elsinore.* He spoke of him, however, and Anne and Michael, their curiosity aroused, made an attempt upon the privacy of the eccentric recluse. They got through the barbed wire but were turned away at the hall-door by the garden-boy.

Yeats's Swift play, with the scene laid in a modern Dublin lodging-house in the room of a medium, was finished at Coole. Perfect alike in what it says and does not say, *The Words upon the Window-Pane* was performed at the Abbey on 17 November 1930. Following it came the original and penetrating essay in which is drawn the parallel and contrast between Vico's view of history and Swift's, and in the eighteenth-century Irishmen – Swift, Berkeley, Goldsmith and Burke – are found four great minds in resistance to what Yeats calls 'Whiggery'.

> Whether they knew or not,
> Goldsmith and Burke, Swift and the Bishop of Cloyne
> All hated Whiggery; but what is Whiggery?
> A levelling, rancorous, rational sort of mind
> That never looked out of the eye of a saint
> Or out of drunkard's eye.†

He was vastly delighted, abused Whiggery in complete innocence‡ and returned to the theme again and again.

---

* *Vide supra*, pp. 21–2.   † 'The Seven Sages'.
‡ It is fair to remember the hostility of both Swift and Berkeley to Newton, whom Macaulay calls 'the glory of the Whig party'.

That Swift foresaw the 'ruin to come, Democracy, Rousseau, the French Revolution' is the theme of Yeats's essay. By liberty – 'this liberty bought with so much silence, and served all through life with so much eloquence' – Swift meant not the rule of majorities, or freedom of speech, but the right of a people to express itself as it would through such men as had won or inherited general consent: the doctrine of Burke in his *Appeal from the New Whigs to the Old*. It seems to Yeats that Swift's *Contests and Dissensions between the Nobles and Commons in Athens and Rome* leads to Burke so clearly as to give Ireland a claim to have recreated conservative thought in the one as much as in the other.*

The whole essay betrays Yeats's desperate anxiety to provide Ireland with an intellectual background, distinct from that of England and also from that of Catholicism. 'Had we a thinking nation,' he remarks in his manuscript-book, 'the Discourse with its law of nations might be for us what Vico is to the Italians.' Contempt for Locke is for him, as for Schelling and de Maistre, the beginning of knowledge, and he makes Locke the typical English thinker, heralding the Industrial Revolution.

> God took the spinning-jenny
> Out of his side.

The 'saint or drunkard's eye' of the poem against Whiggery is a very Catholic (Roman) notion, yet it is notable that Yeats does not seek an ally in the Church for his 'Conservative' thought. A little acquaintance with Irish history may have suggested to him that alliances between Church and aristocracy cannot be lasting. Clericalism frequently produces radicalism (the 'levelling, rancorous, rational sort of mind') as its seed, and aristocracy liberal thought – even against

* There is this reference to Burke in Yeats's manuscript-book: 'Only tolerable in his impassioned moments'. Austin Clarke has noted in Yeats's later work that 'tremulous Anglo-Irish eloquence which one finds in Burke and Grattan'.

their wills. A Church is inclined to favour democracy (because democracy is more credulous), an aristocracy will patronize free thought (because speculative freedom makes people bother less about their individual political rights).*

6

From Swift Yeats returned to an old manuscript, his play on the theme of the Resurrection: young men, a Syrian, a Greek and a Hebrew talking; apostles in the next room over-whelmed by the Crucifixion; Christ, newly arisen, passing silently through. He recast the work, and later added the song ('I saw a staring virgin stand') for the unfolding and folding of the curtain, which greatly enhanced the dramatic tension. The first sketch of *Resurrection*, more dialogue than play, and intended for drawing-room rather than for the theatre, dated from 1925. It had then been read out at 82 Merrion Square to a few people, a Cabinet Minister among them, who were frigid. However, in 1934, the play not only took its place in the volume entitled *Wheels and Butterflies* with *Fighting the Waves*, *The Cat and the Moon* and *The Words upon the Window-Pane*, but was performed in Dublin without any ill effect.

He found the central situation in some book by Sir William Crookes, who relates that he once felt the pulse of a materialized spirit. 'What if there is always something that lies outside knowledge, outside order? ... What if the irra-tional return?' the Syrian is made to say. The thought in *The Hour-Glass* recurs, that 'belief comes from shock'. 'The first nation', runs another entry in the manuscript-book, 'which can possess the three convictions, God, Freedom and Immortality, affirmed by Kant as *free powers*, will control the moral energies of the soul.'

It is, I think, because these convictions must return as free powers that I feel, as so many feel, an unreality in T. S. Eliot's

---

* Catholic Ireland was far more 'liberal' in thought at the end of the aristocratic eighteenth century than it now is.

revival of seventeenth-century divines, in the French neo-Thomist movement. In the time of Swift and Burke and Coleridge the habitual symbols seemed necessary to order. To-day the man who finds belief in God, the soul, immortality . . . must above all things free his energies from all prepossessions not imposed by the beliefs themselves. The Fascist, the Bolshevist seeks to turn the idea of the State into free powers and both have reached . . . some shadow of that intense energy which shall come upon those of whom I speak. When I speak of the three convictions and of the idea of the State I do not mean any metaphysics or economic theory. That belief which I call free powers is free because we cannot distinguish between the things believed in and the belief.

He had been told that the young men of 'the garrets and cellars' were either Communist or Catholic, or both. Here he hit upon something not generally acknowledged in Dublin. Irish Catholics have a Protestant element in them that nothing can eradicate. They consider themselves entitled to hold whatever *political* opinions they choose – even the most subversive, such as the Church must formally denounce. There are many truly devout Catholics in Ireland who maintain that they are Communists, swear by Marx, and would put Socialism into practice tomorrow if they had the power.

The prefaces to the various plays in *Wheels and Butterflies* show how anxious Yeats was to catch the ear of the garrets and cellars. His attitude towards the younger generation had greatly altered; his public personality seemed to expand and develop with his poetic style. He did not rid himself of the studied manner. But now he wanted to be approachable; perhaps Ezra Pound's breezy style and downright transatlantic speech opened his eyes to the fact that the world had changed. Gone were the *savants*, the *salons*, the *cercles*. Poets like T. S. Eliot were surrounded by the young, the unknown, the coming men. Yeats reacted to this rapidly and lost no time in making contact with the younger writers in Dublin. He made F. R. Higgins and Walter Starkie Directors of the Abbey Theatre, and bestowed publicly his benediction

on Frank O'Connor and on Seán O'Faoláin, stating to the
stupefaction of his listeners at a banquet that 'the future of
Irish literature was with the realistic novel'. His commenda-
tion of O'Connor was the more remarkable, since O'Connor
had attacked him fiercely in the columns of AE's *Irish
Statesman*. In this connection Cecil Salkeld writes to me:

> I remember bringing Liam O'Flaherty to one of Yeats' Mon-
> day evenings. I did this with some trepidation; O'Flaherty was
> still struggling for fame and was passionately eager to take
> offence at anything resembling patronage. Yeats was not only
> most courteous but assumed a humility which was almost discon-
> certing. When we rose to go Yeats accompanied us down the
> stairs, saying to O'Flaherty: 'So good of you famous young men
> to look up an old man. . . .' O'Flaherty crimsoned and stammered
> some equally humble reply. The incident shed an interesting
> light on both characters.*

7

Early in November 1930 Yeats took a short English holiday
in which the principal event was a day at Boar's Hill with
John Masefield, who planned a Festival in his music-room to
celebrate the thirtieth anniversary of his first meeting with
the Irish poet. Yeats wrote from the Savile Club to his wife
(8 November),

> Yesterday I met de la Mare at Lady Ottoline's and here is the
> upshot of my talk on a metaphor of Lady Ottoline's:

> > We that had such thought,
> > That such deeds have done,
> > Must ramble on – thinned out
> > Like milk on a flat stone.

> I had a rather moving experience at Masefield's ... he made a
> long eulogy of my work and myself, very embarrassing, and then
> five girls with beautiful voices recited my lyrics for three-quarters
> of an hour. I do not think the whole audience could hear, but
> to me it was strangely moving and overwhelming.

Lady Gregory was now in her eightieth year, and it was
evident that she was near the end of her course. That he

---

*For Yeats's admiration of O'Flaherty's work *vide supra*, p. 384.

might be within call of her, Yeats remained in Ireland for the winter of 1930–31, nor was he any the worse for a winter at home. The Dublin flat being no longer to his liking, nor to his wife's, they found on the hill of Killiney a furnished house, with a view over a eucalyptus grove to the bay of Killiney, ten miles south of Dublin. Here Yeats revised early poems for a collected edition and wrote his essay on Berkeley. 'I have a great sense of abundance', he told Mrs Shakespear. 'Months of re-writing! What happiness!'

The flat at Rapallo was let to Ezra Pound's father, and the children came back from abroad. Later in 1931, when Mrs Yeats sought for a school near Dublin for Michael, Yeats, who was then at Coole, wrote an imaginary letter to a schoolmaster which Lady Gregory thought should be put in verse. It ran:

My son is now between 9 and 10 and should begin Greek at once and be taught by the Berlitz method that he may read as soon as possible that most exciting of all stories the Odyssey from the landing in Ithaca to the end. Grammar should come when the need comes. As he grows older he will read me the Greek lyric poets and I will talk to him about Plato. Do not teach him one word of Latin. The Roman people were the classic decadence, their literature form without matter. They destroyed Milton, the French seventeenth and our eighteenth century. . . . Teach him mathematics as thoroughly as his capacity permits. I know that Bertrand Russell must, seeing that he is such a featherhead, be wrong about everything but as I have no mathematics I cannot prove it. I do not want my son to be as helpless. Do not teach him one word of geography. He has lived on the Alps, crossed a number of rivers and when he is fifteen I shall urge him to climb the Sugar-loaf. Do not teach him a word of history. I shall take him to Shakespeare history plays, if a commercialised theatre permit, and give him all the historical novels of Dumas and if he cannot pick up the rest he is a fool. Don't teach him one word of science as he can get all he wants in the newspaper, and in any case it is no job for a gentleman. If you teach him Greek and mathematics and do not let him forget the French and German he already knows you will do for him all one man can do for another. If he wants to learn Irish after he is well founded in Greek let him – it will clear his eyes of the Latin miasma. If you will not do what I say, whether the curriculum or your own will restrain, and my son comes from school a smatterer like his father may your soul lie chained on the Red Sea bottom.

However, when he went to see the school (Church of Ireland) that was found for Michael, Yeats acted the part of the conventional father. He took the lead with the Warden's wife, Mrs Sowby, who was remarkably impressed by the practical tenor of his inquiries on sanitation, ventilation, heat and so on, until Mrs Yeats, who was walking behind with the Warden, called out, 'Don't mind him, he is only showing off'.

*

In May 1931, Yeats was again in Oxford, this time to receive the degree of Doctor of Letters from the University. The Public Orator, Dr A. B. Poynton, expressed his claims as follows:

Si id tantum hodie mihi proponerem, ut vos docerem adesse eximium sermonis et vincti numeris et soluti artificem, qui quod in litteris esset optimum optima sui parte excoluisset. Vix satis haberem illud Praemium testari, doctarum frontium inter praemia nobilissimum, quod ob eas laudes omnium gentium scriptoribus propositum vates hic Hibernus ante hos novem annos est adeptus. Conarer homo a philosophando alienus explicare qua mentis ratione animam suam praeparaverit ad Veritatis semet ipsam retegentis imagines excipiendas; qua severitate res ac personas veras primus ita tractaverit, ut quidquid finxit ad explendam animae humanae cognitionem faciat. Nunc autem cum vir ad vos redeat quem aliquamdiu nostra nemora et saltus tenuerunt, non ut advenam eum praesentem laudare, sed ut amicum reducem familiarius alloqui mihi liceat. Primum igitur poetae gratulamur qui, postquam ex Parnasso nostro elapsus est, ita pinnis suis calceos mutaverit, ut in senatu Hiberno vocem pro aequitate mittendo vel M. Tullio persuadere posset facilius ex poeta senatorem quam ex consule poetam evadere. Deinde senatorem, qui Heliconis ex saltu, propriis Iernae suae floribus nebulisque amicto, coronam detulerit quae clara per gentes hominum clueat, monemus ne Musa eius diutius quam sit necesse Theatro suo Eblanensi desit, neu rerum civilium inter strepitus ad vespertilionum nenias *Celticis* in *crepusculis* volitantium obsurdescat. Iterum Druida Druidarum suorum prisca carmina subtilitate Platonica, lepore Hiberno, simplicitate Heliconia contingat: iterum lyram modulatus nos secum ad insulam avehat quoquo velit in lacu latentem, ubi una *fabas* et fabulas *seramus.* Denique laureato hederam deferentes optamus ut studia human-itatis, quorum ipse apud populares suos semper fuit hortator, antistes, fax, in patria, quam anima sua dilectiorem habet, magis magisque floreant. Feliciter certe Hibernia adepta suas leges carminis Hiberni alitem in consilium vocavit. Praesento vobis Musarum famulum Willelmum Butler Yeats, ut admittatur ad gradum Doctoris in litteris honoris causa.

In August, writing to Lady Gregory, Yeats announced a new acquaintance, who 'has absorbed my vitality'. This was Dr M. M. Rossi, teacher of philosophy in Bologna and Naples, author of books on Berkeley and on Swift, who spent the summer of 1931 in Ireland. Rossi spoke English copiously, never hesitated for a word, but had never heard English spoken until he came to Ireland. 'We shall send him back to Italy with a faultless Dublin accent', said Yeats. Rossi was invited to Coole for a fortnight, and won the favour of Lady Gregory, who asked him to cut his initials on the bark of the famous copper beech (he must have been the last of her guests to do so). He writes to me as follows about the colloquies at Coole on the circularity of time and Yeats's various rationalizations of his poetic experience.

Even now, after eight years, philosophical ideas come to me not as so many words but as dim shapes projected in a unique landscape against the retiring whiteness of the house at Coole. The vast circle of grass, interrupted only by some moss-grown steps leading up towards the house, the semicircular sweep of the drive which loses itself in the dark dampness of overhanging trees, and Yeats striding patiently with bowed head and inquir-ing about philosophy.

There remains only this memory now to connect me with the happiest moments of my whole life – the few weeks at Coole in the shadow of Yeats and Lady Gregory. Poetry till then was only a deeply-felt pleasure. . . . His face, his words, his silences taught me that it had to be the atmosphere and the blood to be something . . .

Nowhere have I met a more eager interest in metaphysics. Men usually follow only their own thoughts through philosophy. At the end they find themselves just as they were before. But Yeats asked *to know*. He was searching again and again for an explanation. You could not misunderstand his metaphysical interest for a pose. He sought occasions for thinking, for pitting his brain against metaphysics. Perhaps Philistine critics who found it strange that he broke up some commonplace conversation exclaiming suddenly: 'The air is full of the beat of wings' – will console themselves by thinking that there is really *no* need for a poet to drivel metaphysics. . . .

He had no philosophy to offer by chapter and verse. He offered poems – and asked for philosophical theories, for an explanation. He wanted to know how a philosopher sees the world. How his poetical problems could be shaped as logical problems. He asked and listened and asked and listened again. His slow voice which he had deliberately trained on the psaltery, might have seemed pontifical. But he was not proud of himself. He was proud of poetry, of the great things to which he gave voice.

Basically he did not feel philosophy as an abstruse speculation nor was he attracted to it by its technical difficulties. He wanted to solve his problems. He wanted to come in clear about his own mind. He wanted to connect thing and image; to prove that the poet's expression goes further than usual vision, reaches – beyond sensation and word – the intimate transempirical nature of the world, to assure himself that the poet's way of dealing with reality is in fact a metaphysical description of it. . . . The problems evoked by philosophy enhanced and justified the Sibylline quality Yeats saw under the painted veil of words.

On his return to Italy Dr Rossi published a little book called *Viaggio in Irlanda*, and at the time of Lady Gregory's death I translated his chapter on Coole, a beautiful tribute of homage, for a Dublin newspaper.* This and a version which I made of Rossi's 'An Introduction to Swift' brought me several letters from Yeats. In one of these he said:

* The *Viaggio* was subsequently published at the Cuala under the title *Pilgrimage to the West*.

Your translation gives the impression that you are struggling with an over eloquent original, which our language cannot do justice to. I suggest that when you translate Rossi, 'sea' should never become 'ocean' or its 'blue' become 'azure' or 'a wave' 'a billow'. . . . I should have warned you that Eliot, who is himself the most typical figure of the reaction, would refuse the essay on that account. Think of his bare poetry. His position would be compromised by its inclusion in *The Criterion*.

But he was keenly interested in Rossi's *Swift, the Egoist*. 'You have made me for the first time understand Gulliver', he wrote to him. '. . . I do not accept your description of Swift as an egoist yet that description has led you to certain truths of great value: I think of him rather as a solitary, who felt no need to explain or justify his religious conviction just because he was a solitary.'

8

It was now toil for Lady Gregory to go from one room to another:

> Sound of a stick upon the floor, a sound
> From somebody that toils from chair to chair.

But she remained to the last by the side of Irish literature, and it was in her house that Yeats and George Russell discussed the project of an Academy of Letters which should carry on the tradition of their movement, make known the views of Irish authors on such questions as censorship and call attention to the respect due to the intellectual and poetic quality in the national life. Bernard Shaw consented to become President of the Academy, and George Russell drew up the rules and the constitution.

In the last stages of Lady Gregory's illness Yeats was constantly at Coole. There he read during the winter of 1931–2 all Balzac again 'with all my old delight', and *Prometheus Unbound* for the third time. He was also busy with a preface for the autobiography of an Indian monk, named Shri Purohit Swami, an Indian religious man, met with in London, who had reawakened his old sentiment of

Hinduism.* In poetry he made additions to the 'Crazy Jane' series ('Words for Music Perhaps') and fashioned some of the exquisite elegiac passages of 'Coole Park' and 'Coole and Ballylee'. 'I want to exorcise that slut, Crazy Jane, whose language has become unendurable', he wrote to his wife. The Crazy Jane poems, it may be said, were founded more or less upon some stories he remembered about the conversation of an old woman who satirized her neighbours, and whose masterpiece was a description of how the meanness of a shopkeeper's wife about a glass of porter made her so despair of the human race that she got drunk.

3.2.32 *To Mrs W. B. Yeats*

... I am turning the introductory verses to Lady Gregory's 'Coole' (Cuala) into a poem of some length – various sections with more or less symbolic matter. Yesterday I wrote an account of the sudden ascent of a swan – a symbol of inspiration I think.† ... Can you send me Balzac *Harlot's Progress* – Vol. II. I have just finished Vol. I. I want to go right through Balzac again : he has fascinated me as he did thirty years ago. In some ways I see more in him than I did thirty years ago. He is the voice of the last subjective phases, of individualism in its exaltation. When I read of Lucian's [*sic*] return to his native town and his brief triumph there, I see Wilde in his manner of speech and remember that Wilde was a Balzac scholar, perhaps a Balzac disciple – so perhaps were we all. Yet his world was closer to reality that a Goya caricature.

8.2.32. *To Same*

... I have just had the first 3rd of that Indian monk's autobiography – a masterpiece. A book the like of which does not exist, written with the greatest possible simplicity – Mahatmas, cows, children, miracles, a sort of cinema film to the glory of God. I have agreed to write the preface but have urged that Sturge Moore is the proper person.

* *An Indian Monk, his Life and Adventures,* by Shri Purohit Swami, with Introduction by W. B. Yeats. (Macmillan, 1932.)
    † 'At sudden thunder of the mounting swan
      I turned about and looked where branches break
      The glittering reaches of the flooded lake.'

9

On 16 February Yeats went up to Dublin from Coole to
record his vote at the historic election which brought Mr de
Valera and the Fianna Fail party into office, with a mandate
to abolish the oath of allegiance to the British monarch.
Yeats had no objection to the removal of the oath, but he
thoroughly disliked the social outlook of de Valera's followers, and his vote was cast for the defeated side.* Presently
hints reached him that a number of Irish-American societies
were putting pressure on the Government to exercise a censorship at the Abbey. Whereupon he sought an interview
with Mr de Valera, having first stated publicly that he would
prefer to forgo the subsidy rather than permit any such
interference. A passage in a letter to an English friend
records the impression made on him by the Irish leader,
whom he now met for the first time.

I was impressed by his simplicity and honesty though we
differed throughout. It was a curious experience, each recognised
the other's point of view so completely. I had gone there full of
suspicion, but my suspicion vanished at once. You must not
believe what you read in the English papers. They decide moral
questions in the interest of their parties and express their decisions with a complacency that rouses other nations to fury. Here
I think we are generally troubled about right and wrong, we do
not decide easily. The hungry man is nearer to the saint than
the full man. 'A hair divides the false and true' – one should
never be satisfied in any controversy until one has found the
hair – one is liable to think it must look like a ship's cable.

How right Yeats was! In England the mechanism of
civilization has worked towards the obliteration of reality
from public affairs. In Ireland, on the contrary, as Yeats
realized, only realities count. There is never a question of
Tory and Whig – not even of Free State *versus* de Valera.
It is always a question of abstract principle. The briefest
excursion into Irish politics will convince the doubter. Parti-

* Lady Gregory, however, veered towards Mr de Valera's party at
the end.

tion, the Land Question and Industrialization are fought out on this basis and on this alone.

The formation of the Academy was publicly announced at a meeting in Dublin on 18 September 1932, when Lennox Robinson read out the letter, signed by Bernard Shaw and Yeats, which had been addressed to each of those invited to become members. The last was inclusive enough. The 'Celtic' poets were there alongside the 'Cork Realists' of 1910, Gaelic modernists like F. R. Higgins and Frank O'Connor, St John Ervine and Peadar O'Donnell, two Northerners, and Edith Somerville, the 'Big House' novelist. George Moore ignored the invitation, and refusals on various grounds came from Douglas Hyde, Stephen MacKenna and James Joyce. Joyce's refusal was the chief disappointment. He thanked Yeats and Shaw for their 'kind words', and recalled that it was thirty years since Yeats had first held out to him a 'helping hand', but added that his case being as it was, and probably would be, he saw no reason why his name should have arisen at all in connection with such an Academy. On the other hand, T. E. Shaw – Lawrence of Arabia – was simply and unaffectedly delighted at being invited to be a mere Associate.*
He telegraphed his acceptance, and followed up the telegram with several letters. Those familiar with Lawrence's recently published correspondence will have noticed his almost morbid modesty in connection with his literary work: and what gratified him most on this occasion was that Yeats should appeal to him on the ground of nationality. He had but once set eyes on Yeats – in Oxford. 'I wanted then', he wrote, 'to call the street to attention (for lack of power to make the sun blaze out appropriately, instead) but fortunately did nothing. ... I am Irish, and it has been a chance to admit it publicly – but it touches me very deeply that you should think anything I have done or been to justify the honour ...'

---

* The work of 'Associates' was classified as 'less Irish' than that of full members. But the distinction caused some heart-burnings, and one of those invited to be an Associate remained convinced that Yeats elaborated the whole project in order to insult him.

10

After Lady Gregory's death Yeats felt that his long associations with Galway were broken. She had been his fellow and mainstay in all his labours for Ireland for nearly forty years; these labours were in the main crowned with success, but to lose such a comrade was a very heavy blow. Though he had known this would come, he was deeply affected by the dismantling of the old house.

> Where fashion or mere fantasy decrees
> Man shifts about – all that great glory spent –
> Like some poor Arab tribesman and his tent.
> We were the last romantics – chose for theme
> Traditional sanctity and loveliness;
> Whatever's written in what poets name
> The book of the people.

He wrote to Mrs Shakespear (31 May 1932):

You will have known why I have not written, for you will have seen Lady Gregory's death in the papers. I had come to Dublin for a few days to see about Abbey business. On Sunday night at 11.30 I had a telephone message from her solicitors who had been trying to find me all day but she had died in the night. She was her indomitable self to the last, but of that I will not write or not now. . . .

A queer Dublin sculptor dressed like a workman . . . came the day after Lady Gregory's death 'to pay his respects'. He walked from room to room then stopped at the mezzotints and engravings of those under or with whom . . . the Gregorys have served, Fox, Burke and so on, and after standing silent said 'All the nobility of earth'. I felt he did not mean it for that room alone but for lost tradition. How much of my own verses has been but the repetition of those words.

The letter announced a new move on Yeats's own part. For some time his wife had been house-hunting outside Dublin. She had now found exactly what they wanted. This was a small house with a well-stocked garden called Riversdale, a mile beyond the village of Rathfarnham, on rising ground, very convenient to town. The family was scarcely installed when Yeats decided to go on a last lecture tour in America, taking Alan Duncan – the son of an old friend at the Arts Club – as his secretary and 'nurse'. They sailed on the Europa at the end of October. Yeats had a contract for a minimum of twenty lectures, and intended to apply the remuneration to improvements at Riversdale. There was a tumbledown house in the yard which, if put in order, could serve as a perfect playhouse for the children. He also hoped to raise funds for the Irish Academy of Letters by a series of drawing-room lectures.

Mr Alber Wickes had charge of the arrangements for the tour. He saw to the poet's comfort, and never before had Yeats travelled in such luxury. The Abbey company was on tour, and Yeats wrote to his wife on 28 October after its appearance in New York:

... I have just come from the theatre where *The Words upon the Window-Pane* was played before a vast audience, every seat sold and people standing. It was followed by the *Playboy* but I was tired and came back here with Alan who must hurry back in a few minutes to see Mrs Martin who entertained us at Lakeview in Chicago. ... I made a speech at the end of my play.

He wrote from Maine on 4 November:

I picture to myself that little house in the yard put in perfect order, and a play-room there. ... I had a charming week-end at Mrs Harrison Williams' but I think I told you. A great house by the sea with fine pictures, great gardens and a large covered tennis court and a swimming pool – yes, I remember I told you.* Did I describe the room by the swimming pool? A great high room made out of pointed arches covered with silver leaf, fine frescoes over the roof by some Spaniard, Goya-like things made to tone with the general silver and brown.

Yeats's recuperative powers were evident in the way he met the strain of the tour. He fulfilled every engagement, lecturing sometimes twice a day. During short respites from

* He had not.

the desperate routine he read D. H. Lawrence's *Women in Love*, 'a beautiful enigmatic book.' 'I feel in sympathy with him', he wrote, 'as I do not with Virginia Woolf.' From Cincinnati he went for a couple of days to Mr Howe's, where James Stephens was his fellow guest, and at Toronto he gave a day to visiting a Mrs St Lawrence whom he had played with as a child in Ireland. Henry Ford provided him with a motor-car (the same car and driver as had been lent to Mr Winston Churchill); but on cold nights he would refuse to keep the driver waiting. 'Don't wait for me,' he would say, 'I will get a taxi home.' Several times he was characterized as a 'regular fellow', and he felt much flattered.

He wrote from Boston in December:

I have had my first cold. Dr Crandon cured me with tabloids and whiskey. . . . Cold the result of the first snowfall of the winter. Séance very remarkable. They have been experimenting with two separate wooden rings made out of different woods which the spirits are to lock into each other.

There follows a long description of these rings and previous séances.

Dr Patrick MacCartan and Judge Campbell * organized the drawing-room lectures for the Academy, which commenced about Christmas-time. Typical Irish-Americans were still asking questions about *The Playboy*, but he soothed and conciliated, and within a month collected £700 for the institution. Ernest Boyd, the Padraic Colums and other Irish literary exiles of the 'canary-bird' period saw much of him and renewed an old hero-worship. He was physically beautiful, his mind at his best, and age had softened him to his great advantage: his charm, dignity and artistic disinterestedness were not obscured by affectation and petulance. Ernest Boyd recalls that he even went so far as to recite 'The Salley Gardens' – one of his early poems he had at one time been wont to belittle.

* John Quinn had died some years before.

19

Riversdale

The miniature estate – 'The Blueshirts' – Dejection and
recovery – Seventy years of age

——

All his happier dreams came true –
A small old house, wife, daughter, son,
Grounds where plum and cabbage grew
Poets and wits about him drew;
'What then?' sang Plato's ghost. 'What then?'

I

FROM Riversdale the road continues in easy ascent towards
the mountains and gives many views of the bay. Here,
though so close to Dublin, Yeats was in the midst of scenes
truly pleasing to the eye of contemplation – farms and winding streams and old demesnes. The previous tenant of his
small neat house, some good garden-lover, had planned and
nursed and brought to perfection the four acres upon which
it stood. Nothing was missing from the miniature estate;
neither orchard nor velvet croquet lawn (crocket in Yeats's
odd spelling), neither rose nor well-stocked kitchen garden,
neither herbaceous border nor little field.

The rooms were small, and the two at the right of the hall
were turned into one for a study and sitting-room. This long
narrow room had at one corner a glass door which gave
access to the conservatory, where the canaries lived, and to
the fruit garden. Book-shelves filled most of the lemon-yellow
walls, leaving space for a landscape by Robert Gregory and
one or two of Jack Yeats's pictures. Sato's sword lay across
the great oak writing-table. Above the study was the poet's
bedroom; one of its windows looked to the mountains, the

other, where a meat-bone hung for the tomtits, across plum and apple orchard.

Yeats had always dreamed of owning just such a small house and fine garden, but coming to Riversdale so soon after Lady Gregory's death, he was at first heart-broken for the great rooms and great woods of Coole, the house he had loved above all other houses. He wrote to Mrs Shakespear (21 February 1933):

No, I am not coming over for your birthday. I do not think your invitation is pressing enough, besides I have just had the influenza and do not get up till midday. . . .
Have you read *Louis Lambert* of recent years? – I have just re-read it and am thinking of making 'Michael Robartes' write an annotation or even of doing it myself. Perhaps *Faust, Louis Lambert, Séraphita* and *Axël* are our sacred books, man self-sufficing and eternal, though *Axël* is but a spectacle, an echo of the others, as Louis Lambert might have been of that saying of Swedenborg that the sexual intercourse of angels is a conflagration of the whole being . . .*

He played croquet with the children, and started to give Anne, who was artistic, lessons from an expurgated Shakespeare. Michael was in reaction against the literary traditions of the family. His interests were in history and politics. As a little boy he had suddenly announced one day at the luncheon-table that he 'hated poetry'. This was understood to be a revenge upon his father for having passed him unnoticed on the stairs.

Words for Music Perhaps and Other Poems (Cuala) was published while Yeats was in America, and on his return home he found congratulatory letters from John Masefield, Gordon Bottomley and others, full of praise, and there was also in his correspondence an offer of an honorary degree at Cambridge.† Later in the year the contents of this volume were included in *The Winding Stair and Other Poems*, where may be studied the penultimate phase of Yeats's style, the

* *Vide* a year or two later 'Supernatural Songs'.
† He took the degree in June.

'Babylonian turbulence' chastened away into miracles of verbal delicacy. In 'Crazy Jane' and 'A Woman Young and Old' appear occasional traces of the pre-*Tower* Yeats, revised and modernized into something strangely unfamiliar. 'A Last Confession' has the brightness and sprightliness of 'There is a Queen in China' – with a new tenderness and poignancy born of experience. 'Her Vision in the Wood' is Dantesque in its sombre magnificence. 'Parting' echoes Romeo and Juliet:

> No, night's bird and love's
> Bids all true lovers rest,
> While his loud song reproves
> The murderous stealth of day.

while 'Mad as the Mist and Snow' is an incantation seemingly meaningless; rhyme and rhythm, already suggesting his last ballads, force an emotional coherence that convinces the reader beyond reason. 'The Crazed Moon' brings Shelley up to date; and for the charming poem for Lady Gregory's grand-daughter Yeats has for once been in consultation with an orthodox religious man:

> Only God, my dear
> Could love you for yourself alone
> And not your yellow hair.

Mrs Edmund Dulac wrote to him:

Edmund is writing to thank you for your book and the honour of its dedication. But I must write too. The personal dedication gives me greater pride than anything that has ever happened to me of that nature or could happen. But you must know how we feel about you. I am so happy to be linked with Edmund in your friendship. And the words are more than pleasing. ... It is good to see that you have come thro' the Tower and discovered another passion on the other side. This must be very exciting news for all writers – indeed all men. No other poet I have ever heard of has done this. One 'passion of life' they always have of course or they would not be poets; to go on with rich life and vigour and fullness of power to a third is I think unknown except to you.

2

The later contents of *The Winding Stair* dated from about
the time of Lady Gregory's death. After Lady Gregory's
death Yeats wrote no new verse for several months, and he
began to ask himself whether the subconscious drama which
was his imaginative life had closed with Coole. But he also
suffered under endless distractions, one of his employments
being the defence of the Academy against the criticism of
'Catholic Action' and the other nothing less than the construction of a Social theory 'with an ex-Minister, a philosopher and an eminent lawyer' for use against Communism,
which was said to be growing in Ireland as a result of the
toleration extended by the Government to the Irish Republican Army. 'If I were a young man,' he wrote, 'I would
welcome five years of conflict for re-creating unity among
the educated classes and would force de Valera and ministers
in all probability to repudiate the ignorance that has in part
put them into power.' At the same time, he began to take a
greater interest in affairs outside Ireland than he had hitherto done, declaring in another of his letters to Mrs Shakespear
that he had 'rejected' modern England and modern France:
'Europe belongs to Dante and the Witches' Sabbath, not to
Newton'.

He came back to verse by way of politics, and in a moving
poem, 'At Parnell's Funeral' ('Through Jonathan Swift's
dark grove he passed and there Plucked bitter wisdom that
enriched his blood'), he rhymed passages from a lecture which
he had given in America on four moments in Irish history.
To paraphrase one of his avowals, he foresaw public life
moving from violence to violence or from violence to apathy,
and Parliament disgracing and debauching those who entered it, men of letters living like outlaws in their own country. The reign of ignorance would be broken only when some
Government sought unity of culture not less than economic
unity, welding for the purpose museum, school and learned
institution. The Government and party which should under-

take this work would need marching men. Force would be required (the logic of fanaticism, whether in a woman or a mob being drawn from a premise protected by ignorance and therefore irrefutable), and it would promise not this or that measure but a way of life, a discipline.*

A frequent visitor at Riversdale was a certain Captain Dermot MacManus, a student of Eastern mysticism who had fought in the Great War, and then in the Irish Civil War, and spoke with authority upon military matters. Captain MacManus was a member of the Army Comrades Association which in April 1933 adopted the uniform of the blue shirt, and was remodelled as a civil unarmed body pledged to give disciplined service to the country. The movement appealed to the more conservative and orderly sections of the population, and it seemed for a moment that something like a counter-revolution, which would fuse Ireland into a nation, was on foot. Yeats, who (unlike many of his collaborators) never grew cynical or despairing of Ireland as a nation, invited the leader of the Blueshirts, General O'Duffy, to his house, and expatiated on Hegel and Spengler. The interlocutors were somewhat at cross-purposes, but the General left with a promise of a song for his men.

23.7.33. *To Mrs Shakespear*

The great secret is now out, – a convention of Blueshirts – 'National Guards' – have received their new leader with the Fascist salute, and the new leader announces Reform of Parliament as his business. When I wrote to you the Fascist organiser of the Blueshirts had told me that he was about to bring to see me the man he had selected for leader that I might talk my anti-democratic philosophy. I was ready, for I had just rewritten for the seventh time the part of *A Vision* that deals with the future. ... Italy, Poland, Germany, then perhaps Ireland. Doubtless I shall hate it (though not so much as I hate Irish democracy) but it is September, and we must not behave like the gay young sparks of May and June. Swinburne calls September 'the month of the long decline of roses'.

*Commentary on 'Three Songs' in *The King of the Great Clock Tower* (American edition).

Presently the police began to harry and oppress the Blue-shirts, and this gave such importance to the movement that Mr Cosgrave surrendered the leadership of the Opposition to General O'Duffy; a new party called United Ireland was formed, for which Yeats wrote 'Three Songs' to the tune of O'Donnell Abú.

> Those fanatics all that we do would undo;
> Down the fanatic, down the clown;
> Down, down, hammer them down,
> Down to the tune of O'Donnell Abú.

He was disappointed and was also surprised – it is a proof of the credulity which was often observed in him – when politics went on very much as before, the Blueshirts as dema-gogic as the rest. Someone had said to Yeats that the new party had, or was about to have, or might be persuaded to have, some such aim as his. Finding that it neither would, nor could, he rewrote his songs increasing their fantasy, their extravagance, so that no party could sing them.

3

The philosophic poem 'Meru', written after reading *The Holy Mountain*,* and rather Audenesque in certain lines ('Egypt and Greece good-bye, and good-bye Rome'), came spontaneously. Then, perturbed once more by his Muse's absence, he wrote the prose dialogue of *The King of the Great Clock Tower* that she might come back to him with lyrics for its imaginary people. It was at this time (early in 1934) that he heard quite by chance of the Steinach opera-tion. He called upon a friend in a dejected mood, seeming very much out-of-sorts and saying that he had no wish for prolonged life unless he could re-create himself continually,

---

* *The Holy Mountain, being the Story of a Pilgrimage to Lake Manas, and of Initiation on Mount Kailas in Tibet*, by Bhagwān Shri Hamsa. Translated from the Marāthi by Shri Purohit Swami. This work was published by Faber & Faber in September 1934, with Yeats's Introduction.

continually compete with himself, and this friend described the contents of Steinach's book with great impressiveness and the appropriate gesticulations. He hurried away to read the volume in the Trinity College Library. Then after consultation with a doctor, who would give no opinion either way, he made his own decision and went to London to undergo the operation. His friend had merely thought to entertain him with the account of a novelty and was astonished when, a month or two later, he strode into his office looking like another man and said, 'I had it done'.

In June Yeats and his wife made a trip to Rapallo for the purpose of disposing of their flat in the Via Americhe and fetching some furniture home. On his arrival Yeats called Ezra Pound to dinner with a view to getting his opinion on the verse of *The King of the Great Clock Tower*. Pound preferred to praise Mussolini and to denounce Dublin as an ignorant hole because Yeats had said that he was re-reading Shakespeare and was more excited by detective stories than by the economics of Major Douglas. But he took the manuscript, and the next day his verdict came in the word 'Putrid'. Yeats's renewed self-confidence survived this criticism, and during the next few months, as busy with verse as ever he had been, he wrote 'Supernatural Songs', passionate metaphysical verse, in which were such flights of eloquence as this:

> . . . Whence had they come,
> The hand and lash that beat down frigid Rome?
> What sacred drama through her body heaved,
> When world-transforming Charlemagne was conceived?

24.7.34. *To Mrs Shakespear*

Here are two verses out of a poem I have just written:

Natural and supernatural with the self-same ring are wed;
As man, as beast, as an ephemeral fly begets, Godhead begets
    Godhead,
For things below are copies, the Great Smaragdine Tablet said,
Yet all must copy copies, all increase their kind;

When the conflagration of their passion sinks, damped by the
      body or the mind.
That juggling nature mounts, her coil in their embraces twined.

The mirror-scalèd serpent is multiplicity –

and so on. The point of the poem is that we beget and bear
because of the incompleteness of our love. I have another poem
in my head where a monk reads his breviary at midnight upon
the tomb of long-dead lovers on the anniversary of their death,
for on that night they are united above the tomb, their embrace
being not partial but a conflagration of the entire body – and so
shedding the light he reads by.

   Strange that I should write these things in my old age, where
if I were to offer myself for new love I could only expect to be
accepted by the very young wearied by the passive embrace of
the bolster . . .

   Later in the year, *The King of the Great Clock Tower* was
admirably acted and danced at the Abbey Theatre. It was
more original than Yeats had thought, for upon referring to
Salome he found that Wilde's dancer never danced with the
head in her hands. Her dance came before the decapitation
of the saint and was a mere uncovering of nakedness. 'Send
the enclosed cutting to Dorothy,' Yeats wrote to Mrs Shakespear, 'to show to Ezra that I may confound him. He may
have been right to condemn it as poetry, but he condemned
it as drama. It has turned out the most popular of my dance
plays.'

   So far as the theatre was concerned, Yeats had given up
the fight for getting poetry spoken to music in an intelligible
manner. On the occasion of the production of *The King of
the Great Clock Tower* he wrote that 'the plain fable, the
plain prose of the dialogue, Ninette de Valois' dance' were
there for the audience. They could find what was sung in
the book if they were curious, but it would not be thrust
upon them. Nevertheless, in his old age, Yeats was more
than ever haunted by the desire to restore the singing side
of the poet's art, and he constantly discussed the subject with

poets of his acquaintance who had knowledge of music, notably with W. J. Turner and F. R. Higgins. It was in this mood that he started a series of 'Broadsides' at Miss Elizabeth Yeats's press, modelling his own efforts to some extent (as in the case of his song for the Blueshirts) on the tunes of his own country. Turner has told how he was not averse 'to a writer attempting to write new words to old tunes'. '... This seems a strange reversal of the old principle that the words shall come first and determine the music; but ... it seems to elucidate the principle that the success of such a marriage does not depend upon priority, precedent or relative importance but upon a unity of conception.'

In this connection Yeats was much interested in Margot Ruddock, known as Margot Collis on the stage, who came to him in the first instance to seek his help to found a poet's theatre. Meeting her in London, he took her to Edmund Dulac to have her voice rehearsed and to Mr Ashton, the creator and producer of ballets; he also introduced her to his 'religious man' from India, Shri Purohit Swami. Presently he was to venture upon the perilous enterprise of launching her as a poet.

4

In the autumn of 1934 Yeats attended the fourth Congress of the Alessandro Volta Foundation in Rome to speak on the Dramatic Theatre. To this gathering, which was held in the Palace of the Royal Academy of Italy, came many distinguished playwrights and men of the theatre from all parts of Europe. Maeterlinck (whom Yeats had not seen for thirty years), Gordon Craig, Pirandello and Marinetti were among those in the front row. On Pirandello's suggestion the Irish poet took the chair. His theme, once again, was the rise and achievement of 'a small, dingy and impecunious theatre in Dublin'. The speech was printed in English, French and Italian in the *Proceedings* of the Academy.

Certain societies were preparing to celebrate Yeats's next birthday, which was his seventieth. In February 1935, after a visit from a lawyer, who came to see him about Lady Gregory's papers, he collapsed and had to be kept in bed for a time. Alarming rumours spread through Dublin, and the secretary of the Pen Club called at Riversdale to inquire. 'Oh, Mrs Yeats,' he said, 'don't let him slip away before June.'

An upstairs writing-room was improvised, lit by two candles in great sconces which (he told a visitor) had once stood beside a bier. Here he sat busy with the proofs of his scornful analysis of George Moore and Martyn, his *monumentum perenne* for Lady Gregory, called *Dramatis Personae*. Martyn had died some years before Lady Gregory, and Moore had survived Lady Gregory by a year only. Yeats could therefore publish what he chose about the 'preposterous pair', one of them acknowledged to be the author of five great novels. The ill-treatment of Martyn in *Dramatis Personae* is rather curious, as he had been a friendly and appreciated neighbour during Yeats's residence at Ballylee. But Martyn's biographer, Mr Denis Gwynn, had found among his papers, and published, a jocular account of the early years of the Abbey Theatre, which may have aroused Yeats's resentment.

The proof sheets of the definitive edition of *A Vision* followed those of *Dramatis Personae*, and when this work was disposed of, Yeats turned to an anthology of English verse from 1892 to 1935, which the Oxford University Press had invited him to edit. He wrote of this to Mrs Shakespear:

I can never do any kind of work (apart from verse) unless I have a problem to solve. My problem this time will be 'How far do I like the Ezra, Auden, Eliot School, and if I do not, why not?' Then this further problem. 'Why do the younger generation like it so much? What do they see or hope?'

To Mr Maurice Wollman, who was annotating the anthology *Modern Poetry 1922–1934* for the 'Scholar's Library' edition, he wrote:

Your note on 'targeted' is quite correct.* I don't want to interpret the 'Death of the Hare'. I can help you to write a note if that note is to be over your own name but you must not give me as your authority. If an author interprets a poem of his own he limits its suggestibility. You can say that the poem means that the lover may while loving feel sympathy with his beloved's dread of captivity. I don't know how else to put it.

When his birthday came he was fully recovered. John Masefield and Mrs Masefield crossed to Ireland for the occasion and stayed at Riversdale. To a luncheon party given for the Masefields came Oliver Gogarty, Mrs Llewelyn Davies and Julian Bell, the young English poet, who was afterwards killed in the Spanish war. Yeats was charming; it was as though he were saying, 'I am very happy today, and it is you who are giving me this happiness'. He beamed while his Irish playboy Gogarty told one story after another, excellent stories and told inimitably. After luncheon Yeats addressed himself in a very kind manner to Julian Bell and told him to write poetry out of his emotions, not out of his opinions. On leaving, Bell said to Mrs Davies, 'At last I have seen a poet who looks like a poet'.

John Masefield and Desmond MacCarthy (who had come to bring English congratulations) spoke at the Pen Club dinner in the evening. Next day the oldest of the Dublin newspapers, the *Irish Times*, published a supplement on Yeats's work, with contributions by Lennox Robinson, Francis Hackett, F. R. Higgins, and devoted a leading article to his praise, – *Ad Multos Annos*:

It must suffice that he undoubtedly is the greatest poet writing in the English language, that his work will endure while the English tongue is spoken, and that in an age which has produced a large number of brilliant writers – men of the calibre of Shaw, of Synge, of Moore, of Joyce and of O'Casey – the name of William Butler Yeats stands unapproached and unapproachable. . . . From the national point of view W. B. Yeats occupies

* Mr Wollman had inquired whether 'targeted' in Yeats's 'Quarrel in Old Age' meant 'protected as with a target, a round shield'.

an almost unique position in Irish life; for he is virtually the first man since Swift who has been able to bring the Anglo-Irish tradition into line with positive nationalism. ... In his later years he has claimed his place in the line of Swift and Goldsmith, Berkeley and Burke, while clinging to his inheritance as a successor of the Irish bards.

A few weeks after this George Russell died at Bournemouth. His biographer relates that at the end AE was 'pathetically anxious' for a word from Yeats, and that 'happily a letter arrived in time to be read to him'. Friends brought the body back to Ireland for burial. At a big gathering in Plunkett House Yeats sat alone in a front room, unapproachable, sunk in dejection. But at the entrance to the cemetery he took a place behind the hearse with another poet, and walked with head erect to the graveside. 'AE', he wrote some days later in reply to Lady Gerald Wellesley's condolences, 'was my oldest friend. I constantly quarrelled with him but he never bore malice, and in his last letter to me, a month before his death, he said that generally when he differed from me it was that he feared to be absorbed by my personality.'

Of Yeats's early companions in his Irish work there now survived only Douglas Hyde, presently to be raised under the new separatist Constitution to the dignity of President of Ireland and named by de Valera as the 'successor of our rightful princes' – and Maud Gonne. Maud Gonne now lived entirely in Ireland with her son and grandchildren. She had an old-fashioned house in the suburbs of Dublin called Roebuck House, which she shared with Mrs Despard, a ninety-year-old suffragist and a sister of the first Earl of Ypres. Roebuck House was a court and a paradise for animals, and, going up the short avenue, one was assaulted by dogs of dubious temperament. But having faced these, any person could walk on and ask for dinner or asylum for life; she would give either. Whatever the reason – Mrs Despard perhaps – Yeats seldom visited Maud Gonne at Roebuck House. From time to time they would meet and dine at a restaurant in Dublin, and, as politics was always a dangerous subject, he would try to amuse her with stories about the bright young people whom he knew in London. Not very success-fully; she did not care for his 'butterfly' talk; she thought it out of character.

[20]

Old age

———

Picture and book remain,
An acre of green grass
For air and exercise,
Now strength of body goes;
Midnight, an old house
Where nothing stirs but a mouse.

. . .

Grant me an old man's frenzy ...

I

IN November 1935 Yeats published *A Full Moon in March*
and with it an earlier version, *The King of the Great Clock
Tower,* 'Parnell's Funeral', 'Supernatural Songs' and the
'Prayer' – scarcely necessary, one would think – that he
might be saved 'From all that makes a wise old man That
can be praised of all'. The next his friends heard of him was
that he was off for a winter in Majorca with Shri Purohit
Swami, a serious and respectable companion, for a rest-cure
and collaboration in a translation of the Upanishads. His
mind was full of Asia, where Hegel says every civilization
begins, no matter what its geographical origin, and it was in
vain that F. R. Higgins pointed out to him merits in the
Church of Ireland. One could (said Higgins) be a devout
communicant in the Church of Ireland and accept all the
councils before the Great Schism that separated Western
from Eastern Christianity in the ninth century, and for that
reason in course of time the Church of Ireland would feel

itself more in sympathy with pre-Patrician Ireland than could the Roman Catholic Church. But Yeats said that for the moment he associated early Christian Ireland (there were missionaries in Ireland before St Patrick) with India. The Indian monk, protected during his pilgrimage to a remote Himalayan shrine by a strange great dog that disappeared when the danger was past, might have been that 'blessed Cullach who sang upon his death-bed of bird and beast'.* and in literature Joyce and D. H. Lawrence were restoring to use the Eastern simplicity.

The time at Palma passed at first wonderfully well. Yeats breakfasted early; he then wrote in bed for four hours, and spent the afternoons on the shore with the Swami, going through the translation and making such points as that one might call a goddess 'this handsome girl' or even 'a pretty girl' instead of 'a maiden of surpassing loveliness'. In the hotel the Swami, a broad man, saved him from draughts and his heart from undue strain by walking slowly before him whenever he had to go upstairs or downstairs. But it was at Palma that the complication of maladies, a dropsical condition, under which Yeats finally sank, first plainly declared themselves. The most painful symptom was breathlessness. Yeats chose to think it was asthma. The doctor said it was something else, and the Swami recommended an approach to the problem along 'the high *a priori* road'. By the end of January Yeats was evidently so ill that the proprietor of the hotel and the Swami telegraphed to Mrs Yeats, who came out at once and saw that he had the proper treatment.

By April he was much better and could work again in a hillside bungalow, the Casa Pastor, which overlooked a wide stretch of the Mediterranean. The news of his illness had reached London, and St John Ervine, on a cruise, took the chance of his ship calling at the island to go ashore and inquire if he was still there, and how he was. 'I could not have found him more perfectly posed', Ervine wrote afterwards (*Observer*, January 1939). 'He was seated at table with

* Commentary on 'Supernatural Songs', in the American edition.

a Yogi! ... The Yogi, dressed in bright pink and looking like a bright carnation, sat with his hands folded on his ample paunch. ... Yeats sat back in his chair and began to fumble for words but could not find them until a chance remark of mine unloosed his tongue and, with extraordinary recovery of spirits, he began a very entertaining discourse.*

Life at Casa Pastor proved to be more of a nervous strain than a rest-cure. The next face at the window was Miss Margot Ruddock's. She arrived at an even earlier hour than St John Ervine, Mrs Yeats finding her on the verandah, just after breakfast had been brought to W. B. in bed. With Miss Ruddock's visit to Majorca there is associated a wild story, which can be given in Yeats's words to Mrs Shakespear:

The girl, who is quite a beautiful person, came here seven or eight days ago. She walked in at 6.30, her luggage in her hand and, when she had been given breakfast, said she had come to find out if her verse was any good. I had known her for some years and had told her to stop writing as her technique was getting worse. I was amazed by the tragic magnificence of some fragment and said so. She went out in pouring rain, thought, as she said afterwards, that if she killed herself her verse would live instead of her, went to the shore to jump in, then thought she loved life and began to dance. She went to the lodging-house where Shri Purohit Swami was, to sleep. She was wet through so Swami gave her some of his clothes;† she had no money, he gave her some. Next day she went to Barcelona and there went mad, climbing out of a window, falling through a broken roof, breaking a knee-cap, hiding in a ship's hold, singing her own poems most of the time. The British Consul at Barcelona appealed to me, so George and I went there, found her with recovered sanity sitting up in bed at a clinic writing an account of her madness ...

* They were organizing, Mrs Yeats tells me, the day's work on the *Aphorisms* of Patanjali, and not idling, as Ervine hints. Ervine's sudden appearance at the window did take Yeats aback for the moment.

† A pair of slippers among other things.

2

Paragraphs on the Majorcan episode appeared in the London press, and oral traditions were numerous and contradictory.* Both Yeats and the Swami (who left for India shortly afterwards) received anonymous letters, and on his way home Yeats hid from the journalists in the recesses of the Savile Club and at Penns in the Rocks, Sussex, the home of Lady Gerald Wellesley (the poet Dorothy Wellesley), with whom he had formed in the previous year a friendship very precious to him.

He wrote to Lady Gerald on his return to Riversdale (30 June 1936):

On my arrival I was met by the various persons in the *Irish Times* photograph – some of the faces (Gogarty's, Higgins') may interest you as I have much of their work in the Anthology. Dr Hayes is the Government director on the Abbey Board. The fat man is Dr Starkie, who most years spends a couple of months among gypsies in Spain, Austria, etc., playing his fiddle and escaping among the gypsy women, according to one of the reviewers, 'a fate worse than death'. . . . What did you think of the Belloc poem? It is not as good as I thought; I thought it was naïver, simpler. . . . It is amusing but too deliberately so – too facetious. Perhaps on the whole I am for it, but it is your province not mine, for you are English editor . . .

. . . My daughter beat me at croquet. The mallet seemed very heavy. . . . Today I am content with life again – my work has gone well and if the rain would leave off I am certain that the mallet would be light and that I would beat my daughter.† . . . Tomorrow I shall finish the play, then I write the ballad of lovers, the lady and the servant.

* No less than six consuls, including the Peruvian, interviewed Yeats (it was said) at Barcelona, and the Peruvian presented a bill for a valuable dog injured by Miss Ruddock's fall. The reader may be referred for further details to Miss Ruddock's essay 'Almost I tasted Ecstasy' in her volume *The Lemon Tree*, which appeared in December 1936 with an introduction by W. B. Yeats (J. M. Dent & Co.).

† He was quite a skilled player, his one good eye being very accurate, and had played before he came to Riversdale. Where, no one knew, as there was no croquet lawn at Coole.

He wrote much and slept little, often getting up in the morning at four to work at proof sheets (*The Upanishads* and *A Vision*), then returning to bed for breakfast. He wrote poetry between breakfast and noon, entering into competition with Lady Gerald Wellesley in a 'Chambermaid's Song'.* In the afternoon he was taken out in a wheeled chair by Anne or his wife for an hour and pushed along the country roads. For periods he lived on milk, peaches and grapes – all from his own garden. He proclaimed himself an invalid, which indeed he was – 'to get rid of bores, business and exercise', he explained to Mrs Shakespear. 'Why did I not think of this life years ago? Everybody is charming to me and those that I want come to see me.'

His rallies were remarkable, and later in the summer of 1936 he planned the English visit that he made in October. He still attended Directors' meetings at the Abbey Theatre, and after one meeting regaled Mrs Shakespear with the following anecdote of a visiting actress and the stage-producer:

Miss—— is charming pretty and seemingly very shy. After she had left, however, the stage manager reported. 'Did you hear of my *fou pas*? One night I could not find the crown so I went to Miss ——'s room. I knocked and she said "Who is there?" I said "Stage manager". She said "Come in". I went in and there she was, saving your presence, bollicky naked. I turned my head away and there she was facing me in the mirror. I went out and she said "What do you want?" I said "the crown" and she gave it to me, stretching out her long bare arm. I don't mind seeing a comedian in her knickers but nothing like this was ever seen in the Abbey before. At first I was not going to tell you – I did not want to insult your mind with such a story. They do that kind of thing in England but not here.' He was told that it was not a matter for the Board.

It was rather sad to see Yeats climb the stairs to the board-room, stopping on the landing to recover breath so that he

* *Vide* 'The Three Bushes' in *Last Poems* and *Letters on Poetry to Dorothy Wellesley*, a book to which the biographer of Yeats is greatly indebted.

might make a lordly entrance as of old. 'Higgins and I', he said on one of these occasions, 'are both suffering a little from heart' (Higgins at the time was perfectly well). He could not bear that on public occasions he should seem old and ill; always he was elegantly dressed.

F. R. Higgins, Frank O'Connor and Captain MacManus brought him news of contentions in the town, literary and political. The thought of battle still excited him. Was it a private fight, or could anyone join in? One of his relapses was attributed to a visit from Henry Harrison, who as a youth from Oxford had given his heart and service to Parnell. Harrison spoke of a book which he had written to defend Parnell's memory, and what he said made Yeats feel that he, too, should write something in prose or in verse to convince people that Parnell had nothing to be ashamed of in his love. The result was a vigorous song, 'Come, gather round me, Parnellites', and (as 'a footnote to history') an essay on Parnell. A few weeks later came 'Roger Casement' and 'The Ghost of Roger Casement', ballads conceived after reading Dr Maloney's *The Forged Diaries of Roger Casement*. Yeats sent 'Roger Casement' to Mr de Valera's newspaper and the editor gave him a leading article; he was publicly thanked by the Vice-President of the Executive Council. It was as though he lived again in I.R.B. days with his Phoenix. Gone was the 'smiling public man', in his place the rapparee from the Bog of Allen. Only Yeats now felt, as he had not done in his youth, sufficiently confident of his powers to introduce into his poetry the deep-seated nationalistic prejudice. The sadness of sympathy for Irish rebels in his early verse, or in his 1916 poems, is in strong contrast with

> O what has made that sudden noise?
> What on the threshold stands?
> It never crossed the sea because
> John Bull and the sea are friends;
> But this is not the old sea
> Nor this the old seashore.

> What gave that roar of mockery,
> That roar in the sea's roar?
> *The ghost of Roger Casement*
> *Is beating on the door.*

Lady Gerald Wellesley reproached him for encouraging 'hate between nations'. He replied that he was shocked by her thought. 'How could I hate England, owing what I do to Shakespeare, Blake and Morris? England is the only country I cannot hate.' But she herself, at the end of her book, refers to his frequent anti-English outbursts.* The incident with Toller at Claridge's, reported by Ethel Mannin in *Privileged Spectator*, was an exhibition of the same temper. The strange trio walked into Claridge's on a dripping wet night. Toller wanted Yeats to recommend a notable prisoner of the German regime, Ossietsky, to the attention of the Nobel Committee for its prize. Yeats was adamant in his refusal to do anything of the sort. He damned Toller. 'You should know', he told Ethel Mannin afterwards, 'that no Nationalist of the school of O'Leary has ever touched intellectual politics'.

Ballads were to take a very prominent place in Yeats's last book, as they had done in his first. Not all this work was political, some of it was amatory. He was heard to say that 'Oh, Johnny, I hardly knew ye' was the most passionate rhythm in poetry. However, when Mr Bennett, head master of his old Dublin school, asked him for a poem for the school magazine, he found a suitable one for schoolboys, the poem on his four ages with the refrain: ' "What then?" sang Plato's ghost. "What then?" '

3

Yeats's *Oxford Book of Modern Verse* (1892–1935) throws as

* Vide *Letters on Poetry*, pp. 120 *et seq.* and p. 125. Meeting Yeats just after his 'Roger Casement', I was astonished by the ferocity of his feelings. He almost collapsed after reading the verses and had to call for a little port wine. Afterwards he admitted having wronged Alfred Noyes and others, who were named in the first version as persons who had spread stories about Casement's private life for political ends.

much light on his own personality and development of taste as on the poetry of the period. It shows partiality to friends of the moment and to old friends. Some of these friends Yeats really admires, and rightly so, but he does Lady Gregory, for instance, a doubtful service by inserting several pages of her translations from Hyde's Irish while rejecting certain others (in some cases members of his own Irish Academy!) who in courtesy merited at least a poem. From his own poetry, defiantly he chose nothing of earlier date than his fortieth year. His wife and he made separate lists. The final choice was a selection from both lists. Yeats insisted on 'Three Things'; this was their one serious difference of opinion.

It is credibly reported that on seeing the book Sir Arthur Quiller-Couch exclaimed, 'What an Anthology! What a Preface!'; at all events, in bringing his own *Oxford Book of English Verse* (1250–1900) down to 1918, he violently redressed the balance by publishing nothing by Yeats of more recent date than the *Cloths of Heaven*. On the whole, however, now that the shock or surprise at some of the exclusions or inclusions has died down, it will be conceded that Yeats's book is more interesting than most anthologies. He did not play for safety or keep to beaten tracks. At the same time he did his task most conscientiously, collecting his knowledge of recent poetry not merely from friends (as some supposed) but also from the books. He was, at the start, but slightly acquainted with the work of the latest generation. He had read Louis MacNeice on account of his Irish origins, but the productions of Day Lewis, Madge, Spender, George Barker were almost unknown to him.

After the passing of the men of the nineties, several English poets (Binyon, Sturge Moore, de la Mare, the younger Michael Field and, most surely, Davies, to name a few) had won his admiration. Other lights of the Georgian period were not so lucky in his estimation; and in his correspondence with Miss Edith Sitwell and Lady Gerald Wellesley the comments on well-known people were often bitter if enchanting. 'Has Mr B—— ever written a poem that can be called a poem?' he asked, and of another writer's work he said, 'He has made drafts of many masterpieces but all the same [he paused] he is a sheep in wolf's clothing.' He could be obstinate. He chose but one poem by Sir John Squire, and insisted, even when Squire wrote that it was far from being his own preference. On the appearance of the book Lord Alfred Douglas, who was unrepresented, sent him a strongly-worded telegram containing animadversions upon Ireland.

He wanted a theme to follow in the Introduction, and his readings in philosophy suggested to him that neither rhetoric nor humanitarian preoccupations, as the nineties had supposed, were the fault of Victorian literature, but passivity before a mechanized nature.

The despair of his friends in the nineties was preparation for a change that came suddenly with certain poets of the twenties, with W. J. Turner, Herbert Read, the Sitwells. In W. J. Turner Yeats discovers 'the symbol of an incomplete discovery ... mind recognizing its responsibility', and he substitutes Herbert Read's long poem, *The End of a War*, written long after the war, for certain pieces written during it, because 'passive suffering is not a theme for poetry'. Day Lewis, Auden and others of the 'communist' thirties are classified as poets who 'combine the modern vocabulary, the accurate record of the facts learned from Eliot, with the sense of suffering of the war poets, no longer passive'. Anything like a school was certain to excite Yeats's interest, but he must have had a distaste for the un-Homeric subject-matter of the thirties.* He could never quite reconcile himself to 'Mr Prufrock' but one sees from his Introduction how well aware he was of the effect produced by T. S. Eliot – Hopkins left far behind – on the recent outlook. The moderns always found his own hints about technique worthy

---

* He would have agreed with Dr Johnson that 'the source of everything, either in or out of nature, that can serve the purpose of poetry, is to be found in Homer; – every species of distress, every modification of heroic character, battles, storms, ghosts, incantations, etc. . . .'

of attention. A small book could be written on the innovations which he introduced in his later work into the traditional metres, on his restoration into English of the disreputable present participle and his acute use of conjunctions and prepositions. In his skilful employment of phrases taken over from the newspapers ('assault and battery'; 'fearful blast'; 'world-famous') he could beat the young men on their own ground.

4

The publication of the *Oxford Book* was followed by a broadcast from the B.B.C. on modern poetry. Yeats came up from Penns in the Rocks for the broadcast on 20 October 1936, and gave a dinner at the Ivy to 'bring Ethel Mannin and the Dulacs together', then returned to Penns. The dinner at the Ivy was not a success; Yeats fell asleep.

He had a discussion with G. R. Barnes and Miss Hilda Matheson on ways and means of extending the audience for broadcasts of poetry and offered to sponsor two programmes of modern poetry of twenty minutes each. It would be for him to make the selection and introduce each programme, the B.B.C. choosing readers with his approval. He wanted to experiment with the use of drum or other musical instrument between stanzas or between poems so as to heighten the intensity of the rhythm, but never behind the voice, and to experiment in the unaccompanied singing of a refrain. The first of the programmes was to be called 'The Inn Parlour' or 'At the Village Inn', and the second 'In the Poets' Garden'. 'My preliminary statement', he wrote subsequently, 'would explain that the theme was love.' 'The musical instruments', he went on,

used for poems sung or spoken 'At the Village Inn' should be what one might naturally find there – whistle, concertina, drum. B.B.C. Orchestra rejected throughout for both programmes and all forms of chamber music. The musical instrument for 'In the Poets' Garden' should be a fiddle or viola; this one instrument should be sufficient. There must never be an accompaniment, and no words must be spoken through music, though a pause may sometimes be marked by a few low musical notes. They must never be loud enough to shift the attention of the ear. After a song, the gap between that and the next item can be filled up by the repetition of the air on the musical instrument. The difficulty is in the case of spoken recitations; where a few low notes have marked a pause, these might lead up to the air which follows the recitation.

In December W. J. Turner, Hilda Matheson and George Barnes started to rehearse, employing Ronald Watkins and Margot Ruddock as the readers. They found, however, that Yeats's intentions were not clear to them and so decided to postpone the programme until he was again in London. He had originally wanted part of 'In the Poets' Garden' to come from Dublin and to be spoken by a fine male singer at the Abbey Theatre, but the postponement led to the production of a similar programme at the Abbey Theatre which was broadcast from Athlone (1 February 1937) and included 'Roger Casement', 'Come, gather round me, Parnellites' and poems by James Stephens and F. R. Higgins. The performance mortified him. He wrote to Barnes from Riversdale (2 February 1937):

> Broadcast a fiasco. Every human sound turned into the groans, roars, bellows of a wild [*sic*]. . . . I shall attend what rehearsals you ask me to, but it is quite plain that all I can do is to choose the poems and make certain general suggestions. . . . Perhaps my old bundle of poet's tricks is useless. I got Stephenson while singing 'Come All Old Parnellites' to clap his hands in time to the music after every verse, and it was very stirring – on the wireless it was a schoolboy knocking with the end of a penknife or spoon.

To the end he remained unsophisticated, and found romance in the commonplace, and when elected 'by Sir William Rothenstein's grace' a member of the Athenaeum Club, he was hugely delighted. On his arrival in London for the broadcasts in March he wrote from that address to Mrs Llewelyn Davies, in whose house near Dublin he had carried out some rehearsals:

I have rehearsed my B.B.C. broadcast of poems grouped under the heading 'In the Poets' Pub' – poems by Belloc, Chesterton, de la Mare, Newbolt, a woman whose name I forget,* and York Powell's 'The Lady and the Shark'. . . . Though I do not mention Sassoon in my broadcast† – he did not come into the story I was telling – I have put him in the *Oxford Book*. . . . In spite of universal denunciation from the right and left, fifteen thousand have been sold. I admire Auden more than I said in the Anthology (his best work has not been published). The young Cambridge poets write out of their intellectual beliefs and that is all wrong. Am I a barrel of memories that I should give you my reasons? said Zarathustra. My poetry is generally written out of despair – I have just come out of a particularly black attack. . . . Like Balzac, I see increasing commonness everywhere, and like Balzac I know no one who shares the premises from which I work . . .

Between the two broadcasts 'In the Poets' Pub' and 'In the Poets' Parlour' he was for a few days, at Penns, a member of a house party which included Herbert Fisher and W. J. Turner. These visits to Penns were among the greatest pleasures of his last years. Three weeks gave him his fill of London. 'My second programme', he wrote to Mrs Llewelyn Davies, 'is on April 22. I find that a month exhausts my interests here. I have been longing for the cat and the dog, the local gossip of my friends and for you.'

Mr Barnes's story of the broadcasts is this:

Yeats used his 'poet's tricks' with great effect. He made Clinton-Baddeley read de la Mare's 'Three Jolly Farmers' as patter and gave him an excellent imitation of the patter actors which he had heard and admired in his youth. He also made use of the bones with great effect as an accompaniment to Higgins' 'Song for the Clatter-Bones'. The title of the broadcast was changed to 'In the Poets' Pub' and many of the poems which Yeats had chosen – a 'Hardy', a 'Kipling' and an 'Edith Sitwell' – were sternly rejected. Chesterton's 'The Rolling English Road' remained, but at the cost of the last two verses which Yeats described as 'sentimental and rather disgusting'. He would be

---

* Sylvia Townsend Warner.
† The October broadcast on modern poetry.

just as severe on his own work: after the rehearsal of a later
programme when Baddeley read the first lines of 'Sailing to
Byzantium':

> 'That is no country for old men. The young
> In one another's arms; birds in the trees . . .'

and observed that they were difficult to speak, Yeats made a
change to:

> 'Old men should quit a country where the young
> In one another's arms; birds in the trees . . .'

Again, in the interests of British morals, he allowed the second
line of Higgins' 'Song for the Clatter-Bones' to run 'Queen
Jezebel the witch'. Clinton-Baddeley and Margot Ruddock were
eventually chosen as readers and, in spite of Yeats' distrust of
professional actors as readers of poetry, Baddeley became so
indispensable that Yeats cancelled a second broadcast of the
'Pub', arranged in 1938, because 'I don't know anybody who
could take Baddeley's place'.

The other reader, Margot Ruddock, was his chosen instrument.
She possessed one quality which he valued beyond price – the
ability to pass naturally and unself-consciously from speech to
song. Thus in 'I am of Ireland' she would read each verse and
glide into a melancholy tune of her own composition at the
refrain. From my point of view she had one supreme disadvan-
tage; quick to take Yeats' points in rehearsal, she lacked the
professional training to reproduce the effect at transmission. I
pointed this out to Yeats when he suggested that she should
broadcast six or seven of Blake's *Songs of Innocence and Experience* chanted to her own music with an introduction and
interpretation by Yeats. Nevertheless, she had great qualities. I
remember the lilting way in which Yeats taught her to speak:

> 'Ah, dancer; ah, sweet dancer',

and the majesty of fulfilment with which she spoke 'Alexander,
Alexander, the King of the World was he'. She succeeded best in
poems like 'The Curse of Cromwell', where the refrain suited her
song and gave it point. My most vivid memory, however, is her
use of the lowest register of her lovely contralto voice to speak
the climax of 'Into the Twilight', 'And God stands winding his
lonely horn'.

Yeats' distrust of the professional actor was as nothing when compared to his dislike of the professional musician. Something which I had said at our first meeting about Stanford's setting of 'Drake's Drum' brought the rebuke: 'This suggests to me piano or B.B.C. Orchestra, on both of which I stamp with fury'. Forcibly as his ideas about music were expressed, he had no ear for music as it is understood in Western Europe. He could not hum a tune and his notion of pitch was wildly inaccurate, qualities which made his demands upon the professional instrumentalists who took part very exacting. On the other hand, his ear for the sound of speech was so sensitive that it outran comprehension. His sensitiveness to the sound of words made rehearsals long and exacting. Knowing exactly what he wanted himself, he found it difficult to express because he noticed nuances which we could hardly hear. Nor was he helped by his own voice, an instrument inadequate (when I knew him) for conveying his meaning accurately. Margot, perhaps by intuition, could get what he wanted but could not be depended upon to reproduce it later. Baddeley's professional training enabled him to do what he was told over and over again once he had got the effect desired. To get this he would work like a black, but at times Yeats would get exasperated at our insensitivity to his meaning.

'Poetry', as A. E. Housman said, 'is not the thing said, but a way of saying it', and it was Yeats' way of saying lines that made these broadcasts memorable. In 'An Irish Airman' he made Clinton speak the lines 'A lonely impulse of delight Drove to this tumult in the clouds' as though he was experiencing the physical sensation of flight. 'Ecstasy, Baddeley!' he would cry, and repeat the lines lovingly to himself. The pleasure of rehearsal was to hear him trying to convey the sounds which were running in his head, and when he succeeded they remained unforgettably in the ear. The subtle differences of stress which separated the twice-repeated line 'Seventy years have I lived'; the Irish names 'Said Pearse to Connolly', and 'My country is Kiltartan Cross, My countrymen Kiltartan's poor'; the rhythm of 'And showed her hills green'; the tension of 'I came on a great house in the middle of the night'; and lastly, those wonderful refrains which he made Margot sing and which he longed to sing in some way himself: 'The little fox he murmured, Oh, what of the world's bane?', and 'Oh what of that, oh what of that, what is there left to say?'

5

Yeats also proposed a broadcast debate between himself and James Stephens; when Stephens declined the invitation Dulac offered to fill the gap. Yeats stated his thesis as follows:

That it is not the duty of the artist to paint beautiful women and beautiful places is nonsense. That the exclusion of sex appeal from poetry, painting and sculpture is nonsense (are the films alone to impose their ideas upon the sexual instinct?). That, on the contrary, all arts are an expression of desire – exciting desirable life, exalting desirable death. That all arts must be united again, painting and literature, poetry and music. Bless synthesis; damn Whistler and his five o'clock.

'My idea', he wrote on 3 June, 'is to work it all up into a kind of drama in which we will get very abusive, and then one or the other of us will say with a change of voice "Well, I hope they will have taken all that seriously and believe that we shall never speak to each other again". The other will say "Stop, the signal is still on us. They can hear us." Then the first speaker will say "God", or if that is barred by the B.B.C. – "Hell".'

Unfortunately the arrival of some Americans and of Professor Bose necessitated Yeats's instant return to Dublin, and the debate was cancelled. Professor Bose brought a gift, *The History of the Upanishads*, from another Indian scholar, Professor Ranada, and called at Riversdale in company with Dr Wilbraham Trench of Trinity College (the 'man of known sobriety'), to present it. Yeats, who was in an excited mood, opened the conversation by saying that his friend Tagore wrote 'too much about God'. 'My mind [he said] resents the vagueness of all such references. Another sort of mysticism which is harmful to poetry is that of Peter Bell and the primrose.' DOCTOR TRENCH: 'But what about Wordsworth's little poem on the primrose-tuft in the rock? Flowers clinging to stem, stem to rock, rock to earth, "constant to her sphere", and God over all through the season's changes.' YEATS (waving the implied rebuke aside): 'I have fed upon the philosophy of the Upanishads all my life, but there is an aspect of Tagore's mysticism that I dislike. I find an absence of tragedy in Indian poetry. Indians should write in Urdu or in Bengali.' BOSE: 'Our problem is not so much to get into conflicts as to get out of them.' YEATS: 'When I talked to Indians in Oxford I found just one, only one, who disdained trying to express himself in English. That was because he was a Nepali and had therefore never lost independence or bowed to the yoke. Let Tagore cast off English.' BOSE: 'The question is a complicated one. We have the different traditions of the Moslems and the Hindus to contend with. Can you give me a message to India?' YEATS: 'Let 100,000 men of one side meet the other. That is my message to India, insistence on the antinomy.' He strode swiftly across the room, took up Sato's sword, and unsheathed it dramatically and shouted, 'Conflict, more conflict.'

Later in June Yeats returned to London for the third programme 'My Own Poetry', in which Edmund Dulac was to assist. He had a sudden quarrel in the B.B.C. studios with his collaborator, who, like other musicians, had hitherto shown him a remarkable indulgence.* However, Mrs Dulac's tact led to a compromise, and Yeats drafted an announcement to show that he dissociated himself from Dulac's setting of his words.

A little before this Dulac had earned Yeats's gratitude by taking him on a visit to Nora Heald and her sister, Miss Edith Shackleton Heald, in their beautiful village home, Chantry House, Steyning. Yeats was delighted with the place and with his hostesses; the visit was repeated in September and thereafter whenever he came to England. 'My window', he wrote to his wife, 'looks on the village street; behind are large gardens "circum-mured" with brick.' Miss Shackleton Heald was extraordinarily clever in getting

---

* Of this he was conscious. He had made a character in one of his Michael Robartes stories say, 'I have always had an idea that some day a musician would do me an injury'.

exactly the right sort of people to meet him, in keeping away members of Book Societies, 'Whigs' and other rationalists, and in seeing that he rested at the right times. Mr and Mrs Dulac were frequently his fellow-guests at Steyning, and another who came was R. A. Scott-James, who had known him at Woburn Buildings and was now publishing his poems in the *London Mercury*, side by side with the moderns. Scott-James found him 'in some ways far more practical' than he had been in earlier years. His interests were wider than had formerly been the case; he was ready, for instance, to discuss details of international politics. A neighbour of the Misses Heald, whose company he relished, is described in a letter to Mrs Yeats: 'He has some kind of paralysis that makes him shake perpetually. I drew him out and heard all about his property. He owns three ducks, four geese and an apple tree. One of the geese eats all the fallen apples. He has put barbed wire all round the apples but the goose gets over. He has lived many years in Africa "turning the natives into soldiers" where he was the only white man, and he had a pet monkey, etc. etc. It is many years since I have seen anybody smile so; timidity, shyness, boundless benevolence. I saw a Chinese actor smile like that.'

6

In New York, earlier in the year, a Testimonial Committee was formed under the direction of Mr James A. Farrell, retired President of the United Steel Corporation, for the purpose of expressing in a practical manner the admiration and affection felt for the great poet and the great Irishman by his American friends of Irish ancestry or birth. The Committee underwrote a fund which assured Yeats a moderate income for his declining years. He was so touched by the gesture that he insisted on making the matter public at a banquet of the Irish Academy of Letters held on 7 August 1937. He further expressed his gratification by publishing at the Three Candles Press in Dublin an eleven-page pamphlet entitled *A Speech and Two Poems*, as a gift for the fifty members of the Testimonial Committee. Writing to Mr James Healy after the banquet, he said:

> I said that I would thank the other subscribers later. I spoke of my renewed visits to the Municipal Gallery where my friends' portraits are – visits made possible, or at any rate easy, now that I could go by taxi. I spoke of my emotion in the gallery where modern Ireland is pictured, and said that I had a poem on this subject in my head and would send it to the subscribers ...

He recalled in 'The Municipal Gallery Revisited' Arthur Griffith ('starring in hysterical pride'), Kevin O'Higgins, Lady Gregory, Robert Gregory, Hugh Lane ... 'that tale As though some ballad-singer had sung it all'.

5.9.37. To Lady Gerald Wellesley
My dear Dorothy,
– I hear you have been working over old scraps of verse and I am eager to see the result. I have just finished a poem which for the moment I like exceedingly. It is on the Municipal Gallery. ... It is very much what my speech foreshadowed – perhaps the best poem I have written for some years unless the 'Curse of Cromwell' is. After I had left the Academy Banquet somebody called for the 'Curse of Cromwell', and when it was sung a good many voices joined in. I have no very clear plans except to be back in Ireland in November and December (where I have to keep an eye on the Abbey) and then get to a warm climate with friends and dig myself into some inexpensive spot until spring. Then I hope ... to put the Cuala Press into shape that it can go on after my death, or incapacity through old age, without being a charge upon my wife. Then I can fold my hands and be a wise old man and gay.

He went to London at the end of September for a fourth broadcast. His subject again was 'My Own Poetry', and he read most of the poems himself. Except for 'Coole and Bally-lee' all the selections were from his early work, and his comment was mainly autobiographical. It was very moving and he read with great feeling. He was tired after the per-formance but insisted upon taking Miss Margot Ruddock and Barnes out to supper. The Ivy was suggested, but it was shut; whereupon Yeats, without hesitation, ordered the cabman to drive to a small 'Italian' restaurant, telling on the way of succulent meals he had had there in the past. Alas for his memory, a stern Scottish waitress denied the party drink and the feast consisted of white coffee and hard-boiled eggs.

Plans were made for a revival of the 'Pub' and for another programme in which Starkie was to play the fiddle, but Yeats's health prevented both, and he wrote, 'I have no chance of being able to fix dates ahead. My broadcasting is finished. I am sorry considering all the trouble you have taken with me.'

7

Before setting forth for the Riviera with Miss Edith Heald, he wrote the introduction to the Swami's translation of the *Aphorisms* of Patanjali, brought out *Essays* (1931–6) and a new play, too ribald to be produced, *The Herne's Egg*. Also he released at long last the final version of *A Vision*, enormously improved in plan and balance but as embarrassing to reviewers as ever. Cecil Salkeld, the writer of the most intelligent notice of the book, while suggesting a parallel between it and Wittgenstein's *Tractatus Logico-Philosophicus*,* gave these reasons why *A Vision* could not be treated 'critically':

(a) There is no critical terminology wherewith to treat of a technical work having no border-line between metaphysics, astrology, history, spiritualism, 'school' philosophy, poetry, symbolism, geometry (conic sections), and a great deal of humour (an unfortunate man whose Guardian Angel is jealous of his sweetheart is a case in point).

---

* Where the doctrine is advanced that a relation between objects can ultimately be only indicated 'not by a symbol, but by a relation between symbols, so that the symbolic structure of the expression *shows forth* – it does not in the strict sense "symbolize" the structure of the fact, but expresses the meaning by a kind of pictorial relation'.

(b) Symbol and Dogma are both modes that invalidate analysis.
This whole section [The Great Wheel] might be termed Dogmatic Symbolism and, as such, either personally valid or
invalid *in toto*. In no case can the original and arbitrary
symbol be questioned since we are at no time on common or
verifiable ground.

To some of Yeats's friends it seemed that he was less
satisfied than formerly with his modern interpretation of the
Babylonian star-cult, considered as a contribution to the
body of mystical literature. Indeed, he informed Ethel Mannin that he was 'not a mystic'. 'No, I am a practical man. I
have seen the raising of Lazarus and the loaves and fishes and
have made the usual measurements, plummet, line, spirit-
level, and have taken the temperature, over from [?] mathematics. But on the other hand, the author of the last chapter
of the half-Russian novel* is not a materialist.' Lady Gerald
Wellesley reports him as saying: 'Individual immortality is
proved now beyond a doubt; there is sufficient evidence to
prove it again and again in a court of law'.† When, on one
occasion, she tried to make him speak with exactitude about
his views on the after-life, his answers made her say, 'Well,
it seems to me that you are hurrying us back to the great
arms of the Roman Catholic Church'.

* Miss Mannin's *Darkness my Bride*.
† With a jury of metaphysicians? How can the empirically verifiable prove more than survival? In Yeats's introduction to his *Oxford
Book* he might have credited the Victorians with his own preoccupation with the doctrine of immortality, so singularly absent from recent
poetry.

Last days

Last Poems – On the Boiler – Summer, 1938 *– Purgatory*
and epitaph – Death at Cap Martin – Tributes

═══

No marble, no conventional phrase.

I

THE last book of verse that Yeats saw through the press was
New Poems, the proofs of which he corrected at Mentone
in January 1938, for publication at the Cuala Press in April.
There is a terrifying quality in this last book. 'Conduct and
life grow worse and coarsen the soul', and in this changed
world ·

> Now that my ladder's gone,
> I must lie down where all the ladders start,
> In the foul rag-and-bone shop of the heart.

All the elements of 'blood and mire' are there, submerged
now in the simple language of the soil; the thing he had
wanted to achieve in the chaste idealism of his youth only
became possible via Byzantium – Sligo via Byzantium. The
wheel to which he so often refers has come full circle in *New
Poems* and in *Last Poems and Plays*. 'I have got the town out
of my verse', he wrote to Lady Gerald Wellesley from Mentone on 26 January. 'It is all nonchalant verse – or it seems to
me – like the opening of your "Horses".' And writing to Sir
William Rothenstein about Diana Murphy's designs for
Cuala embroideries, he exulted in his incorrigible roman-
ticism :

In England . . . the average man guys the dream. With us it is
the opposite. Some of the best known young men who got themselves killed in 1916 had the Irish legendary hero Cuchulain so
much on their minds that the Government has celebrated the

event with a local statue. For us a legendary man or woman must still be able to fight or to dance.

Roughly speaking, in Yeats's verse there are three periods, and much of his verse of all three periods is mystical and amatory. His sense of love developed from a boy's awe through a man's passion to a sense of common love and appreciation of the quintessence of love. His early poetry uses language more mystical than amatory; in his middle period his poetry was based upon associations of a definitely personal sort.

If with a few strokes an artist can give the very spirit of a tree, there is no need to add details like leaves. Yeats, in his last period, was in the position of such an artist. By concentration (an idea, a phrase, often haunted him for weeks) he could sift his thoughts to give expression in purest form to his ideas. It is important to emphasize that the preoccupation with love so apparent in his last poems was evident, just as his mysticism was evident, in his early work. As a young man he garnished a paucity of ideas with a great deal of mysticism. As an old man, hard, bright and clear in intellect, he had no need to garnish, nor for circumlocution.

One of his critics, Dr Bronowski, in an essay *The Poet's Defence*, goes so far as to say that from middle age onwards Yeats rejected the ideal of poetry for living; at the end he saw the mystical as the sexual life. 'Yeats stands against the line of poets whose ideal was poetry. And he stands away from the little poets of the nineteenth century who tried to fit poetry into a social use. He is a poet of great living and of the senses. Yeats is a poet great enough to stand against poetry.'

2

Yeats was pleased with Mentone, writing to Edith Shackleton (Heald) from the Carlton Hotel that 'the life is good for my mind and body – my life is fixed henceforth, the winter here or near here'. 'I am writing poetry', he added, 'and the big essay is finished. The *Irish Church Gazette* has given *A*

Vision a long, eloquent, enthusiastic review which makes up for the stupidities of men who attribute to me some thought of their own and reply to that thought. They all think I was bound to explain myself to them. It is just that explaining which makes many English books empty.'

The 'big essay' was planned as the first number of an occasional publication something in the style of the old *Beltaine* or *Samhain*. But whereas *Beltaine* and *Samhain* had been a defence of his theatre, its actors and plays, the coming publication, all written by himself and appearing at irregular intervals, would deal with a variety of topics, with whatever excited him at the moment, like Ruskin's *Fors Clavigera*. He devised a picturesque title; this was *On the Boiler*, whereby he recalled a mad ship's carpenter called McCoy, of whom his Pollexfen grandparents used to speak. McCoy went to bed from autumn to spring and in the summer broke off work from time to time to read the scriptures and denounce his neighbours from an old boiler on the Sligo quays:

> Why should not old men be mad?
> Some have known a likely lad
> That had a sound fly-fisher's wrist
> Turn to a drunken journalist;
> A girl that knew all Dante once
> Live to bear children to a dunce;
> A Helen of social welfare dream,
> Climb on a wagonette to scream . . .

Every country is a mirror of the world, and though Yeats's pamphlet was Irish in subject-matter, his English friends were told that they would learn from it his attitude towards European agitations. Never had he announced a book with greater joyousness and confidence. He was particularly curious to see what effect his animated assertions and improvisations would have upon Maud Gonne. What would she say to this? –

The whole State should be so constructed that the people should think it their duty to grow popular with King and Lord

Mayor instead of King and Lord Mayor growing popular with them . . .

Or to this? –

Forcing reading and writing on those who wanted neither was the worst part of the violence which for two centuries has been creating that hell wherein we suffer . . .*

Or to this (after all he had no objects out of Ireland)? –

Do not try to pour Ireland into any political system. Think first how many able men with public minds the country has, how many it can hope to have in the near future, and mould your system upon those men. It does not matter how you get them, but get them. Republics, Kings, Soviets, Corporate States, Parliaments, are trash, as Hugo said of something else, 'not worth one blade of grass that God gives for the nest of the linnet'.

He recalled that in the nominated group of the first Irish Senate were to be found most of its able men. Wisdom is to be the sole virtue of the rulers, and so great is Yeats's dislike of democracy that he gives no place at all to the passions, not even that (reversing the common ideal) of a check upon wisdom. Yet Yeats remains attached to nationalism – a passion.

More than once the appearance of *On the Boiler* was announced to be imminent, but Yeats went on adding features, notes on Cuala embroideries and the 'Broadsides', on a novel by his brother, and making the whole more violent and alive. He wrote that the choice before Europe was between decay and civil war, 'with the victory of the skilful, riding their machines as did the feudal knights their armoured horses'. He had read a great number of popular books on Hitler's Germany, and someone told him – he repeated it with great satisfaction – that there was 'a new law in that country whereby ancient and impoverished families can recover their hereditary properties'. His conversation ran on eugenics, which he had been studying in Cattell's *Psychology*

---

*Here he followed his compatriot George Moore, who in *Conversations in Ebury Street* had already denounced popular education as the grossest injustice ever inflicted upon the masses.

and Social Progress and from material supplied by the
secretary of the Eugenics Society; and he spoke of the necessity of the unification of the State under a small aristocratic
order which would prevent the materially and spiritually
uncreative families or individuals from prevailing over the
creative. In the Fascist countries, as much as, or even more
than, in the democracies, quantity seemed to be put before
quality.

A 'race philosophy' appears to have been in his thoughts
for some time, to judge from some pages among his papers,
probably dated 1926, in which he depicts society as the
struggle of the family and the individual. From the struggle
of the individual to make and preserve himself comes intellectual initiative. From the struggle to found and preserve the
family come good taste and good habits. Equality of opportunity, equality of rights have been created to assist the
individual in his struggle; inherited wealth, privilege, precedence, to assist the family in theirs. The business of government is not to abate either struggle. Because the antinomies
cannot be solved, both the dialectical materialism of Karl
Marx and his school, and the modern philosophy of Italy,
also influenced by Hegel, are inadequate. There is no final
aim, neither the losing of the individual, class, nation in the
whole, nor the return of classes to the mass bringing their
gifts. Neither the proletariat (which having nothing can
reject all) nor history can be justified.

3

When Yeats returned to Ireland in May, he was ill for a
time, and a plan for dining with Maud Gonne and discussing
with her the very controversial ideas of *On the Boiler* fell
through. However, he was able to finish a long meditative
poem on Greek statues and write some lines, the happy-
thoughted 'Politics', that had been suggested in part by the
panic-stricken conversation of a guest whom he had met at
Lady Gerald Wellesley's. Here he turns from 'wars and war's

alarms' to look at a girl and wish that he were young again:

> How can I, that girl standing there,
> My attention fix
> On Roman or on Russian
> Or on Spanish politics?
>
> .   .   .   .
>
> But O that I were young again
> And held her in my arms!

He spent about half the summer of 1938 in England. He was now at Penns in the Rocks, now at Steyning, with flying visits to the Athenaeum in between. From Steyning in June, he replied to some questions which Maud Gonne had put to him in regard to her autobiography:

Yes, of course, you can quote those poems of mine, but if you do not want my curse, do not misprint them. People constantly misprint quotations. I do not know if Agnes Tobin is still living. A week or two ago I was talking to Mrs Moody, the tennis player, about the Tobin family. She lives in San Francisco and knows them well, but had never heard of Agnes Tobin . . .

I am staying with an old friend here, Miss Shackleton Heald, one of the best-paid women journalists in the world. She found she had no leisure and so she gave up the most of it. On Tuesday I go to Penns in the Rocks, Withyham, Sussex, to stay with Lady Gerald Wellesley, another good friend, then back here and then to Ireland for the first performance of my one-act play *Purgatory*.

God be with you.

There had latterly been gaps between Yeats's meetings with Maud Gonne, due to his refusal to excite himself about Partition, which question the I.R.A. had made a burning issue. She had written to him that it would be wiser to wait until he was in a better political frame of mind, and he had replied from aggravation or ennui that he found the inhabitants of the lost province of Ulster so disagreeable that he hoped they would never reunite with the rest of Ireland. But when she came to see him at Riversdale in the late summer of 1938, all was well again between them. He was sitting in an armchair from which he could only rise with difficulty. As she got up to leave he referred to the glorious ends they had once sought together. 'Maud,' he said, 'we should have gone on with our Castle of the Heroes.' She was so surprised at his remembering that she could not reply. She had thought him 'contaminated with the British Empire', and yet when he read a few weeks later in the newspapers that a letter, or a portion of a letter, signed Maud Gonne MacBride, had been found by the English police on one of their I.R.A. captives, he threw up his arms in elation. 'What a woman!' he exclaimed. 'What vitality! what energy!' And he wrote to Sir William Rothenstein to beg him to find some way of making a drawing: 'No artist has ever drawn her, and just now she looks magnificent. I cannot imagine anything but an air raid that would bring her to London – she might come to see the spectacle – do you ever go to Dublin?' The drawing, had it been made, would have been reserved as an illustration for the definitive edition of his work which Macmillan had proposed and for which he was busy revising his text once more. There was no painting or drawing of the enchantress in her youth or prime that altogether satisfied him, nothing that showed 'that bright look as though she had gazed into the burning sun'. But a plaster head painted bronze by the young sculptor Laurence Campbell inspired a last statement from the great love-poet:

> No dark tomb-haunter once; her form all full
> As though with magnanimity of light,
> Yet a most gentle woman; who can tell
> Which of her forms has shown her substance right?
> Or maybe substance can be composite,
> Profound McTaggart thought so, and in a breath
> A mouthful held the extreme of life and death. . . .
>
> Or else I thought her supernatural;
> As though a sterner eye looked through her eye
> On this foul world in its decline and fall. . . .

Two other interesting callers at Riversdale were Vernon Watkins, a young Welsh poet, and Mary M. Colum (Mrs

Padraic Colum) from New York. In the poem 'Yeats in Dublin', Vernon Watkins made a word-for-word record of his visit.* Yeats thanked him. 'I like,' he said, 'to be thought of in that charming way and certainly I have no objection to your publishing the scraps of conversation it contains.' In the 'scraps' was an attack on 'those Londoners' who try to substitute 'psychology' for 'the naked sky of metaphysical movement'–

> All is materialism, all
> The catchwords they strew
> Alien to the blood of man . . .

Mary Colum found him much changed since she had last seen him in America. The old energy now only came in patches. 'We are both changed', he said to her. 'You were once my ideal of a youthful Nihilist.'

At intervals he made notes for a second number of *On the Boiler*.† 'To-day', he tells Lady Gerald Wellesley (Riversdale, 22 June 1938),

I am full of life and not too disturbed by the enemies I must make. This is the proposition on which I write: There is now overwhelming evidence that man stands between eternities, that of his family and that of his soul. I apply those beliefs to literature and politics and show the change they must make. Lord Acton said once that he believed in a personal devil, but as there is nothing about it in the Cambridge Universal History which he planned he was a liar. My belief must go into what I write, even if I estrange friends; some when they see my meaning set out in plain print will hate me for poems which they have thought meant nothing. I will not forget to send you that poem about the Greek statues, but I have not yet had it re-typed.

4

His last public appearance was in August, when the Abbey gave his *Purgatory*, a one-act play written round the idea

---

* Printed in *Life and Letters*, February 1939. Mr Watkins had already written *Yeats' Tower*, a meditation at Ballylee.

† This number never got further than the stage of notes.

that a family can never purge itself of a crime inherited with
its blood, but repeats its transgression until the last evil
consequences to itself and others are completed. Two ghosts
appear at the window of a burnt-out house before which the
son of the house, now reduced to a pedlar, and the grandson
are talking; the dialogue is in irregular metres and there are
no choral interludes. T. S. Eliot has drawn attention to the
'virtual abandonment' of blank verse in *Purgatory* and to the
extraordinary skill with which so much action is put within
the compass of a small scene of but little movement. Right
down to the end Yeats was experimenting.

At the fall of the curtain he came forward to say that he
had put nothing in the play because it seemed picturesque,
but had put there 'his own convictions about this world and
the next'.* It was a gala week at the Abbey Theatre, with
revivals of *On Baile's Strand* and other early masterpieces,
and lectures by Lennox Robinson, F. R. Higgins and others,
on phases and figures of the Irish Dramatic Movement. In
the lecture hall, a Jesuit, a pleasant but persistent man, who
had come all the way from Boston to penetrate into the
mysteries of Irish intellectual life, rose to ask for enlighten-
ment in regard to Yeats's theological doctrine, which he
apprehended to be inexact and confused. His questions
threw the platform into some confusion and Yeats's eulogist
could do no more than answer that a poet should not be
expected to be explicit. Yeats had retired to bed, exhausted
by his efforts at the Festival, but he sent a short letter to the
press to repeat that he had expressed his convictions in
Purgatory.

Writing to Lady Gerald Wellesley of the incident (15
August 1938), he said:

... The mass of the people do not like the Jesuits. They are
supposed to have given information to the Government in 1867.
This story which may be quite untrue has made the Franciscans
the chief religious influence in Dublin. The chief character in

* *Vide* the ghost story told at one of Charles Ricketts's Friday
evenings. *Supra*, p. 287-8.

my play was magnificently played by a player who could probably go to the Barn.* The other character was played by a fine
actor too old for the part. There was a fine performance of my
Baile's Strand. Cuchulain seemed to me a heroic figure because
he was creative joy separated from fear. I have found a book of
essays about Rilke waiting me, one on Rilke's ideas about death
annoyed me. I wrote on the margin:

> 'Draw rein, draw breath,
> Cast a cold eye
> On life, on death.
> Horseman, pass by!'†

In September he was off once again to his friends in
Sussex. He spent a day at Oxford, and driving with Miss
Heald from there to Steyning, stopped at R. A. Scott-James's
cottage in Berkshire to lunch, to read his recent poems, and
to talk about Spender, Charles Madge and George Barker.
Soon after he had returned to Dublin he was saddened by the
news of the death of Olivia Shakespear. 'For more than forty
years', he wrote to Lady Gerald Wellesley on 8 October,

she has been the centre of my life in London, and during all
that time we have never had a quarrel, sadness sometimes, but
never a difference. When first I met her, she was in her late
twenties but in looks a lovely young girl. When she died she was
a lovely old woman. You would have approved her. She came of
a long line of soldiers and during the last war thought it her
duty to stay in London through all the air raids.

A further gift reached him from the American Testimonial Committee, and in thanking the treasurer, Eugene F.
Kincaid he wrote that, apart from small gifts to his sisters,
the money would be applied entirely for the expenses of the
winters in the dry climate which had become essential to
him. It had been planned that he should leave for the Riviera

---

* Miss Edith Craig's theatre.
† *R. M. Rilke: Some Aspects of his Mind and Poetry*, a book sent
him by William Rose, who wrote the section 'Rilke and the Conception
of Death'. There is no note on the margin of Yeats's copy.

early in October, stay with his friends in Sussex for some weeks, and then meet his wife in London for the journey south. Lady Gerald Wellesley, feeling that England was near to war, warned him by telegram to remain at home. He ridiculed the notion that he would let a war deter him from doing as he chose, but in fact, during the dangerous days, he was laid up with lumbago (really kidney trouble) and unfit to move. 'When you do come,' Lady Gerald Wellesley wrote to him, 'we had better talk poetry, not politics.'

A long poem, 'His Convictions', concluded with the lines he had made on reading Dr Rose's essay on Rilke.* They were to serve as his epitaph. The prose draft of the poem was written in August, and the final version was read out to F. R. Higgins on the night before he left Ireland for the last time. It sounded like a crack at the rootless and analytical thirties; never had he been more arrogantly Irish or more arrogantly metaphysical. 'We parted', Higgins wrote afterwards, 'on the drive from his house. The head of the retiring figure, erect and challenging, gleamed through the darkness as I turned back; while on the road before me my thoughts were still ringing out with the slow powerful accents of his chanting:

> Swear by those horsemen, by those women
> Complexion and form prove superhuman,
> That pale, long-visaged company
> That air in immortality
> Completeness of their passions won;
> Now they ride the wintry dawn
> Where Ben Bulben sets the scene . . .
>
> Irish poets, learn your trade,
> Sing whatever is well made,
> Scorn the sort now growing up
> All out of shape from toe to top,
> Their unremembering hearts and heads
> Base-born products of base beds.

* He left out the 'Draw rein, draw breath'. 'Under Ben Bulben' was the title finally given to the poem.

Sing the peasantry, and then
Hard-riding country gentlemen,
The holiness of monks, and after
Porter-drinkers' randy laughter;
Sing the lords and ladies gay
That were beaten into the clay
Through seven heroic centuries;
Cast your mind on other days
That we in coming days may be
Still the indomitable Irishry.'

5

He made the prose draft of his last play, *The Death of Cuchulain*, at Chantry House, and then left for the Riviera with his wife. They took rooms at the Hôtel Idéal Séjour, Cap Martin, which they had liked in the previous year. It was on the hill, far away from the noise of the cosmopolitan coast. Michael came out for his Christmas holidays, and friends were near by: the Misses Heald at Mentone; Dermod O'Brien and Mrs O'Brien at Cap d'Ail; Lady Gerald Welles-ley and Miss Hilda Matheson in a villa above Beaulieu. Lady Gerald Wellesley has recorded that, on the first evening she saw him, she was astonished at what seemed a miraculous return to health. He was in bed, excited by the completion of *The Death of Cuchulain*, which he read out to her 'with great fire'. Some days later he dined with her to meet Schnabel the pianist, and W. J. Turner. He talked of Rilke and Stefan George. On Christmas Day he was again at her villa with Mrs Yeats and seventeen-year-old Michael. On this occasion he told charming stories out of the Indian monk's autobiography, intending them (as he said after-wards), for Michael. The B.B.C., through George Barnes, in-vited him to send a short New Year's message to the country in a programme to which John Masefield, de la Mare and E. M. Forster had promised to contribute. He replied: 'I am sorry I could not do what you wanted, but surely a man as intelligent as yourself understands that if I were to write what I would most like to say to the country as a whole, or to my family as a whole, it would be altogether unprintable'. The poet bird could not be caged.

Appearances were deceptive and the doctor was in no doubt that his condition had much deteriorated since the previous winter. On 4 January he wrote to Lady Elizabeth Pelham:

I know for certain that my time will not be long. I have put away everything that can be put away that I may speak what I have to speak and I find 'expression' is a part of 'study'. In two or three weeks – I am now idle that I may rest after writing much verse – I will begin to write my most fundamental thoughts and the arrangement of thought which I am convinced will complete my studies. I am happy, and I think full of an energy, of an energy I had despaired of. It seems to me that I have found what I wanted. When I try to put all into a phrase I say, 'Man can embody truth but he cannot know it'. I must embody it in the completion of my life. The abstract is not life and everywhere draws out its contradictions. You can refute Hegel but not the Saint or the Song of Sixpence.

On another day Mrs Yeats, Lady Gerald Wellesley, W. J. Turner, Mrs Turner and Miss Matheson, coming back from an excursion to La Turbie, found him up, and awaiting them in the hall of the hotel. He looked very spruce in his light-brown suit and blue shirt. He read out what would be his last poem, 'The Black Tower', and invited Miss Matheson to make a tune for it. On the Sunday before his death the Dermod O'Briens called, and Mrs Yeats being out, he received the visitors in his bedroom and gave them tea. They were amazed by the liveliness of his conversation and his excellent spirits. He had a heap of papers beside him. He entertained his visitors with an account of how, though F. R. Higgins failed to answer his letters, he had at last managed to get rid of his responsibilities for the Abbey Theatre. He was feeling so happy, he said, that he had given up reading detective novels and was deep in poetry again.

On Tuesday 24 January, he wrote to Mrs Josephine

MacNeill, expressing sympathy with her on the death of her husband, a former Governor-General of the Irish Free State: 'What can I say except that he was a wise and charming man who did his country considerable service...'

On the Thursday following, Lady Gerald Wellesley saw him both in the morning and afternoon. In the afternoon he wandered in his speech, but he rallied towards nightfall and gave Mrs Yeats corrections for 'Under Ben Bulben' and for the play. On Friday he had bouts of pain and breathlessness, which were relieved by morphia. He died at two in the afternoon on Saturday, January 28.

6

He looked indescribably noble that evening when Canon Tupper, whom the O'Briens brought from Monte Carlo, repeated some church prayers in the quiet little room. Unfortunately it was impossible to have a photograph taken, and on Sunday there was too much change for Dermod O'Brien to make a drawing, as Mrs Yeats had wished, and as O'Brien would have liked ('I had never before realised', he wrote to Miss Sarah Purser, 'what a beautiful face he had').

The body was taken on Sunday evening at 7.15 to lie in the chapel of the cemetery of the little rock-built town of Roquebrune, which overlooks Cap Martin and Monaco. In the afternoon Mrs Yeats, Lady Gerald Wellesley, the Misses Heald, Miss Hilda Matheson and the Dermod O'Briens toiled up the long stone path between walls to the graveside, where the Anglican Burial Service was read. In an account that she wrote of the scene Lady Gerald Wellesley noted that there were many drowned sailors near Yeats's grave (which would have pleased him) and an obscure follower of Garibaldi beside it. 'Yeats alive or dead brought distinction wherever he came.'

The Irish Government telegraphed condolences, and a message came too from the German Foreign Office. The Irish Cabinet in its telegram hoped that Yeats would be brought back for burial in his own land. He had expressed at some recent time a wish to be buried at Drumcliff. The alternative, he had said, was Roquebrune ... if he should die in France, and he had added that, if convenient later on, they could 'dig him up' and take him to Sligo. A gesture he never foresaw and would have appreciated came from the Dean of St Patrick's, Dean Wilson, who offered an interment in the Cathedral – none had taken place for over a hundred years! The spot offered was not far from the place where the dust of Jonathan Swift and of 'Stella' lies. 'Swift haunts me, he is always round the corner', Yeats once said. The Cathedral itself he revered, and during the time that he lived in Merrion Square he often wandered there to meditate. He had hoped that Protestant Ireland would ask permission to bring back the body of Henry Grattan from Westminster to St Patrick's. He would have had the street lined with soldiers that it might appear that St Patrick's meant more to all Ireland than Westminster, but at the head of the procession he would have put all the descendants of those who voted for independence in the eighteenth-century Irish Parliament.

His burial took place in the cemetery of Roquebrune, which lies high above the village, looking out to sea. There were memorial services both in London and in Dublin: in London at St Martin-in-the-Fields, and in Dublin at St Patrick's, where the Archbishop pronounced the Benediction. Tributes in verse were published by W. J. Turner and several of the younger generation of English poets, and John Masefield mingled verse and prose of personal reminiscence in a Cuala Book, *Some Memories of W. B. Yeats*. In an article for the *London Mercury* H. W. Nevinson, going back still further, recalled his entry in the early nineties into *The Celtic Twilight*, when he followed *The Wanderings of Oisin* and beheld 'The Rose Upon the Rood of Time', and knew how Cuchulain died, and perceived far away the 'Isle in the Water' and went 'Down by the Salley Gardens'. T. S. Eliot came to Dublin to speak on one whom he called 'the greatest poet of our time – certainly the greatest in his language, and so far as I can judge, in any language'. 'There are some poets', he said, 'whose poetry can be considered more or less in isolation, for experience and delight. There are others whose poetry, though giving equally experience and delight, has a larger historical importance. Yeats was one of the latter; he was one of those few whose history is the history of our own time, who are a part of the consciousness of their age, which cannot be understood without them.'

Epilogue*

YEATS died on 28 January 1939. The grave at Roquebrune
was intended only as a temporary resting-place; a plain stone
with the inscription W. B. YEATS, 1865–1939 marked the spot.
After her return to Ireland and consultation with the family,
Mrs Yeats decided that his body should be brought home;
the French Government offered the services of a destroyer,
but the outbreak of the war that autumn brought all plans
to a standstill.

A plot of ground had been secured in Drumcliff churchyard, and in September 1948, nine years after his death, the
body of the great poet was brought back to his own countryside. After lying in state in the town square of Roquebrune,
where a poet from Menton delivered his tribute, the coffin
went by road to Nice and was there taken aboard the Irish
corvette *Macha*, reaching Ireland eleven days later. As it
was feared that the channel at Sligo might be too shallow
for a safe landing, the boat entered Galway Bay. Mrs Yeats,
her children, and Jack Yeats, the poet's brother, went aboard
and the coffin was piped ashore. From Galway the funeral
procession made its way by road to Sligo where a military
guard of honour waited. The Government was represented
by Mr Seán MacBride, Maud Gonne's son, Minister for External Affairs; the Mayor and Corporation of Sligo attended,
and friends and admirers of the poet gathered in the churchyard of Drumcliff; the last resting-place was reached. A
stone, inscribed as he had directed, now stands there, 'under
bare Ben Bulben's head'.

* An adaptation of the Epilogue in *The Letters of W. B. Yeats*, ed.
Allan Wade (Hart-Davis, 1954), pp. 923–4.

No marble, no conventional phrase;
On limestone quarried near the spot
By his command these words are cut:

> *Cast a cold eye*
> *On life, on death.*
> *Horseman, pass by!*

Notes

I. POEM ON ANCESTORS (page 2)

I find that the lines in the original edition of *Responsibilities*

> ...You that did not weigh the cost,
> Old Butlers when you took to horse and stood
> Beside the brackish waters of the Boyne
> Till your bad master blenched and all was lost.

were subsequently altered to

> A Butler or an Armstrong that withstood
> Beside the brackish waters of the Boyne
> James and his Irish when the Dutchman crossed.

It had been brought to Yeats's notice that his Butler ancestor had fought on William's side, not on that of James, at the Battle of the Boyne. Elsewhere, except where I stated, I have quoted Yeats's final versions.

II. THE ORDER OF THE GOLDEN DAWN AND THE SOURCE OF ITS TEACHINGS (page 72)

A typescript among Yeats's papers dated 1923 records that the cypher MMS. on which the old G. D. and its successor S. M. were founded were discovered by a clergyman, the Rev. A. F. A. W., on an old bookstall in London in 1884. Attached to the cypher was a letter saying that if anyone could decipher the MMS. and would communicate with Sapiens Dominabitur Astris, c/o Fräulein Anna Sprengel in Hanover, they would receive interesting information.

Dr Wynn Westcott, the London coroner, declared that at the start of the Order he received letters from Anna Sprengel, who was a member of a German Rosicrucian Order. But it was never known for what purpose the cypher MMS. was drawn up and left on the London bookstall. Dr Westcott had cyphers of the

Outer Rituals, but the greater part of the original Order lectures were based upon Mrs Mathers's clairvoyance. Later, when difficulties arose with Mathers, Dr Westcott received a postcard from the German Order which said : 'Have no fears, Mathers cannot harm you'. In Dr Westcott's opinion Mathers was an adventurer from the first, and in the early Order days knew nothing more than what he had read in the British Museum. Mrs Mathers asserted, on the other hand, that her husband had never believed for a moment in Sapiens Dominabitur Astris, but had to investigate the extraordinary statements made by this woman – an American, not a German – whom he considered from the first an emissary from some enemy of the Order.

The Mathers's letters to Yeats are mostly of early date and written from 87 rue Mozart, Paris. Mathers signs as 's. r. m. d.' and his wife as 'Vestigia'. After the death of Mathers his widow came to London, where she read with great displeasure the statements about 's. r. m. d.' in Yeats's *Autobiographies*, such as that 'he was to die of melancholia' and that he was 'self-educated, unscholarly, though learned', whereas he had received one of the best English educations at Bedford Grammar School. Yeats visited Mrs Mathers, and they were reconciled, but he did not make any alterations of consequence in the second edition of *Autobiographies*. Madame Gonne MacBride, who used to see Mathers in Paris during the war, had an impression, similar to that of Yeats, of the cause of Mathers's death.

III. COOLE

In Chapter six I write as if Coole were still standing. During Lady Gregory's last years house, garden, fields and woods passed into the hands of the Forestry Department; she rented the house and garden from the Department. While this book was going through the press, the Department sold the house to a purchaser who had pulled it down. Yeats's prophecy of 'nettles waving upon a shapeless mound' in 'Coole Park, 1929' has been fulfilled sooner than he thought. Of the three famous 'literary' houses in the West of Ireland, Moore Hall, Coole and Tulira, only Tulira now survives.

IV. WILLIAM SHARP AND FIONA MACLEOD (page 144)

Among Yeats's papers are letters in entirely different hand-writings, some signed William Sharp, others Fiona Macleod. Before his death in 1906 Sharp left this letter with instructions that Yeats should receive it immediately upon his death:

You will think I have deceived you about Fiona Macleod. But, in absolute privacy, I tell you I have not, howsoever in certain details I have (inevitably) misled you. Only, it is a mystery. Perhaps you will instinctively understand, or may come to understand. 'The rest is silence.' Farewell. *William Sharp.*

It is only right, however, to add that I, and I only, am the author – in the literal and literary sense – of all written under the name of Fiona Macleod.

Bibliography

Appreciations published after Yeats's death, by Gordon Bottomley,
Austin Clarke, Mary and Padraic Colum, St John Ervine, Stephen
Gwynn, Desmond MacCarthy, Frank O'Connor, Dorothy Richard-
son, R. A. Scott-James, W. J. Turner, *The Times, Irish Times,
Irish Press, Observer, Sunday Times,* etc.

Autobiographies, W. B. Yeats.

Benson, A. C., Letters to W. B. Y. MS.

Bibliographies, William M. Roth and Allan Wade.

Boyd, E. A., *Ireland's Literary Renaissance.*

Collected Poems, W. B. Yeats (1933).

Craig, Gordon, Letters to W. B. Y. MS.

Curtis, E. C., Yeats's Gaelic Sources. MS.

Daiches, David, *Poetry and the Modern World.*

Das, Mr H., MS.

Dramatis Personae, W. B. Yeats.

Dulac, Edmund and Mrs, Letters to W. B. Y. MS.

Eglinton, John, *Irish Portraits and A Memoir of AE.*

Eliot, T. S., Yeats Memorial Lecture at Abbey Theatre. MS.

Ellis-Fermor, Una, *The Irish Dramatic Movement.*

Farrell, Michael, MS. 'Indian Homage to Yeats'.

Feilding, Hon. Everard, Correspondence. MS.

Fitzgerald, Desmond, MS.

French, Cecil, Letters to W. B. Y. MS.

Full Moon in March, A, W. B. Yeats.

Gregory, Lady, *Our Irish Theatre.*
    Correspondence. MS.
    A Memoir of Hugh Lane.

Gwynn, Stephen, *Irish Literature and Drama.*

Healy, John A., American Memorial Committee. MS.

Hempel, His Excellently Eduard, MS.

Hopkins, G. M., *Further Letters.* Edited by C. C. Abbott.

Horniman, A. E. F., Correspondence. MS.

Horton, W. T., Correspondence. MS.

Johnson, Lionel, Correspondence. MS.

Letters to the New Island, Edited by Horace Reynolds.

Lowinsky, Thos., Yeats Ghost Story.

MacBride, Madame, *A Servant of the Queen.*

MacCartan, Patrick, MS.

Martyn, Edwards, Letters to W. B. Y. ms.

Mathers, MacGregor, Letters to W. B. Y. ms.

Mathers, Mrs MacGregor, Letters to W. B. Y. ms.

Moore, George, *Hail and Farewell*.

Moore, T. Sturge, Correspondence. ms.

Murray, Sir Gilbert, Letters to W. B. Y. ms.

O'Faoláin, Seán, W. B. Yeats. ms.

O'Leary, John, Correspondence. ms.

O'Sullivan, Donal, *The Irish Senate*.

On the Boiler, W. B. Yeats.

Packet for Ezra Pound, A, W. B. Yeats.

Pollexfen, George, Letters to W. B. Y. ms.

Quinn, John, Correspondence (with acknowledgements to Lennox Robinson).

Ricketts, Charles, *Self-Portrait*.

Rossi, M. Manlio, Yeats and Philosophy. ms.
   Spaccio dei Maghi.

Ruddock, Margot, *The Lemon Tree*, with Introduction by W. B. Yeats.

Russell, George (AE), Correspondence. ms.

Scattering Branches. Edited by Stephen Gwynn, with contributions by Maud Gonne, Lennox Robinson, William Rothenstein and others.

Sharp, William (Fiona Macleod), Correspondence. ms.

Shirley, Ralph, Yeats's Horoscope.

Squire, Sir John, *Essays on Poetry*.

Sturm, Dr F. P., Letters to W. B. Y. ms.

Symons, Arthur, Letters to W. B. Y. ms.

Tynan, Katharine (Mrs Hinkson), Correspondence, ms.
   Twenty-Five Years.

Walsh, E. R., Reminiscences of Yeats. ms.

Watkins, Vernon, 'Yeats in Dublin'.

Wellesley, Lady Gerald, *Letters on Poetry to Dorothy Wellesley*.

Yeats, J. Butler, Correspondence. ms., and *Some Chapters of Autobiography*. With acknowledgements to Jack B. and Lily Yeats.

Very few of Yeats's letters to Madame Gonne MacBride have been available, as many were left in Paris and others were lost in Ireland during the troubled times.

Index